Psychometrics and Psychology

PAUL KLINE

Department of Psychology,
University of Exeter,
Exeter, UK

1979

ACADEMIC PRESS

LONDON   NEW YORK   SAN FRANCISCO

A Subsidiary of Harcourt Brace Jovanovich, Publishers

ACADEMIC PRESS INC. (LONDON) LTD.
24/28 Oval Road
London NW1

United States Edition published by
ACADEMIC PRESS INC.
111 Fifth Avenue
New York, New York 10003

British Library Cataloguing in Publication Data

Kline, Paul
  Psychometrics and psychology.
  1. Psychometrics
  I. Title
  152.8   BF39   78–18023

  ISBN 0–12–415150–7

Printed and bound in Great Britain by
Morrison & Gibb Ltd., London and Edinburgh

PREFACE

In "Psychometrics and Psychology" I attempt to set out the contribution of psychometrics to psychological knowledge. I have done this because in my view, books about psychometrics are concerned too much with tests and methods and pay insufficient attention to the substantive findings that have arisen from their application. Similarly, in most psychology books, the findings from psychometrics other than in the field of intelligence are largely ignored. As I argue throughout this book, there are substantive results from psychological testing that deserve to be incorporated into the body of experimental psychology. Furthermore, and this is also fully discussed, there are clear indications of research as yet undone which could be most fruitful.

In the first chapter psychometrics is defined, essentially as psychological testing and a study of the desirable attributes of good tests and the methods of test construction demonstrates the power of factor-analytic tests, and the psychological meaningfulness of factored variables. This leads on to a discussion in Chapter 2 of the special statistical methods peculiarly suited to the analysis of psychological test results, multivariate methods, with special emphasis on the most widely used technique, factor analysis. In Chapter 3 there is a brief description of the main varieties of psychological test that have been produced by the methods previously discussed—intelligence, aptitude, temperament and motivation tests, providing examples of each kind. These three chapters prepare us for the substantive results that have been obtained from the application of these tests, and they are set out in the following chapters.

In Chapter 4 the main factors discovered in the field of abilities are discussed. Various attempts to weave these into a theory of cognition are examined, together with the problems of creativity and the inheritance of intelligence. In all these topics the substantive findings are set out. In Chapters 5 and 6, a similar approach is adopted to cover human temperament, mood and dynamics. Here the main variables isolated by factor analysis are described and their psychological significance discussed. In Chapters 4 to 6 the most powerful psychological variables, it is argued, have been described.

In succeeding chapters, the impact of these variables on different aspects of psychology is discussed. Here, the present and future contributions of psychometrics to knowledge are most clearly seen. In Chapter 7, the influence of these findings on theories of learning with special reference to the work of Cattell and Eysenck is examined. In Chapters 8 and 9, the substantive results in the areas of educational, industrial and clinical psychology are described

v

and discussed. In Chapter 10, the value of psychometrics in cross-cultural psychology is examined. In this chapter, especially, the contribution of psychometrics can be seen to be potential rather than actual.

Finally, in Chapter 11 the bearing of all these results on theories of psychology is examined and an attempt is made to show how factored psychometric variables can be incorporated into a theory of their own, as ultimately they must be if a properly quantified psychology is desirable.

In this way the full psychological significance of psychometrics, one of the oldest branches of psychology, is brought out. I hope that experimental psychologists will begin to utilize in their experimental designs the factors discussed so that a full and empirically based integration of psychometrics and psychology can be brought about.

February, 1979   PAUL KLINE

CONTENTS

1

The Meaning of Psychometrics

Etymologically (from the Greek) psychometry means measuring the mind. Since, however, the concept of mind tends to be eschewed by scientific psychology, as belonging to the world of metaphysics rather than science, the word has now shifted its meaning. In modern psychology psychometry is that branch of the field concerned with psychological testing. Parenthetically it should be noticed that in parapsychology, psychometry has quite another meaning. There it refers to the art of guessing the history and nature of objects from manual contact with them. In this book this meaning of psychometrics will not be further considered. Psychometrics, then, is psychological testing.

The aim of this book is to set out the contribution to psychological knowledge that has been made and could be made by psychometrics. To understand this fully, however, it is necessary in the light of this definition, to define the nature of psychological tests, for their contribution to psychological knowledge stems in large part from their special qualities.

THE SPECIAL QUALITIES OF PSYCHOLOGICAL TESTS

As any textbook in elementary psychometrics makes clear (e.g. Cronbach, 1970) psychological test constructors have traditionally aimed to make their tests valid and reliable. Validity can be defined as the accuracy with which a test measures what it purports to measure. Reliability on the other hand is essentially the reproducibility of the scores from a test, although it can also refer to the internal consistency of the components of a test score. These definitions demonstrate, of course, that a test is unlikely to be valid if it is not reliable (although in certain cases this is possible) which is why reliability has been considered to be a desirable characteristic of tests. In addition to this test constructors have attempted to supply good norms for their tests thus enabling comparisons to be made between individuals and between individuals and groups. One further point is important in appreciating the special qualities of psychological tests—they have an empirical (rather than an intuitive) basis. Thus validity, reliability and the standardization of norms all entail trying out the test and demonstrating that it works.

It might seem to readers unacquainted with the problems of measuring human behaviour that reliability and validity are so obviously important that they would be a *sine qua non* of any test rather than be regarded as special characteristics. However, this is far from the case. For example, studies of tests used in schools and in public examinations of educational achievement (including university degrees), as discussed in Vernon (1950) have almost always revealed them to be of poor reliability and hence poor validity. Perhaps, therefore, it is not surprising that Hudson (1960) found that many Fellows of the Royal Society did not in fact have particularly distinguished first degrees. It is certainly true to say, also, that the questions in such public examinations have not been previously tried out. In short, they do not have the characteristics which psychometrists attempt to build into their tests.

It must also be said, at this point, that many psychological tests fail to meet the psychometric criteria or ideals that have been described. To call a test of a psychological test, confers upon it, no magic qualities of reliability or validity that have not been specifically built into it. Perusal, indeed, of the psychometric bible, Buros' "Mental Measurement Yearbooks", indicates clearly that many psychological tests are not reliable and not valid and that many other tests are reliable and not valid. Only a minority are valid. Since this is the case even with celebrated psychological tests such as the Rorschach Test (Rorschach, 1921), whose fame spreads beyond psychometrics and psychology, it is necessary to examine how psychological tests can be made valid and reliable. It is only by constructing tests of this kind that psychometrics is able to make a contribution to psychology. In this context one has to remember that the natural sciences have progressed because their measuring instruments are precise. A good microscope magnifies the specimens on its slide as it claims to do. What one sees is not something else. Furthermore the observations one makes through it are identical each time and can be checked by different observers. The microscope is highly valid and almost perfectly reliable. This means that the observations can be trusted. Good psychometric tests so far, cannot be said to have achieved such quality, although the best, can approach this degree of accuracy. This leads to the question of how reliable and valid psychological tests, the essence of psychometrics, can be constructed.

Reliability

As indicated there are two distinct meanings of reliability. The first refers to the internal consistency of the test. Although there is no similar analogy in the example of the microscope, a ruler or thermometer is perfectly internally consistent. If one were to break the ruler in half there would be a perfect correlation between the measurements made with the two halves. It should be noted that if this were not the case, one should quite rightly decide that there was something wrong with the original ruler. Most psychological tests, when split in half, do not yield perfectly correlated scores, i.e. they are not completely reliable.

This internal consistency has to be measured. As the example of the ruler implies if a test is not consistent, it is difficult to argue that it *could* be valid. There is almost no need for further evidence that it is invalid. There are, as a consequence of its importance, various methods of measuring the internal consistency of tests, which should be mentioned since they bear upon the proper evaluation of this construct in using tests to establish substantive psychological findings. Split-half reliability is a common method where the first half of a test is correlated with the second half. This suffers from two defects. First, in tests of ability or aptitude, items are arranged in order of difficulty. The correlation between the first and second halves will be distorted. To overcome this, an odd-even split can be used where scores from even-numbered items are compared with scores from the odd-numbered items. The second defect applies equally to both methods—namely that each is but one of a large number of possible splits. Kuder and Richardson (Richardson and Kuder, 1939) have developed special formulae for estimating internal consistency which take into account all possible groupings of the items and these are preferable as an accurate estimate of internal consistency. Since reliability is related to length, the split-half methods underestimate the reliability of the whole test and the effects of this can be corrected by the Spearman-Brown formula. Hoyt (1941) has also developed an analysis of variance approach to the problem where variance due to subjects is compared with variance due to items which is hopefully small.

Most psychometric texts, e.g. Guilford (1956) argue that the internal consistency of a test is satisfactory when it is around the 0·7 figure. Lower than this, each part of the test must be measuring something different and no test can correlate with anything (i.e. be valid) more highly than with itself. A higher correlation than this, on the other hand suggests that the test is too narrow and too specific, in which case it can again hardly be valid. After all if one constructs items that are virtually paraphrases of each other, the result would be high internal consistency and very low validity. This is the dilemma of the psychometrist. If two items are perfectly correlated, i.e. perfectly consistent, one adds in no new information relative to the other, so it may as well be dropped. Ideally one wants items correlating 0·0 with each other and +1 with the criterion of validity; a vain hope as yet in psychometrics. Usually human behaviours are not narrow or specific (unlike distance or temperature) so that good measures cannot be too consistent. Low consistency, on the other hand, means or can mean poor validity. Thus, when one examines how best to construct psychological tests with the characteristics that are demanded, this will be an important parameter to ensure internal consistency of around 0·7.

Reliability over Time

This is probably the more important meaning of the term. It is obvious that if a test gives a different score for the same subject on different occasions, then on at least one of them it is in error, unless one has some *a priori* reason for thinking that the subject's status on the variable should have changed. This means that the correlation between a set of scores from the same test given twice should approach $+1$. In fact, with some psychometric tests of intelligence and attainment this is the case. With many other psychological tests test-retest reliability is extremely poor, dropping, in some cases as low as 0·2 or 0·3 and with no obvious reason to account for the changes. Indeed, in research projects I have known, scores on some well-known personality tests changed so drastically that subjects classified "high" on one occasion fell into the "low" category on the other and vice versa. The factors, therefore, that produce such fluctuation apparently unrelated to genuine changes must be considered. Obviously if one is to claim that psychometric tests have contributed to psychological knowledge one must feel confident that the results discussed are stable.

One fact that must be faced is that some very high test-retest reliabilities may really be overestimates of the true stability of the test. If the interval between the two tests is short, subjects may remember their previous responses. This, of course, contributes to a spuriously high correlation. Again if a test is given that is far too difficult for subjects they are equally in difficulty on both occasions. With a different set of subjects the reliability could be lower. Hence all test-retest reliability coefficients must be interpreted as applying only to the population from which they were obtained. A highly reliable test among students may be less so among psychiatric groups. However, these are the less important instances of factors producing spuriously high reliability, factors producing low reliability are of more general significance.

Some degree of unreliability on retesting is inevitably introduced by factors such as how subjects happen to feel when they are tested and the temperature and conditions of administering the test. These, however, are relatively trivial and are unlikely to produce the high degree of unreliability that is not uncommon. Where items are phrased in difficult English, or are tangential to subjects' knowledge and interest, then random responding, leading to low reliability, is likely. An obvious source which most psychological tests avoid, is scoring. Where scoring is objective, i.e. there is only one keyed response, then this cause of unreliability is ruled out. Where judgements have to be made, as in many projective tests and tests of educational attainment, reliability can easily be reduced. Indeed sources of error can be specified as: variance due to markers, variance due to occasions and interactions. It is almost essential that psychological tests if they are to be reliable must be objective. However, all this still fails to account for the low reliability of some objectively scored psychological tests.

One possibility which I shall briefly examine, but which will be fully dealt with in Chapter 5, is that the changes in scores known as unreliability, in fact reflect real changes even though our psychological knowledge is not such as at present to enable us to understand or predict them. With certain variables that are regarded as labile such a view makes sense. Anxiety is a good example. One might not be able to predict with any accuracy how an individual's anxiety score might change on retesting simply because one could not be aware of all that had happened to him in the interval. Nevertheless change *per se* almost supports the validity of an anxiety measure. This indeed is recognized and many tests of anxiety distinguish between trait and state (the labile one) anxiety (e.g. Spielberger, 1966). Moods such as joy or elation would be expected to be unreliable if validly measured. It could be the case that unreliability which appears to be error only appears so through the ignorance of its true nature. While this is so, at present I must conclude that the test-retest unreliability of tests is not fully understood.

One final point remains to be made: the reliability of tests is particularly important in the study of individuals. Indeed, as I have fully discussed in my book on tests in vocational guidance (Kline, 1975), for use with individuals as distinct from groups a reliability of at least 0·7 is essential. This is simply because the standard error (s.e.) of a score is related to the reliability of the test. The formula for the s.e. is $\sigma^2 t / \sqrt{1 - rtt}$ where $\sigma^2 t$ = s.e. of the score and rtt is the reliability. Clearly, therefore, the lower the reliability, the larger the standard error. Thus with an obtained score of 10, 95 % of true scores would fall between 10 ± 2 s.e. If the reliability is poor, the meaning of any individual's score becomes vague. Reliability must be high.

From the discussion it is clear that tests must have high test-retest reliability unless one has reason to think that the variables they measure are likely to fluctuate from occasion to occasion. Tests too should be consistent but not too specific, a point to be discussed while examining what is far more important ultimately—the validity of tests. High reliability is only aimed at because it tends to high validity.

Test Validity

As pointed out above, it is possible to construct tests which are reliable but not valid. One must turn one's attention to validity to ensure as far as possible that the psychological tests used to establish basic facts in psychology are really suited for this purpose. The meaning of validity, the extent to which a test measures what it purports to measure is simple. What is difficult is to demonstrate that a test is valid. Over the years various methods have been employed to investigate test validity which itself has become a term with effectively different meanings. In fact, psychometric tests recognize different types of validity and these are discussed briefly, pointing out their problems and advantages in the light of being able to recognize and construct valid tests. Oviously test results from invalid tests are worthless, and no psychology could be based upon them.

Before considering the different types of validity, I must first expound the notion of validity in general. The basic question is: How is a test to be demonstrated as valid, even in principle? Usually one has to set up some kind of criterion by which a test may be judged. Just what this criterion, or more usually criteria, is/are varies with the kind of test and is the essence of the problem of validity. If it is possible to establish good criteria then it is relatively simple to demonstrate test validity. A few illustrations will clarify the point and highlight difficulties with criteria.

To take an intelligence test for example, the criteria used to validate this could be any or all of the following: correlations with other well-established tests of intelligence are an obvious demonstration of validity. Here, however, faced with the difficulty of satisfaction with the validity of the well-established test, one could well question the point of another test. If one is dissatisfied with the validity, it is clearly absurd to use correlations with it as evidence of validity for the new test. This approach to validity can only be used when the new test has some outstanding feature compared with the old, e.g. if it is brief and suitable for all age groups, not a characteristic of the best individual intelligence tests such as the Wechsler Intelligence Scale Children (WISC) (Wechsler, 1958). Obviously this method can only be used where another well-accepted measure exists. Actually, there are few fields other than intelligence where there is good agreement that certain tests are valid. Perhaps in the area of personality, most psychometrists would accept that the Eysenck Personality Questionnaire (EPQ) (Eysenck and Eysenck, 1975) measures extraversion and neuroticism although certainly not all psychometrists would agree with the nomenclature (Cattell and Kline, 1977).

Different evidence for validity would be provided by demonstrating that certain groups scored more highly than others on the test. Thus, in keeping social class constant and dealing with professional occupations, by careful job analysis one could hypothesize that administrative civil servants, research physicists and barristers for example, should score more highly than funeral directors, stockbrokers or store managers. In the civil service and armed services, superiors' ratings are available for job success and a positive correlation should be expected between these and the intelligence test scores. Similarly, positive correlations should be expected between the test scores and educational attainment, especially if the figures are computed within each social class.

Yet another highly effective method of demonstrating the validity of an intelligence test, albeit time-consuming, is to follow up a group of testees over a period of years. Children tested at eight could be investigated at, say, 30 years old. A positive correlation should be expected between I.Q. score and criteria of job success such as money earned, amount of responsibility, number and class of degrees, number of patents and number of books published. This is not to argue that intelligence is the only factor influencing such performance, only this it is important. This was the method employed by Terman (1926) in his study of gifted children. High scorers did indeed do better at almost everything, thus providing strong support for the validity of his intelligence test which is still in use today as the Stanford-Binet (Terman and Merrill, 1964).

I have shown above three distinct methods of demonstrating a test to be valid. Each separately would provide support for validity. Together all three yield positive results which would demonstrate almost beyond reasonable doubt that the test was a valid intelligence test. This would be particularly true if further studies indicated clearly what the test *was not*. This old Socratic device for arriving at a definition is always valuable in the study of validity. Thus if a test is not A, B, C, D, then there is that much more likelihood (if these were still possible in the light of the results) that it is *x*, as I wish to demonstrate.

The example was specially chosen to illustrate the different approaches that may be adopted towards validity. However, as it happens, the concept of intelligence is sufficiently clear to allow these relatively rigorous essays. This is not the case unfortunately, with many psychological variables. For example (Kline, 1971) I have recently constructed and validated a test of the Freudian anal character (Freud, 1908). The methods advocated above were used but the results were obviously more equivocal. Correlations with other anal tests were only of limited value for most of these were flawed. Moderate positive correlations were hypothesized. Special groups of highly anal or non-anal subjects could not be obtained. The best possible alternative was to have people rated for the anal triad—orderliness, obstinacy and parsimony—and compare ratings and scores. Since ratings of personality are notoriously poor (e.g. Vernon and Parry, 1949), unless done under special conditions involving raters and subjects living together for long periods of time, as described by Cattell (1957), high positive correlations between ratings and tests could not be expected, although some degree of agreement would be hypothesized. It was, of course, impractical to follow up the sample nor is it clear what criterion could have been adopted had this been done. Thus, attempting to validate a scale of anal traits brings home with great clarity, the problem of defining the criterion.

Since many personality tests tend to measure the two major personality factors, extraversion and anxiety, it was necessary to demonstrate that the anal test was unrelated to these. In doing this I was able to use a technique for demonstrating validity that is not so useful with a concept such as intelligence. It is possible to hypothesize that a valid test of anal traits would be related in certain ways to other quite separate personality variables. For example, in Freudian theory one would expect it to load up with superego (Cattell's factor G) and with id tension (Q4), although correlations with these variables should be small.

This illustration of personality test construction shows that the demonstration of validity is not a simple procedure. There is no one validity figure that can be obtained for a test. Usually the validity of psychological tests is attested by a series of findings which have to be evaluated. To that extent the validity of a test is a subjective matter. However, as a study of Buros' "Mental Measurement Yearbooks" shows, on certain tests there is a large measure of agreement among experts. Furthermore, tests are valid usually with respect to some particular purpose—for selection, or screening or diagnosis. They are not necessarily valid for all purposes unless demonstrated to be so.

In interpreting studies of validity two statistical artefacts need to be noted. These are restrictions in the size of correlations due to homogeneity of samples and unreliability of the criterion measure. If, for example, following up an intelligence test administered at 11 years old among university students, one would be plagued by both these problems. Thus, in Great Britain at least, generally only students of I.Q. 115 + get to university due to the selection procedures. Thus our university sample is exceedingly homogeneous for I.Q. This factor inevitably lowers all correlations with I.Q. among this group. Furthermore university examinations of the essay type are highly unreliable, and low reliability attenuates correlations. This is why correlations between I.Q. and university degree are almost always low (e.g. Hamilton, 1970). Formulae are available for "correcting" observed correlations for both these factors. However, the propriety of such procedures especially where the resulting correlations are subjected to further statistical analysis is dubious. Thus low but significant positive correlations (in the region of 0·2) between university success and intelligence test scores mean, almost certainly, that I.Q. is strongly related to university performance.

I have mentioned, briefly, the essential problem of validity studies—the establishment of a sound criterion. With my test of anal characteristics the only possibility was ratings which are far from satisfactory. With almost all tests this difficulty is the major one. How to devise, for example, criteria for measures of interest or for personality variables such as dominance, tough-mindedness or naivety? This problem must always be borne in mind when evaluating test validity.

To summarize the general position on validity, I am arguing that essentially for most tests there is no one way of establishing validity and no one figure. Rather, bearing in mind the nature of the test variable and the purpose of the test, the test constructor should present a series of results no one of which need be solely convincing: the overall effect is the critical issue. Basically evaluating test validity is subjective rather than objective.

Against this background of the problems of demonstrating that a test is valid, we are now in a position to examine the different kinds of validity which are invoked in different investigations. This can be discussed briefly.

Face Validity

This term refers to the appearance of a test. If a test seems to be measuring what it purports to measure it is said to have face validity. It is essential in the testing of adults to retain the cooperation of the subjects, that tests have face validity. Without it subjects may refuse to do a "stupid test". However, there is no relation in many kinds of tests between face validity and true validity. Except in tests of attainment which are largely outside the sphere of interest of this book, since little psychological knowledge other than developmental could arise from their results, face validity can be misleading. This is recognized by many test constructors who construct items entirely empirically. Strong, for example (1943), in the development of his interest test was prepared to use any items which would discriminate one occupational group from another regardless of why this should be the case. Although the

Strong Interest Blank has overall face validity, despite this form of construction, certain items are curious, e.g. "I dislike people with hooked noses", although these have now been removed from the latest version of this test. Where face validity can be particularly misleading is in the field of personality. Many psychometrists who have genuinely attempted to use psychological tests to establish psychological theories have fallen into this trap. Barnes (1952), for example, constructed questionnaires purporting to measure psychosexual syndromes as described in Freudian theory (Freud, 1905). He established that the scales were internally consistent and each measuring a factor common to their items. However, what these factors were was decided purely by item content. No other evidence of validity was adduced. That this is totally unsatisfactory is well exemplified by the study of the Authoritarian Personality (Adorno *et al.*, 1951) which will be discussed in Chapter 5. Here, scales which seemed in terms of item content to be highly face valid for the measurement of the fascistic personality turned out to be contaminated by two response sets—acquiescence, the tendency to put "Yes" to items regardless of content and by social desirability, making oneself seem as good as possible. Thus item content is not necessarily a reliable guide to what a test is measuring. It must now be considered why face validity fails to relate to true validity.

The pernicious influence of response sets which has already been mentioned
is the major reason. Since response sets were first fully discussed by Cronbach (1946, 1950) an enormous research effort has been expended upon them, probably out of all recognition of their importance. Guilford (1959) has argued in the case of acquiescence, that this is more likely to occur when the items are vague and difficult and not relevant to the subject's feeling and behaviour. Usually the effects of acquiescence are minimized by constructing items such that the keyed responses are equally "Yes's" and "No's". Scales such as the EPI N scale (Eysenck and Eysenck) where all the items are keyed "Yes" may well be contaminated by acquiescence. Edwards (1957) has
unquestionably contributed most to the study of social desirability. He demonstrated that response rate to items was correlated with their social desirability, as estimated by judges. This factor therefore must underly much of the variance in personality tests. As an exercise, Edwards (1959) constructed the Edwards Personal Preference Schedule to obviate the effects of this response set. Items were of the forced-choice type and each choice was of equal social desirability. Unfortunately, however, it has been shown that when two items are thus juxtaposed, slight differences in social desirability between them are magnified, thus nullifying the extremely time-consuming test construction procedures (Corah *et al.*, 1958).

Normally in testing, I have argued (Kline, 1973) that social desirability effects can be minimized by careful item writing and item analysis. Thus while few subjects would endorse the item "Are you jealous?", the item "Do other people sometimes accuse you of jealousy?", may be more acceptable. However, my emphasis is on *may*. If it is shown that the scales are valid, it is not possible to impugn them on the grounds that they are contaminated by social desirability or any other response set. Furthermore, if items are chosen that are endorsed by about 50% of the population, it is difficult to argue that they are socially desirable. One further point about social desirability must be made. So far I have talked about eliminating its influence. However, it can be argued (e.g. Cattell, 1973) that this tendency is itself an interesting personality variable. While this is no doubt true, there have to be attempts to counteract its influence when measuring other personality variables.

These are not the only factors that tend to make face validity so poor a guide to true validity. There are obvious effects of deliberate distortion, which may occur when tests are used for selection, although this is less likely in the guidance or psychiatric situation where testees are voluntarily doing the tests and wanting to be helped. Again, some subjects have illusions or even delusions about their own feelings and behaviour so that almost all their responses will be false. While there is no knowing when this occurs, if validity has been demonstrated these objections are irrelevant. Eysenck and Eysenck in their EPI and Cattell (Cattell *et al.*, 1970) with the 16 PF test, adopt the rationale for their tests that the truth or falsity or accuracy of the responses is irrelevant. All that matters is whether the response that subjects make does or does not load on the apposite personality factor. The objective fact of putting response X is the empirical fact. Cattell (1957) indeed distinguishes Q data (where the response is not believed) from Q' data where it is assumed to reflect a subject's feelings and behaviour.

The face validity of some attainment tests can also be highly misleading. If the instructions are complex, despite the content, a test may become a measure of understanding the instructions, i.e. an I.Q. test. Tests of practical subjects in verbal form may look valid to those inexperienced in psychological testing. However, they inevitably involve verbal skills which in turn reflect I.Q. and education level. These factors can easily produce invalidity.

This discussion must have made it clear that the appearance of tests (their face validity) for a number of reasons is no guide to their true validity—a fact especially true of tests other than tests of ability, although even here face validity can be misleading.

Content Validity

This approach to validity applies only to tests where the subject matter is fixed and specific. It is thus most applicable to tests of ability and attainment. To measure the vocabulary of children, content validity is important. If the test consists of defining English words and if one is able to show that the test items constitute a sample of the most common nouns, verbs, etc., in the proportions found in the language and if the instructions are clear, then the test is *ipso facto* valid. Its task is simple a sample of the criterion task. Even in tests of this sort, however, evidence for reliability and validity should be given. Tests can have good content but be subjectively marked, for example, thus leading to low reliability and in this case low validity.

Concurrent Validity

This is the validity obtained when a test is correlated with other similar tests on one occasion. As has been discussed, if there are no other satisfactory tests, this is not a powerful technique. If other good tests exist, then the new test must have some special worthwhile features.

Predictive Validity

With the current emphasis on the hypothetico-deductive method in scientific psychology, despite some doubts whether this fits the particular problems of the subject matter (Cheshire, 1975), predictive validity, where the evidence is the test's predictive power, its correlation with a criterion subsequent to the test, is considered to be highly convincing. As discussed in the examples which considered following up I.Q. test results, a major difficulty lies in establishing a good criterion. If this can be done, there is no doubt that predictive validity is good support for any psychological test.

Construct Validity

This is a term introduced by Cronbach and Meehl (1955). To demonstrate construct validity a number of hypotheses are set up that would be tenable if the test were valid. In the discussion of validity above, this included showing what is and is not correlated with the test and what groups score high and low. It thus embraces both concurrent and predictive validity. Cronbach and Meehl (1955) accept that it is unlikely that any one result can provide unequivocal evidence for the validity of a test. However, a whole series of results can build up a composite picture, as a mosaic, which overall, demonstrates that a test is valid: each result is seen as fitting into a nomothetic network. For tests of personality and motivation where almost by definition there can be no clear criterion, construct validity is the most useful approach to the problem of validity. Nevertheless it has to be admitted that when the experimental results provide neither clear support or condemnation of the test (as is usually the case), considerable subjective judgement enters into the estimation of construct validity—more than is desirable in an objective science.

In this general discussion of validity the examples deliberately embraced the different kinds of validity that have been defined and these are undoubtedly of the greatest importance for the extraction of psychological significance for test results—which is the aim of the book. However, there are other kinds of validity whose main utility is to the practical test user who wants discrimination rather than meaning.

Incremental Validity

In selection a test may correlate low with the criterion compared with other tests. However, if there is no overlap with these other tests, the test is contributing something to the selection procedure and may be said to possess incremental validity *for this procedure.*

Differential Validity

A test may be useful in predicting relative success in, for example, university, i.e. intelligence tests give positive correlations with all types of university degree course. However, an interest test score can predict *relative* success even though their actual correlations are low. Thus for university courses an interest test score may be said to have differential validity.

It is to be noted that these two terms apply to specific selection procedures or criteria. They have little general significance. Construct validity, in comparison, has a general significance.

Finally, mention should be made of the Campbell and Fiske (1959) validation by the multitrait-multimethod matrix. This demands that at least two traits be measured together by at least two methods. In this way the variance specific to a particular type of test, "instrument variance", can be eliminated. In my view, however, this influential paper puts the commonplace notion that tests purporting to measure the same trait should correlate highly together and should not correlate with other traits. It would appear that the multitrait-multimethod matrix is a specific instance of a construct validity study.

The true meaning of reliability and validity as applied to psychological tests—the characteristics at which psychometrists aim—have now been seen. With these in mind it will be possible to examine rationally the various methods of test construction for, as will be argued, not all are equal to their task.
myself to what has been described as the classical procedures of psychometrics

In this discussion of reliability and validity I have deliberately restricted myself to what has been described as the classical procedures of psychometrics (e.g. Levy, 1973). This is not to deny the importance of the work by Lord and Novick (1968) or Birnbaum (1968) on the statistical properties of items. However, as yet the contribution to knowledge from psychometrics has arisen from tests developed in the classical tradition. The substantive results from tests developed by the modern itemetric methods is not considerable. Similarly, the studies on generalizability theory by Cronbach and his colleagues (Cronbach *et al.*, 1972) which reconceptualize reliability as generalizability and validity as decision-making, and which attempt to pin down the sources of error in tests experimentally, have not been considered. This again is because as yet the contribution to substantive psychological knowledge by tests constructed in the light of the criteria which they advocate is not large. Where one of the particular methods advocated by the workers seems particularly valuable (as for example the work of Rasch (1960) for cross-cultural work), it will be discussed.

Norms

Psychometric tests usually possess norms—sets of scores from various groups with which it is possible to compare a subject's score. Obviously in the use of psychological tests for establishing psychological facts, norms could be one of the most important characteristics. Thus, with sufficiently good norms one could discover the developmental course of any psychological trait. Although most psychological tests have norms, they cannot be considered a characteristic of such tests in the same way as reliability and validity. Norms are simply collected by using the test in a certain way. Very poor tests can have excellent norms and because norms are useful, how they should be best collected is important.

The collection of adequate norms for a test, its standardization, essentially depends upon sampling. If there is an interest in age trends, as in developmental studies, it is clear that there must be sufficiently homogeneous age groups to enable sensible comparisons to be made. Thus, in measuring infant vocabulary, such is the rapidity of its growth that the standardization groups should be at three monthly intervals. How large such intervals are depends both upon the variable being measured and upon the age of the subjects, since generally, growth rates slow with age, thus enabling larger groupings to be made with older subjects.

When forming norm groups all the variables that usually affect samples: social class, urban-rural residence, occupational status, I.Q, sex and age, for example, all have to be taken into account. Thus a "normal adult sample" would have to reflect the actual population in respect of these parameters. In addition to these sampling demands, the N used would have to be substantial. In all cases before trusting norms it is essential to know their provenance. Similarly for special groups such as schizophrenics or criminals, numbers must be sufficient to make the results trustworthy and details of the sample should be given. For example, all the schizophrenics at one hospital would not, owing to the difficulties of diagnosis, be an adequate sample of schizophrenics in general. In brief, therefore, one must be sure that the normative groups have been properly sampled and are in other ways (age homogeneous, for example) suitable for comparative work.

Only a brief discussion of the statistical form of the norms is necessary. It seems best if some form of standard score is used such as a T score with a mean of 50 and a standard deviation of 10, or, as is used with the Wechsler Intelligence Scales, scores with means of 100 and standard deviations 15. This makes comparisons simple and accurate. Percentiles are not advisable since these are not amenable to statistical analysis.

A well-standardized, reliable and valid test will enable us to make the kind of precise measurements that have, in part at least, led to the advances of the natural sciences. How are such tests to be constructed? In the last section of this chapter I discuss the rationale and logic of psychometric test construction.

TYPES OF TEST

A distinction is often drawn in psychological testing (other than of abilities) (e.g. Vernon, 1964) between psychometric and projective tests. Psychometric tests usually consist of items, often a great number as in the Minnesota

Multiphasic Personality Inventory (MMPI) (Hathaway and McKinley, 1951) which has 559, all of which are objectively scored. Generally they seek to establish the common dimensions along which individuals differ and to thus elucidate the underlying structure of individual differences. Some psychometric tests are aimed to discriminate criterion groups for the purposes of diagnosis, treatment, counselling or selection. Cronbach (1970) regards psychometric tests as nomothetic, attempting to lay down general laws accounting for differences in ability and personality.

Projective tests, on the other hand, are thought of as idiographic (Vernon, 1964) concerned with the delineation of what is unique to an individual, his idiodynamics, (Rosenzweig, 1954). By their adherants they are claimed to reveal innermost feelings, conflicts and wishes. Generally, as Semeonoff (1973) described, projective tests consist of more or less ambiguous stimuli to which subjects have to respond often descriptively. The stimuli can be visual, aural or tactile. Responses can vary in their freedom: sentence completion being perhaps the least free; drawing a house, tree and person, as in the house, tree and person (HTP) test (Buck, 1948) has almost no restraints. It should be noted, that the term projective does not imply that these tests depend upon or make use of the Freudian defence mechanism of projection, as described in the diaries of Dr. Schreber (Freud, 1911). Rather it refers to the fact that, since projective test stimuli are ambiguous, any description must reflect something of the individual as well as the stimulus itself. Something is, therefore, projected onto the stimulus.

Eysenck (1959) launched a ferocious attack on the Rorschach test in particular and projective tests in general, on the grounds that for almost none of them was there good evidence for validity mainly because of the hopelessly subjective scoring system implicit in such tests. These objections are well made and they would appear to demonstrate that projective test results could play no part in the establishment of a scientifically viable psychology. However, attempts have been made to alleviate these flaws such that some projective test findings are far from worthless and these will be discussed in the relevant chapters. Certainly, the work of Holtzmann (1968) with the Rorschach test and the implication of G analysis for this test (Holley, 1973) cannot be dismissed in an overall condemnation of projective tests.

There is a third category of tests, which are highly reliable and in some cases valid—objective tests (Cattell, 1957) also called performance tests (Cronbach, 1970). Objective tests are defined by Cattell as tests of which the purport is hidden from subjects thus making deliberate distortion, as distinct from psychopathic sabotage, unlikely and difficult, and whose scoring is objective. This definition embraces projective tests if, as is possible, an objective scoring scheme is devised for them. Objective tests are fully discussed in Chapter 3 and in the chapter on motivation where they have been most employed. These tests are varied in nature, ranging from questionnaires with items with standard psychometric qualities to single tasks such as, balloon blowing.

This discussion of different types of psychological tests makes clear, it is hoped, that I do not draw this rigid distinction between psychometric and other tests, or even between nomothetic and idiographic measures, although both distinctions are meaningful. I regard psychometrics as the branch of psychology concerned with all kinds of psychological test and that results from all kinds of tests *can* be used as scientific data if they are based upon reliable and valid scoring methods. This introduction is not intended to be comprehensive and takes no account of such special procedures as repertory grids (Bannister and Mair, 1968) or Shapiro's individual method of patient assessment (Shapiro, 1961). However, it does include the vast majority of published tests reviewed in Buros (1972) and is certainly sufficient for its purpose—to clarify the following discussion on test construction.

TEST CONSTRUCTION

At present test construction is both an art and a science: the science lies in the techniques to select items and to demonstrate reliability and validity, the art is in the item writing and it is difficult to describe. To my knowledge there is no account of how it is done. If an algorhythm could be developed, it would, of course, become a science. This is not to make a mystery of it. If, however, one is asked how one sets about writing an essay or making jokes, indeed any similar creative activity, there is the same problem.

The Art

With ability and aptitude tests, the test constructor attempts to devise the kind of problems he has good reason to think will prove useful. For example, a study of the more effective intelligence tests indicates that analogy problems (A is to b as C is to ...) and series problems are good items. Since intelligence is not identical with knowledge, the content of the item will be restricted to subjects with which most individuals for whom the test is intended will be familiar. Thus the item Locke is to Plato as Clarendon is to .... Herodotus would appear to demand both logical analysis and knowledge whereas the item Δ is to ∇ as Δ is to ... ∇, requires only the former. In all types of test construction the aim is to produce far more items than will be needed because, most forms of item analysis cause around half the items to be rejected. With tests of aptitude and more specific abilities, experts in the areas should be consulted to ensure that these items give a proper coverage of the subject matter.

In the case of tests of personality and motivation, instructions about item writing are even more dubious. However, bearing in mind what has been written about test reliability, one is virtually restricted to objectively scored items. One can have forced-choice type items as in the EPPS (Edwards, 1959), items demanding subjects to note their degree of interest on 5 or 7 point scales for example, trichotomous items, requiring subjects to indicate "Yes",

"Uncertain" or "No", or finally dichotomous items where the middle category (often all too alluring) is left out. These are the common forms of personality inventory items.

Again, if one refers to our examination of response sets, especially social desirability and acquiescence, one is bound at the very least, to think carefully whether people would be willing to admit to the various characteristics implied in this item content. In addition there would be an attempt to balance the scale so that some items were keyed "Yes" and others "No". Since this discussion has also shown that a lack of ambiguity and relevance were important in reducing the effect of response sets, the writing of inventory items has parameters such that to a large extent, one's hand is bound.

With reference to content, most test constructors use their psychological knowledge of the variable involved as a basis for item content. This is best illustrated for these purposes by my own tests (since with these alone was I privy to the thought processes involved). I shall look at the rationale of certain items in Ai3Q, a test of anal character (Kline, 1971), and in OOQ and OPQ (Kline and Storey, 1978) tests of oral characteristics.

The anal character (Freud, 1908) is described as parsimonious, obstinate and orderly. In constructing items, I was aware that many would have to be phrased so as to avoid social desirability effects especially those tapping obstinacy and meanness. Thus, "Are you mean?" and "Are you obstinate?" were ruled out. Since, as Guilford argued (1959) one wants to know how subjects are placed on a dimension, rather than how they think they are placed, items were made to refer to behaviour as far as possible. If one asks subjects whether they are unhappy, they have a genuine problem in responding: what is meant by unhappy? how unhappy do you have to be to call yourself unhappy? and so on. If, however, the item presented is behavioural the problem can be overcome. For example: "Do you find that you cry at least once a month?" or "Do others often say that you are unhappy?" Notice that this is not a claim that these two items will be successful at measuring unhappiness. All would depend upon the item trials. They are simply examples of items referring to behaviour rather than feelings. They should be more reliable than the latter type of items because subjects either do or do not cry at least once a month, and are or are not called unhappy.

To tap parsimony an item was used: Is the old adage: "Take care of the pence and the pounds will take care of themselves" just nonsense? Although this is not behavioural it requires subjects to state their views about a proverb. It seems to eliminate entirely social desirability and is keyed "No". (This item, incidentally, did not prove successful.) Another example of a parsimony item, based upon the descriptions of the anal character in the psychoanalytic literature which was searched and rephrased in item form, as far as possible, was the following—again unsuccessful. "Money spent on a good holiday is never wasted." This item, (keyed "No"), taps the parsimonious tendency of the anal character to prefer for his money the solid to the evanescent. Again, it is unlikely that this item is strongly affected by social desirability.

Items to tap obstinancy are again, in our culture, likely to be beset by problems of social desirability. Example of items are: "When you're given orders, do you often immediately feel like doing the exact opposite?" "Do you let your ideas and opinions be overridden without a struggle?"

Items to tap orderliness are likely to be over-endorsed rather than under-endorsed through social desirability since this is a desirable trait especially in schools and institutions. "Are you one of those people who find figures and statistics a complete bore?" (keyed "No") and "Do you have a special place for important documents etc.?" (keyed "Yes"), are two typical items. In all these cases these actual behaviours (liking statistical tables, immediate resistance to orders) had been mentioned in descriptions of the anal character (Abraham, 1921 and Jones, 1923). The fact that none of these items was successful and was not used in Ai3Q does not affect the illustrations of item writing.

More recently questionnaires have been constructed to measure oral optimism and oral pessimism. Typical oral traits are dependence, cheerfulness, sociability, high valuation of words and a liking for comfort. Similar item writing techniques based on psychoanalytic descriptions of orality (e.g. Glover, 1924) were used. A few items from these tests will clarify the process of item writing, the creative "arts" aspect of test construction. Ultimately a test can never be better than its items.

"Are your efforts usually in vain?" (keyed "Yes") this item taps pessimism. "Are you a good patient when ill?" (keyed "No") this item taps independence. The rationale was that for an independent person there is nothing worse than to be ill in bed, helpless and dependent on others. It was also hoped that in this form, the item was neutral for social desirability. "Do you enjoy arguing?" This item, keyed "Yes", taps love of talking and argument—reputedly oral characteristics.

These items attempt to illustrate the rationale for constructing or writing test items. Failed items were deliberately chosen, to avoid the claim of immodesty and to keep the confidentiality of the test items in the three sets. The rationale for the successful items was no different. It has been demonstrated, how a number of typical personality items came to be written. This is the art of item writing about which I make no claims. The science of test construction must now be reconsidered. Given these items, how are final revisions of tests to be developed?

The Science

Essentially, given an item pool, there are two approaches to test construction which are likely to yield tests with very different characteristics. It is not relevant to discuss these methods in so detailed a way that readers could construct tests themselves. This is a task for books specifically aimed at test construction (e.g. Anstey, 1966). What is needed here is a discussion of the logic behind these two approaches. With this it will be seen that for the purposes of establishing sound psychological data as a basis for a science of psychology, the methods are not of equal value.

Criterion-keyed Tests

In this type of test items are selected if they can discriminate a criterion group from a control group. Perhaps the two most widely used tests of this type are the Strong Vocational Interest Bank (Strong *et al.*, 1971) and the MMPI (Hathaway and McKinley, 1951). A description of how the MMPI was constructed will clearly reveal the severe problems with this method of test construction as well as showing up its actual utility.

A large MMPI item pool, consisting of items manifestly related to clinical descriptions of neurotic and psychotic symptoms, was administered to the most important categories of psychiatric patients, as defined by Kraepelin (1907). These included paranoids, schizophrenics, manic depressives and psychopaths. Items were included in a particular scale if they could discriminate one criterion group from the other groups and from controls. For example, if an item discriminated the depressives from the others, it went into the depression scale. Originally there were nine clinical scales in the MMPI, but the authors were well aware that the 559 items of the MMPI could be regarded as an item pool to form new scales by administering them to other nosological groups. Indeed, Dahlstrom and Welsh (1960) were able to collect together more than 200 criterion-keyed scales which had been developed from the MMPI items.

If one wants to use psychological test scores as a basis for psychology, this method of test construction has several severe problems, which are set out below:

(1) The nature of the criterion groups. Psychiatric classification is notoriously unreliable (Beck, 1962). Thus one may be selecting items which discriminate groups which in another experiment might not appear again! Schneider (1958), for example, prefers a tenfold classification into psychopathic types while Sjobring (1963), has yet another categorial system. Thus the MMPI highlights both the difficulty of reliably categorizing subjects into groups (admittedly more acute within psychiatry than in certain other fields) and the problem of whether the groups are groups at all. Of course if the groups are dubious, the method must inevitably fail.

(2) The nature of the discrimination. Even if it had been possible to establish criterion groups more obviously homogeneous, such as the vocational groups used in the Strong test, there is the difficulty of establishing in what way they differ from each other. How, in other words, is the discrimination made? For example, schizophrenics might differ from manics on a wide variety of psychological characteristics: liveliness, volubility, cheerfulness, intelligence and vocabulary. A scale designed to discriminate these two groups could contain a mixture of items tapping all the traits. If this were the case, what psychological significance would it have? How could scores on such a scale, collected from normals, be interpreted? Thus it can be argued that such a scale has almost no psychological meaning. In fact my example actually oversimplifies the case! It is not known actually how such psychotic groups do differ from each other. Thus the psychological meaning

to be attached to a scale which happens to discriminate the groups is very dubious. This being the case it becomes obvious that criterion-keyed scales, being psychologically meaningless, cannot yield psychological knowledge.

Practical utility of criterion-keyed scales. Buros (1972) has reached 3291 references for the MMPI and more than 1000 for the Strong Blank test, so that clearly a large number of psychologists carry out research with these tests. If my arguments are correct, it is necessary to enquire why this should be so. If the scales produced by criterion-keying have been cross-validated, there is little doubt that they can effectively discriminate between groups. Thus a hard-pressed clinical psychologist in an out-patient department can rapidly assign patients to groups as a preliminary classification with the MMPI just as a vocational guidance officer with the Strong test can see what vocational group his clients most resemble. This can be helpful in practice and certainly this is what such tests are most often used for. However, as I have argued with respect to Vocational Guidance in the "Psychology of Vocational Guidance" (Kline, 1975) and to clinical and educational psychology in "The Scientific Analysis of Personality and Motivation" (Cattell and Kline, 1977), this practical utility is in the long run specious. Thus all these researches showing differences between clinical and occupational groups on these tests, because of the lack of psychological meaning in the scales, give us little information about the psychological nature of these differences. Without this information it is not possible to investigate the aetiology of these differences, which are important in the study of abnormal groups, or factors influencing the variables which in the case of occupational groups would become, if known, important determinants of job choice. Without all this essential information I would argue that the practical utility of these tests is more apparent than real.

It would serve to contrast this psychologically barren testing with the data that can be obtained from the second major type of psychological test—those constructed by utilizing factor analysis or some analogous technique. Factorially-derived dimensions can have psychological meaning, although much experimental work needs to be done in many cases to define it. Nevertheless if one knows that group X differs from Y on a meaningful psychological variable, almost by definition there is some insight into the nature of the two groups.

Factor-analytic Tests

Definition of a factor. In a previous description which still seems succinct (Kline, 1975) I argued that a factor was "...a construct defined by its factor loadings (which are correlations of the factor with variables) and accounting for the correlations between the variables loading on it". Thus in the case of test construction, if one computes the correlations between all the items in the item pool and submits these correlations to factor analysis, the resulting factors by this definition will be the constructs or dimensions underlying the test, for they will account for the inter-item correlations. Thus if a common factor loading on all items emerges from factor-analysing the items, it is evidence that the test is really measuring some common factor. This, briefly, is the rationale for factor-analytic tests. It still remains, of course, for further research, to identify the factor.

However, there are considerable technical problems in factor-analytic test construction which must be discussed first, because they have led many test constructors to turn to analogous procedures which effectively produce the same result but with far less computational effort—important before the advent of the present generation computers—and also because in evaluating the merits of factored tests, one must be at least aware of these difficulties.

Analagous techniques. The aim, as has been seen, of factor-analysing test items is to ensure that they are measuring some common dimension. One other possible method of achieving this is to compute the item/total biserial correlation for each item. Items are then selected which correlate beyond usually 0·3 with the total score. The rationale of this method which is simple, to compute since tables have been produced (e.g. Fan, 1952), which enable this correlation to be estimated accurately from the tails of the distribution, is best shown by illustration. Suppose that a test was administered consisting of items in Turkish, Urdu, Greek and Aramaic, items testing geography, history, petrology, tribology and sociology and finally items requiring extensive knowledge of Maxwell's equations. Virtually none of these items would correlate with the total score of the test. There is obviously no common dimension among them.

The disadvantage with this method of test construction lies in the fact that the items may be relevant not to one, but to two correlated factors. Where two such factors underlying items the item/total biserial correlation is unable to reveal this. Nevertheless, in practice, sound homogeneous tests can be constructed by this method which avoids the technical problems besetting the factor analysis of item correlations.

Difficulties in factoring items. These problems have been extensively examined by Cattell (1973) and in a more summary form by Cattell and Kline (1977). They stem mainly from the statistical artefacts arising in the correlation of dichotomous data. These correlations are usually not reliable and this strongly affects subsequent factor analyses which essentially attempt to reproduce the correlations. The tetrachoric correlation, not only assumes a continuous and normal distribution for the two variables but in addition has a very large standard error (Guilford, 1956), a particularly serious flaw where the coefficients are to be factor-analysed. In addition where the item split is uneven, the correlation is limited in size. Since in most tests one wants items to range in facility value from about 10–90% (i.e. to some items only 10% will put the keyed answer, in others 90%) this is again a serious flaw. Owing to these disadvantages many test constructors turn to the phi coefficient (ϕ). This, although strictly meant for truly categorical data, which the "Yes" "No" and

"True" "False" of tests are not, does not have the large standard error of r_{tet} but is unfortunately still affected by unevenness of item split.

I have found in my own tests that the practical effects of the unreliability of correlations are seen most clearly in that emerging factors account for only a small proportion of variance. Sandler and Hazari (1960) working with the obsessional symptom items of the Tavistock Self Assessment Inventory (Sandler, 1958) bear out this point precisely. With the oral tests OPQ and OOQ (Kline and Storey 1978) it was found that factor analysis of the phi coefficients yielded factors that could not be easily identified, all being, in addition, of small variance. Yet using the technique of biserial correlation between item and total score both these tests were consistent.

Cattell and his colleagues at Illinois, in their extensive essays into test construction over the years since the war have obviously encountered this problem. Their solution has been to use item parcels rather than individual items as the basic unit of analysis (see Cattell, 1973). Resulting factors are then larger and more stable.

Kline and Storey (1978) have attempted a novel solution to this problem which deserves brief mention. OPQ and EPQ were subjected to G analysis (Holley, 1973) which then revealed that almost all items were powerfully discriminating high and low scorers on both tests. The G index (Holley and Guilford, 1964) is yet another statistic for correlating dichotomous variables. However, unlike ϕ and r_{tet} it is *not* affected by item splits. Readers may be wondering why I have not mentioned G before since it obviously overcomes most of the disadvantages of the two statistics discussed above. Unfortunately as shown by Levy (1966) G indices between items, when factored, tend to give rise to factors which relate to the facility level of the items. However, in G analysis, Q factor analysis is carried out, i.e. subjects are factored not items. The factors thus load on people. Then D estimates are computed which indicate which variables pick out best the people in the Q factor groups. Such is G analysis and it is clear that it is a powerful method for item analysis especially since using Burt's reciprocity principle (Burt, 1940) if Q factors can be formed from items, R factors should also be present.

In the development of OPQ and OOQ, the top 15 and bottom 15 subjects' responses to each item were subjected to G analysis. Since in each case the subjects fell clearly into two groups it was argued that a common factor must run through each test. D estimates revealed that almost all items were contributing to this discrimination between groups. Since the results agreed well with a standard item analysis, and since G analysis refers through the reciprocity principle to factors and demands less computation than item analysis, G analysis is a further useful method of item selection.

The solution advocated above needs further research with a variety of tests and subjects before it can be confidently used. I attempted this rather than the item parcelling referred to earlier as the method favoured by Cattell and colleagues at Illinois. This is because item parcelling has problems of its own. Sometimes items in the parcel virtually form scales so that resulting factors are not first-order (i.e. factors underlying item correlations) but second-order, factors underlying first-order factors. This may well be, as has been argued by Cattell and Kline (1977), what has occurred in the research of Comrey (Comrey, 1970) where his factors based upon FHID's, factored homogeneous item groups, appear to be second-order rather than first. I shall return to this point when looking at the contribution of psychological tests to the knowledge of personality in Chapter 6.

Even if despite these problems one manages to obtain from the factoring of items a general factor of sufficient variance to be useful, by no means has one completed the item selection. This equally applies to the other techniques for selecting items whether by biserial correlations or G analysis. All that has been achieved is the demonstration that a common factor (or with item analysis, possibly factors) runs through the items. *This factor must now be identified.*

Factor identification. Factor identification is absolutely essential in test construction. It is identical to demonstrating the validity of a test—which is fully discussed (see pp. 5–12). Suffice to say that it is not enough to label the factor from the content of the items loading on it. This is no more than face validity. If one is truly empirical and constructing more than one scale at a time, scales may emerge with items, intended for different scales, loading on them. This is true of Cattell's 16 PF test (Cattell *et al.*, 1970). This makes labelling by item content impossible. As discussed in the section on validity, one has to show that the scale is not homogeneous due to response sets such as social desirability or acquiescence and is not measuring what other tests measure. Usually experimental demonstrations of validity are necessary. With many tests construct validity studies are the only means of properly labelling the factor.

From this discussion it should now be clear why a factorial scale has, if demonstrated to be valid, psychological meaning. The dimension underlying the items has been shown to possess certain characteristics, otherwise it could not be labelled or identified. This is not, of course, to say that *all* factors have psychological meaning. It is possible to develop scales where all items load on a meaningless factor. This will arise in later chapters where various results that have been claimed in almost all branches of psychology, on the basis of factored tests are discussed. A few examples will clarify this point.

If a series of items which are largely paraphrases of each other were written, e.g. Do you enjoy a good party? Do you like going to lively gatherings? Do you like to stay quietly on your own? Are you the person who can keep a party going? and so on, these items might well load up on a common factor. However, whether such a factor could be said to have psychological meaning is doubtful. Although the meaning of a factor is not determined by the speculation in which we are indulging for the sake of clarification but is established by empirical evidence, such a factor is likely to be moderately correlated with extraversion, but mainly specific. In other words this factor is common to these items and little else. Such a factor has been called by Cattell (1974) a bloated specific and by Eysenck and Eysenck (1969) a T (tautological) factor. Such bloated specifics can be recognized when one identifies the factor by the fact that they correlate with almost no other psychological variables and make no meaningful discriminations between criterion groups and are unable to predict other test results or behaviours. The variance which they encompass, therefore, must be specific to the items.

GUILFORD MODEL OF VARIANCE

This example leads on to a useful but arbitrary distinction to be drawn between factors. Common or group factors load on a number of psychological variables, specific factors on one variable only. The arbitrary nature of this distinction is obvious when it is realized that a factor can only load on the variables put into the particular investigation. In a battery of ability tests, if there were only one mathematical test, the N factor would appear to be specific. However, that would only reflect my poor sampling of the universe of variables. Variable sampling (and subject sampling) has to be correct if factor-analytic studies are to be psychologically meaningful. However, this is a different question which shall be discussed in Chapter 2. It is sufficient here to note that the distinction between specific and group factors, although arbitrary, is important.

If the factorial variance underlying tests is considered, it can be broken down into group factors, specific factors and error variance. Thus the WISC (Wechsler, 1958) can be shown to load highly on two important factors gf and gc, fluid and crystallized intelligence (see Chapter 4). The specific factors are those that underlie the particular form of this test (e.g. that it is speeded, that it has one particular set of questions and not others). The error variance is the variance left unexplained by the common and specific factors.

This analysis of test variance has most clearly been stated by Guilford (1956) and as a final conclusion to this chapter on the nature of psychological tests, it will be helpful to discuss it. With this model, a number of points become clear. First one can see that a test can be reliable but not valid. For the reliability of a test depends upon the true variance, i.e. the common, general and specific factor variance. A test can be highly reliable if most of its variance is specific or its group factors those of social desirability or acquiescence. It is also clear how a test can have the wrong group factor variance running through it, (making it invalid), thus confirming the importance of experimentally identifying the factor as discussed. It incidentally highlights a common lay argument about tests of intelligence. It is often claimed that these tests show nothing but ability at intelligence tests. In Guilford's terms, this means that their variance is all specific. If this were the case, of course, intelligence test scores would not correlate with anything else or predict academic or occupational success. In fact, there is little doubt that perhaps of all psychometric tests, intelligence tests pick up the variance in abilities that is the most distributed among tasks of every kind, as will be discussed in Chapter 4.

Guilford's (1958) model can be regarded as a classical approach to understanding test variance. However, more recently in psychometrics attention has been turned to the very nature of the item variance by such workers as Rasch (1960), Birnbaum (1968) and Lord and Novick (1968). One of the important problems they have been concerned with is to disentangle the effects on item response, of the item's response eliciting power for the trait it measures and the status on the trait of the particular subject. This is obviously important in group comparison where items may differ in their strength for the different groups who may really be no different in respect of this trait. Since this work has been little used in practice, item response models will not be developed here; good surveys of this work can be found in Lord and Novick (1968) and in Levy (1973). However, where any results do have substantive implications for psychological theory, they will be be discussed in the relevant chapters.

PROJECTIVE AND OBJECTIVE TEST CONSTRUCTION

This completes a brief discussion on the construction of psychological tests that are likely to have the attributes which have been argued to be essential for good measurement. All that has been said about test construction applies to tests with items. However, it provides no guide for the construction of projective tests or T, objective, tests. In both these cases, one has to use creative imagination applied to well-known psychological principles. The selection of a projective test, once the idea has been conceived, must depend entirely upon the results achieved with it. In the case of T, objective tests, all depends on their factor loadings. If they load up as wished, they will be used. If not, they are abandoned.

However, what are these "well-known psychological principles" which have to be applied with imagination? Cattell and Child (1975) list 66 for the construction of T tests of motivation and Cattell and Warburton (1967) contain similar useful information as well as a taxonomy of tests in terms of test instructions, test stimuli and subjects' responses which can prove helpful in systematic test construction. Examples of the psychological principles taken from Cattell and Child (1975) are set out below. Increases in the following variables are expected to reflect increased interest. Threat reactivity: PGR drops when interest is threatened. Learning: learning of interest-related material is better. Availability: readiness to associate interest-related material to a given cue. All the variables can be inferred from clinical motivational theory so that, at least as far as objective tests are concerned there are principles available for guiding test construction.

In the case of projective tests one has to be guided by intuition and one's particular personality theory. Thus Murray's (1938) TAT pictures are closely related to his motivational theory of needs and presses. Blum (1949) and Corman (1969) have based their projective tests upon Freudian theory—

especially developmenal theory. For example, to test orality, Blum shows pictures of Blacky (his eponymous hero dog) suckling and Blacky tearing his mother's collar. Corman shows his piglet suckling and suckling from a goat. In 1977 I was tentatively developing a projective oral test (to be objectively scored however) where three pictures are used: a ravening wolf, a ferocious vampire and a baby sucking luxuriantly at the breast. In the development of tests of this sort all depends upon results. If clinicians and researchers find a stimulus elicits data they want, then it is a useful test. If it fails to do this, then regardless of rationale and provenance, it is worthless.

This completes the introductory chapter on the nature of psychometrics and psychometric tests. Their attributes have been delineated and their construction discussed sufficiently to evaluate their worth when one comes to examine the mass of psychological test results in the various fields of psychology. Before this, however, in Chapter 2 the special kinds of statistical analysis must be discussed which, I shall argue, are especially suited to analysing psychometric test data. My argument runs that psychometric tests are the special instruments of a psychological science but powerful data analysis is particularly important if their true worth is to be realized.

SUMMARY

(1) The special qualities of psychological tests: Reliability: internal consistency, test-retest reliability were described. Validity: face validity, content validity, concurrent validity, predictive validity, construct validity incremental validity and differential validity were discussed. Effects of response sets were examined. Norms and standardization were described.
(2) Types of test: psychometric, projective tests and objective tests were scrutinized.
(3) Test construction: The art of test construction: item writing was described. The science was discussed: criterion-keyed tests, item selection: advantages and disadvantages. Factor-analytic tests, item selection: advantages and disadvantages.
(4) The Guilford model of test variance and other item models were discussed.
(5) Projective and objective test construction were described.

2

The Statistical Methods of Psychometrics

PSYCHOMETRIC DATA

The ideal characteristics of psychological tests yield data of a special and typical kind (see Chapter 1). This is not to say that these data are unique or radically different from the data obtained by other psychological methods. Nevertheless, test data do have features which demand correspondingly special statistical analyses if the maximum possible information is to be obtained.

In this chapter, therefore, I shall discuss typical psychometric data and indicate the kinds of problems to which they are most apposite. This introductory section enables one to see more easily the logic and rationale of the statistical methods which have been largely developed by psychometrists to solve their special problems.

The important distinction often drawn between nomothetic and idiographic tests was discussed, and it was seen that contrary to the view of many workers in this field (notably Eysenck) idiographic tests could yield scientifically useful data, if they were both valid and reliable. This distinction is particularly relevant to the discussion of the characteristic data yielded by tests.

Nomothetic Data

By definition nomothetic data are aimed to establish laws, the regularities underlying the test responses. In practice over the years in psychometry, nomothetic tests have been used to define the basic dimensions accounting for individual differences. In this approach individuals differ from each other along certain dimensions of ability, personality and motivation. If one knows what these dimensions are, as is the case with electrons and neutrons, so one can understand the whole of which they are parts.

Since, therefore, nomothetic tests aim to uncover fundamental dimensions, then it is obvious that in any properly conducted investigation one needs a large number of tests. Without this, important factors could be easily missed out. Since these dimensions are related to individual differences, large numbers of subjects—or, more accurately subjects with a considerable variance on the variables under investigation are needed. Thus nomothetic tests demand that investigations utilize a large number of variables on large numbers of heterogeneous subjects. Psychometric statistical methods must be able to deal adequately with these.

However, the nomothetic aim demands also that the statistics can answer certain questions of which the most basic is, in terms of scientific parsimony, what is the smallest number of variables that can account for the observed individual differences in this large number of variables, in this large sample? That is the question that the statistical methods of psychometrics must be able to answer for nomothetic data.

Idiographic data

Again by definition these data seek to describe the individual. What is distinctive about this person, special, unique to him? Idiographic data, therefore, are the antithesis of nomothetic. In their concentration on the uniqueness of the individual (as advocated by Allport, 1937), it is reasonable to ask how they may ever be regarded as scientific. There are two separate answers to this point, and each demands its own statistical analysis.

In the first place the uniqueness of each individual may itself be lawful. For example, measuring regularly the fluctuations in moods of an individual over a considerable time period, one might find that for him his anger was always roused by his spouse's sitting late over her knitting, his fear by having to make long car journeys. For this kind of idiographic data, tests are needed with the same degree of reliability and validity as are demanded in orthodox nomothetic psychometry. Furthermore, within each subject these variations may themselves be accountable in terms of a few more simple dimensions. This *within subject* analysis of individual differences (truly idiographic work) could lead to powerful clinical insights. It could be that apparently unique features turned out to be common, after such analysis. This type of within subject analysis is no different from the nomothetic analyses, discussed in the previous section, in the demands made upon statistics. Essentially identical statistical methods would suit both.

The second argument concerning the unscientific nature of idiographic tests relates to the type of data (and what statistical treatment it is amenable to) that usually emerges from such tests. Generally, as in the Thematic Apperception Test (TAT), for example, or the Rorschach, typical projective tests, and it is projective tests that most frequently seek to assess the idiodynamics (Rosenzweig, 1954) of individuals, subjects have to describe stimuli. This produces responses which have to be interpreted by scorers and generally, as has been discussed, reliability and validity are necessarily low. This being the case, such responses could not form part of a scientifically useful testing procedure.

However, objective content analysis by dichotomous scoring (0 or 1) for the presence or absence of a particular feature enables objective scoring procedures to be used for almost any projective test. Although these techniques and their results will be discussed in later chapters relevant to the findings, Holley (1973) utilized them in investigations of the Rorschach test which showed impressive clinical discrimination of depressives and schizophrenics. More recently Hampson and Kline (1977) utilized, in a study of criminals, similar objective scoring methods on a wide variety of projective tests and even interviews. However, these idiographic data were used in these studies nomothetically since subjects were factored, rather than variables, and placed into clinical and criminal groups. Nevertheless, it is clear that objections to the nature of the test responses in projective tests can be overcome. As indicated, for these studies special statistical methods have been developed and these will be discussed. Thus even projective test, idiographic, data require their own statistical analysis, concentrating on within individual rather than between individual variance and on special methodologies designed for dichotomous data.

In summary it can be seen that the data of psychometry require statistical analyses that can handle large numbers of subjects and variables. The purposes of psychometric investigations generally further demand that the statistical analyses can uncover underlying dimensions or factors and can give simple, elegant and parsimonious accounts of highly complex initial observations. Against this background one can now examine the special methods that if not actually developed in psychometrics have been widely and until recently, almost exclusively used in this field. I am only concerned with the mathematical models implicit in these methods where they impinge upon the interpretation of results—with their rationale and logic. If this is properly understood, it becomes possible to evaluate investigations that have used these statistical procedures. I shall also define the terms that arise in such discussions, although every effort will be made to avoid statistical or psychological jargon and elaborate certain technical rules agreed upon by most psychometrists to ensure that results are not but statistical artefacts.

MULTIVARIATE AND UNIVARIATE ANALYSIS

In statistical analysis a highly important practical distinction can be drawn between univariate and multivariate methods. Cattell, who is one of the leading exponents of psychometrics in the tradition of Spearman whose research assistant he was, has perhaps most consistently made this point (Cattell, 1946, 1957, 1966).

The essential difference between univariate and multivariate analysis is a practical one. The univariate method, as its name suggests, involves manipulating one variable to ascertain its effect on another. It is the method primarily of experimental laboratory psychology. It necessitates that one can control completely the variable under manipulation. Multivariate analysis, on the other hand, operates on a large number of variables at once and can use them, as they occur in the real world: a laboratory is not necessary. These very brief, and necessarily over-simplified definitions, which are amplified below, enable us to see however, that in the content of the demands made by psychometric data, univariate methods are clearly inadequate. One needs to deal with many variables thus making it plain that multivariate analyses by the first criterion (of variables) is clearly the methodology suited to psychometric data. What is needed is multivariate analysis that can simplify complex data.

This careful distinction between univariate and multivariate analysis has to be made so as to stress its practical aspects. This is because, as has been cogently argued by Van de Geer (1971), as regards mathematical assumptions there are no major differences between the various techniques of multivariate analysis and multivariate analyses of variance. However, this implies further that there is no difference between the univariate method (one-way analysis of variance) and multivariate methods.

Practically, the differences between the two methods are large. In the univariate case one controls the variable with great precision or at a stretch, in analysis of variance, a few variables. Precise hypotheses are formulated which are or are not refuted. In multivariate analysis as many variables as possible are measured as they occur in nature. The manipulations are those that may be found in the real world, e.g. one parent families, children in families larger than five and so on. All variables are analysed taking into account their mutual interactions. It is in this basic philosophy, the scientific laboratory or the laboratory of life, that univariate and multivariate methods present so striking a contrast. Again, this distinction emphasizes the utility for psychometric data of multivariate analyses.

At this point analysis of variance must be mentioned. This technique which has been elaborated (e.g. Snedecor, 1956) and although basically an extension of the univariate method, does allow several variables to be simultaneously manipulated and their interactions can be measured. However, it does not meet the demands of psychometric data as well as multivariate analyses because the number of variables that can be utilized in any one study is limited. This limitation arises from sampling problems (unequal numbers in the cells leads to interactions of dubious veracity) and because the interpretation of interactions of more than three variables is almost impossible.

Such studies can and do play an important part in understanding the results of psychological tests. For example, if one wants to discover sex differences on variables, the most sensible form of analysis is a univariate comparison. The point is that the data from psychometric tests on the whole are best suited to multivariate analyses. These answer both the nomothetic and idiographic questions that the proper use of psychometry puts up. Certainly, as shall be seen in later chapters, the contribution of psychometrics to psychology has resulted from just such multivariate analyses.

MULTIVARIATE ANALYSES

There are now in existence a large variety of multivariate analyses each of which has a particular purpose. In this section I shall briefly describe the various types concentrating on their logic and their practical usage. This whole field of multivariate analysis is highly technical and complex. It is important to know the strengths and weaknesses of each technique so that its worth can be evaluated as it is used or not in the investigations to be examined in later chapters. (Further discussion on multivariate techniques can be found in Cattell, 1966 and Cattell and Kline, 1977.)

Since, however, the major discoveries from psychometrics have been made from the application of one particular technique, factor-analysis, it is upon this that this chapter concentrates, and an examination of this technique will be found at the end of this chapter.

Multiple Correlation

In this technique the aim is to maximize the correlation between a set of variables (the predictors) and a criterion variable. Obviously in doing this, optimum weights for each variable have to be worked out (the beta weights) and these indicate the importance of each variable in the overall total correlation.

From this description it is evident that multiple correlation is a valuable technique when using psychometrics to establish psychological facts. For example, a multiple correlation of ability, personality and motivation measured against academic success at university could establish with some precision just what qualities are or are not important in such success. This, therefore, could constitute a clear statement in educational psychology. In Chapter 8 there are discussions of investigations of this type at the secondary school level, conducted by Cattell and Butcher (1967).

However, this technique has a number of problems. First, beta weights are notoriously unreliable (e.g. Anderson, 1966) so that it is essential that all results are replicated on fresh samples. A further difficulty lies in knowing what predictor variables to include in any investigation. Where the field is known this is not difficult, but if it is known there is, perhaps, little point in this type of research. Thus generally multiple correlation studies are undertaken after the area of research has been clarified by other methods (often factor analysis). Finally, the most serious defect in the method is the criterion variable, (see pp. 6–7). However, in most fields of psychology a single criterion is manifestly unsatisfactory although my example of academic success is probably an exception which is why it was chosen. This last problem is overcome by canonical analysis.

Canonical Analysis of Canonical Correlation

In this method by Hotelling (1936), which is only much used recently now that rapid computing facilities are available, sets of predictors are correlated with sets of criteria. In other respects it resembles multiple correlation and may be regarded, for practical purposes, as an elaborated version of it.

As has been indicated these two techniques have obvious application in clarifying what has been discovered through psychometrics. It is necessary to mention some other multivariate techniques although they are not so relevant to psychometricists' aims.

Discriminant Function Analysis

This technique examines differences between two groups. Although this can be done variable by variable by t-tests, this ignores correlations between variables and gives each unit weighting, whereas discriminant functions take these into account. For the establishment of a basic psychology it could be useful if there is some prior reason to investigate two groups. For example, discriminant functions of dyslexics versus controls might clearly discover what the differences (if any) were between these and normals. This could lead to a proper understanding of the syndrome. As yet, however, few such studies exist. Practically, a difficulty with discriminant function analysis arises from the fact that the results are very dependent upon the particular sample and set of variables. Thus, it is always necessary to replicate any results before utilizing them in any way.

Latent Class Analysis

Lazarsfeld (1950) was responsible for this method which can assign subjects to groups on the basis of dichotomous data. It is, therefore, useful in the study of projective and objective tests (making idiography scientifically respectable). As yet it is a technique that is rarely employed.

Configural Analysis

This method (Cattell, 1949) which classifies response patterns is suited to clinical case studies. It can, therefore, be useful in confirming theories by putting them to the test in the individual case—one contrary case being a refutation.

Type Recognition

Cluster analyses are the usual method employed in the recognition of types. Many different varieties have been developed (see Sokal and Sneath, 1963). Tryon (1939), one of the pioneers in the field, thought cluster analyses, usually grouping subjects, not tests, together, to be superior to factor analysis because factors were not verified.

Sneath and Sokal (1973) in an excellent review of these methods argue that there are two basic types—"Association Analysis" and "Agglomerative methods":

(1) Association analysis is divisive: the sample is divided successively into smaller and smaller sub-groups. Each sub-group is monothetic, i.e. is defined by a unique set of attributes (perhaps only one) which every member of the group possesses. Sneath and Sokal (1973) argue that a weakness of the methodology is that a subject can be misplaced at early stages of the process. They prefer polythetic techniques where membership of a group consists of the greatest possible number of shared characteristics. This type of cluster analysis "association analysis" can again be useful in establishing group identities, although a careful choice of variables has to be made and there is no necessary psychological meaning in the grouping.

(2) Agglomerative methods of which a well-known variety is pattern analysis (McQuitty, 1967) proceed by combining individuals into larger and larger groups. Broadly a type is defined in this methodology as a set of subjects whose intercorrelations are higher than their correlations with subjects not in the group. This is a limited definition of a type and limits the value of forms of pattern analysis which use it.

As Tryon (1939) pointed out, cluster analyses of subjects are similar to factor analyses (see factor analysis). Fruchter (1954) has shown that in cluster analysis each person is placed exclusively in one cluster which is unlikely to fit the data well, since most variance is multifactorial, not unifactorial.

Cattell (1966) has also argued that a further advantage of Q factor analysis over cluster analysis lies in the meaningful nature of rotated Q factors, compared with clusters of types which are heavily dependent on the particular sample and variables. This psychological meaningfulness of factors is a critical topic in this book.

From this discussion I hope it is clear that type analysis can play some small part in establishing the kind of basic psychology relevant to our needs. However, as shall be shown later, cluster analysis is probably inferior for this purpose to factor analysis. Readers can be referred to Sneath and Sokal (1973) or to Hampson (1975) for a very clear discussion.

The Work of Guttman

Guttman (e.g. 1957) has provided an even more parsimonious account of correlation matrices, according to his arguments, than that provided by factor analysis. He has been able to reveal certain underlying structures which neatly describe correlation matrices: the Radex (Guttman, 1954), the Simplex (Guttman, 1955) and the Circumplex (Guttman, 1966). However, Cattell (1966) notes that these structures may well not reveal the "real world". Instead there is a temptation for psychologists to construct a world of tests and items to fit these models. This is a very real danger and it is a point discussed in various chapters where the substantive findings from psychological tests are examined. It is perhaps best exemplified in the argument between Burt (1966) and Lewis (1966) concerning the normal distribution of intelligence. As Lewis (1966) points out, the fact that test scores are normally distributed is not *per se* a powerful argument for normal distribution since it is a function of the particular set of items in the test and the subjects. Intelligence test items could be constructed of prodigious difficulty: in this case the distribution of scores would be very different.

Guttman's work has been little used to establish any substantive findings so that its relevance is not high. However, one should be aware of its existence because it is an arguable case that it could provide results of considerable importance in certain difficult areas, as shall be seen in later chapters.

Factor Analysis

I have dealt briefly with seven types of multivariate analysis, all of which could prove useful in the task of creating a psychology based upon psychometrics, and some of these have indeed provided valuable results. However, of all the multivariate techniques, factor analysis has been the most widely used in psychometric analysis and factor-analytic results have demonstrated, time and again in varied fields of psychology, the power of psychometrics. Indeed, without a sound understanding of the logic and rationale of factor analysis and a mastery of the special terminology, the main corpus of this book cannot be understood. Findings must be evaluated rationally, and the following section clarifies the essentials of factor analysis, excluding mathematics, but concentrating on its logic and function.

Factor Analysis in Test Results and Test Construction

At this point an apparent contradiction must be disposed of. Here I am claiming that factor analysis is an ideal method for analysing test data yet in the first chapter it was argued that it was an ideal method of test construction. The answer is that both of these claims are true. Ultimately, they are not different claims either. Thus, to demonstrate that a common factor pervades a set of items not only allows a test to be constructed (as in Chapter 1) and enables that test to be used along with others to establish the nature of the factor and the structure of the psychological domain (as in Chapter 2), it is also of psychological interest itself that a factor does exist, that a test can be constructed. The fact of test construction can be a psychologically substantive result.

ESSENTIAL FACTOR ANALYSIS

For computational aspects of factor analysis readers must be referred to Harman (1964) for an excellent survey of different techniques and to Child (1971) for those who need the simplest possible explanation. Nunnally (1978) is also excellent.

Definition of a Factor

Eysenck (1967c) has defined a factor as a condensed statement of linear relationships between variables. However, it can be objected to that this is too general. Royce (1963) searched the literature for definitions and was able to find the following descriptions: dimensions, determinants, functional unities, parameters and taxonomic categories. In other words these terms are what Eysenck's condensed statement is. Royce (1963) however, supplies his own definition which is broadly the one that will be adopted throughout this book, since it embraces most descriptions and is certainly agreeable to the leading psychometrists. According to Royce a factor is "*a construct operationally defined by its factor loadings*". Factor loadings are the correlations of variables with factors. Examples will clarify this definition.

Suppose the intercorrelations between Latin, Greek, French, German, Physics, Chemistry, Biology and Maths are factor-analysed. If one obtained a factor loading on the languages but not on the sciences, and a factor loading on the sciences and not on the languages, it is no great effort of deduction to argue, using Royce's definition, that factor 1 is a language ability factor and factor 2, a numerical or scientific ability factor. If one had obtained a common factor loading on all subjects, again it would clearly be labelled as general ability. It is to be noted that these constructs, language ability and numerical ability, are quite different from these terms in general use. This is because they are defined by their factor loadings. They are not dependent on verbal descriptions. It may happen as in this example that there is a good overlap between common use and factorial definition, but often factors emerge which have no vulgar equivalents.

There is a further scientific advantage in utilizing factorial concepts of this kind. When one puts factors in these investigations, these are replicable variables (defined by their loadings) that other researchers can follow up. In addition and even more important, the proper identification of factors does not depend only on their loadings, as it did in these examples. If one had identified a factor of numerical ability, one could test this tentative identification experimentally. For example, physicists, engineers and mathematicians should score more highly than the rest of the population. Cambridge Wranglers should exceed pass degree students on the factor. It should be able to predict university success in the sciences.

This example has, I hope, clarified the meaning of Royce's definition of a factor as a construct defined by its loadings. However, to complete the clarification it is necessary to discuss further the nature of factor loadings.

Factor Loadings

It has previously been mentioned that factor loadings are correlations of the variables in the analysis with the factors—the constructs which they define. However, it must also be pointed out that, as Eysenck's definition stressed, the factors are a *condensed* statement. This condensation arises from the fact that there are considerably *less* factors in a factor analysis of a correlation matrix than variables. Thus one can account for the observed correlations between the variables with relatively few factors, i.e. by cross-multiplication of the factor loadings one can arrive back at the original correlations. Thus factors are not only operationally defined constructs. In addition they can account for the observed correlations, i.e. variances and covariances by a few precise constructs. This is why factor analysis can be regarded as a scientific method. It is elegant and parsimonious (a few factors instead of many variables) and precise, each construct being mathematically defined by its factor loadings.

From this definition of factor and factor loading it becomes clear why factor analysis is so fitting a statistical technique for the psychometry of individual differences. It precisely simplifies complex data, and the resulting factors mathematically, at least, account for the observed correlations. However, there now arises the question of the psychological meaning and status of factors. Are they mathematical entities or have they some further psychological meaning reflected in the real world?

Status of Factors

This is one of the most crucial issues in factor analysis and there are divergent opinions even among the leading authorities in the field. The basic question concerns factors as, in Cattell's (1966) terminology, causal agencies. There is no doubt that the early pioneers of factor analysis did regard factors as having causal implications. This is evident in the work of Spearman (1927) and Thurstone (1947) in the field of abilities. Thus, for example, g the general ability factor isolated by Spearman and appearing at the second-order even in Thurstone's work can be seen as in some way causing the observations the term subsumes: performance in a wide variety of school subjects is correlated because of the part in such performance played by general ability. If we have high general ability, most subjects lie open to us, if not we are restricted to domestic science, sociology or some other of those subjects beloved of modern universities and polytechnics: these tax the adult earner rather than the mind.

This example where one can see that a well-established factor g does seem to have some causal status (some factors, therefore, if not all, could be causal agencies) introduces another associated difficulty. Burt (1940) was well aware of the danger of reifying factors. In abilities g is a neat construct which encapsulates a mass of complex data. Nevertheless, it cannot be said to exist in the sense that some part of the brain does and hence, may be observed, e.g. the optic chiasma. There is a misleading tendency to think of factors as things rather than concepts. Sometimes, however, as Eysenck (1969) illustrates, these factorial concepts have precise equivalents in the world strongly supporting, of course, the power of factor analysis to uncover basic dimensions. In his example from medicine, he points out that the factorization of symptoms would lead to a factor loading on coughing, spitting blood, weight loss, brilliant eyes, sweating at night and so on, i.e. the symptoms of tuberculosis. This factor would be causal and would correspond in fact to the tubercle itself.

Cattell (1966) takes a more extreme view. His argument is that the mathematical model of factor analysis implies that factors are determiners especially if simple structure, i.e. the simplest solution is reached. This point can only be properly evaluated after simple structure has been examined. This is so important in understanding the full implications of factor analysis and in interpreting factors that there is a section on this topic. Many of the disagreements between factorists and misunderstandings of factor analysis in psychology generally are due to a failure to understand the notion of simple structure.

Rotation of Factors and Simple Structure

A common and *prima facie* reasonable objection to factor analysis by the uninitiated (e.g. Heim, 1975) is that there is no unique solution. There are as many solutions as factorists. Since there is no *a priori* method of determining the position of the factors or axes relative to each other, Thurstone (1947) argued that rotation to simple structure would overcome the difficulty.

Rotation to simple structure is curiously a complex affair. The summary here is based upon a brilliant and detailed analysis of the topic by Cattell (1966) and a simplified version of it in Cattell and Kline (1977) to which readers are referred for greater detail.

Thurstone (1947) defined simple structure essentially as the attainment of factors with a few high loadings and many low loadings. This definition is thus an exemplar of the law of parsimony—the simplest explanation of the observations is the best. However, the question now arises as to how such simple structure is to be reached. Cattell (1966) argues that it is here that many factor analyses fail.

First, some technical terms have to be defined: orthogonal and oblique rotations and higher-order factor analyses. In *orthogonal rotation* the axes are kept at right-angles to each other—thus being uncorrelated. So an orthogonal rotation will produce uncorrelated factors. Except in rare cases this means that it is unlikely that simple structure can be reached. Generally it happens that in the real world influences on variables are correlated. *Oblique rotation* produces correlated factors, the correlation being related to the angle between the axes.

In a large scale study the correlations between the factors can themselves be factored—thus producing higher-order factors (in this example—second-order). Second-order factors load on first-order factors which load on variables. As we continue into the realms of higher-order factorization so our factors become, of course, further removed from reality, from observation. Thus, in factor analysis the simplifying power can be easily illustrated: m variables can be accounted for by n factors, which can be accounted for by p second-orders, which can be accounted for by Q third-orders ... where $m > n > p >$ Q.

Thurstone (1938) originally rotated factors graphically. Simple structure was obtained by eye. This procedure is lengthy, demanding great skill and can only approximate simple structure. I have already pointed out that orthogonal rotation is unlikely to reach simple structure so that oblique solutions have to be reached. Cattell (1966) has claimed that simple structure is attained best if one maximizes the hyperplane count, which is effectively the number of nil loadings. In practice the value of the loading one regards as zero can be set, at, e.g. 0·05 or 0·1, and the different solutions can be compared. What is needed, therefore, according to Cattell, is an oblique rotation programme aimed at maximizing the hyperplane count. Indeed, three criterOPia for estimating whether simple structure has been obtained are suggested by Cattell (1966). These are: the demonstration that further rotations produce a drop in the hyperplane count, the application of Bargmann's (1953) statistical test for simple structure and the fact that the percentage of variables in the hyperplane count lies between 55 % and 85 %. If simple structure has been obtained by these three criteria, the method by which it was obtained is of no significance, although Cattell (1966) argues that in fact, topological computer programmes, such as Maxplane (Cattell and Muerle, 1960) which actually locate clusters of variables, are far more likely to reach simple structure than analytic programmes which maximize the dispersion of factor loading by raising them to the fourth power in their rotation procedures. Recently, however a study by Hakstian (1971) showed an analytic programme producing a result slightly better than Maxplane. Nevertheless, generally topological programmes by these criteria of simple structure do seem more efficient than others.

From this discussion it is now clear that one can reach simple structure objectively by computer programme with some kind of agreement by external criteria that one has arrived there. This, therefore, enables the psychometrist to reach the most simple solution, thus fitting in with the scientific law of economy, and to overcome the disadvantage with factor analysis that there is an infinity of solutions.

An entirely different approach to simple structure—confactor rotation (Cattell, 1944)—should be mentioned. Here it is argued that if factors are causal agencies, then factor patterns in different experiments will have predictable relationships. Indeed from experiment to experiment, loadings should be replicable in terms of a constant. Full details can be found in Cattell and Cattell (1955). At present this grandiose method has been little used and there is no need to discuss it further.

To summarize factor analysis. A factor is seen as a construct operationally defined by its loadings. The factors in an analysis when simple structure has been reached, by definition give the most parsimonious account of the observed data. Certainly often such factors have a causal status. From this the power of factor analysis in the study of individual differences as they emerge from the application of psychological tests should be clear.

In fact Eysenck (1953) has suggested that there are three distinct uses of factor analysis. First there is a purely descriptive aspect. Here one could simply take the principal components solution before rotation and set that out as a parsimonious account of the intercorrelations. Each factor might not be interpretable, but it would be a simplified, if meaningless, description. This use is not common in psychometric work.

The second approach is to allow the rotated factor analysis to suggest a hypothesis. This would then be refuted or not in further experimental studies. The hypothesis suggestive use is extremely valuable in psychometrics in clarifying exceedingly complex data.

Finally there is the hypothesis refuting or supporting use. I have employed this in the study of Freudian theory (Kline, 1968, Kline and Storey, 1977). In the first case from psychoanalytic theory an anal character factor was hypothesized loading on tests of obsessional traits but not symptoms and independent of the 16 PF factors and EPI extraversion and anxiety. In the second study a similar approach was adopted in an investigation of the more nebulous concept of the oral personality. Both these investigations will be fully discussed in the chapter on personality.

So far in this section I have indicated some of the problems of factor analysis and shown how these can be overcome. However, the nature of factors and the purpose and aims of factor analyses are only possible if certain practical technical rules are observed. If these are broken the logic of factor analysis, as discussed above, is irrelevant: statistical artefacts will predominate.

BASIC PRACTICAL RULES FOR FACTOR-ANALYTIC STUDIES

In this section, I discuss therefore, the basic rules (of sampling both subjects and variables) that ensure replicable results. These rules are generally agreed upon by most experienced workers in the field. For various reasons in many researches, these rules are often flouted. Thus, it is essential for a proper estimation of the worth of factor-analytic research to understand not only its logic but the basic research practicalities. Some of these rules stem from the logic of the technique, others from simple statistical demands for reliable figures.

Cattell (1973) sets out eight requirements for factor analysis if it is hoped to define unitary traits. These are concerned with the following points: (a) sampling of variables, (b) sampling of subjects, (c) number of factors, (d) communalities, (e) oblique rotation, (f) simple structure, (g) significance of simple structure, (h) invariance of pattern across researches and (i) invariance of higher-order structure. Cattell (1973) and Cattell and Kline (1977) discuss these requirements in detail. However, for the purposes of evaluating the merits of factor-analytic researches I shall concentrate on what are undoubtedly the most important, i.e. the first two.

Sampling Variables

An objection that is often made to factor analysis (e.g. Heim, 1975) is that one can only get out what one puts in (as if this made it in some way different from and inferior to traditional univariate methods). This objection is implicitly aimed at the problem of fully sampling variables. Thus, if through factor analysis one tries to describe the fundamental dimensions of ability or motivation but inadvertently leaves out a set of variables the results will be inevitably awry. Taking motivation as an example, suppose one measures the drives to be found in the literature; sex, aggression, achievement, self-sentiment and so on, but omits hunger and thirst. These last can then never appear in the factor-analytic picture of motivation. In this sense the objection is correct: no tests, no factors. However, in a more important sense the objection is false. Often factors can arise which constitute concepts no one has previously conceived. The medical example of tuberculosis exemplifies this. Nevertheless one thing is clear. In factor analysis, when it is used to delineate and define a field, one must be sure that the universe of variables has been fully sampled. Without this guarantee, results can be misleading. Of course, this raises the problem, different in the various fields of psychology, of how variables can be sampled. This will be discussed in the relevant chapters.

Sampling Subjects

Subject sampling can also affect the factors emerging from factor analyses. Guilford (1957) has argued that samples should be homogeneous and that scores from different groups should not be put together unless they have been demonstrated to be the same. However, there are two difficulties here. In the first place a sample is supposed to reflect a population and this may not be homogeneous. Secondly, homogeneity reduces correlations and thus lowers the variance of factors. Ideally I should like to see factoring of large heterogeneous samples with checks on more homogeneous sub-groups.

Furthermore Guilford's (1956) suggestions can lead, it seems, to actual error. Suppose one was to investigate the determinants of academic performance. If one restricts oneself to open scholarship winners at Oxford or Cambridge (whose I.Q. is generally very high), intelligence test scores would not load highly on the attainment factor. If one investigated all institutions of Higher Education (including degrees in Pollution Studies or Ecology and Man (with Honours)) there would be a far greater variance of I.Q. scores and a corresponding rise in the loading of this variable on an academic performance factor. However, if Guilford were correct such populations (differering in I.Q.) should not be put into the same factor analysis. Furthermore, it cannot be argued that among Oxford scholars I.Q. is not an important determinant of academic success, thus making sense of the results. It is simply that it plays little part on the differences between them and they all have sufficient.

A further example of the problems involved in homogeneous samples is again illustrated in the motivational field, by hunger. In studies of human motivation (e.g. Cattell and Child, 1975) factor analysis has not always revealed a hunger drive. It is nonsense to try to argue that hunger is not a drive among human beings. However, most factor-analytic studies of motivation have been carried out with well-fed western students. A cross-section of a large Indian city would reveal a very different pattern.

Sample size is also important in technically sound factor analyses. Guilford (1956) in advice that would find general agreement among leading factorists argues that a sample size of 200 is the minimum for ensuring statistically reliable results. The aim here is to minimize the standard error of the correlation coefficients, particularly important in a technique which seeks to reproduce the original correlations by cross-multiplication of the factor loadings. However, given that this aim of 200 is a conservative figure, there would seem little reason to doubt the reliability of factors derived from samples of 100 subjects. It must be stressed that this discussion of sample size is concerned with its statistical suitability for factor analysis. It ignores the equally important question, which is relevant to all psychology, of how adequately the sample reflects the population.

It is also generally agreed that (for reasons of matrix algebra) there should be at least twice as many subjects as variables in factor-analytic investigations. This means that in a large scale study on this account alone, one should have to use more than the minimum 100 subjects.

From this discussion of these first two requirements one can now see that a statistically adequate factor analysis demands proper sampling of both variables and subjects. Since subjects must be twice as numerous as variables, most investigations will be on a large scale. With correct sampling psychologically meaningful results can be obtained provided that the more technical requirements which are briefly discussed below are also met.

The six other rules which introduced this section have the aim of obtaining simple structure. The rationale for demanding simple structure has been fully discussed above so I shall restrict myself to comments which have not been previously raised and I shall ignore the mathematical assumptions and models of factor analysis. (Cattell, 1966 or Harman, 1964.)

The number of principal components rotated obviously must affect simple structure. De Young and Cattell (1973) have shown that if too few components are rotated, second-order factors tend to be thrown up at the first-order. A common solution is to rotate all factors whose eigen values are greater than one. Cattell (1966) has developed the Scree test which seems (in known cases) to give sound results. Fixing communalities is a technical point aimed at improving simple structure while the other rules have already been discussed. However, I shall comment briefly on the last two rules. The point here is that these checks ensure replicability of results. In any statistical procedure such as factor analysis where a best fit is obtained—the reproduction of the correlation matrix from the factor matrix—there is bound to be an element of chance in each individual case. However, as Cattell (1966) has argued, if the simple structure factors are revealing functional unities or causal agencies, there should be considerable agreement from analysis to analysis. The check on higher-order factors similarly ensures that the first-order factors have the same position in factor space relative to each other in each research.

These technical rules can be summarized by arguing that they are aimed at three points: to sample properly the universe of variable, to sample properly the universe of subjects and to find the invariant simple structure. When these requirements are met, one can feel some confidence in making sense of the factor analysis.

I have now described the logic and rationale of factor analysis, defined the status of factors and discussed the importance of obtaining simple structure. A number of technical rules which reduce the likelihood of statistical artefacts obscuring the results have been set out. In the examination of the status of factors one saw how Eysenck had claimed that there were broadly three functions of factor analysis, the descriptive, the hypothesis suggestive and the hypothesis testing (p. 38). To achieve these various aims, factor analysis can be used in different ways and I shall now turn to exploring what have been called by Cattell (1952) factor-analytic designs.

FACTOR-ANALYTIC DESIGNS

R Technique

R (regular) factor analysis is, as the initial suggests, the usual form. Variables, test scores, are factored and the factors are, therefore, dimensions accounting for differences between people. R factors have unquestionably yielded the best and most solidly based psychological findings compared with other forms of factor analysis. Well known R factors are gf, fluid ability, N, neuroticism and tough-mindedness, to take examples from three fields of psychology.

P Technique

In P technique the traits within one person are correlated and factored. Resulting factors are, therefore, unique to this individual. If P and R factors in an individual were known, theoretically, powerful predictions about his behaviour should be possible. P technique has been little used partly because it demands repeated measurement of subjects who must, therefore, be well disposed to psychology or the experimenter. I (Kline, 1976b) have utilized P technique in the study of motivation with two subjects. In each case the P technique revealed useful information strongly suggesting that it is a neglected form of factor analysis.

Q Technique

Q technique factors correlations between people. The normal data of psychological testing are inverted: subjects become the variables; the variables become subjects. Q factors, therefore, load on people and each factor represents a group. Q technique is, therefore, *prima facie* highly useful in the study of any kind of group. Compared with cluster analysis techniques (see p. 32) Q factorization has the advantage that, at least with some kinds of data, the factors are equivalent to R factors. However, Q analysis has not been as widely used as cluster analyses and more work is needed regarding the meaning of Q factors, before one can fully understand Q factor results.

O Technique

Scores of the same subject on two occasions are correlated and factored. If one were to add in other variables such as measures of psychotherapeutic processes or classroom interactions, highly valuable factors influencing behavioural change might be discovered. The two final designs are possible, in that the data can be obtained but the results have not been widely used. These are T technique, involving the factor analysis of test-retest reliability coefficients and S technique where responses of two persons on several occasions, as a study of social interaction, are subjected to factor analysis.

Conclusions about Factor Analysis

This discussion of factor analysis has attempted to demonstrate how the technique is peculiarly suited to the analysis of psychometric data. An oblique, rotated factor analysis of simple structure can lead to a fundamental understanding of a field, beyond what is possible by initial observation (unless this is done by persons of exceptional insight) since it reveals basic and often causal dimensions which can then be experimentally verified in further research. Various objections to factor analysis have been discussed and sound technical rules and possible designs have been outlined to make possible proper evaluation of factorial research and to demonstrate how factor analysis can be used to test and to formulate new hypotheses.

SUMMARY

(1) The nature of psychometric data: the distinction between nomothetic and idiographic data was drawn. The demands of such data on statistics were discussed.
(2) Distinction between multivariate and univariate analyses: the suitability of the former to typical psychometric data was demonstrated.
(3) Different types of multivariate analysis: these were described and their main functions delineated: multiple correlation, canonical analysis, discriminant function analysis, latent class analysis, configural analysis, type recognition, the work of Guttman and factor analysis were compared.
(4) Essentials of factor analysis: the definition of a factor, factor loadings, status of factors, rotation and simple structure, confactor rotation and the uses of factor analysis were discussed.
(5) Technical requirements of factor analysis: these were described and the problems of sampling subjects and sampling variables were outlined.
(6) Factor-analytic designs: various different research designs utilizing factor analysis were described.

3

Psychological Tests

INTRODUCTION

To examine the substantive psychological findings that have arisen from psychological testing, it is clearly necessary to delineate and categorize the results into a coherent picture. I have chosen to do this in two ways. First, the varieties of psychological test are set out, for each can be expected to produce a body of related results. Thus, from tests of motivation for example, the results will bear most closely on the psychology of motivation but in addition the results will be relevant to educational and industrial psychology. The second method has been to examine whole areas of psychology, such as clinical psychology, to see what has been discovered from all kinds of tests.

This chapter is concerned with the varieties of tests. Obviously if no good tests of a variable exist, the contribution of testing it must be small. Thus, the different types of psychological test that have been devised and which have some reputation for validity are set out. Since, however, there are considerable problems in attempting such a feat, it is necessary to discuss these so that the full import of the list can be understood.

One major problem is the vast number of tests. In a book not primarily concerned with tests *per se* but with test results, some drastic selection procedure has to be adopted. In Chapter 1 the qualities of good psychometric tests were shown to be of high validity and reliability together with good standardization. These were the criteria that were applied to the tests listed in Buros. The results from invalid tests cannot have any psychological implications other than that the findings are not necessarily as observed. These criteria automatically reject a very considerable proportion of psychological tests.

However, in the study of test construction there are two important categories: criterion-keyed tests and factor-analytic tests. Chapter 1 demonstrated that the psychological meaning of criterion-keyed test variables, even though they might be useful for screening or selection purposes was often dubious. Factor-analytic tests on the other hand, when properly constructed, yielded variables of considerable psychological significance. Thus, the second criterion has been that the test is of a factor-analytic kind. However, in some cases through sheer weight of research, some criterion-keyed tests have yielded substantial psychological findings. As was also shown an exception can be made, in principle, of projective tests. Where evidence has occurred of the validity of some projective test, it has been included. In the following sections of this chapter there are tests which have adequate evidence for validity and which have factored variables. In addition a few other psychological instruments have been included.

The method of categorizing the tests is another difficulty. To group tests into ability, personality and interest tests is already to have made decisions concerning the psychological findings of test data. Thus, to claim a test in an intelligence test implies that the variable intelligence is a meaningful psychological term. The justification for the other categories would be perhaps even more complex. The solution here is to adopt the well-accepted categories of psychometrics; those used in the Mental Measurement Year Books. Then as in each subsequent chapter the results obtained with a particular variety of test are examined, the category can be justified or rejected and shown to be but a label of convenience. In this chapter the use of these psychometric test categories does not mean that I necessarily accept them with all their implications.

Although, as has been previously indicated, I do not necessarily accept the following labels of psychological tests, a brief definition of the variable or variables measured by the tests is appended. Tests to be described are those from which the majority of substantive results were obtained.

INTELLIGENCE TESTS

The brief definition of intelligence, as measured by tests, is a general reasoning ability factor which is important in most tasks. It is the factor which was first somewhat roughly discerned by Spearman (1927), produced at the second-order by Thurstone (1938) and sharpened into two by Cattell (1971). It is this factor which accounts for the high performance in adult life of the gifted children, followed up by Terman et al. (1926) and for the overall correlation of intelligence and occupational success in over 10 000 studies, reported by Ghiselli (1966). There have been many tests devised to measure this most pervasive of factors so that even with the criteria set out for selection only some typical examples can be described.

INDIVIDUAL INTELLIGENCE TESTS

These are tests which are designed to be given to individuals (in contrast to groups). The advantage of such tests over group tests is that the psychologist can see how a subject tackles the various test problems. This can be a useful clue to sources of difficulty. A child, for example, may refuse to go on to a new item until he has solved the one he is working on even though this is obviously too hard. This is a poor strategy for efficient use of talents. Two individual intelligence tests stand out from the rest. These have been extensively used in child-guidance clinics throughout the English speaking world. Recently a new British test, the British Intelligence Scale, threatens to challenge this domination. These three tests are:

(1) *The Terman-Merrill Scale* (Terman and Merrill, 1964). This is a test for children of around 4–15 years. Items are arranged in groups suited to an average child of a particular age. It takes about one hour to administer.

(2) *The Wechsler Adult Intelligence Scale and the Wechsler Intelligence Scale for Children* (Wechsler, 1958). In this test the items are grouped by kind—and each group is ordered in difficulty.

(3) *The British Intelligence Scale* (in press). This test, which has had a gestation period of ten years attempts to bring up to date the tests above, by basing its items on Guilford's approach to intelligence (see Chapter 4).

The style of item used in these tests immediately reveals the nature of the factor which they measure. In the Terman test (known as the Stanford-Binet because it is based on Terman's revision of Binet's early work in Paris, carried out in the University of Stanford), there are items such as: vocabulary, recognition of absurdities, working out similarities, being able to name the days of the week, being able to define abstract words, copying a bead chain from memory, paper-cutting, sentence building from given words, digit repetition and explaining proverbs. This is only a sample of the widely ranging Terman items. If one recalls the factorial nature of tests one can see that it is unlikely that the Terman test is measuring a bloated specific. Rather it follows the pattern advocated by Cattell (1973) for personality tests where full coverage of the criterion rather than homogeneity is the aim: in other words validity before reliability.

An obvious objection to many of the item types described above although not all (e.g. bead stringing) is that they are verbal. Since children from homes where there is a low educational level have less verbal stimulation than children from articulate middle-class homes (e.g. Bernstein, 1967) class-conscious sociologists have argued that scores are affected by such socio-economic factors and are unlikely, therefore, to be measures of pure ability (see Chapter 4). The WISC and WAIS items go some way in overcoming this because half the scales are verbal, half non-verbal. The verbal scales are: information (general knowledge), comprehension, arithmetical computation, similarities, digit span and vocabulary. The non-verbal set consists of digit symbol (where the symbols and digits are matched), picture completion, block design, picture arranging (into correct sequences) object assembly and a mazes test. Although there is good evidence that these tests do measure the general reasoning factor it is perhaps, less obvious from the items. However, the argument is in picture completion for example, that the subject has to *work out* what is missing from a picture (e.g. the shadow of an object) and in picture arrangement he has to *work out* what the story in the out-of-sequence pictures must have been. However, there is little doubt that scores from both these tests are strongly affected by the level of education of both the subject and (in the case of a child) of his parents.

The new British Intelligence Scale was developed both to be less sensitive to such educational and social influences and to take into account the work of Guilford (1967) which in its multiplicity of factors tended to place less emphasis on g. Furthermore, it attempted to assess stages in cognitive development as postulated by Piaget and colleagues in Geneva (e.g. Piaget, 1952). However, because of these manifold aims (in addition to measuring the general factor) the scales in this test are not a guide to the nature of the general factor so they are not quoted. This scale is introduced simply because it is effectively an updated version of the other tests.

The first two tests are regarded by most educational psychologists as standard measures of intelligence, although as shall be seen in Chapter 4, modern psychometric work has rendered these tests almost obsolete. Their practical disadvantages, namely that they are time consuming and have to be given individually, can be overcome by group tests. When group tests are developed, evidence for their validity is usually attested by correlations with one or both of them. And because group tests are as brief as in consonant with reliability, all items must be loaded highly on g so no weak items can be afforded. And because they must be given almost without instructing subjects the items must be simple in form. This means that the items of the best group tests illustrate even more clearly what intelligence tests measure.

GROUP INTELLIGENCE TESTS

There are so many highly reliable group intelligence tests of well-proven validity that comments and descriptions shall be restricted to the most widely used and to those of some special interest. Verbal and non-verbal tests are not discussed under separate headings, since some test constructors have devised both types intending them to be used together while many others, as was the case with individual tests discussed above, have utilized verbal and non-verbal items.

(1) *Raven's Matrices* (Raven, 1965). This test first developed by Raven just before the war now has a considerable number of revisions which allow testing of children from five years old through to superior adults. The matrices items in all forms are of one kind. Sequences of diagrams are shown and subjects have to select the next one in the sequence. What is needed in this test, therefore, is the ability to work out the relationship between the diagrams and to apply the rule in a new instance. This item form has turned out to be superbly successful as an intelligence test. They are relatively simple to construct at many different levels of difficulty and they are largely non-verbal. In terms of the psychometric test model in Chapter 1, one can see that because all items are of the same type there is a danger that a factor specific to these items could

confound the scores. In fact this seems to occur in a few cases where subjects (presumably high on this S factor) score far higher than would be predicted from other criteria and other subjects (presumably those low on the specific) score lower.

(2) *Mill-Hill Vocabulary and Crichton Test* (Raven, 1965). There are two vocabulary tests designed to be used in conjunction with the Raven's Matrices, thus yielding a verbal score to parallel the non-verbal matrices. It is highly interesting that despite the obvious environmental influences, vocabulary remains the best brief measure of intelligence of all sub-scales of intelligence tests (Vernon, 1950). Large differences in either direction between the matrices and the vocabulary scales can be revealing although in all cases interpretation must be made in the light of the individual case.

(3) *The Culture-Fair Intelligence Test* (Cattell and Cattell, 1959). The three forms of this test allow testing of subjects from three years old to superior adults. This test was devised to allow the comparison of groups from alien and non-comparable cultures, the rationale being (Cattell, 1971) to use items with the content of which all subjects would have had an opportunity to be acquainted, and items with which no subject would have prior knowledge. All items are non-verbal and fall into five groups—analogies, series, classifications, matrices and conditions topology. As with the Raven's matrices test, these items powerfully stress the eduction of correlates, the very essence of the general reasoning factor. A public school background and braying voice will avail nothing in the solution of these problems.

Most other intelligence tests tend to use these item types so that it will be convenient to give examples of each. For the sake of test security they have been invented, and I make no claim that they are valid. It is to be noted that each type of item can be made at almost any level of difficulty.

Types of Item in Group Intelligence Tests

Analogies

With these items level of ability is easily manipulated and both verbal and non-verbal material can be utilized.

Easy examples:

(1) Rough is to smooth as hard is to...

(2) Adder is to snake as lion is to...

Difficult examples (Kline, 1976):

(1) Sampson Agonistes is to Comus as the Bacchae are to...

(2) Television is to microscope as telephone is to ...

With these items the difficulty level does not spring simply from the fact that obscure knowledge is necessary, as in the first of these difficult examples. It arises from the nature of the relationship in the actual analogy. Thus, to take our four examples in order one finds opposition, classification, double classification (by author and type of play) and a different kind of opposition. Here are some non-verbal examples:

(1) 0 is to $\boxed{0}$ as $\triangledown$ is to ... with a multiple-choice of five drawings

(2) is to as is to...

Heim and her colleagues (Heim *et al.*, 1970) have produced the A.H. series of group tests ranging in difficulty from below average to extraordinarily hard (A.H.6). She specializes in non-verbal clock analogies which in some cases are shown slow and reflected in mirrors. These analogies are essentially a form of series item.

Series Item

Examples:
   (1) minute, small, big, large...
   (2) 3, 6, 12, 24...
Non-verbal series items essentially take the form of matrices where changes in patterns have to be worked out:

(3)

This is a typical non-verbal series item of great simplicity. With these series items the relationships can of course be varied as with analogies.

Classification

These items are frequently known as odd-men out items, a name given to them because subjects have to select from a list, the item that fails to fit. The reasoning task involved is, therefore, to find the classification scheme which embraces all but one item. Obviously items can take verbal and non-verbal form.
   Examples (Kline, 1976):
   (1) carrot, turnip, swede, beetroot, cabbage.
The classification to solve this item is *root* vegetable. Notice that vegetable or edible matter is useless. Red or white might be possible solutions, but one would think that classification by such inessential characteristics would not be done by high I.Q. subjects. However, item analysis would decide this empirical point.
   (2) valley, coomb, hillock, gorge, chasm.
Here the classification is basically hole in the ground. These items require, however, in addition to the simple classification reasoning a certain knowledge so that they would be suitable only for adolescents and adults.

(3)

This example is a simple non-verbal classification item.

Matrices Items

These have been fully discussed previously in the brief description of Raven's Matrices.

Topological Conditions

This is an item type mainly utilized by Cattell in the Culture-Fair Intelligence test. Since these are hard to invent one of the examples of this item type is used from the test itself. Subjects have to indicate into which of the five boxes a dot could be placed so that it would be inside a circle, but outside a square, as illustrated in the test example. All these group test item types reveal clearly that the essence of such tests is educing relationships and applying them to new material. All these types offer enormous possibilities of varying the difficulty level of the relationship. They also show how items may be difficult for reasons that are due to content not reasoning ability. Such items, however, would be unlikely to be valid and retained after proper analysis.

Finally, there are similarities, items which feature in most individual intelligence tests although the necessity to provide multiple-choice items for group tests make their use in these tests rare. To find the similarity between an apple and a cherry is a particularly good exercise of the reasoning ability tapped by intelligence tests (given that the subject is a young child). Thus responses such as you can eat both, both red, they have skins, or pips, are obviously not incorrect. However, they fail to penetrate to the core of the problem, that both are fruit. This is the analytic categorization of the bright child. The response, for example, "they both shine" is not indicative of high reasoning ability.

To conclude this section on group intelligence tests the names of some well-known tests have been listed: the A.H. series (Heim *et al.*, 1970), the Otis tests (1954), the celebrated Moray House tests, used for secondary school selection in Great Britian and finally Miller's Analogies (1970) designed for the selection of graduate students and needing an encyclopaedic knowledge, if nothing else, for successful completion.

From the discussion of group and individual intelligence tests and their items, it is hoped that the nature of "g" is clear. In Chapter 4 the substantive findings that have emerged from the application of these tests and aptitude tests (see below), their psychological nature as distinct from description of the factor, will be discussed.

Not all factor analysts, even in the early days of the subject before the war, were agreed that this general ability factor was the most useful either for practical selection procedures or as a help to conceptualizing the structure of human abilities. Thurstone (1938) was the most influential figure who supported the concept of group factors and this led ultimately to the construction and design of aptitude tests.

APTITUDE TESTS

I have always maintained (Kline, 1975) that the term aptitude refers to two quite different sets of psychological characteristics. Furthermore, this distinction has considerable bearing on the psychological meaning of the results of aptitude testing. Some aptitudes may be relatively factor pure. For example, verbal or numerical aptitude. When one says an individual has mathematical aptitude for example, one means that he tends to be able to learn easily the mathematics involved in the whole range of sciences. Such an ability is related to the N factor (which, however, is computational speed) and to the abstract reasoning factor. Verbal aptitude, as evinced by those with a gift for languages (of whom the most spectacular example is the great explorer Burton) is almost certainly unifactorial, being related to the verbal factor V. This is why aptitude testing was introduced by reference to Thurstone's group factor analyses.

The second class of aptitudes, however, is a collection of psychological traits, of both ability and personality in some instances, which happen to be valued in a particular culture. Computer programming aptitude for which tests exist is a mixture of mathematical, abstract reasoning and general reasoning abilities with a considerable specific factor for the particular kinds of task involved. Clerical aptitude is even more diverse. Here one finds in those who are good clerks, speed and accuracy in simple computation and copying, conscientiousness in checking, vigilance and resistance to boredom, and orderliness for its own sake. This is, as has been said, a disparate collection of attributes.

The question may have arisen now in some readers' minds as to the relation between aptitude tests and the general intelligence tests that have been previously examined in this chapter. This is a crucial issue which is fully discussed in Chapter 4. Here, however, it can be said that many aptitude tests have the general intelligence factor accounting for a good deal of their variance. Nevertheless the term aptitude is still meaningful in both its senses. Thus there are individuals whose general intelligence is similar but whose verbal and numerical aptitude is totally different: the poet and the mathematician are clear examples. Similarly individuals differ in their non-factorial aptitudes, knowledge which can be valuable in vocational guidance.

Aptitudes related to the group factors require tests that are loaded on these factors and in the subsequent sections the best of such tests are mentioned and their items illustrated. The heterogeneous aptitudes are not factorial. Hence, tests of these are designed usually by criterion keying, and are used mainly in industrial psychology and for selection and guidance. Generally as discussed in Chapter 1, the factorial aptitude tests can throw light on the theoretical nature of abilities. The criterion-keyed aptitude tests are not necessarily psychologically meaningful although their manifold factor loadings can highlight the demands of particular occupations.

In examining some typical aptitude tests and their items, it is hoped in this way to illustrate the nature of the variables involved. However, it is argued, in

Chapter 4, that the findings from aptitude tests are not of substantial psychological importance.

(1) *The Differential Aptitude Test* (*Bennet et al.*, 1962). This aptitude test intended for pupils of 14 years and upwards meets the criteria of good tests with ease (discussed in Chapter 1), except in terms of validity. It is highly reliable and has very large normative samples. The scales in the DAT are: verbal reasoning, numerical ability, abstract reasoning, clerical speed and aptitude, mechanical reasoning, space relations, spelling and grammar.

As Quereshi (1972) points out in an excellent review of the DAT, this is usually regarded as the best aptitude battery. However, the difficulty is that it is not differential. The power that the DAT has in predicting occupations arises from its loading on the general intelligence factor. Thus clerks are not the highest scorers on clerical aptitude (more intelligent groups score higher) neither is it always their highest score. This is fully discussed in Kline (1975) and clearly diminishes the psychological importance of this psychometrically impeccable test. However, since it is a good example of its kind, the items in the scales are a useful indication of the meaning of the variables.

DAT Items

The verbal reasoning and abstract reasoning items are of the standard group test variety which have been described under verbal and non-verbal intelligence test items. Similarly the numerical ability, spelling and grammar scales have items exactly as would be expected from their titles.

One of the clerical scale sub-tests clearly indicates the concept of clerical aptitude held by the authors of the DAT. This consists of two columns of addresses. Subjects have to identify errors in the right hand column which is supposed to be the same as the left. This is a speeded test measuring accuracy and possibly resistance to boredom.

Mechanical Reasoning

These tests (different versions for boys and girls, which may now possibly be illegal) consist of illustrations of mechanical devices—series of cogwheels, or systems of pulleys for example, and subjects have to indicate which system will pull the heaviest weight or in which direction a cogwheel is revolving. Although (as I maintain) certain specific information is needed to solve these problems (one has to know what a cogwheel is and to be used to its functioning) it is assumed that this will be acquired in most Western environments. That is the reason for a separate female version since in the original test standardization, there was a large sex difference in the male items.

Space Relations

These items would appear to be highly loaded on what Cattell would call gf (fluid ability) see p. 83. Typical space relation items resemble the topological conditions items (in Cattell's Culture-Fair test). A commonly used type is to show flattened out a design for paper folding with folds indicated. Below this is a series of folded paper constructions. Subjects have to indicate which of these the flat design would have made.

This test has been carefully constructed and standardized. Yet as has been mentioned its practical utility is in doubt because all these aptitudes tend to be correlated because of the importance of general ability in human performance. However, this does not take up all the variance and the items indicate the nature of these aptitudes.

(2) *The General Aptitude Test Battery* (U.S.A. Government, 1970). This test is used by government employment agencies in the U.S.A. for vocational guidance. It has to be given by officers who have had little test training so that it has been made as simple in content as possible. This test, given to around 1 000 000 subjects a year is psychometrically sound with excellent norms and high reliability, although it is clear from the manual (U.S. Govt., 1970) that it tends, as the DAT, to measure the general intelligence factor. Thus, correlations between the sub-tests are as high as the correlations with the DAT. Furthermore, as Cronbach (1970) points out, who incidentally favours the GATB more than I do, taking all the scores into account simultaneously improves predictions—as one would expect with a test that is strongly loaded on g.

However, the GATB is of interest to this chapter because its scales are not all composed of paper and pencil items, thus linking this general battery to tests of more specialized aptitudes, to which a general factor would not be relevant, which are discussed later in this chapter.

GATB Scales

Nine factors are measured from eight sub-tests. General ability (g) is derived from the vocabulary scale. Numerical aptitude (N) is tested by computational and arithmetic reasoning tests. Spatial aptitude (S) is measured by the three-dimensional space test. The fact that the general ability factor is composed of the V, N and S scores is an admission that general ability accounts for much of the variance in these tests. The items in these scales are similar to those discussed in the sections on intelligence tests.

However, the five other factors measured by the GATB use items that deserve further scrutiny. Of these the clerical perception test is the least relevant because its items (name comparison) are similar to those in the DAT.

Form Perception

This is measured by two tests—form and tool perception. In each subjects have to match shapes. Tools are used to give face-validity to the procedure.

Motor Coordination

This is measured by the mark making tests in which subjects have to put dots into as many squares as possible within one minute. Notice that is an example of motor coordination. If this is a general trait it must *per se* be a valid test.

Finger Dexterity

Here the rivet test is used. Subjects have to screw washers and rivets into place and then unscrew them. This is a performance test.

Manual Dexterity

The place and turn test is used to measure manual dexterity. Here 48 pegs are placed into holes and then these have to be replaced upside-down. This again is another performance test.

The rationale of these scales and their items is clear. The testers have taken a typical sample of the behaviour they wish to measure and used this as items. Thus the place and turn test demands manual dexterity. If you can do it, by definition you are dextrous, if not you are not. These items are therefore, especially the performance tests, good examples of how specific aptitude tests can be constructed.

The description of these items has enabled us to see what is conceived of as aptitudes by the authors of these two tests which are unquestionably the best of their type. However, as indicated, I do not regard the concept of aptitude as useful either theoretically or practically. The fact is that the substantive finding that the notion of aptitude is best otherwise conceived comes from the results achieved with these tests. Most of our knowledge of aptitudes arises from them. Thus to understand properly the arguments refuting their value, these tests have to be known.

All differential aptitude tests are permeated by the general ability factor which robs them largely of their differential quality: their total scores are useful, their profiles are not. However, this argument would not necessarily apply to more specific tests of aptitudes or abilities, especially those which are very different from the general reasoning factor.

Special Aptitude Tests

There is, naturally, a very large number of special aptitude tests. Many of these have been designed to enable employers who need individuals with skills highly specific to a particular job to select applicants most likely to learn them. Such tests generally have contributed little to psychological knowledge although some results will be discussed in the chapter on industrial psychology.

Finger and Manual Dexterity

Over the years a variety of performance tests of these variables which would appear to be important in a wide range of engineering have been developed. Almost all of them require subjects, as the GATB test above, to perform some task demanding the requisite dexterity, e.g. the Purdue Pegboard (1968) and the Stromberg Dexterity test (Stromberg, 1951). The Stenquist Mechanical Aptitude test actually required subjects to perform engineering tasks using small tools. However, as scrutiny of the "Mental Measurement Year Books" indicates, few of these tests had much evidence supporting their validity especially against the criterion of success in engineering training courses. Whether this is on account of the importance of g in success at almost anything, or whether it is due to the importance of non-cognitive factors in success such as personality and motivation is not clear.

The tests from which substantive psychological findings have arisen have been described and their items illustrated so that one can see the nature of the test variables. Readers are referred to Buros (1971) or Cronbach (1970) for a full list of tests. However, measures of musical aptitude have revealed important facts about musical ability.

Measures of Musical Ability

Shuter (1968) has listed and discussed all musical ability tests up to that date. Most results have been obtained with two tests, the Wing Test, for which research began in 1936 (Wing, 1936) and which has been updated recently (Wing, 1967) and the Seashore test, ancient by the standards of psychology (1919), and even this, according to McLeish (1950), still needed validation.

(1) *The Wing Test.* There are seven sub-tests played on a piano. There are norms on around 10 000 subjects and the whole test is highly reliable, even the sub-tests being sufficiently reliable for profile use. It can be used with children as young as eight years old. The sub-tests are: chord analysis, pitch change, memory, rhythm, harmony, intensity and phrasing. The validity of the test is well supported by a number of studies. It is able to predict success at music school, and all members of the National Youth Orchestra scored the highest grade.

Scores on such a test must be affected by musical experience, but as the history of music makes clear, so is musical ability itself. Exemplified in the lives of Bach, Mozart and Beethoven, a musical background is a supreme advantage. What the Wing test essentially does is tap the various skills which are demanded by good musicianship.

(2) *The Seashore Test.* This tests broadly similar variables but utilizes, instead of a piano, pure tones. These include pitch, loudness, time, timbre, rhythm and tonal memory. However, this test, because of its non-musical stimuli, offends the musical and is thought by them to be valueless (i.e. to have low face validity (Wing, 1953)) and since it is less reliable than the Wing test, is probably the less desirable of the two.

Motor Ability

Since a wide variety of occupations demand motor abilities, it might be expected that batteries of such tests would now exist and the field would be charted and clear. This is not the case. There is, indeed, little agreement as to what are the most important motor ability factors. Fleishman (1966) in Bilodeau (1965) lists the most important motor ability factors as: control precision, multilimb coordination, response orientation, reaction-time, speed of arm movement, rate control, manual dexterity, finger dexterity, arm-hand steadiness, wrist-finger speed and aiming. According to Fleishman, these factors may be regarded as enduring traits which underly skills defined as proficiency on specific tasks. All these factors have special tests to measure them. However, as Cronbach (1970) points out, their generality is much in doubt because there is little evidence of their involvement in occupational success.

Distinction of Aptitude and Attainment

This discussion of aptitude tests introduces a point which must be clarified: the distinction between aptitude and attainment. In the case of verbal aptitude it is clear. One can say someone has verbal aptitude and no attainment in Hindi implying that he will learn Hindi more quickly than subjects with less verbal aptitude. Mechanical aptitude should have the same implications for mechanical tasks. However, as has been seen, even in the verbal DAT mechanical test, the items are really attainment items. They pose a mechanical question. I would argue that aptitude refers to the basic factorial dimensions of verbal, spatial and mathematical ability which are important in a wide variety of tasks, whereas other aptitude tests in the main tend to be essentially attainment tests. Musical ability falls between these two categories, since it seems to be a basic ability but requires considerable experience for it to flourish.

ATTAINMENT TESTS

Attainment tests measure how much, in a particular field, a person has learned. Aptitude and ability tests try to predict how much a person might learn (that is, given he is trying) in a variety of attainments. Attainment tests, therefore, are almost numberless. If a task of skill can be conceived, an attainment test can be constructed to measure it. Except in special cases, therefore, such as Reading tests, attainment tests are of little general psychological interest.

Attainment tests are perhaps most important in the educational field. For example, it is generally agreed that mathematics is not well learned in British schools. Investigations of factors influencing mathematical attainment could well yield useful and theoretically valuable results (for example, in relation to Piagetian theory or teaching by teaching machine) and these would involve the use of valid attainment tests of mathematics. However, this example deliberately highlights a major problem with all attainment tests—their contents. If an attainment test covers a different curriculum from that which the subject studies, for that subject it is bound to be inaccurate. One of the putative advantages of attainment tests is that they can be well standardized, thus allowing national comparison of individuals and, therefore, accurate assessment of progress. However, this is only true if all pupils have followed the curriculum covered by the test.

In my view this problem, which with the greater freedom of modern education is likely to increase rather than not, makes the value of most attainment tests dubious certainly for purposes of establishing psychological truths or facts.

Reading Tests

A possible exception to this are reading tests. Since the psychology of reading is not well understood, nor the factors influencing the difficulty or ease of attainment and since in its own right the psychology of reading is highly interesting as a problem in cognitive psychology (e.g. Smith, 1971), reading tests are or should be of great value to the psychologist. It is to be noticed that they avoid the curriculum problem because the reading curriculum is finite, although with children, care should be taken to sample well-known vocabulary.

I shall not illustrate items from reading tests. Suffice it to say that each item is an example of the skill required, usually graded for difficult or by average age of a normative group. Reading aloud (barking at print) and reading for comprehension are two separate and not necessarily highly correlated variables to be measured in tests of reading. Given the task it should be hard to make an invalid test. Tests vary mainly in their reliability and the adequacy of their norms. However, scrutiny of the reviews of reading tests in Buros (1972) indicates that some test constructors have managed to achieve this! Some well-regarded reading tests are: the Gates-MacGinitee Reading Tests (Gates and MacGinitee, 1965) and the Schonell Tests (Schonell, 1951).

In arguing that the construction of reading tests is simple I have been unfair. The problem concerns sampling reading matter, i.e. obtaining a reasonable difficulty level for each age group. Even more considerable is the problem of measuring comprehension. In principle, however, the construction of reading tests is not difficult and the items are obvious.

I shall now consider personality tests. In Chapter 1, I examined the art of item writing which is, perhaps, best exemplified in the construction of personality tests. The rationale of item writing was examined and here I shall list the tests that are most widely used and give examples of their items. Since there are in most tests a considerable number of scales and since items are not necessarily face valid, I shall restrict myself in the case of questionnaires, to giving sample items. For reasons of test security the items will not be those actually used in the tests themselves.

PERSONALITY QUESTIONNAIRES

(a) Factored questionnaires. By volume of research carried out into the psychological nature of their variables, two personality questionnaires stand alone. These are Eysenck's tests of Extraversion (E) and Neuroticism (N), e.g. the EPI (Eysenck and Eysenck, 1964), and the series of personality questionnaires arising from the 16 PF test (Cattell *et al.*, 1970).
(1) *The Eysenck Tests.* These have measured two factors E and N as stated above, although the most recent version, the EPQ (Eysenck and Eysenck, 1975) has a third variable, Psychoticism (P).

The Eysenck Factors

Extraversion: The extravert is sociable, cheerful, expressive and stimulus hungry. The introvert is the opposite of this, interested not in the external, but in his own private world of feeling. Neuroticism: The neurotic is anxious, moody, unstable and worried, by disposition rather than as a result of unpleasant events. Psychoticism: This is the variable which discriminates psychotics from neurotics and normals who usually score low. The high scorer is, as Eysenck and Eysenck (1975b) admit, not so clearly delineated as is the case with the extravert and the neurotic. However, in the test manual he is described as: solitary, not caring for people, troublesome, inhumane, lacking in empathy, insensitive, hostile and aggressive.

The actual tests developed by the Eysencks have been: the Maudsley Medical Questionnaire (MMQ) (Eysenck, 1952b), a 40 item measure of N. Then followed the Maudsley Personality Inventory (MPI) (Eysenck, 1959), which tested E and N and the Eysenck Personality Inventory (EPI) (Eysenck and Eysenck, 1964) which was an improved version of the MPI with an L scale (to detect subjects whose responses were affected by social desirability). It was also more reliable and in more simple English than the MPI and care was taken that E and N were entirely independent. Finally, comes the Eysenck Personality Questionnaire (Eysenck and Eysenck, 1975) which measures the new variable P, psychoticism, and is a yet further improvement on the EPI. There are junior versions for use with children of the MPI, the JMPI and the EPI, the JEPI. The EPQ has a junior version of the same name.

This series of tests whose rationale and development is scrutinized in the chapter on personality, has without doubt yielded a large amount of information about personality and these tests have made an important contribution to knowledge. However, it is disappointing that the most recent

EPQ test is, despite its claims, less well supported by evidence of validity than the earlier EPI as I have pointed out (Kline, 1978).

(2) *The Cattell Tests*. Cattell has identified not three, but 16 factors of personality which are oblique and yield five second-order factors. Two of these, Anxiety and Exvia, closely resemble the E and N of the EPQ. As with Eysenck, there has been prodigious research into the nature of these factors resulting in more than 350 papers and 30 books. More recently, yet further factors have been identified including those in the abnormal sphere (Cattell, 1973). Much of the psychometric contribution to a knowledge of personality derives from the use of this series of tests.

The basic test in this set of questionnaires is the 16 PF Test (Cattell *et al.*, 1970) of which there are parallel forms for adults, a short-form and a simplified version for the lower ranges of intelligence. There are also versions for pre-school children, the PSPQ (Pre-School Personality Quiz), the ESPQ (Early School Personality Quiz) for children up to about eight years old, the CPQ (Childs' Personality Questionnaire) up to 12 years old and the HSPQ (High-School Personality Questionnaire) up to about 15 or 16 years old. In addition to all these, there is the CAQ (Clinical Analysis Questionnaire) which measures 12 abnormal pathological factors. All primary factors, normal and abnormal, are oblique. All these tests are fully described in Cattell and Kline (1977).

The Cattell Factors

Normal: First I set out adult personality factors which have also been identified in ratings of behaviour. Factor B is intelligence, which is included in the 16 PF test. The descriptions are those used in Cattell (1973). The Q factors are so labelled because they have not been found in ratings.

The missing factors D, J, K and P, have been found in ratings of behaviour but until recently not in questionnaires. However, Cattell (1973) had managed to identify seven extra factors which are set out below. Three of them, as their labels suggest, have not been found in ratings. The seven new factors are: D, insecure excitability; J, coasthenia; K, mature socialization; P, sanguine casualness; Q5, group dedication with sensed inadquacy; Q6, social panache and Q7, explicit self-expression. These are Cattell's 23 adult factors.

Among children, most of these source traits appear, there being fewer at the younger age groups. There are no child factors which fail to appear at the adult level.

Pathological: In Table 3.2 12 adult pathological factors have been set out.

The relation of the two sets of personality factors from the two most widely used factored personality tests and the bearing of their results on the knowledge of personality will be discussed in Chapter 4. So too, will be the factors derived from other tests of whom the most important and original are those of Guilford. His work on personality where he was a pioneer is well summarized in Guilford (1959).

TABLE 3.1

Source trait index	Low-score description	High-score description
A	SIZIA Reserved, detached, critical, aloof, stiff	AFFECTIA Outgoing, warmhearted, easygoing, participating
B	LOW INTELLIGENCE Dull	HIGH INTELLIGENCE Bright
C	LOWER EGO STRENGTH At mercy of feelings, emotionally less stable, easily upset, changeable	HIGHER EGO STRENGTH Emotionally stable, mature, faces reality, calm
E	SUBMISSIVENESS Humble, mild, easily led, docile, accommodating	DOMINANCE Assertive, aggressive, competitive, stubborn
F	DESURGENCY Sober, taciturn, serious	SURGENCY Happy-go-lucky, gay, enthusiastic
G	WEAKER SUPEREGO STRENGTH Expedient, disregards rules	STRONGER SUPEREGO STRENGTH Conscientious, persistent, moralistic, staid
H	THRECTIA Shy, timid, threat-sensitive	PARMIA Venturesome, uninhibited, socially bold
I	HARRIA Tough-minded, self-reliant	PREMSIA Tender-minded, sensitive, clinging, overprotected
L	ALAXIA Trusting, accepting conditions	PROTENSION Suspicious, hard to fool
M	PRAXERNIA Practical, "down-to-earth" concerns	AUTIA Imaginative, bohemian, absent-minded
N	ARTLESSNESS Forthright, unpretentious, genuine, but socially clumsy	SHREWDNESS Astute, polished, socially aware
O	UNTROUBLED ADEQUACY Self-assured, placid, secure, complacent, serene	GUILT PRONENESS Apprehensive, self-reproaching, insecure, worrying, troubled
Q_1	CONSERVATISM OF TEMPERAMENT Conservative, respecting traditional ideas	RADICALISM Experimenting, liberal, free-thinking

TABLE 3.1 (*continued*)

Source trait index	Low-score description	High-score description
Q_2	GROUP ADHERENCE Group-dependent, a "joiner" and sound follower	SELF-SUFFICIENCY Self-sufficient, resourceful, prefers own decisions
Q_3	LOW SELF-SENTIMENT INTEGRATION Undisciplined self-conflict, follows own urges, careless of social rules	HIGH STRENGTH OF SELF-SENTIMENT Controlled, exacting willpower, socially precise, compulsive, following self-image
Q_4	LOW ERGIC TENSION Relaxed, tranquil, torpid, unfrustrated, composed	HIGH ERGIC TENSION Tense, frustrated, driven, overwrought

Printed with permission from IPAT, Champaign, Illinois.

The Work of other Factorists

(1) *The Guilford–Zimmerman Temperament Survey* (G-ZTS) (Guilford and Zimmerman, 1948). The factors (orthogonal) measured by Guilford are: G, general activity; R, restraint; A, ascendance; S, sociability; E, emotional stability; O, objectivity; F, friendliness; T, thinking introversion; P, personal relations and M, masculine emotions and interests.

(2) *The Comrey Personality Inventory*. The work of Comrey (e.g. Comrey, 1961) deserves note if only because of his attempt to overcome the problems of correlating items by using factored homogeneous item dimensions and because he uses a seven-point response scale for his items instead of the more usual dichotomous "Yes"/"No" items (EPI) or trichotomous "Yes", "Uncertain" and "No" items (16 PF). Factors in the Comrey Personality Inventory are: T, trust; O, orderliness; C, social conformity; A, activity; S, stability; E, extraversion; M, masculinity and P, empathy. There are two further scales concerned with the validity of subjects responses.

(3) *The Dynamic Personality Inventory* (*Grygier*, 1961). Grygier has developed the Dynamic Personality Inventory through a series of factor analyses summarized in the manual to the test (Grygier and Grygier, 1976). Although the evidence for the validity of many of the scales is not good as shown by empirical studies by Kline (1968; Kline and Storey, 1978), there is no doubt that this test measures useful personality variance since there are substantial

TABLE 3.2

PRIMARY SOURCE TRAITS IN CLINICALLY DEVIANT PATHOLOGICAL BEHAVIOUR (PART II OF CAQ)[a]

Source trait symbol	Low-score description (1–3)	High-score description (8–10)
Hd or D_1	LOW HYPOCHONDRIASIS Is happy, mind works well, does not find ill health frightening	HIGH HYPOCHONDRIASIS Shows overconcern with bodily functions, health, or disabilities
Sd or D_2	ZESTFULNESS Is contented about life and surroundings, has no death wishes	SUICIDAL DISGUST Is disgusted with life, harbors thoughts or acts of self-destruction
Bd or D_3	LOW BROODING DISCONTENT Avoids dangerous and adventurous undertakings, has little need for excitement	HIGH BROODING DISCONTENT Seeks excitement, is restless, takes risks, tries new things
Ad or D_4	LOW ANXIOUS DEPRESSION Is calm in emergency, confident about surroundings, poised	HIGH ANXIOUS DEPRESSION Has disturbing dreams, is clumsy in handling things, tense, easily upset
Fd or D_5	HIGH-ENERGY EUPHORIA Shows enthusiasm for work, is energetic, sleeps soundly	LOW ENERGY, FATIGUED DEPRESSION Has feelings of weariness, worries, lacks energy to cope
Gd or D_6	LOW GUILT AND RESENTMENT Is not troubled by guilt feelings, can sleep no matter what is left undone	HIGH GUILT AND RESENTMENT Has feelings of guilt, blames self for everything that goes wrong, is critical of self

	LOW	HIGH
Md or D_7	LOW BORED DEPRESSION Is relaxed, considerate, cheerful with people	HIGH BORED MISANTHROPIC DEPRESSION Avoids contact and involvement with people, seeks isolation, shows discomfort with people
Pa	LOW PARANOIA Is trusting, not bothered by jealousy or envy	HIGH PARANOIA Believes he is being persecuted, poisoned, controlled, spied on, mistreated
Pp	LOW PSYCHOPATHIC DEVIATION Avoids engagement in illegal acts or breaking rules, sensitive	HIGH PSYCHOPATHIC DEVIATION Has complacent attitude toward own or other's antisocial behaviour, is not hurt by criticism, likes crowds
Sc	LOW SCHIZOPHRENIA Makes realistic appraisals of self and others, shows emotional harmony and absence of regressive traits	HIGH SCHIZOPHRENIA Hears voices or sounds without apparent source outside self, retreats from reality, has uncontrolled and sudden impulses
As	LOW PSYCHASTHENIA Is not bothered by unwelcome thoughts and ideas or compulsive habits	HIGH PSYCHASTHENIA Suffers insistent, repetitive ideas and impulses to perform certain acts
Ps	LOW GENERAL PSYCHOSIS Considers self good, dependable, and smart as most others	HIGH GENERAL PSYCHOSIS Has feelings of inferiority and unworthiness, timid, loses head easily

The notation suggested for pathological factors used two letters mnemonically related to the name (for example, Sd = suicidal disgust) to distinguish them from the normal factors, which use the alphabet by order of approximate variance: $P, A, B, C, \ldots, P, Q_1, Q_2$, and so on.

ᵃ From "Personality and Mood by Questionnaire" by R. B. Cattell with the permission of Jossey-Bass.

TABLE 3.3

VARIABLES IN THE DPI[a]

H	HYPOCRISY
	Self-satisfaction with own moral standards, lack of insight
Wp	PASSIVITY
	Liking for comfort, warmth and mild sensual impression
Ws	Seclusion and introspection as a defence against social anxiety
O	ORALITY
	Interest in food; liking for sweet creamy food
Oa	ORAL AGGRESSION
	Pleasure in biting and crunching, liking for strong drinks and savoury foods: suggestion of free floating aggression and anxiety about its control
Od	Oral dependence, especially on parents and parental substitutes
Om	Need for freedom of movement and emotional independence; a reaction formation against oral dependence
Ov	VERBAL AGGRESSION
	Verbally and/or intellectually aggressive behaviour
Oi	Impulsiveness, changeability, spontaneity, reactive speed, emotional expressiveness
Ou	Unconventionality of outlook
Ah	ATTENTION TO DETAILS
	Orderliness, conscientiousness and perfectionism
Ac	Conservatism, rigidity and tendency to stick to routine
Aa	Submissiveness to authority and order
As	ANAL SADISM
	Emphasis on strong authority, cruel laws and discipline
Ai	INSULARITY
	Reserve and mistrust, social and racial prejudice
P	Interest in objects of phallic symbol significance
Pn	NARCISM
	Concern with clothes and appearance: sensuous enjoyment of luxury
Pe	EXHIBITIONISM
	Conscious enjoyment of attention and admiration
Pa	ACTIVE ICARUS COMPLEX
	Psycho-physical drive, drive for achievement
Ph	Fascination by height, space and distance: aspirations at the fantasy level
Pf	Fascination by fire, winds, storms and explosions: vivid imagination
Pi	ICARIAN EXPLOITS
	Interest in active exploration, a love of adventure
S	SEXUALITY
	Conscious acceptance of sexual impulses
Ti	Enjoyment of tactile impressions, interest in handicrafts and creative manipulation of objects
Ci	Creative, intellectual and artistic interests
M	Masculine sexual identification, masculine interests, attitudes and roles
	or
F	Feminine sexual identification, feminine interests, attitudes and roles
MF	Tendency to seek roles regardless of their sexual identification

TABLE 3.3 (*continued*)

Sa	Interest in social activities
C	Interest in children, need to give affection
EP	EGO-DEFENSIVE PERSISTENCE
	Tendency to act with renewed effort in the face of difficulties
Ei	Initiative, self-reliance and a tendency to plan, manage and organize

[a] 33 variables are measured in the DPI.
I have constructed (1971) a simple 30 item test of anal characteristics Ai3Q and two measures of oral personality traits OOQ, oral optimisms and OPQ, oral pessimism (Kline and Storey 1978b). These are intended to improve upon the DPI variables.

correlations between some of the scales and academic success at the university (Hamilton, 1970). This test deserves note because it was deliberately designed to test the Freudian conception of personality development and is thus of some interest to personality theory.

Criterion-keyed Inventories

For reasons which have been fully discussed in Chapter 1 criterion-keyed tests are by virtue of their construction less likely to produce psychologically important results than factored tests. For this reason I have selected only one test of this variety, which, however, has yielded significant information. This is the MMPI.
(1) *The MMPI* (Hathaway and McKinley, 1951). A 556 item pool which can yield over 200 scales (Dahlstrom and Welsh, 1960) but which contains nine standard clinical scales. In addition there are a number of other scales to check the reliability (in the non-technical sense) of subjects' responses.

Since the MMPI was developed to screen out abnormal, psychiatric subjects, there are problems in using this test with normals, the main one being the lack of variance: normals, almost by definition, do not show neurotic symptoms. As a result various attempts have been made to produce a sane man's MMPI of which the most notable is probably Gough's California Psychological Inventory (Gough, 1969), which has almost 800 references in Buros (1972). However, as Walsh (1972) points out, the method of scale construction makes the psychological meaning of the CPI variables unclear and of little generality.

Indeed, this objection to criterion-keyed scales, such as the MMPI, is so strong, that unless much further research has demonstrated the psychological meaning of the scales, they cannot be used as a basis for psychological findings of any generality and hence are not useful for the purposes of this book.

In Chapter 1 projective and objective tests were discussed under the heading types of test. Although there are strong objections to projective tests, certain of them have yielded data capable of supporting psychological hypotheses with some rigour and these tests deserve mention.

TABLE 3.4
THE NINE STANDARD CLINICAL SCALES

Hs	The hypochondriasis scale is a measure of the amount of abnormal concern over bodily functions
D	The depression scale measures the depth of the clinically recognized symptom complex, depression
Hy	The hysteria scale measures the degree of resemblance to patients who have developed conversion symptoms
Pd	The psychopathic deviate scale measures the similarity of the subject to a group of persons whose main difficulty lies in their absence of deep emotional response, their inability to profit from experience and their disregard for social mores
Mf	The masculinity scale measures the tendency towards masculinity or femininity of interest pattern
Pa	The paranoia scale measures the paranoid (suspicious, brooding, with delusional persecutory feelings) tendencies in the subjects
Pt	The psychasthenia scale measures the similarity of the subject to psychiatric patients who are troubled by phobias or compulsions—the obsessional neurotics
Sc	The schizophrenia scale measures the similarity of the subject to those diagnosed as schizophrenic
Ma	The hypomania scale measures the personality factor characteristic of persons with marked overproductivity of thought and action

In addition there is a further scale, Si, social introversion, which is similar to the E of the EPI.

PROJECTIVE TESTS

(1) *The Rorschach Test* (Rorschach, 1921). This consists of ten symmetrical inkblots which subjects are asked to describe. Highly ingenious scoring systems have been developed by Klopfer *et al.* (1956) and Beck (1952) to embrace the undoubtedly rich data of the responses. Holley (1973) has demonstrated that some of these data are powerful in discriminating nosological groups, work which will be discussed in Chapter 9.

(2) *The Thematic Apperception Test* (Murray, 1938). This test consists of a series of cards portraying human beings in ambiguous situations. The description of these cards was held by Murray (1938) to reveal a subject's needs and presses the critical motivational variables in Murray's own theoretical work—Personology. Thus the original TAT was designed to measure the most important needs and presses, i.e. the pictures were chosen deliberately to be likely to reveal them. In fact, much empirical work has shown that the TAT is useful in the assessment of a huge variety of variables (e.g. Murstein, 1963). Of course, all the objections to projective tests in general apply to the TAT. Again, as with the Rorschach test, however, some work has emerged which meets these criticisms.

As was the case with personality inventories, there is a huge number of projective tests most of which are not capable of supporting any substantive psychological findings. Nevertheless a few others have been used and scored in such a way that the results have some scientific value, as will be discussed in the relevant chapters. These tests include:

(3) *The Blacky Pictures* (Blum, 1949). This is a TAT-like set of cards portraying a family of dogs in typical psychoanalytically important situations, Blacky being the eponymous hero son. Descriptions reveal, it is claimed, psychosexual fixation.

(4) *The PN test* (Corman, 1967). This is the French cousin to the Blacky Pictures, PN being Patte Noire of a family of pigs. Based upon the Blacky Pictures, by using improved drawings (less crude and comic-like) and a more free method of administration, the PN test attempts to measure both psychosexual fixation and defense mechanisms.

Both these tests attempt deliberately to assess subjects' psychodynamics as conceived in psychoanalytic theory. They are, therefore, potentially useful in the study of psychoanalysis but are necessarily limited to that orientation.

(5) *The Children's Apperception test* (Bellak *et al.*, 1974). This test is effectively a childrens' version of the TAT, suitable for children up to the age of eight or nine years old. Although psychoanalytically oriented (*not* related to personology), it is not so closely relevant to Freudian variables as the Blacky Pictures and the PN test which makes it a more flexible instrument which can be used simply to gather information about childrens' personality.

(6) *The House Tree Person Test* (Buck, 1948). This test requires subjects to draw a house, tree and person and to answer certain questions about these drawings. Two manuals (Buck, 1948; Buck and Hammer, 1969) have collected together a mass of clinical data which has been interpreted in the most spectacular style of projective testers: the comments show enormous insight and imagination but there is little objective evidence to support them. However, the data from this test are well suited to the type of analysis suggested by Holley (1973) for the Rorschach test and Hampson and Kline (1977) showed that highly interesting results with this test by this method were possible.

(7) *Le Gribouillis* (Corman, 1967). This test, the scribble test, requires subjects, mainly young children, to scribble and write their names. Inferences are then drawn from the position of the name relative to the scribble. Although strong evidence for the validity of this test is lacking, its simplicity and the objective nature of its data could render it a genuinely scientific measure. It, therefore, deserves investigation.

(8) *The Defence Mechanism Test* (Kragh and Smith, 1970). Kragh and Smith have collected together a number of studies with the DMT and explained its rationale in some detail as have both Sjoback (1967) and Kline (1973). The DMT consists of three pictures shown in a tachistoscope at gradually increasing exposure rates beginning well below threshold and continuing until veridicity is reached. Subjects describe and draw what they see at each exposure. The rationale of the test is bound up with percept-genetic theory

(Kragh and Smith, 1970) which states that a normal percept is related to the whole history and experience of the individual which is naturally instantaneously incorporated with the ongoing stimulus. This process becomes "fractionated" or broken down by the serial tachistoscopic exposure technique of the DMT. Thus the genesis of a percept may be observed. When this is done, not only may characteristic defence mechanisms be clearly seen but individual traumatic experiences of a subject can be observed. Kragh and Smith present clinical evidence for this claim but there is no need to follow this percept-genetic theory in using the test. The work of Dixon (1971) makes it quite plausible that defense mechanism could be seen in such a technique without involving percept-genetics and this, of course, is simply an empirical question. Kline and Cooper (1977) certainly were able to observe such defences, and Kline (1977) has produced an experimental version of the DMT with entirely different stimuli, known as "The Vampire" and designed to test psychoanalytic hypotheses concerning orality.

The DMT which is truly a projective test nevertheless may also be classified provided that an objective scoring system is adopted as an objective test. Objective tests discussed in Chapter 1 are defined, it will be remembered, as tests which can be objectively scored and (the crucial point) the purport of which is hidden from the subject (Cattell, 1957). Thus all projective tests can be classified as objective tests, although the DMT resembles the typical specially designed objective test, far more than the older projective tests which have been described.

OBJECTIVE TESTS

Cattell (1957, 1973) has frequently argued that ultimately objective tests will replace all other methods of personality assessment in the scientific study of human behaviour. This is largely because they avoid distortions and do not require any special skills or cooperation on the part of subjects. They are more like the standard measuring instruments of the older sciences. However, scrutiny of the compendium of objective tests (Cattell and Warburton, 1967) shows that as yet few of these objective tests have clearly demonstrated validity.

In fact, only one objective test has been at all extensively used—the Motivation Analysis Test (MAT) (Cattell *et al.*, 1970) and its version for use in school with adolescents, the School MAT—*SMAT* (Sweney *et al.*, 1970). Although an objective test, the MAT is of a questionnaire type and thus can be administered to groups. The 208 items are grouped into four types: forced-choice items in which subjects are required to indicate preferences for spending their time and resources; items where subjects estimate the length or difficulty of certain tasks; a word-association test, and information items on the rationale that a person is best informed on those topics in which he is most interested.

The variables measured by the MAT are strictly motivational rather than temperamental and it is in the section on human motivation that the results from this test are discussed. Five ergs, best regarded briefly as biological drives—narcism, mating (sex), self-assertion, pugnacity and fear—and five sentiments, which are culturally acquired drives—sweetheart spouse, career, parental and home, superego and self-sentimental—are measured by this test. Cattell and Child (1975) and Cattell and Kline (1977) have fully discussed the rationale of the construction of this test and have shown how the results fit various motivational theories.

The only other objective tests which have yielded results of substantive interest are those in Schuerger's objective Analytic Battery (Schuerger and Cattell, 1975) devised for clinical work and its adolescent version (Schuerger and Cattell, 1971). This battery was based upon the research reported by Cattell *et al.* (1972) and discussion of these tests is in Chapter 9.

The reason that objective tests have yielded little in the way of substantive findings is that until recently, easily administered batteries were not to be found. Researchers had to scour the literature and abstract tests which were often difficult to administer.

Interest Tests

The objective MAT is an obvious bridge to the standard interest tests which are the only tests that can be considered motivational. The most well known of these is:

(1) *The Strong Vocational Interest Blank* (Strong *et al.*, 1971). This test which was first produced in 1927 has undergone steady development up to the latest edition considerably modified by Campbell (1971). Together with the MMPI, the outstanding example of criterion-keyed tests, the SVIB, has been extensively utilized in occupational psychology and in Buros (1972), there are cited over 1000 references. However, as we have pointed out, criterion-keyed tests do not necessarily yield psychologically meaningful scales so that despite the vast amount of research with this test, the substantive yield of solid findings is not as large as might be expected.

As regards variables, the SVIB in its latest form measures a subject's resemblance on 400 items to 54 occupational profiles. In addition there are 22 basic interest scales which, however, are correlated since some of them share items (Katz, 1972). The SVIB is not an interest test but an occupational discrimination test, which works but gives us no real clue as to why this should be.

The basic interests measured include, for example, adventure, agriculture, music, social activities and teaching, broad variables such as underly, intuitively, a number of occupations. The occupations which are, of course, specific include: dentist, osteopath, forest service-man and chamber of commerce executive, just as examples.

As I have fully discussed in Kline (1975) to which readers must be referred, occupational profiles of this kind are too specific to give results of much generality. Furthermore, I must stress here, and this will be critically examined in the chapter on occupational psychology, that the whole notion of interests is not necessarily meaningful. It may be that to say a person is interested in a subject means no more than that he spends time on it voluntarily. Further to this even if the concept of interests is held to be useful these may reflect only other more fundamental aspects of personality and motivation. In brief, the description here of the SVIB does not mean that I accept the implicit psychology of the test.

Despite all these problems the SVIB has to some extent provided some information relevant to occupational choice and success. Other well-used American interest tests are the Kuder tests, of which the latest is the Kuder General Interest Survey (Kuder, 1970), which measures ten interest areas, outdoor, mechanical, computational, scientific, persuasive, artistic, literary, musical, social-service and clerical. However, despite its popularity, I shall not use its results, because of its ipsative scoring.

Stahmann (1971) reviewing the KGIS, points out that the ipsative scoring of the tests, renders the scores almost meaningless. The items consist of triads to which subjects have to indicate most and least liked. Hence it follows that all scores are interlinked. Thus correlational and factor analyses are of dubious meaning. If a subject chooses one item he must score less on the interests represented by the other two items of the trial. Thus for any one subject the scores represent *his* ranking. However, this does not enable subjects to be compared with each other. As argued before, the light drinker and the dipsomaniac could rank, Brandy, Whisky and Rum in that order but the meaning of the rankings would be different (Kline, 1975). This flaw of ipsative scoring makes subject comparison meaningless and means that norms should not be utilized and the test is only valuable for individual discussion rather than quantitative research.

Since these problems of ipsative scoring apply to the majority of interest tests no further mention is necessary. Indeed the only other interest test that merits description is the Brook Reaction Test (Heim *et al.*, 1966). This test consists of 80 ambiguous stimulus words orally administered one per twelve seconds to subjects who are required to write down their first association and then their next, and so on. The ambiguity of the stimulus may lie in the meaning e.g. swift (bird or adjective) or the sound bred or bread. The test is scored by classifying the associations into one or more of 22 interest categories which seemed to the authors to cover the most important areas. This scoring system, although subjective, has been shown to be highly reliable (Kline, 1969). The interest categories measured by the Brook Reaction Test are: aesthetic, business, clothing and appearance, dancing and social functions, entertainment, food, agricultural, humanitarian, intellectual, practical, literary, legal, military, outdoor, people, political, religious, biological science, physical science, secretarial, sport and travel.

In addition scores can be derived from the Brook indicative of personality disturbance. The number of omissions (suppression or repression) of bizarre responses, of sexual or aggressive responses, all counting towards these scores. There is some evidence with school children (Heim *et al.*, 1977) that these are effective indices of maladjustment and disturbance.

As yet the Brook Reaction test does not have particularly powerful evidence supporting its validity. However, it overcomes many of the disadvantages of normal interest tests especially the annoyance of the forced-choice type of item where subjects have to choose between equally hated alternatives. Deliberate distortion is difficult also since the rapid delivery of stimuli every 12 s means that suppression or alteration brings in its wake omissions or bizarre responses. The scores too are almost free from the problems of ipsative scoring although with this type of test, putting one response does prevent, obviously, other responses. For example, to respond to swift, swallow, martin, would mean that a subject received for this item four points (the maximum per item) for biological interest. This response prevented him from responding, as perhaps he might had he the time: Bean, Talbot, which would have given him (for the sake of the example) four points of practical interest since both these responses are now defunct makes (as is Swift) of cars. If all four responses had been made the subject would have scored two points for biological interest and two for practical. From this it is clear that the Brook scores cannot be wholly independent of each other, although the linkage is of a different kind from the ipsative scoring of most interest tests. This Brook Reaction test has been included amongst these tests more for its potential than any actual substantive findings that have been made with it. Finally I should point out that this potential arises from more than the fact that the Brook overcomes testing problems. In addition its rationale—the psychological meaningfulness of free association—lies deep in the history of clinical psychology. Jung (1918) was certainly among the first to use associations to uncover complexes to use his terminology and Freud regarded free association as an instrument of scientific investigation of the mind. More modern work (e.g. Cattell and Warburton, 1967) has shown that such word associations are indeed relevant to personality assessment. The Brook Reaction test *should* work, therefore. However, more evidence is required.

I have described these tests in the most important areas of psychology which meet the criteria of scientific measuring instruments, as defined in Chapter 1, or, in the case of projective tests, which could meet the criteria if subjected to special scoring procedures and statistical analyses. In the main I have only described those tests from which substantive psychological findings have been made. In a few cases tests have been included on account of their potential rather than actual results.

In the remaining chapters I shall examine the psychological results that have been obtained from the application of these tests. Obviously not all the results discussed are based on tests described in this chapter. Where necessary, therefore, any new tests will be described. However, in fact, most of the substantive results from the application of psychological tests have been reached by means of these tests especially in the field of personality. In the area of ability where tests are both easier to construct and as a result more numerous than in other areas of psychology, this is not the case. However, the tests used are virtually identical with some of those described in this chapter.

SUMMARY

(1) Various types of test are discussed and criteria for selecting and describing specific tests within each category are outlined.

(2) Individual intelligence tests are described.

(3) Group intelligence tests are discussed.

(4) Aptitude tests are described.

(5) Special aptitude tests, manual dexterity and musical ability, are described.

(6) Attainment tests are discussed.

(7) Factored personality questionnaires and criterion-keyed personality tests are described.

(8) Projective tests are described.

(9) Objective tests are described.

(10) Interest tests are described.

4

Psychometrics and Human Abilities

HISTORICAL BACKGROUND

The history of psychometrics and its associated multivariate methods is inextricably tied up with the study of human abilities. Although the first ability testing began without a rationale, but based itself firmly on empirical results (the work of Binet at the turn of the century in France), there is little doubt that the first contributions from psychometrics to psychological insight into the nature and structure of human abilities emerged from the work of Spearman (1927) in London. Indeed Spearman and Pearson who were among the first to develop and utilize factor analysis as an analytical technique for psychology virtually founded a London school of psychology, factor analysts of whom the best known are Burt, Eysenck, Cattell and Vernon. Spearman, indeed, was early on responsible for the concept of "g" or general ability. For him an ability test was composed of "g" and s, a specific factor.

While this work was developed in Great Britain, especially by Burt and his colleagues, work in America was proceeding but on a somewhat different tack. Here the great exponent of factor analysis was Thurstone who developed multiple factor analysis (1931) which enabled a far more flexible analysis of complex matrices to be carried out than the methods favoured by Spearman. Indeed Thurstone's methods are the essential foundation of the modern factor-analytic methods advocated by the leading workers in the application of factor analysis to psychology, the methods described in Chapter 2. Thurstone (1938) in his study of abilities produced not one general factor, but nine primary ability factors. His oblique factors were correlated and at the second-order a general ability factor did in fact emerge.

However, the fact that factor analysis could yield two such apparently different sets of findings led many psychologists to distrust factor analysis as a technique. The argument was that you got out what you put in or that rotation would enable you to arrive at any result you want: otherwise how could Spearman claim that there was one general ability factor and Thurstone, nine?

It is necessary to introduce these two great names from the past because from their work has arisen research which has now given psychometrists some knowledge of the structure of abilities. It is this knowledge which is the great contribution from psychometrics to the field of abilities and it is these findings which are examined in this chapter.

INTRODUCTION

Since there has been so huge a volume of research in the sphere of human abilities, in a book devoted to the contribution of psychometrics to all fields of psychology, a full description of all investigations would be hopelessly daunting to read and to write. Indeed Guilford (1967), Cattell (1971) and Eysenck (1973) have all produced entire large volumes devoted solely to the subject of abilities, and none of these is able to document at all thoroughly the early development of the field.

My approach, therefore, is to be selective. I shall select and examine the results that now, in 1979, appear to rest on a secure foundation, those findings that, in the judgement of the leading workers in the field, constitute a substantive contribution to knowledge. I shall not examine all studies, therefore, and I do not discuss in any detail the brilliant early, and original work of Thurstone and Spearman. Modern factorial techniques have enabled large samples to be tested on many variables and simple structure to be reached; researches, thanks to computers, that earlier workers would have been totally unable to carry out. Thus modern findings have generally superseded the early work.

After listing the main ability factors, I shall scrutinize what is known about them and discuss how they have been constructed into what might perhaps be called a theory of cognitive abilities. How such a structure of abilities derived from factor analysis fits other descriptions, for example, the information-processing approaches of Hunt (1971), will be discussed.

Recently, there has been considerable scientific and popular debate concerning the heritability of intelligence and possible racial differences in intelligence. Since this is a scientific book, I shall try to examine the evidence as a scientist should, without emotion and prejudice. The polemics have not been entered into neither is there use of perjorative terms such as racist or elitist, both of which are irrelevant to the truth or falsity of any argument.

At this point the argument by Kamin (1974) should be rebutted; to adopt any position on the I.Q. debate concerning the relative importance of heridity and environment is inevitably a political act. Certainly it may be the case that in the U.S.A. some advocates of I.Q. testing as measuring innate abilities, adopted before the war, racist not to say Fascist attitudes concerning the abilities of immigrants. Kamin certainly produces evidence supporting this. However, this is not inevitably the case. After all it is possible that there are national differences in intelligence test scores, differences that are genetic in origin. To investigate the source of such differences is to do nothing political. However, to advocate the euthanasia of low scorers is fascistic, just as presumably to advocate the longer and more careful education of low scorers is not. Certainly there may be political consequences of this kind of research, but the research *per se* is no more political than the study of sodium.

The Meaning of Abilities

One of the problems facing psychology is that often the definition of its subject matter is difficult. If the term intelligence is considered, a wide variety of verbal definitions has been given. In fact, as shall be seen, the best definitions of intelligence are not *a priori* but those based upon the results of empirical work. In fact, therefore, I do not want in this chapter to give careful verbal definitions of intelligence or any other ability. Instead I shall define these terms operationally. Each factor will be defined by its factor loadings. Thus the variables to be discussed will not mean different things to different people, *tot homines quot sententiae*; nor in the clumsier words of construct theory will one have to know how each individual construes the world.

However, to have a rough idea of the variables one can say that intelligence or general ability is the capacity to think abstractly, to learn, to generalize and to adapt to new situations. Similarly verbal ability is the capacity to use words well, and numerical ability to use numbers well. This, however, assumes that there are such abilities and that they are separate and that there does exist a general reasoning ability. This is a further reason why psychometrists eschew verbal definitions because such definitions presuppose an answer.

PSYCHOMETRICS IN THE STUDY OF ABILITY

The brief discussion of the problems in verbally defining abilities makes clear the place of psychometrics and its associated multivariate analyses in the investigation of human abilities. The questions I am implicitly asking when seeking such definitions concern the number, nature and interrelationship of human abilities. These are questions which factor analysis is especially suited to answer, as shown in Chapter 2. Thus the research design one needs is essentially simple. One needs as many tests as one can devise of all the varied human abilities and skills. Ideally the tests should sample from the whole universe of abilities. For clearly if one is trying to lay down the fundamental dimensions of ability, to leave out a particular set of skills will inevitably flaw the results. With no tests of numerical ability, no numerical factor could emerge. The correlations between the test scores are then subjected to rotated factor analysis. The simple structure obtained will then yield the major dimensions of ability. To study these ability factors is to study statistically the most important (accounting for the most variance) variables.

Thus the first contribution of psychometrics to the study of ability must be to set out what the main ability dimensions are. Since these dimensions have emerged from factor analysis, each dimension can be precisely defined by its loadings. There are no measurement problems, in as much as each factor will have its set of tests which at least are sufficiently valid to define the factor, although this does not mean that tests cannot be improved.

The Main Ability Factors

In the previous paragraph it was pointed out that the basic research design to discover the structure of human abilities was essentially simple and this is indeed the case. However, problems in sampling the whole ability sphere, differences in factor-analytic methods and also subject differences among samples have given rise to a variety of findings, which in some cases are contradictory. Before one can set out the list of ability factors, these problems will have to be discussed in relation to the investigation of abilities.

Differences in Rotation

Differences in rotation can give rise to apparently different factors. As shown in Chapter 2, the Thurstonian and Cattellian principles of rotating to simple structure have been followed, as being in accord with the scientific principle of parsimony. However, Guilford, who is one of the major workers in factor analysis, prefers orthogonal factors on the grounds that uncorrelated factors are *ipso facto* more simple than correlated. Thus Guilford's work on ability to some extent cuts across other lists based upon oblique factors, as is inevitable from the geometrical constraints of the two systems. Guilford's work will be discussed separately.

Rotational differences can affect the issue of whether one extracts a general factor of ability, (and the first principal component is always a general factor) because to varying extents the different rotational procedures reallocate the variance of the first general factor. Furthermore, and this is an important point which is often overlooked, the criteria for simple structure as laid down by Thurstone (1931) and fully discussed in Chapter 2, are antithetical to a general factor. By the act of seeking simple structure thus defined, one is deliberately making a general factor impossible. Of course the general factor can reappear at a higher-order, as in fact it does in the case of abilities.

Sampling Problems

Subjects

Vernon (1961) in his attempt to show that Spearman and Thurstone were not as far apart as some psychologists had maintained, not only proposed an hierarchical model of ability factors but pointed out also that some of the differences were due to the nature of the two samples. Where the whole range of ability is tapped, a general factor is more likely to emerge than in a highly educated homogeneous sample which is likely to reveal group factors.

Abilities

This is also a major difficulty in the field of abilities. How are we to assume that all variables are sampled? Cattell (1971) has proposed a total realm of ability performances summarized in the ability dimension analysis chart (ADAC) which is a taxonomy of abilities, based upon a theoretical analysis of what constitutes human ability (see p. 90).

This contrasts with Guilford's model (1959b) which is an *a priori* analysis of abilities (according to Cattell (1971)) and one which enables tests to be constructed since it claims to embrace all possible abilities. Thus Guilford's work differs from that of Cattell not only in the orthogonality of factors, but in its basis of sampling abilities.

A further difficulty which, although often treated as being one peculiar to factor analysis, is strictly one of sampling, concerns the definition of group and specific factor. A group factor has loadings on a number of variables, a specific factor on one alone. In the case of factoring ability tests, a factor loading on text X only and thus by definition a specific, can be apparently changed into a group factor if one was to construct new tests A, B, C, D, E, all similar to X. Such a factor has been called by Cattell (1971) not a group factor but a bloated specific. Ultimately the two can be distinguished by their relations with external criteria. A group factor should show correlations with external criteria, a bloated specific, being specific to a set of tests, is not likely to correlate with such external criteria. It can be argued that some of Guilford's ability factors are but bloated specifics (Cattell, 1971).

These are the problems which make the production of a definitive list of abilities so difficult, problems that mean in any particular research the factors might be peculiar to the sample or the tests or to an interaction between the two. There is the further difficulty of matching factors across investigations for, however robust a factor is, by the laws of probability the loadings will not be identical. If they were, Kamin and his like would doubtless regard it as evidence of poor reporting or worse. Since two different laboratories, e.g. Guilford's and Cattell's favour different rotational methods, it might be thought prudent to abandon the attempt to list factors. Perhaps indeed no such list can be produced. If this is so, of course, then much of our argument concerning the efficacy of factor analysis as a scientific investigatory method is overthrown.

However, as Horn (1976) points out, carefully designed studies with clear markers, large samples and rotation to simple structure, can go a long way to overcome the problems. If the main factors from other investigations are included, it follows that the relation of these factors and the establishment of identities can take place. A study which Horn (1976) singles out as meeting these criteria for the definition of the ability sphere is that of Hakstian and Cattell (1974). This study is particularly important because it throws light not only on the primary ability factors but on Cattell's triadic theory of abilities (1971).

As Hakstian and Cattell argue there are two purposes in this paper—(1) to clarify the nature of the primary ability sphere and (2) to clarify the relation between primary and higher-order factors. For according to the Cattellian theory (1971) one can consider third-order broad factors, such as fluid intelligence, gf, as capacities, the second-order factors such as visual and auditory powers, as powers, while the primaries may be regarded as agencies. These terms are not arbitrary labels (see discussion of the theory p. 90), but are related to their neural and cultural aetiology. As a check on such a theory, however, it is essential that one has an all-embracing and accurate picture of the primary factors and this is the principal aim of the paper.

Variables

For the purposes of defining the primary ability sphere, this study is particularly powerful because the variables were selected from the most extensive lists up to that time so that there can be little doubt that the 57 variables do embrace what has so far been found. The sources were Horn and Cattell (1966), Guilford and Hoepfner (1971), so that the two most important theoretical positions in the study of abilities are compared, and the single best source, the French Ekstrom and Price (1963) "Kit of reference tests for Cognitive Factors". This list of almost all cognitive factors and the tests loading on them, some of which, however, are certainly specifics or bloated specifics and many of which, from different studies, are almost certainly equivalent, is indispensible in the study of abilities if we want to ensure that the whole ability sphere is examined. The only possible omission is auditory ability.

Sample

As heterogeneous a sample as possible was used. A total of 343 subjects, 176 males and 167 females age range 15–55 years, $\bar{X}$ 23·70, s.d. 8·67 years. It reflected the distributional characteristics of those living in or around Alberta.

From this it is clear that both the subjects and the tests are such as are likely to produce a clear picture of the structure of adult human abilities, provided that adequate rotational procedures were adopted.

Rotational Methods

As was shown in the discussion of simple structure and the rules for adequate factor analyses, a critical feature is the number of significant factors in the rotation. If there are too many simple structure is not obtained; too few and second-order factors tend to appear at the first-order. Various methods were used, to ensure the correct number of factors were rotated including a maximum likelihood factor analysis and a scree test and there was general agreement that 19 factors best accounted for the variance. Finally 19 factors were subjected to oblique rotations by various methods, and the clearest solution was that of Harris-Kaiser (1964) independent cluster technique which constitutes the reported results.

It is because of the careful selection of variables which was based on the best work of different schools, the heterogeneity of the sample and the care in rotation, that these results can be considered as a sound basis for listing the primary ability factors—a conclusion supported by the fact that most of the better known primaries were found together with some more recently discovered. Table 4.1 contains this basic list of primary factors.

TABLE 4.1
PRIMARY FACTORS WITH BRIEF DESCRIPTION

V	VERBAL ABILITY—understanding words and ideas. Loading on synonyms, meaning of proverbs, analogies. Probably the best indicator of gc—crystallised intelligence
N	NUMERICAL FACTOR—this is facility in manipulating numbers which is factorially distinct from arithmetic reasoning
S	SPATIAL FACTOR—the ability to visualize two or three dimensional figures when their orientation is altered
P	PERCEPTUAL SPEED AND ACCURACY FACTOR—which involves assessing whether pairs of stimuli are similar or different
Cs	SPEED OF CLOSURE OF FACTOR—this taps the ability to complete a gestalt when parts of the stimulus are missing. Speed of verbal closure correlated 0·61 with word fluency suggested that familiarity with words plays a part in the results
I	INDUCTIVE REASONING—this involves induction, reasoning from the specific to the general
Ma	ASSOCIATIVE OR ROTE MEMORY—memory for pairs for which no mediating link exists. There are substantial correlations between the word number pairs test and figure-number pairs test although according to the Guilford model (see p. 87) these should be orthogonal
Mk	MECHANICAL ABILITY OR KNOWLEDGE
Cf	FLEXIBILITY OF CLOSURE—this involves disregarding irrelevant stimuli in a field to find stimulus figures. According to Hakstian and Cattell (1974) this factor is a manifestation of Witkin's field independence (Witkin, 1962) and is related to the personality factor independence
Ms	SPAN MEMORY—This is the short term of digits or letters, as has long been used in the WISC and WAIS tests (Wechsler, 1958). It is noteworthy that the mean correlation of the MS tests with the Ma tests (factor 7) is only 0·18
Sp	SPELLING—recognition of mispelled words. Hakstian and Cattell (1974) point out that spelling has not appeared as a factor in previous researches because usually there was only one test, thus making the emergence of a factor impossible. Since there are good correlations with V and W, whether spelling is a narrow primary or dependent on these two factors is not yet clear

TABLE 4.1 (continued)
PRIMARY FACTORS WITH BRIEF DESCRIPTION

E	AESTHETIC JUDGEMENT—the ability to detect the basic principles of good art. Like Mk, this would appear to depend much on previous experience
Mm	MEANINGFUL MEMORY—this involves the learning of links between pairs in which there is a meaningful link. The mean correlation of Mm with Ma tests is only 0·35, suggesting that Ma and Mm are behaviourally distinct
O1	ORIGINALITY OF IDEATIONAL FLEXIBILITY—This loaded on the multiple grouping tests of Guilford and Hoepfner (1971) which fall into the divergent production of semantic classes cell of the Guilford model. There are substantial correlations between this O1 factor and O2 and FI
FI	IDEATIONAL FLUENCY—the ability to reproduce ideas rapidly on a given topic. This is distinct from WI word fluency and associational and expressional fluency which were not included in this study, although discussed by Guilford and Hoepfner (1971)
W	WORD FLUENCY—the rapid production of words, conforming to a letter requirement, but without meaning. This factor was found as early as 1933 by Cattell and has regularly occurred ever since.
O2	ORIGINALITY 2—as with O1 this is a relatively new factor loading on the Guilford tests where subjects have to combine two objects into a functional object. Originally the test was designed to mark the convergent production of semantic transformations but it actually loaded on a divergent production factor (Guilford and Hoepfner, 1971)
A	AIMING—involving hand–eye coordination at speed
Rd	REPRESENTATIONAL DRAWING ABILITY—drawings of stimulus objects scored for precision of lines and curves

Finally Hakstian and Cattell (1974) compared the correlations in their study between five of the most long established factors, V, N, S, I and W, with those found in the work of Thurstone and Thurstone (1941). It was found that they were as similar to the earlier studies as were the earlier studies to each other.

These 19 factors in Table 4.1 are impressive support for much of the earlier work in primary abilities. Some newer factors were confirmed (memory factors, ideational fluency and two originality factors) while four factors although clearly distinct in this study, may represent combinations of more basic traits (Mk, Sp, E and Rd). Clearly this is not the complete list of primary factors. As the work of the Guilford laboratory demonstrates (Guilford and Hoepfner, 1971) there may be a large number of what are little more than specific factors—certain very narrow group factors. Nevertheless the factors in Table 4.1 can be regarded as covering much of the ability variance.

Horn (1972) and Royce (1973) in their survey articles on individual differences in ability also demonstrate that these Cattell and Hakstian factors are replicable across studies and that they are robust descriptive dimensions of ability. However, as Horn (1976) argues, the similarities of loadings patterns in all these cases are subjective. Harris and Harris (1971) in an effort to overcome this problem utilized a variety of factoring procedures to try to obtain comparable common factors, all based on the same data, in this case fifth grade students. If the common factors were also replicable across samples, Harris and Harris, argue that they can be regarded as stable. These are severe criteria and of the factors in Table 4.1 only V, I, Ma, P and Fw were able to meet them. However, what causes doubts is the fact that N and S did not emerge as stable—there being, in the case of N, sex differences. Since these factors seem clearly to emerge in almost all studies and are highly meaningful, it may be the case that Harris and Harris (1971) have developed inappropriate criteria.

Nevertheless, subjective though the identifications be, it does appear that the factors in Table 4.1 represent the major primary ability factors. However, there are other well-substantiated factors and these are briefly indicated.

Cattell (1971) contains a list of primary factors based upon previous work, in the field. For reasons that have been fully discussed, this at the present state of knowledge cannot be complete. Furthermore, he only inserts those of the Guilford factors which would be likely to occur in oblique rotation to simple structure. The additional factors to those in Table 4.1 are set out in Table 4.2.

These eight further factors made up a tentative list of 27 primary ability factors. Before trying to indicate their nature, I must point out that such a list makes no attempt to construct a taxonomy of such factors. This will be done in later sections of the chapter. Guilford and Hoepfner (1971) in their extensive work on ability factors have produced many more factors than the 27 in my tables. However, not only are these orthogonal but many of them are specific to the model they were written to suit and are so narrow that it is doubtful if they correlate with any behaviour outside the test situation. All these 27 factors

TABLE 4.2
FURTHER PRIMARY FACTORS IN ABILITY STUDIES

D	DEDUCTIVE REASONING
Mc	GENERAL MOTOR COORDINATION This is tested by the pursuit meter, among other tests
Amu	MUSICAL PITCH AND TOTAL SENSITIVITY Found in the Seashore (musical aptitude) test
Fe	EXPRESSIONAL FLUENCY Found in Guilford (1967) verbal expression for assigned ideas
ams	MOTOR SPEED Found in Guilford (1967)
asd	SPEED OF SYMBOL DISCRIMINATION Found in Guilford (1967)
—	MUSICAL RHYTHM AND TIMING
J	JUDGEMENT Ability to solve problems where judgement and estimation plays a part. Again found in Guilford (1967)

have been found in a variety of researches and I shall now briefly describe the largest of these factors so that the nature of these fundamental dimensions of human ability can be grasped.

Verbal ability is that skill which enables us to seize on the meaning of what we read. It is essentially verbal comprehension and is highly loaded on crystallized intelligence tests and high academic performance in the arts.

The numerical factor N is concerned with computational speed and accuracy and is not therefore necessarily implicated in ability in higher mathematics which is highly loaded on "g" and 1. The individual high on these two important factors will strike the onlooker by his quickness of understanding and work. The spatial factor S involves keeping orientations in mind. Cattell's (1971) example is excellent: if a three inch cube is painted red and sawn into one inch cubes, how many will have paint on one, two, three or four sides? It is to be noted that S is independent of visualization—a finding which indicates how common sense cannot reveal the ability structure.

The 27 ability factors in Tables 4.1 and 4.2 do not and cannot constitute a complete and definitive list of primary abilities, although there is no doubt that the most important factors are there. Among the smaller factors, however, there are problems of definition especially among the various fluency and originality factors: Fe, O and O2, F and W. These are the factors which Guilford and his colleagues (see Guilford and Hoepfner, 1971) have extensively studied and which are often referred to as divergent thinking factors (e.g. Hudson, 1966). These factors will be discussed in the examination of Guilford's model, and in the section on creativity.

There are similar difficulties with the memory factors and here it is hoped to impose order on the primaries when considering these findings in the light of cognitive psychological work, especially the work of Carroll (1976) and Hunt (1976).

Since, from the nature of the factors involved and the difficulty of tapping the ability sphere, a definitive list of primary factors is hard to produce and would be excessively long, it becomes evident that what is needed is some taxonomy of primary ability factors. Although the 27 factors are straightforward in meaning, their number and the knowledge that there are others even if of small variance, provided a further demand for some kind of structuring in the domain of ability. This then must be examined.

The Taxonomy of Primary Ability Factors

Since the primary factors in Tables 4.1 and 4.2 are correlated, the simplest form of ordering them is to subject them to higher-order analyses. This would appear sensible except that such a solution leaves out the results of some of the best research in the area—the work of Guilford whose factors are orthogonal and are, therefore, not amenable to higher-order analysis. Guilford himself (1967) has elaborated a model to encapsulate his factors and Cattell (1971) has also produced an elaborate model. Indeed a number of workers in this field have done this, e.g. Eysenck (1967). In the following discussion, therefore, I shall examine the results of higher-order factorization of the primary factors. The models of Guilford and Cattell because these are capable of embracing the primary factor results, together with the work of Carroll (1976). This will be reviewed because it explicitly seeks to tie in the psychometric factorial work with the informational processing approach to cognitive psychology, as exemplified previously by the work of Hunt (1976). This is, therefore, important because it begins to indicate how psychometrics can contribute to cognitive psychology.

When it is seen how the primary factors are best ordered, then there is psychological knowledge of some power. For if one measures the fundamental dimensions of ability, one has essentially measured the abilities accounting for the most variance in tasks demanding ability. This is far more parsimonious and effective than attempting to cover ability with an enormous battery of variables or even trying to measure all the primary factors.

Horn (1976) in his review of work done on human ability makes a neat point concerning the first set of investigations which shall be examined—attempts to order these primary factors in terms of broader general traits. He argues that there are two types of study, those that attempt to examine the components of "g", the intelligence factor, and those that attempt to locate important broad ability traits that are independent of intelligence. In these terms Cattell's (1971) work on fluid and crystallized ability, and Jensen's (1974) claims concerning levels of intelligence fall into the first group while the research of Guilford and his colleagues clearly belongs to the second category.

The approach to this topic is closely bound into the aims of this book. Thus my purpose is to state as clearly as possible the contribution from psychometrics to psychological knowledge, not dogmatically but supported by evidence and interpretative argument. However, in this field there is a huge corpus of researches. To discuss them all when their variables, statistical analyses and samples differ would be hopelessly confusing. Instead I shall examine what are regarded as key investigations which buttress my claims.

Second-order Structure

The first study is Horn and Cattell's (1966). The primaries in this study were: matrices, inference, induction, memory span, verbal ability, originality, associational fluency, ideational fluency, irrelevant associations, flexibility of closure, aiming, perceptual speed, visualization, writing speed, cancellation speed and backward writing. This list of ability factors demonstrates that the main primaries in Tables 4.1 and 4.2 were measured and that the divergent thinking or creativity measures of Guilford were also present. The subjects in this study were 480 males of mean age, 28 years. Five second-order ability factors emerged. These are set out in Table 4.3.

This investigation by Horn and Cattell (1966) thus postulates that at the second-order one can conceive of human ability in terms of five capacities, fluid and crystallized intelligence, visualization, retrieval capacity and cognitive speed. If one knows a subject's scores on these factors, given their loadings on other primary factors one should be able to predict scores on the primaries.

This means that when one thinks of performance in ability tests it should not be in terms of general intelligence, as Spearman claimed, or even two intelligence factors but in terms of five. Since these results have not yet been absorbed into the general knowledge of psychology, a few points need to be explicated. First these factors have been found in other researches at age ranges from five upwards (Cattell, 1963, 1967a, 1967b). Furthermore, these factors are independent of the main personality factors, indicating that the spheres of ability and personality are independent. However, one weakness of

TABLE 4.3
SECOND-ORDER ABILITY FACTORS (HORN AND CATTELL, 1966)

gf	FLUID INTELLIGENCE Loading on the Culture-Fair test, inference, induction memory span and flexibility of closure. Also it loads on intellectual speed and level tests.
gc	CRYSTALLIZED INTELLIGENCE This is the factor of traditional intelligence tests. Loading on verbal, mechanical, numerical and social skills factors.
gr	(now Pv) VISUALIZATION Loads all skills where visualization is helpful, spatial orientation, formboards. This factor loads some of the tests of the Culture-Fair test thus demonstrating that even here visualization can be useful. Cattell (1971) points out that in some research earlier, visualization had appeared as a primary but this work by Horn and Cattell clearly shows this not to be the case.
gr	RETRIEVAL CAPACITY OR GENERAL FLUENCY Loading on ideational fluency, association fluency and irrelevant association test, it is the general retrieval power which accounts for a variety of skills.
gs	COGNITIVE SPEED FACTOR This affects speed in a wide range of tasks although it is a minor factor in solving gf problems. This factor is speed in mechanical performance, e.g. writing or numerical computation.

these studies must be pointed out. As has been argued my list of primaries is far from definitive—because of rotational problems, and sampling difficulties. For this reason one cannot argue that these five factors are the only second-order ability factors. Moreover, most of Guilford's factors being deliberately orthogonal are not suited to oblique second-order analysis. Finally, a whole host of skills have no psychometric tests to measure them: the cheesemaker's art, the gardener's skill with plants, a horseman's understanding of his charge. Indeed as Cattell (1971) argues the concentration by ability testers on educational-style pencil and paper tests has largely ruled out the emergence of factors related to auditory, olfactory, tactile and kinaesthetic skills. In short, then, it can be claimed that psychometrics has failed to cover the ability sphere. Hence neither the primary nor the secondary list can be definitive. Indeed ultimately ability factors will not be classified by stratum or order of emergence only, but by other parameters such as content and process. At present, however, where all tests are basically similar, of the pencil and paper kind, classification by factor-order is meaningful. These points will be amplified when discussing the model which Cattell has developed in an attempt to encompass both the primaries and secondaries which have been so far discussed and those that are likely to emerge when a better selection of tests has been developed.

Since these secondary ability factors were oblique, to arrive at simple structure, it is obviously possible, given sufficient hyperplane stuff (see Chapter 2), to submit the correlations between them to factor analysis. What are these third-order factors?

Third-order Factors

Cattell (1971) is one of the few factorists to have attempted third-order analysis of ability factors. As he argues there are considerable technical difficulties in obtaining replicable solutions at this level because unless a large number of variables is included there are too few points for accurate rotation and if only gc and gf have emerged clearly at the second-order, there is almost inevitably going to be one general third-order factor. Since, too, ability variables are all positively correlated (Thurstone's positive manifold) we need variables that are in the hyperplane as a basis for rotation so that our researches need to include motivational and personality factors. Finally at the third-order it becomes necessary to establish the correlations between variables by the factor analysis itself, i.e. by the angle between the vectors, rather than from the test score themselves and this is at best a rough procedure (Cattell, 1956c). All these difficulties mean that the execution of researches adequate for third-order factor analysis is difficult and that inevitably there are few of them and that at present any results must be regarded as tentative rather than definitive.

In the studies already discussed by Cattell and Horn which gave rise to the second-order factors in Table 4.3, third-order analyses were carried out with the following results. With the age groups 5–14 years, a gf(H) factor emerged loading on fluid and crystallized ability, and an educational effectiveness factor loading on crystallized ability and certain personality factors which were difficult to identify. In the Horn study with adult criminals, a gf(H) factor emerged loading on gf, gr, gs and Pv (but not gc), together with an educational effectiveness factor similar to that previously found. It is to be noted that in the younger age groups gr, gs and Pv were not clearly represented at the second-order.

How can these results be interpreted? The factor gf(H) is regarded by Cattell as the historic, childhood-fluid ability which has produced the present fluid ability and the crystallized ability which is the ability at tasks demanding intelligence and required of children in a culture (e.g. school subjects). Its failure to load on gc in the criminal group is attributed to the fact that criminals have not oriented their fluid ability to culturally acceptable tasks. The educational effectiveness factors, a combination of ability and personality indicate that gc, crystallized ability and personality traits play their part in enabling people to utilize their abilities effectively. Thus the critical third-order ability factor is the historical fluid ability gf(H). It is clearly not the common factor "g" of Spearman or the second-order Thurstone factor, because it loads more highly on gf than gc, the factor measured by most conventional I.Q. tests.

How this gf(H) develops and influences behaviour is examined (p. 93) by the model of cognitive abilities which Cattell (1971) has erected to account for these results. At present, however, one can say that the empirical work demonstrates five second-order ability factors—gf, gc, gr, gs and Pv—and one third-order gf(H).

So far the work of Cattell and his colleagues has been scrutinized because they have pursued to its logical conclusion the factor-analytic rationale—the attainment of simple structure at its highest level. Indeed as Cattell and Kline (1977) have argued this is how factor analysis can be most usefully used in psychology and one can see the results of such applications in other chapters of this book notably those on temperament, mood and dynamics.

Guilford, however, like Cattell one of the great figures in factor analysis, has pursued a different line, in that he has consistently preferred orthogonal rotations. As Fulgosi and Guilford (1972) put it, although loadings on oblique axes commonly make it appear that tests are factorially simpler, in view of correlations among such axes, that appearance is illusory. In effect, Guilford is adopting a definition of simple structure different from that of Cattell and Thurstone. One problem, of course, with orthogonal factors is the impossibility of obtaining higher-orders. Elsewhere (Guilford, 1967) this difficulty has been overcome by using the intercorrelations between the tests as the basis for correlations between the factors.

The basis and essence of Guilford's work lies in the Structure of Intellect Model, fully described in Guilford (1967) and Guilford and Hoepfner (1971) but which appeared in 1959 in a well-known paper "The three faces of intellect". There can be little doubt that this has been, and indeed still is a most influential theory. Tyler (1972) has described it as a major contribution to our knowledge of intellectual functioning, and it has inspired a large research output into divergent thinking and creativity (e.g. Torrance, 1966; Getzells and Jackson, 1962; Hudson, 1966). Despite its influence this model has been severely criticized and one paper (Horn and Knapp, 1973) so savages it, that it really has to be discarded. There is a brief description of the model so that the criticisms can be understood.

THE GUILFORD STRUCTURE OF INTELLECT MODEL

The structure of intellect theory states that there are 120 independent abilities, each characterized by an intersection of one of five mental operations (cognition, memory, divergent thinking, convergent thinking and evaluation) on one of four contents (figural, symbolic, semantic and behavioural) to produce one of six products (units, classes, relations, systems, changes, implications). This is therefore a three-dimensional model with $5 \times 4 \times 6$ intersecting cells, each representing an independent ability—hence the 120 factors. Factor analyses quoted by Guilford (1967) and Guilford and Hoepfner (1971) are taken as supporting this model.

One feature of the model seems to produce general agreement even among its severest critics (e.g. Horn, 1972, Cattell, 1971) namely that as a schema for thinking about human abilities it has been stimulating and this is especially true if one is attempting to construct tests of ability. Yet even here it can be criticized. The Cattell and Warburton compendium (1967) of objective psychological tests (see Chapter 3) contains a more extensive list of the operations which are possible in completing tests, a point which has also been made by Fisher (1971). Indeed the distinction of convergent and divergent for which this model is perhaps best known is itself dubious because the best tests of flexibility and fluency do have restrictions concerning how they should be answered although it is true that free and playful settings, as Wallach and Kogan found (1965), seem to affect the quality of the responses.

However, not only are the operations not comprehensive, but the category of products is also arbitrary. Other products could equally well be included. Butcher (1973) has argued that this category is actually otiose. Eysenck (1967) has also pointed out the model has a fatal flaw namely that all the tests thus developed should be independent whereas in fact, as all studies demonstrate, they are correlated.

All these points are serious. However, a more fundamental criticism concerns the provenance of the model. As Eysenck (1967) has argued, it highlights the divorce of psychometry and psychology. Basically this model represents an intuitive attempt to categorize abilities. It has neither been developed in the light of empirical factorings of ability (it was indeed constructed to provide a rationale for such studies) nor in the light of the findings of modern cognitive psychology on mental processing, as advocated for example by Hunt (1971). Cattell (1971) has argued that in constructing tests to fit the model, to the extent that the model fails to fit the real world, so the tests must inevitably fail to measure what abilities in fact operate. That fairly large factors have emerged is attributed to the fact that by developing several similar tests, specific factors can be made to resemble group factors, i.e. they are bloated specifics.

One answer to these criticisms has always been proposed by Guilford and his associates and the work of Guilford and Hoepfner (1971) contains these findings—namely that the factorial studies support the structure of intellect model. Arbitrary it may be in origin but the factors confirm it. A typical study conducted with Americans and Yugoslavians by Fulgosi and Guilford (1972) makes just this point, that the structure of intellect model was confirmed.

Horn and Knapp (1973), however, have demonstrated that these factorial studies do not in fact support the model. First, Horn is especially careful to define two terms that are central to the argument. As he had previously pointed out (Horn, 1967) it is convenient in the discussion of factor analyses to extend the meaning of objective and subjective. A factor method is said to be objective if investigators using the same data and the same method but different hypotheses (the extension) arrive at the same result. A procedure is regarded as subjective if under these same conditions it can lead to different results. The Varimax rotation (Kaiser, 1958) is by these criteria objective: the Procrustes programme (Harley and Cattell, 1952) and similar rotational methods are subjective. Thus the Procrustes rotation produces identical results given the same target matrix (which of course contains the hypotheses of the experimenter). Given different target matrices, the results will be different. In short, therefore, any rotation procedure (whether by hand or computer) which fits data to hypotheses is defined as subjective.

As Horn and Knapp (1973) argue, the factor-analytic methods used to support the Guilford model are subjective. Indeed these authors quote Guilford and Hoepfner (1971) to the effect that where theoretical considerations guided rotations, 93% of attempts to demonstrate abilities were successful compared with only 32% where a mathematical description of simple structure was used. Horn and Knapp (1973) note a number of important points here. First if a method is so successful, it is pertinent to ask whether it *could* reject hypotheses. Secondly, there is little agreement as to what is psychologically awry (which helps guide the rotation). Finally Horn (1967) used Procrustes procedures to fit random variables to a previously stated theory, findings which have been replicated by others, e.g. Armstrong and Soelberg (1968).

Even if random variables can be forced into factors, it is possible that variables with a given set of relationships cannot be forced into a pattern of factors that is not consonant with such relationships. Thus the Guilford factor analyses could still be regarded as confirmatory evidence of the model. To put this to the test Horn and Knapp (1973) reanalysed the data from three studies by Guilford and his colleagues which covered a wide range of subjects, young adults to ninth grade students, and more important, embraced a large portion of the three-dimensional Guilford model. The data were subject to Procrustean analysis. Two kinds of target matrix were used, one representing hypotheses determined by random procedures and the other representing hypotheses determined partly by a random procedure and partly by consideration of theory and results that were not based entirely on the Guilford model. Factors found in the SI model, together with factors in the French *et al.* (1963) list were put into target matrices.

As a basis for comparing results, three descriptive indices were adopted:
(1) Hits (H). The number of variables in a solution with loadings greater than 0·3 on factors where such loading were postulated in the target matrices.
(2) Misses (M). The number of variables in a solution with loadings less than 0·3 on factors where loadings greater than 0·3 had been hypothesized. H + M is, of course, the number of variables in the study.

(3) Extra (E). The number of variables with loadings greater than 0·3 where zero loadings had been specified.

From these indices a number of informative ratios can be computed. The two most illuminating are: (1) H/(H + M) the proportion of hits relative to the attempts and (2) E/(H + E) the proportion of salient loadings that had not been hypothesized. Ratio (1), the proportion of confirmed hypotheses, is certainly that which implicitly or explicitly forms the basis of subjective judgements of fit of results to theory while ratio (2) is not often used, although as Horn and Knapp point out, it is useful.

The results of these studies are clear. Procrustes solutions can support random hypotheses as well as those based on SI theory or the list of French *et al.* (1963). In fact, ratio (1) was around 0·90 for all hypotheses whatever their provenance. Ratio (2) does indicate a slight difference in that more extras were found in the random than the factors hypothesized from theories. However, while this is perhaps evidence that factor-analytic procedures can sort out random from non-random factors, it does not affect the argument that the factor studies purportedly supporting Guilford's model could "confirm" any set of results. This is because as Horn and Knapp (1973) argue, variables that load as extras were not taken as disconfirmatory in evaluating the fit, indeed as Guilford and Hoepfner (1971) make clear in their discussion of their methods, the presence of such extras is regarded as error and manipulations of the vectors are made such as to diminish their number. Thus if extra loadings in Procrustean solutions are fully taken into account it is possible that such methods could disconfirm theoretical positions. If they are not, as they are not, Procrustean solutions appear able to fit virtually any set of results.

In brief, then, Horn and Knapp (1973) have shown that the factor-analytic results purporting to confirm the Guilford model are based on a methodology that can confirm virtually any hypotheses. This means that the model is left only with the rather weak support of criterion studies of the various factors as reported in Guilford and Hoepfner (1971). As a model, therefore, there is no reason to consider it further. However, this is not to say that as a means of classifying tests it is not useful and the divergent thinking tests which it has spawned, even though these abilities had been studied before, have proven interesting. However, as a model of intellect and one of particular significance for this book because of its psychometric origins, it cannot now be seriously considered.

So far, we have seen the structure of abilities as revealed by higher-order factor analysis with simple structure and as hypothesized by Guilford in his structure of intellect model. The model proposed by Cattell (1971) is now examined.

CATTELL ABILITY DIMENSION CHART (ADAC) MODEL

This model contains three facets or domains:

Domain A Action Phases

Involvement of Input

This is largest in the perceptual abilities. It involves the extent to which the ability depends upon sensory input. Raven's Matrices is clearly a test in which this aspect of domain A is important. This is why the matrices may not be an ideal test cross-culturally.

Involvement of Internal Processing and Storage

Cattell (1971) argues that this is largest in measures of memory. It involves the extent to which the score is determined by cognitive processes such as retention or retrieval. The memory span test of the WAIS is clearly a relevant test here.

Involvement of Output

This is seen most vividly in performance tests. Obviously this is important in measures of instrumental musical ability.

Domain C Content

Involvement of Experiental-cultural Dimensions

This includes subdimensions such as verbal, numerical, social, mechanical knowledge and art, just as examples. Notice that we can have measures testing say rhythmic output (Domain A3) in terms of music or words, involving, that is, different content dimensions.

Involvement of Neural-organizational Dimensions

For example, visual, kinaesthetic, auditory, tactile. As argued previously, most of the factors so far found in the sphere of abilities (which by the ADAC model is clearly largely uncharted) involve only the visual dimensions. There are certainly no well-established psychometric tests involving kinaesthetic or tactile dimensions.

Domain P Process Parameters

Demand in Terms of Complexity Level of Relation Eduction

This relates to the complexity of relations handled, as well as to the eduction of correlates. This is a process typified in the typical gf, test. How the complexity of relations is to be measured is, in fact, as Cattell (1971) admits, difficult.

Demand in Terms of Multiplexity of Sets

This concerns the amount of complication in processing (independent of P1), as evinced by, for example, number of items to be handled, number of simultaneously applied sets and the number of sets in successive steps.

Amount of Committing to Memory

This parameter does not only apply to the storage phase (A2). Since other phases all depend to some extent on storage, itself related to C3, then this demand will affect all abilities.

Amount of Retentive Activity Involved

This is an obvious parameter seen clearly for example in mechanical knowledge.

Amount of Retrieval Activity Involved

This again must play its part in many abilities and is dependent on the previous ability in 4. Retrieval is essential to fluency.

Flexibility versus Firmness

Every dimension or function which has been so far discussed could vary along the dimension of flexibility versus firmness.

Speed Demand

Clearly speed is a variable demand of a wide variety of tasks both among tests and in real life. It can be found equally in such disparate activities as problem-solving and flute-playing.

Rationale of the Model

The basis of this model lies in the concept of behaviour in terms of SOR, stimulus-organism-response. With this basis it is clear that three components are needed and these are to be found in the three categories of the first domain, and any ability can be categorized by the demands it makes on these three phases.

However, all these three activities are carried out on content and two dimensions of content in Domain C will apply to any tests and all abilities. It is to be noted that input and output for an ability are not necessarily the same. To take flute-playing again, the input is visual, the output spatial-kinaesthetic. Thus content C is totally different from that in Guilford's model, since here these are two independent categories, as described above.

In the processing parameters of Domain P, Cattell (1971) has argued from the original factor-analytic work of Spearman where the ability to handle complex relations was the essential definition of his g factor, from logical considerations of cognitive processes and from more recent experimental work in this area, that there are seven essential processing parameters. Speed is a problem for it is not clear whether there is a general speed factor and even if there is, whether in fact it belongs to the ability or personality sphere. Nevertheless, because it is a factor in speeded tests, Cattell argues that it is a worthwhile category.

The first point to notice about this model is that it is both a taxonomy of tests and a description of people. A test can be described in terms of categories within the three domains and so can a person who is high on x, average on y, but low on z. This is, as Cattell (1971) points out, a clear example of the equivalence of Q and R factors (see Chapter 2).

The 12 dimensions of this ADAC model make it impossible to represent it as a three-dimensional figure. If we consider only above and below average scores on each dimension there are 2^{12} (4096) types of ability. However, many of these are non-viable but there are still about 500 types. However, there is no implication in this model that there are as many factors as types.

As Cattell (1971) admits some of the criticism that we have mentioned in relation to the Guilford model (but not all, as we shall see) could be applied to ADAC. For example, although the analysis of processes seems more sound and is based upon cognitive psychological research, the connection is loose: there is no set of experiments tied to each dimension. Furthermore it would be possible to construct tests and thus emerge with factors that fitted the model (bloated specifics) without using the highly suspect Procrustean procedures (Horn and Knapp, 1973).

However, there are two important distinctions between the ADAC and the Guilford model. The point is that the ADAC model does not hypothesize that a factor will be found for each combination. Rather it claims that there will be a factor for each dimension and some of the sub-dimensions. Furthermore, the model is able to account for correlated factors (a fact of life in the ability sphere, as all researchers know, evinced by the positive manifold, and all teachers who see the effects of these ability factors in the work of their pupils) and is able to accommodate the ability factors so far discussed in our tables. Thus Spearman's "g" is the ability to handle complex relations, the general speed factor is gs, the general retention factor is rote memory and the retrieval factor is implicit in fluency.

The other major difference is the way that the model is applied. Cattell (1971) takes great care to stress that it should not be used so that research is directed towards an outcome. Cattell advocates factor analysis to discover the relationships between traits. He argues directly against the use of the model to construct tests. Now as we have seen from the work of Horn and Knapp (1973) Procrustean methods of factor analysis will support any set of hypotheses. To put the case more generally, subjective (in the Horn and Knapp sense) factor analyses will not do. Objective methods, and rotation to simple structure (as argued in Chapter 2) can lead to a definitive and replicable mapping of the structure of abilities. The ADAC model can be helpful in this provided that objective methods are used. Thus then the ADAC model can accommodate the findings of factor analysis which the Guilford model cannot, and it does provide a coherent taxonomy of abilities.

The ADAC model is able to encompass the factorial findings discussed earlier in this chapter and summarized in Tables 4.1 to 4.3. However, Cattell and his colleagues have developed a theoretical account of the findings which must be discussed before turning to an examination of a further model of abilities which tries to tie in the psychometric data more closely with cognitive psychology. These theories of the development of abilities which Cattell has based entirely on the factors in Tables 4.1 to 4.3 may be regarded as a theoretical contribution to the field of abilities from psychometrics while the factors themselves may be considered as a factual contribution.

Investment Theory

The investment theory of gf and gc claims that in the development of the individual there is "initially (perhaps after two or three years of maturational shaping from birth) a single, general, relation perceiving ability connected with the total associational, neuron-development of the cortex". Because this is a general power applicable to all motor and sensory areas and all selective retrieval, it is called fluid intelligence, gf. Crystallized ability, on the other hand, gc, develops and takes its specific form (different in different cultures) as a result of investing the general capacity gf(H), in suitable learning experiences. Thus school performance is related to gf (if low the calculus is impossible) opportunities, motivation and memory. Gradually the crystallized ability skills where gf has been invested separate from other skills acquired through experience at home and school of tasks requiring little gf. Thus in a child who is well adjusted to school (i.e. one who is investing his gf in the skills demanded by the school and not rebelling) gc may be clearly seen in the more abstract parts of the curriculum. According to this investment theory gc will be closely related to gf at an early age, but later beyond school where other skills may play their part, this may not be so. Thus, I find in my studies gc related to gf(H), the historic fluid ability.

Investment theory seeks to account for the relation of the third-order historical fluid ability to crystallized and fluid ability as they are measured. Cattell (1971) has developed a more comprehensive theoretical account of the factors implied in the ADAC model and those listed in Tables 4.1 to 4.3. This he has called Triadic theory.

Triadic Theory

Triadic theory derives its name from the fact that there are three elements in it. Three distinct types of ability are held to contribute to cognitive behaviour (along with a variety of temperamental and motivational variables which are irrelevant to the chapter on ability but which are fully discussed in Chapters 5 and 6). The theory describes the nature of these different ability categories and their mode of interaction in cognitive behaviour. The three kinds of ability are:
(1) General capacities.
(2) Local organizations or provincials.
(3) Agencies which correspond largely to primary abilities.

The Capacities

These are limits to brain action and emerge as general cognitive factors. The capacities are gf, fluid ability, gs, speed and the retrieval factor (fluency).

The Provincials

These powers include factors corresponding to sensory organizations—visual or auditory for example—and to motor areas.

The Agencies

These correspond to the primaries. The primaries, e.g. verbal ability are held to arise from the repeated use of fluid ability in learning in a particular kind of situation. Thus in an educated family, verbal ability will be reinforced (more so than in the home of an illiterate) and the skill becomes an agency by which the child achieves his ergic goals, i.e. fulfills his needs (see Chapter 6 for discussion of ergs). Thus the primary factors are instruments or agencies in civilized life and these are constructed from the application of fluid ability which is, therefore, a second-order among them. It must be noted that by this criterion gc, crystallized ability is really an agency; the set of skills favoured by a particular culture.

While the capacities especially fluid and crystallized ability have been extensively studied and described, the second class of powers, the provincials have been largely neglected. However, visualization, on reflection, is likely to be important in many kinds of artistic endeavour, working with maps and plans and in the selection of geometric rather than algebraic solutions, just as examples. Thomson would be high on this provincial. Auditory imagination (note that this power has been so neglected that there is no single commonly-used word for it in English) would clearly be significant in musical tasks, other than those demanding motor skills. Similar functions can be assumed for the other provincials.

The relation of the agencies and provincials is also interesting. Although in the description of an agency it was pointed out that it was determined partly by the level of fluid ability which is involved in any ability demanding the perception of relations, an agency must have some dependence on some provincials. Thus verbal ability will be aided by high skill in auditory and visual perception of words and probably by the kinaesthetic perceptions involved in utterances.

Thus then the primary factors, the agencies, are the products of the capacities and provincials, together with the experiences that each individual has. As in the example above, verbal ability is a product, say, of gf and visualization, for the sake of the argument, and the experience of the child with words. If rewarded by his family and school, verbal ability will be one way of reducing ergic tensions. Now this concept of ergic tension brings in Cattell's theory of motivation and his notions of structured learning theory. These two topics are beyond the sphere of abilities and readers must peruse them in Chapters 6 (motivation) and 7 (structured learning theory) or for a fuller discussion they must turn to Cattell and Kline (1977). Suffice it to say here that triadic learning theory is the link between the spheres of ability, and motivation and learning theory.

These are brief descriptions of the triadic theory and the ADAC model which demonstrate a notable attempt to integrate the basic factorial findings in the sphere of abilities into a coherent theoretical account. They also provide links with factorial work in other spheres of human behaviour. Thus as argued they represent the theoretical contribution to the psychology of human abilities from psychometrics. At present the triadic theory is still speculative and I do not feel that in a book attempting to point up the psychometric contribution to psychological knowledge a more detailed presentation is in order. The theory is included as an example of how the findings can be used in theory construction. Far more supportive work is necessary before it could be fully accepted. For a detailed study of this theory, readers must turn to Cattell (1971).

COGNITIVE PROCESSING AND INTELLIGENCE

As discussed previously, almost all critics of Guilford's structure of intellect model have objected to the arbitrary nature of the cognitive processes involved. Guilford (1967) has attempted to fit his model to that of Crossman (1964) but clearly the temporal sequence is wrong, since Guilford's model came first. Cattell's (1971) ADAC model can be similarly criticized, although Cattell claims that he did take into account the findings of modern cognitive psychology in constructing it. However, his accounting was general rather than specific and precise.

Hunt (1971, 1973, 1976) has attempted to link intelligence test scores precisely to a cognitive model based on experimental cognitive psychology, thus overcoming the objections to the work which have been examined so far. The first two models are the product of brilliant factor analysis which have surveyed cognitive psychology. Hunt's model is the obverse of this.

HUNT'S MODEL

The theoretical basis of Hunt's work is a distributed memory model of cognition, which is a computer analogy. Central to the model is the claim that information storage and transformation occur in three stages which can be informally described as pre-conscious thought, conscious thought and long-term memory (LTM). Within each stage there are a number of sub-stages, organized as in the distributed memory model (Fig. 4.1).

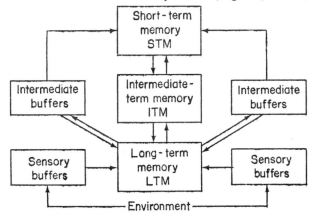

FIG. 4.1 From Hunt (1976). Printed with permission from L. Erlebaum Associates.

In this model information is passed up towards short-term memory (STM) in a series of progressively higher-order codes. The codes are based upon matching sensory input with patterns in LTM. When information in a buffer is recognized, the appropriate pattern name is placed in the next higher buffer. This continues until information is placed in STM where it becomes conscious. Active information-processing takes place in STM and intermediate-term memory (ITM). STM contains an echoic memory of recent stimuli, ITM an information-structure capturing the meaning of ongoing events. The STM lasts seconds, ITM lasts minutes or hours, LTM contains the permanent information.

In this model thought is the transformation of information in the STM-ITM system, and these transformations follow what Newell and Simon (1972) refer to as production rules which are of two sides. The left side is a pattern-recognition rule describing a class of states into which the STM-ITM system may fall. The right side is an action rule which can produce changes in information in STM, ITM or LTM or an overt response. When a left hand pattern is recognized, the corresponding right hand side is activated.

As Hunt (1976) points out this system is driven by pattern-recognition based upon the contents of LTM. Consequently the availability of this information must affect system-action and it is pertinent to distinguish between speech information (stored in the left brain position of LTM) and other kinds, some of which may be stored in the right brain position, since some buffers are assumed to have direct access only to one side of the brain.

This model of cognitive abilities is of interest for a wide variety of reasons. First, as Hunt points out, there are many places where individual differences might be expected. If these are shown to occur one must examine their relation to the list of ability factors. Secondly one has to consider the implications of this model of cognition in the light of the lists of factors. Finally one can see how well the psychometrically-based cognitive models fit this model which seems generally acceptable in cognitive psychology.

Individual Differences Implicit in the Model

(1) The model must be able to carry out lexical recognition. Hunt argues that there are likely to be differences in the speed with which logogens (cantabrian term (Morton, 1969), for a concept associated with a pattern) are aroused—a vital process for example in reading.

(2) People are likely to differ in the rapidity with which information can be manipulated in STM.

(3) Is storage in the STM-ITM system a separate ability, distinct from storage in the LTM system?

(4) Are there significant differences in the speed with which individuals transmit information within the system?

(5) Can individuals shift information processing to different components of the system with or without loss of efficiency?

Hunt and his colleagues have tried to produce experimental evidence demonstrating that some of these individual differences in processing do occur and that these are related to intelligence test scores. For example, Hunt *et al.* (1975) and Hunt *et al.* (1975) demonstrated that low verbal ability was associated with slow access to codes by comparing reaction times to pairs of identical letters and pairs of letters varying in type case (which demand conceptual coding). Similarly Hunt (1976) reports that among adults verbal subjects were more sensitive to changes in semantic categories in studying the release from proactive inhibition. There are, Hunt concludes, reliable and important individual differences in the ability to recognize and assign meaning to arbitrary physical stimuli—a very important dimension of human performance.

There are obvious differences in long-term memory. Cognitive psychologists have attempted to answer the question of whether this is due to different data in the LTM or whether those data are differently organized. One approach regards the data as organized in Euclidean space as do the studies of meaning, for example, Anderson and Bower (1972). Hunt (1976) argues that the relevance of these cognitive models to intelligence testing lies in the fact that many of the high loading g items, such as analogies, are problems solved by searching for an ideal solution conceptualized as a point in a specifically defined Euclidean space. A solution is obtained by finding an occupied point as close as possible to the ideal. With the Euclidean model, Hunt claims that there are two sources of individual differences in problem solving: differences in defining the space and differences in locating the points. In the network model, concepts are nodes, and relationships between them arcs. Here individual differences in problem solving will depend on the structure of this network. Hunt cites work by Loftus (1973) who demonstrates this point. Here reaction times are compared in two tasks, one of which is supposed to serve as an index entry into a subject's semantic net. Thus there is a difference in reaction time to: "Think of an example of a class X . . . beginning with Y" and "Think of something that begins with Y that is an X". From this type of study there is no great mass of data but Hunt (1976) strongly suggests such investigations should be carried out.

Since the model proposed by Hunt, and virtually all information-processing models of cognition, posit a working memory and a long-term memory, an obvious test of this approach lies in examining the relationship between memory tasks where the material has to be remembered for different periods. Again there seems no doubt that memory is not a unitary ability, since there were in a study by Nelson (1971) zero and negative correlations between number of errors to criterion of perfect learning and memory at six weeks. Love (1973) has demonstrated this same point impressively by showing that excellent mnemonists are superior to undergraduates in working memory but no different if long-term memory is tested. However, this is probably only true of meaningless material. Where meaningful material is used, the encoding of mnemonists and subsequent retrieval may be superior to normals. Nevertheless, the point is clearly taken: working memory is different from LTM.

Hunt and his colleagues in their studies of high and low verbal ability subjects have studied two other cognitive processes which may be regarded as sources of individual differences: the capacity to manipulate data rapidly in STM and the ability to retain information concerning the order of entry of items into STM. High verbal scorers are superior to low scores in both these capacities.

An example of a study illustrating this point is that of Hunt *et al.* (1975). They used tasks in which additions had to be done using complex codes, e.g. those based upon days: Sunday is zero and Saturday is six. What is Monday + Wednesday? Similar problems were constructed using day names, month names and letters. The differences between high and low verbal subjects in reaction time to these problems increased with increasing problem difficulty, defined in terms of base size (seven for day, 26 for letters) and whether carrying was necessary. This is to be expected, Hunt argues, if short-term memory information is more rapidly manipulated in the high verbals.

In respect of order information in STM, Hunt repeats a study where high verbals are better judges of the order of dichotically presented stimuli with a difference in arrival time of only 50 ms. Both these studies may well indicate, as Hunt argues, the manipulating and ordering capacities in STM of high verbals. They are also both strong evidence of the gf factor of our tables, which was defined as a general mental capacity. The high gf individual has a brain that simply operates more efficiently than those lower on this factor. Finally, Hunt reports a study where STM of gestures and words was investigated. The correlation between word recall and gesture recall was 0·09, suggesting that STM is not a unitary capacity.

In these investigations discussed here Hunt has demonstrated a clear relationship between verbal intelligence test scores and various mental processes implicated in his model of cognitive processing, viz. (1) rapid access to codes; (2) organization of data in LTM; (3) rapid manipulation of data in STM and (4) a better capacity to retain order of entry of information into STM. In addition STM and LTM capacities (at least for meaningless material) are clearly distinct and it appears to be necessary to posit separate STM's for different types of input, visual or verbal for example. These then are the cognitive processes found by Hunt to be related to intelligence test scores.

Hunt (1976) concludes this excellent paper by trying to state the relation of his model and these findings to psychometric work. He argues that his approach implies that an individual is a highly non-linear combination of basic abilities. He writes:

> In fact by choosing different control strategies, two individuals may make their performances on the same task depend upon different non-linear combinations of their structural capacities. If this is correct then a psychology of individual differences cannot possibly be recovered from data analyses based upon linear models...

The Relation of Hunt's Work to Psychometry

This is especially important because as one can see from the quotation above, Hunt clearly regards his work as demonstrating that traditional psychometrics cannot contribute to a knowledge of abilities—"the psychology of intelligence must be part of the psychology of cognition" is his concluding remark. Since I do not agree with Hunt on this point, I want now to examine the relation of this work to the psychometrics of abilities, as described earlier in this chapter.

The first point to notice is that Hunt has proposed the possibility that individuals use non-linear combinations of their abilities. Now it is perfectly true as has been argued in Chapter 2 that multivariate analyses assume the linear combination of variables. As Cattell and Kline (1977) have argued this hypothesis, the simplest, is justified until refuted by the evidence. Hunt has produced no evidence that non-linearity prevails. (If it is correct he writes.) However, the factorings of ability that have yielded the factors in the three tables in this chapter also yield no evidence of non-linearity. Indeed, the substantial factor loadings on test items of the kind discussed by Hunt (analogies for example) gives strong support to the claim that these psychometric factors can account for the variance, which they would fail to do if tasks were non-linear in their relations. Thus, I would argue that it is not necessary to introduce the problem of non-linearity among ability variables until the evidence forces one so to do. Thus the claim that psychometrics, via multivariate analyses, is bound to fail in the study of intelligence is only true if non-linearity prevails; and of this as I have argued, there is no evidence.

Suppose, however, that this cognitive process approach to the study of ability were to be taken up and extended. What would emerge, it seems, would be a series of processes correlated with gc or gf. In this case these processes would be equivalent to the primary factors discovered by Cattell, unless it turned out that they were all uncorrelated. This, however, is unlikely since the studies already quoted show different processes to be correlated since verbally high subjects are superior on several of them.

How then do the processes discussed by Hunt compare with the factors listed in Table 3.1. Of course, it could be the case if these processes are implicated in a wide variety of tasks that they should not be primary factors, as Hunt (1976) hints, but secondary powers or even third-order factors. Thus, it is also worth scrutinizing Tables 4.2 and 4.3. What one looks for is access to codes, rapid manipulation of data in STM and the capacity to retain entry order information in STM.

Accessing codes as tested by Hunt and colleagues is certainly close to P perceptual speed and accuracy in Table 3.1, which involves subjects making rapid comparisons between pairs of visual stimuli, a procedure similar to the experimental procedures from which this cognitive process was inferred. The STM factors are certainly found among the primaries in Table 3.1. Ms is span memory, involving short-term retention of meaningless digits. Ma is rote-memory which is the ability to recall pairs with no mediating link, this clearly resembles the mnemonic STM ability, so high in certain individuals. Finally, Mm is meaningful memory, which is found in Table 3.1, a supposition which is confirmed by Hunt's warning that different findings are obtained with meaningful and meaningless material. From this I would argue that the cognitive study of abilities is eventually likely to end up with the same factors as those revealed by factor analysis, but given labels more closely tied to hypothesized processes. The factor labels on the other hand used by analysts are broader in meaning but less tied to a particular cognitive model.

It is, therefore, false to claim that the study of abilities must be the study of cognition. For it is clear that the study of cognition is leading to the establishment of abilities essentially the same as those that have emerged through factor analysis. However, abilities established by experiment have a less sound statistical basis than those established by multivariate methods on large samples, and the relation between the abilities is unknown. This is not to say that cognitively-based psychological enquiry into abilities in terms of models is not valuable. Such experiments can throw much light on the interpretation of psychometrically discovered factors. All methods should be used in the study of factors and cognitive processes. However, to claim that the cognitive process method is superior to that of psychometrics is clearly wrong. It is not good at revealing abilities but it is good at revealing what they are.

Ideally, therefore, a combination of psychometrics and cognitive process psychology would be a powerful tool in the study of abilities.

Carroll (1976) has attempted to do just this—produce a rapprochement of Hunt's model and the French *et al.* (1963) list of factors. One further point about Hunt's work needs to be examined: how do the Guilford and the ADAC models compare with this model rooted in cognitive psychology?

While it is clear that the Guilford model bears little relation to that of Hunt, the ADAC model is not so far removed. In Domain or Panel P, the process parameters, many of the capacities implicit in the Hunt model are discussed. Perhaps the greatest difference lies in the P1 demand in terms of complexity of relation eduction. Cattell is content to speak of this as though it were a process, whereas in Hunt's model such reasoning is analysed into more constituent processes. This difference is due largely to the different universes of discourse, with which the models are concerned: one with the end result of the process, the other with the process itself. Generally, however, the ADAC model is not grossly at variance with modern cognitive views.

CARROLL'S WORK

Carroll has attempted to apply this cognitive approach of Hunt directly to the psychometric work discussed in this chapter and it must be described and commented on before drawing conclusions concerning the value of this cognitive work. What he has done is to classify the cognitive processes underlying 24 factors drawn from the reference kit of French *et al.* (1963). Table 4.4 presents the summary of his results.

Carroll (1976) while admitting that these are process-descriptions of factors offers them as examples of the kind of research that should be in progress. The implication of the descriptions is, according to Carroll, that none of these factors is pure or simple in the sense that each demands a number of memories of different kinds and of control processes. That so many tasks demand this processing core accounts for the positive correlation between ability factors. If this is the case then it follows that gf which factorially accounts for the correlations is the total efficiency level of all these processes.

This paper by Carroll (1976) illustrates the relationship of psychometrics and cognitive psychology which seems likely to be most fruitful for psychological knowledge. The experimental study of cognitive processing enables psychologists to describe in some detail the nature of the ability factors recognized by psychometrics. As already seen from Hunt's work, the processes which he has studied and which were related to crystallized intelligence, were highly similar descriptively to some of the primary factors in Tables 4.1 and 4.2. Thus by enabling factors to be tied down to cognitive processing, the large scale multivariate study of ability factors, showing environmental and genetic influences on their development can be related to the cognitive processes themselves, work which would be of great interest in cognitive

TABLE 4.4

CARROLL'S VIEW OF THE COGNITIVE PROCESSING INVOLVED IN SOME PRIMARY ABILITY FACTORS

Individual differences in cognitive processes and memory stores associated with 24 FA factors[a]

Factor	Principal memory involved	Cognitive process operations				Strategies	Response rendering
		Addressing sensory buffers	Addressing ITM or LTM	Manipulations in executive and STM			
Ss SPATIAL SCANNING		Visual search for connectedness of lines and paths (T, C)				Search from goal rather than start (P)	
Le LENGTH ESTIMATION	STM (visual)			Compare distances (T, C)			
P PERCEPTUAL SPEED	STM (visual)	Visual search for specified items (T)					
Cf FLEXIBILITY OF CLOSURE	STM (visual)			Image figure-in-ground (T, C)			
S SPATIAL ORIENTATION	STM (visual)			Mentally rotate spatial configuration (T, C)			
Vz VISUALIZATION	STM (visual)			(1) Mentally rotate spatial configuration (T, C) (2) Perform serial operations (T)			
Xa FIGURAL ADAPTIVE	STM (visual) [LTM, general logic]		Search hypotheses in LTM (T, C)	(1) Image figure-in-ground (T, C) (2) Perform serial			

Factor	Memory store				
MEMORY SPAN	STM (non-specific)	(1) Store in STM (T, C) (2) Retrieve from STM (T, C)		Chunk or group stimulus items (P)	
Ma ASSOCIATIVE MEMORY	ITEM (non-specific)	(1) Store in ITM (T, C) (2) Retrieve from ITM (T, C)		(1) Find mediators in LTM (P, C, T) (2) Rehearse associations (P)	
Cs SPEED OF CLOSURE	LTM (visual-representational)	Search for match of cue (T, C?)		(1) Search hypotheses in LTM (P, C) (2) Search different portions of LTM (P) (3) Restructure perception (P)	Writing Speed?
Fw WORD FLUENCY	LTM (lexicographemic)	Search for instances (T, C)		(1) Search different portions of LTM (P) (2) Use alphabet as mnemonic (P)	Writing Speed
F EXPRESSIONAL FLUENCY	LTM (lexico-grammatical)	Search for instances (T, C)		(1) Search different portions of LTM (P) (2) Use of grammatical mnemonics (P)	Writing Speed
Fa ASSOCIATIONAL FLUENCY	LTM (lexico-semantic)	Search for instances (T, C)		Search different portions of LTM (P)	Writing Speed
V VERBAL COMPREHENSION	LTM (lexico-semantic)	Retrieve word meanings (C)			
N NUMBER FACILITY	LTM (numbers and numerical operations)	Retrieve number associations and algorithms (C)	Perform serial operations with algorithms (T, C)	(1) Chunk intermediate results (P) (2) Record intermediate results (P)	
I INDUCTION	LTM (abstract logical)	Search hypotheses (C, T)	Serial operations to construct new hypotheses (P, T)		

TABLE 4.4 (*continued*)

CARROLL'S VIEW OF THE COGNITIVE PROCESSING INVOLVED IN SOME PRIMARY ABILITY FACTORS
Individual differences in cognitive processes and memory stores associated with 24 FA factors[a]

Factor	Principal memory involved	Cognitive process operations			Strategies	Response rendering
		Addressing sensory buffers	Addressing ITM or LTM	Manipulations in executive and STM		
Rs SYLLOGISTIC REASONING	LTM (lexico-semantic, abstract logical)		Retrieve meanings and algorithms (C, T)	Perform serial operations (T, C)	Attention to stimulus materials (P)	
R GENERAL REASONING	LTM (abstract logical, algorithms for quantitative relations)		Retrieve algorithms (C, T)	Perform serial operations (T, C)		
Fi IDEATIONAL FLUENCY	LTM (experiential, general)		Search for associations (T, C)		Search different portions of LTM (P)	Writing Speed
O ORIGINALITY	LTM (experiential, general)		Search for "unusual" instances (C, T)		Search different portions of LTM (P)	Writing Speed?
Re SEMANTIC REDEFINITION	LTM (experiential, uses of objects)		Search for associations (C, T)		Search different portions of LTM (P)	Writing Speed
Xs SEMANTIC SPONTANEOUS FLEXIBILITY	LTM (experiential)		Search for associations (C, T)		Search different portions of LTM (P)	Writing Speed
Sep SENSITIVITY TO PROBLEMS	LTM (experiential, abstract logical)		Retrieve associations (C, T)	Perform serial operations (T, C)	Search different portions of LTM (P)	Writing Speed
Mk MECHANICAL KNOWLEDGE	LTM (mechanical knowledge)		Retrieve associations (T, C)			

[a] Individual differences in: (C) contents or capacity of memory store involved; (T) temporal parameters of the process; (P) probability of a strategy. From Carroll (1976). Printed with permission of L. Erlbaum Associates.

psychology. My conclusion is, therefore, that these two approaches to the study of ability, the pychometric and the cognitive, are not antithetical, nor should the latter replace the former. Rather they are complementary and together they should contribute richly to the stock of psychological knowledge.

CONCLUSIONS ON ABILITY FACTORS AND THE STRUCTURE OF ABILITY

So far I have argued that the factor analysis of ability has revealed the most important dimensions of ability. The largest primary factors, which can be small and of which, ultimately, there will be a considerable number, were listed in Tables 4.1 and 4.2. The differences in different lists produced by different investigators were shown to be due largely to technical problems in factor-analytic methods and to sampling problems. (The length of this list of primary factors makes it unwieldy and some ordering of them was held to be desirable.) Table 4.3 contained the second-order factors that have been obtained from these primaries and even higher-order factors can be extracted. The meaning of these higher-order factors was discussed.

Another approach to ordering the primaries is to construct models of cognitive processes. Guilford's (1959) SI model was examined and found wanting in various ways, especially because it bore little relation to the findings of modern cognitive psychology and because, contrary to research findings it implied that all abilities were independent. Finally an important research (Horn and Knapp, 1973) was reviewed which showed that there was little sound evidence in favour of the SI model.

Cattell's (1971) ADAC model was examined together with the related investment and triadic theories of ability. These seemed to order the factors a meaningful way, although the hypothesized cognitive processes, were not in all cases closely based in experimental psychology. The triadic theory of abilities, though speculative was regarded as a good example of how psychometrics could in the future contribute to theory in this field of psychology.

Finally the work of Hunt (1971) was examined, who has argued that the study of intelligence is best undertaken as part of experimental cognitive psychology and that the factor analysis of abilities was unlikely to be successful. This claim was shown to be ill-founded. Rather I concluded that both approaches were complementary and that together powerful contributions to knowledge could be expected.

The chief contribution to psychological knowledge in the field of abilities lies in the establishment of the main dimensions of ability. The models and theories are still in advance of knowledge but illustrate what kind of contribution psychometrics is likely to make in the future.

Now the factual contribution to the knowledge of abilities from psychometrics has been seen, the primary- and higher-order factors and their structure whether in the form of models or simple structure oblique rotations, psychometrists are now able to answer questions that are of great interest in this field. All findings are closely relevant to (1) the nature of intelligence (cf. the attempts to define it by Miles, 1957); (2) the nature of creativity and (3) the genetics of intelligence. The next section, therefore, will be concerned to elucidate these points. These questions are not so complex or difficult to answer as might be thought from the lengthy and continuous discussions which they normally provoke. As shall be seen, many of the problems arise from an inadequate grasp of the factorial structure of abilities and even more profound, an inadequate grasp of the nature of factors.

INTELLIGENCE

Generally, in the light of the evidence in Table 4.1 to 4.3, I should like to regard intelligence much as did Spearman—the ability to educe correlates, i.e. basic ability in abstract reasoning. However, I am not over-concerned with verbal definitions since there is an inevitable confusion over the meanings of words, meanings being ultimately private and subjective. Instead I prefer to define intelligence operationally by its factor loadings and by the correlations of the intelligence factor with external criteria. In this way the definition becomes public and there can be no doubt what is meant.

Intelligence, as measured by the standard intelligence tests, is a mixture of two factors gc and gf, crystallized and fluid ability. Crystallized ability shows itself in the primary verbal factor, V, the computation factor V and the reasoning factors R and I. It can also be seen in knowledge and social skills. But, as has been argued, gc is a reflection of gf; it is gf, evinced in the particular set of skills valued in a culture. Gf, itself, appears in those tests where knowledge is minimal and reasoning all, series, matrices, and synonyms and analogies where the words are well known to all subjects and the difficulty lies in working out the relationship. In brief, gc demands the same reasoning abilities as gf, together with a knowledge deemed valuable by the culture. Because of this gc can underestimate the basic intellectual potential (which depends on gf) of those from deprived or anomalous backgrounds who may not have the requisite knowledge and overestimate the ability of those from cultured and literate homes who may virtually know the answers.

In real life terms the implications of conceiving of intelligence as two factors are considerable. Horn and Cattell (1967) have examined the development of these factors. Fluid intelligence increases through childhood and into young adulthood, levels off and declines. Crystallized intelligence on the other hand increases until late maturity. Thus in most tasks one is unlikely to notice failings due to age because most tasks demand crystallized intelligence. Fluid ability is needed if there is something radically novel to be grasped. The introduction of computing into jobs was a good example of a skill which, being new, required fluid ability. In departments of psychology, for example, many older staff members found it unnecessary for their research to master computing. Horn and Donaldson (1976) have recently rebutted claims (e.g. Baltes and Schaie, 1976) that there is no decline with age.

The dual nature of intelligence accounts also for apparently disparate findings that both the environment and genetics play a major part in the determination of intelligence test scores. Thus Gordon (1923) found that Canal Boat Children has extremely low I.Q. scores, a fact attributable certainly in part to their unfavourable (for learning) environment. On the other hand, the twin studies and other better methods of estimating heriditary influences on intelligence test scores show around 80% hereditary determination (see question 3 of this section). This anomaly is explicable in that it is gf that one should expect to be largely genetically determined while gc is involved in many intelligence tests.

Finally in the discussion of the nature of intelligence I want to examine the reasons why most psychometrists consider it to be so important an ability trait. A common argument raised against intelligence test scores is that they just measure ability on the intelligence test, an argument apparently reinforced by the definition of intelligence as what intelligence tests measure. This is entirely false for the following reasons:

(1) In factor-analytic terms the claim means that gf and gc are specific factors, specific to the tests measuring them. As my factor analyses demonstrate, this is simply not so, gf and gc load a very wide variety of tests, so wide that it is quite improbable that the factors are bloated specifics.

(2) If these factors were bloated specifics they would not correlate with external criteria. As discussed in detail in Chapter 8 on the contribution of psychometrics to educational psychology, this is simply wrong. Intelligence test scores correlated with educational achievement and as Ghiselli (1966) showed in a survey of predictors of occupational success, I.Q. correlates 0·3 on average with performance in any job. This is conclusive proof that intelligence tests do not just measure skill at the tests. Finally mention should be made of Terman's (1926) old studies, before factored tests were common, of gifted children. Here children selected as highly intelligent on the Stanford-Binet Test, when compared with controls, were enormously successful as adults, creating a flood of scientific papers, books and patents and reaching positions of wealth and eminence.

Both these arguments entirely refute the claim that intelligence scores reflect only skill at intelligence tests and demonstrate (especially the work of Ghiselli) the pervasive nature in all tasks of gf and gc.

(3) There is a final third point. From the discussion in Chapter 2 on the nature of factors, it is clear that factors are dimensions underlying or accounting for observed correlations and that in many cases when rotated to simple structure they reflect causal agencies. Thus from the very nature of factors it is likely that gc and gf will be pervasive dimensions underlying a wide variety of human abilities, rather than some narrow test variable.

In summary, therefore, gf and gc, are seen as basic reasoning abilities which underly our cognitive skills in a wide variety of tasks. This is not to deny the significance of specific abilities, perhaps musical ability is a good example, but the evidence points unequivocally to the importance of intelligence, gf and gc, in all abilities.

CREATIVITY

Guilford (1959) in his APA address first turned attention onto tests of creativity. Based upon his model of intellect, whose defects have already been discussed, much was made of the divergent thinking category of tests, tests which required not one correct answer but a variety of responses. These were contrasted with the typical convergent gc or gf loaded question. Guilford (1967) lists a considerable number of divergent thinking tests which cover the content categories and products of his model. From these three scores are derived: (a) fluency, usually determined by the number of responses; (b) originality, which may be a subjective judgement or a statistical one derived from scores and (c) flexibility, scored from the number of conceptual categories used in the responses.

Although Guilford and his colleagues have been able to develop creativity tests to fill the cells of the SI model, this is not sufficient evidence that these measures form a useful category. These questions have to be considered. Can divergent thinking tests be accounted for by factors rotated to simple structure? Are these tests independent of general intelligence? And are these tests related to creativity in the real non-test world?

First the primary factors in Tables 4.1 and 4.2 include factors which are indubitably related to those in the Guilford model. Thus O1, ideational flexibility loaded on factors which fell into the divergent production of semantic classes cell of the SI model. In addition, as expected, there were substantial correlations with O2 and Fi. Fi, is ideational fluency which is the ability to reproduce ideas quickly on a given topic. The O2 factor of originality was a new factor loading on tests requiring subjects to combine two objects into a functional object. In addition to these, in Table 4.2, one finds the well-established Fe, expressional fluency factor. These oblique primary factors demonstrate that Guilford in his emphasis on creativity and divergent thinking was certainly dealing with well-established factors that are not specific and do not disappear on rotation to simple structure.

Table 4.3 indicates that at the second-order, much of the variance in these factors can be accounted for by gr, the retrieval capacity factor. Thus it appears that ability in these primary factor skills depends upon the capacity to retrieve information in our long-term memory. This second-order structure brings us to the second question—the relation of Guilford's divergent factors to the general intelligence factors.

To answer this question one has to think clearly about the nature of these factors. The paragraphs above demonstrate that some of Guilford's divergent factors (constructed originally to fill the cells of his SI model) are retained in simple structure. These are independent largely of gc and gf and as shown load on the retrieval from memory factor. Thus one can say that they are independent of intelligence. However, this does not mean that Guilford was correct to argue this in his SI model. His divergent factors were orthogonal and as such were not factor-pure, i.e. they picked up variance from several oblique factors as is inevitable if orthogonal vectors are used to match oblique descriptions of the same factor space. Thus if Guilford's divergent factors are factored with intelligence factors, *they* are not independent but load moderately on them as Cropley (1968) and Hasan and Butcher (1966) found. Indeed, although, as Butcher (1973) argues, results have varied from no correlation to correlations as high as 0·7 between divergent and convergent tests, depending on particular measures and samples, generally as the survey of Nuttall (1973) demonstrates, there is a moderate correlation. Bennet (1972) in an investigation of 1000 children from the whole range of ability also showed that Guilford's divergent tests and conventional I.Q. scores were not independent.

There seems little doubt that the Guilford divergent tests are moderately related to convergent thinking tests, although measuring some extra variance. The figures have to be treated cautiously because as with all correlations with a variable of such heterogeneity as general ability, results differ from sample to sample depending on the homogeneity of the sample. Thus where divergent tests are found most discriminating is usually where convergent scores are high and homogeneous as in the studies by Hudson (1966) and Getzells and Jackson (1963). Indeed, where all subjects are highly intelligent so that most problems present little difficulty, it is clear that variance on test scores is likely to be attributable to some factor other than intelligence. Secondly, as shown above, research using the Guilford tests is not strictly relevant because they are not factorially clear.

In conclusion, therefore, I would argue that the basic dimensions underlying Guilford's divergent tests are independent of the two intelligence factors, being in fact related to gr, the retrieval factor. The actual divergent thinking tests are, however, not independent of gc and correlate with it around 0·4.

The last point concerning the correlation of the divergent thinking factors with creativity, as it is understood in the non-test world—the production of great art and science, can be dealt with fairly briefly. In fact, there is little evidence linking scores on divergent tests to creative performance. As the work of Guilford and his colleagues show, the vast majority of studies used students or some group undergoing training. Ratings of originality by teachers were the usual criterion and Barron (1955) with air force officers found correlations between these and divergent tests of 0·3. Taylor *et al.* (1963) have argued that the criterion of creativity is so complex that this problem alone could account for the failure for divergent tests to correlate well—as they found with a sample of research scientists. Indeed, Lytton (1971) has pointed out that there is no evidence that divergent thinkers are or will become creative people. I must, therefore, conclude that as yet there is no evidence that creativity and scores on divergent thinking tests are linked.

I am forced to argue, therefore, that the emphasis on divergent thinking tests in the study of creativity is probably not a sensible strategy. They are not clearly linked to creativity and are not independent of gf and gc. Indeed great creative people, if one examines their lives are noted not only for great ability, but their personality and dynamics which would appear to be different from those of less talented individuals. The labour alone of Bach in writing out his own music would be excessive for the majority, even of able musicians. Indeed, it is far more likely that an understanding of creativity will come from the study of personality and motivation rather than from ability alone.

HERITABILITY OF INTELLIGENCE

This is a question which causes feelings to run high and in some cases reason to be over-run. Again this is a vast subject which cannot be comprehensively surveyed.

Anastasi (1961) has argued that the nature/nurture question is of little importance, that what one wants to know is not the extent to which environment effects intelligence, but how it does so. Hudson (1974) in his introduction to Kamin's (1974) book makes a similar point, by questioning what differences would be brought about in education or in any other societal institution if the nature/nurture ratio were 80:20 or 20:80. In my view both these points are irrelevant. The question is a scientific one. To what extent is intelligence inherited in any given culture? The practical consequences that may or may not follow the answer are irrelevant to the question as such. These are in the field of ethics or politics. To know the answer implies much about the nervous system and behaviour of men. Psychometrists' concept of the physiology and psychology of the intellect must be different if on the one hand one thinks of abilities as entirely genetic or on the other as entirely learned.

Two further critical issues follow from this first point. As Cattell (1971), one of the psychologists who has most clearly stated the case for the importance of genes in the determination of intelligence, has stressed, no worker in this area suggests an either genetic or environmental determination: there is an interaction between the two. Those unfortunate children, usually illegitimate, who are reared without human contact will clearly not develop their potential.

The second point is that any determination of the nature/nuture ratio is made from a sample from a population, and as such it can only refer to that population. Ratios that have been demonstrated in the U.S.A. or Great Britain are by no means applicable to other populations. Where the environment is extremely diverse, as in India, then it is inevitable (if there are any environmental affects) that the contribution from genetic differences will be smaller. The converse is the case in a homogeneous culture.

As indicated, this topic is one of the more controversial in psychology to such an extent that workers often utilizing the same basic studies come to entirely opposed conclusions. Cattell (1971) and Eysenck (1971) both conclude that in the West at least, there is about 80% of variance in I.Q. scores attributable to genetic causes. Kamin (1974) on the other hand concluded that "there are no data sufficient for us to reject the hypothesis that differences in the way in which people answer the questions are determined by their palpably different life experiences".

Kamin has examined in minute detail the original papers reporting, in the main, the intelligence test scores of dizygotic and monozygotic twins (MZ). In this process he has discovered inconsistencies, errors and in all cases, in his view, incorrect interpretations of the findings. Before subjecting this book to critical scrutiny, Burt's findings (Burt, 1966, Burt and Howard, 1956) have to be discussed. Kamin demonstrated that Burt had reported his studies of MZ twins reared apart over the years with considerable inaccuracy and inconsistencies. For example, correlations remained identical when the number of subjects was different. The number of subjects in apparently the same investigation was sometimes different in different reports. Details of test procedures and administration were not clear. Jensen (1974b) in a careful study of all Burt's work in this area recorded 22 such errors and was forced to conclude that the data (which are much the clearest demonstration of the genetic determination of I.Q. scores) were scientifically worthless. This is certainly the view adopted by Kamin, who hints in his writing that this was something worsé than carelessness. I have (Kline, 1975, 1976) utilized Burt's data previously as supporting the genetic determination of intelligence. The inconsistencies I regarded as careless reporting, but not so careless as to invalidate the results. This is especially the case since Burt's findings are not significantly different from those of others in the field (Jensen, 1974b). However, Jensen and Kamin have catalogued so many inconsistencies that it seems safer to ignore his findings.

Some writers (e.g. McAskie and Clarke, 1976) have impugned Burt's honesty arguing that the figures were deliberately distorted to support his theoretical position. This attack seems monstrous since Burt is unable to reply. It is a topic which is not discussed further, but I do not believe this to be the case. However, granted that Burt's figures are not included in my argument, and that Kamin has made his case here, how do Kamin's arguments stand scrutiny?

The task has been simplified by a superb review of this book by Fulker (1975), with whose views I am in close agreement. Newman *et al.* (1937) carried out a famous study of 19 pairs of MZ twins reared apart. They reported a correlation of 0·67 between the twins which was apparent evidence for a considerable genetic determination. According to Kamin, however, this correlation results from the imperfect standardization of the Stanford-Binet test, and is an artefact of the effects of age on measured I.Q. In the sample, age and I.Q. in fact correlate -0.22, i.e. they account for just over 4% of the variance. If this were so, the correlation would be reduced to 0·65.

Kamin, however, does not accept this reasoning. Instead, he breaks down the 19 pairs into sub-groups and examines the correlations. For 14 male twins, age and I.Q. correlate -0.78 and -0.11 for females. Subdivided into groups matching in age, older than and younger than the males, the correlations are −0·60, −0·27 and +0·99. Thus, the sample appears heterogeneous. But, as Fulker (1975) points out, this heterogeneity is the result of breaking the sample into such small groups. There are only two pairs of twins in the +0·99 correlation. Since −0·60 and −0·27 are not significantly different with these small samples, whether the females are regarded as heterogeneous depends on the two pairs of young twins. Now these twins are as pairs different, although the members of each pair are similar, thus accounting for the +0·99 correlation:

Pair *X* 12 years 9 months scores 122, 127.

Pair 16 11 years 5 months scores 90, 88.

As Fulker (1975) cogently points out, to argue that this correlation represents the correlation of age and I.Q. (and not a statistical abnormality of a small sample) implies that I.Q. is increasing 20 points a year at this age. This is one example of Kamin's attempts to demonstrate that a sound correlation in MZ twins reared apart is, in fact, attributable to a statistical artefact. Ironically the demonstrated result itself is an artefact. Few psychometrists (hated figures to Kamin) would cite correlations based on two pairs. Kamin also puts on a further impressive display in connection with this study. He carried out pseudo-pairing of the twins such that each pair is matched for age, but is not in fact related. Calculation of the intra-class correlation indicates the effects of pure age matching effects. For males the r is 0·67 (greater than for related pairs!). For females of equivalent age one finds 0·47 and 0·65. For older females one finds 0·06 and 0·48—perhaps a small genetic effect here. It is concluded by Kamin that the 0·67 reported by Newman is meaningless—on account of the correlation with age.

However, as Fulker (1975) demonstrates, these pseudo-pair correlations are again artefactual. If one was to break down any correlation by taking small sub-samples one should find the same thing. Fulker in fact used the pseudo-pairing technique with the Otis I.Q. scores and the r was −0·02. Using the Binet scores, he worked out other pseudo-correlations with slightly different age groups and obtained r's of 0·16 and 0·12. Finally, using all possible pseudo-pairing the r was −0·02. Kamin's figures, therefore, represent the fluctuations in r expected of very small samples. These same arguments apply to Kamin's attempt to overthrow the Juel-Nielsen study (1965). The final *coup de grace* of these figures is the correlation worked out by Fulker—that between Kamin's reworked figures and sample size, −0·75 (highly significant). Thus two of the studies which support the genetic determination of I.Q. scores still stand.

Shields' (1962) studied 40 MZ twins reared apart. Strangely, age effects were not observed here. Instead this investigation, according to Kamin, is totally invalidated by testing bias and selective placement. Testing bias is shown by the fact that the mean difference in the scores of the five twin pairs not tested by Shields is far greater than the mean difference of those he did test.

However, Fulker (1975) again demolishes the argument. Two of these five pairs had discrepancies no larger than one-quarter of the pairs tested by Shields. This means the argument of testing bias rests on three cases. In one of these, one twin failed to understand the instructions and scored one on the dominoes test. In the first pair one twin had a medical history of recurrent blindness, congenital syphilis and amnesia. There was also a huge discrepancy in the neuroticism scores. The second pair were daughters of a drunken ship's carpenter. One twin was sold to a doctor and settled in South America. The other had little education and at nine years old was sold in Europe. They grew up speaking different languages (not English). It is hardly surprising that there was a discrepancy in scores. Kamin, who demonstrates in his attempts at refutation, that he pays careful attention to details and castigates workers in this field for imperfect examination of their sources, must have known these facts. How, therefore, he could claim that unconscious bias invalidated the testing defies reason. Indeed, it could be asked how such bias could affect pencil and paper tests. Thus, Shields' study is certainly not invalidated by testing bias.

I now come to the question of selective placement, a factor always raised in arguments about MZ twins reared apart. Kamin points out that 27 pairs were reared in related families, e.g. the real mother and the aunt. Thirteen pairs were raised in unrelated families. For the 27 pairs, the correlation is 0·83. For the unrelated families, it drops to 0·51. Kamin argues that the drop demonstrates that the environment has a powerful effect. Nevertheless, Fulker (1975) again destroys Kamin's claims.

Most of the 27 twins reared in related houses were nurtured by aunts or grandparents. In this case, therefore, they should resemble each other as do cousins. However, the I.Q. of cousins correlates around 0·25; these twins showed a correlation of 0·83. This difference surely demonstrates a powerful genetic determination. However, the correlation of 0·51 for twins in unrelated homes is probably excessively low. For these include the three bizarre and highly discrepant cases we have seen used to illustrate the argument for testing bias. Without these three the correlation rises to 0·84. In other words with small samples (13) one again finds that the figures can be distorted by a few special cases.

These arguments clearly demonstrate that Shields' twin study is not invalidated either by selective placement or testing bias. Three of the four twin studies can thus be utilized safely in the argument for the genetic determination of intelligence. Kamin either deliberately or through inexperience with parametric statistics which are little used in his special field of operant work, has made too much of fluctuations in coefficients among small sub-samples.

As has been indicated Kamin has certainly established that Burt was a careless reporter of his researches into twins. I agree with Jensen (1974b) that it is probably better not to utilize his results in arguments concerning the heritability of intelligence since critics can always dismiss them on these grounds of carelessness. Nevertheless, as Fulker (1975) points out, his results are not that different from those of the studies which have already been examined. Since, if one ignores the work of Burt, Kamin's arguments about three of the twin studies are shown to be hollow, these twin studies still stand. If they still stand, then they show ineluctably the considerable (around 60%) genetic determination of I.Q. scores, and Kamin's thesis, that no data exist, such that a prudent man would accept the genetic determination of I.Q. scores is totally refuted.

Fulker (1975) destroys Kamin's other arguments concerning adoption studies. Nevertheless, Fulker makes a more general point that deserves note. It is implausible in the extreme that the similarity in I.Q. of twins reared together should be only a matter of shared environment. For example, the r of MZ twins is about 0·9, which is virtually the test-retest reliability of the test. Thus, the differences in the homes of MZ twins must explain virtually all I.Q. variation— i.e. an investigation of how pairs of MZ twins differ in treatment would reveal all the determinants of I.Q. It is curious how such critical differences have so far remained undetected. Finally, as Fulker fantasizes, it would follow that "if we could pass off a child as an MZ Co-twin, perhaps with a few falsehoods and some alteration to his appearance, we could determine his I.Q. to about 5 points". Fulker (1975) has powerfully made his point. Kamin's arguments cannot stand scrutiny and these twin studies of MZ twins reared apart still stand as powerful evidence for the importance of genetic components in the determination of intelligence in U.S.A. and Great Britain.

Before going on to examine further arguments relevant to the heritability of intelligence, one final point needs to be made about Kamin's book. Just as he demonstrated that Burt's papers contained inaccuracies and inconsistencies, so also he has shown that certain well-known papers which discuss these twin researches report findings and results with irritating errors which may not be sufficient to infirm the conclusions, but which nevertheless rob these papers of much of their power. This is particularly unfortunate in the case of Jensen's (1970) paper which reanalyses the twin studies and draws some highly interesting conclusions. Nevertheless, these errors together with the fact that Burt's data were used make the results less than definitive.

The position reached so far is: Kamin's thesis that no evidence exists for the heriditary determination of intelligence is clearly not supported in his book. Three of the four studies which show that monozygotic twins reared apart have highly similar I.Q. scores still stand as sound evidence for the genetic determination of intelligence.

Nevertheless, problems still remain. First, (although Kamin (1974) makes no mention of this) one has to decide whether, in fact, MZ twins are genetically identical. If this is not necessarily the case, then the force of the four published studies is less than might be thought. Again twin studies are relatively crude methods of determining the genetic determination of a trait. Cattell (1971) and his colleagues have developed a method, MAVA (multiple analysis of variance), which allows a more sophisticated analysis. Even more informative are the biometric genetic methods stemming ultimately from Fisher's work in Cambridge, methods which, as developed by Mather (1949) and elaborated by Jinks and Fulker (1970) and Mather and Jinks (1971), allow the fit of different models to the data to be estimated. These methods are so powerful that given reasonable data, all the objections to results with simple basic investigations (in terms of interactions of genetics and environment and the effects of dominance and assortative mating for example) can be answered.

As has been argued, the force of those MZ twin studies with one twin reared apart is strongly in favour of a high genetic determination of I.Q. scores. However, this assumes, among other things, that twins are in fact genetically identical. However, this is not necessarily so. Eysenck (1973) succinctly summarizes some of the difficulties which have been discussed by Darlington (1970). For MZ twins there are sources of discordance which are neither environmental nor genetic in the ordinary senses of those terms. These special factors can be classified. (a) There are nuclear differences which arise by gene mutation or chromosome loss or gain in one of the two products of splitting; (b) there can be cytoplasmic differences which arise though the action of deleterious genes in an assymetrical cytoplasm; (c) there may be embryological differences which are caused by errors due to late splitting and (d) there can be nutritional differences which came about through unequal placentation.

Since these discordances can arise in MZ twins it follows that it is a faulty assumption that the discordances of such twins must be attributable to environmental differences. It therefore follows that estimates of heritability based upon MZ twins must be underestimates. This must be borne in mind for further research.

Problems with Twin Studies

Apart from the fact that MZ twin studies provide an underestimation of heritability, there are numerous other problems which make it preferable to use some other method. Apart from the plain fact that the number of MZ twins reared apart is small, there are the factors of selective placement and the obvious difficulty of generalizing from twins to singletons. However, there is a more fundamental problem, namely that the twin method assumes that the genetic and environmental influences are uncorrelated and that they combine in a simple additive way without interaction. Since this is clearly not the case (e.g. bright children tend to go to stimulating environments such as universities rather than production lines), and the evidence in relation to this will be discussed, it is clear that more sophisticated statistical methods are necessary.

The MAVA (Multiple Analysis of Variance) Method

Cattell (1960) and his colleagues have developed over the years the MAVA method for teasing out the effects of heridity and environment on psychological traits, and this is capable of taking into account the fact that both influences may be correlated and that there are, as has been seen, likely to be interaction effects. This method is highly complicated. The emphasis will be to describe the essentials without the results. This is because there is a yet more elegant set of procedures (which are in many respects similar) which give an even more definitive answer to our question. Essentially, the MAVA deals with four sources of variance:

(1) σwg^2 This is the variability among siblings due to *within* family genetic variance.

(2) σwt^2 This is the variance *within* the family due to environmental influences.

(3) σbg^2 This is the variance *between* families due to genetic influences.

(4) σbt^2 This is the variance *between* families due to environmental differences.

In addition covariance and interaction terms can be added. However, if one ignores these complicating factors for ease of explanation one can see that σo^2, i.e. the observed variance on a trait:

$$= \sigma^2 wg + \sigma^2 wt + \sigma^2 bg + \sigma^2 bt. \qquad (1)$$

These unknowns can be obtained thus. The observed variance among family means:

$$\sigma^2 FO = \sigma bg^2 + \sigma^2 bt$$

and it is calculated from the mean of siblings in each family, being the variance between the means. So one can subtract this now from the basic equation (1):

$$\sigma o^2 - \sigma^2 FO = \sigma wg^2 + \sigma wt^2. \qquad (2)$$

One next takes pairs of identical twins and measures their differences from the family mean which leads to within family variance for identical twins raised together $\sigma^2 ITT$. Since (Darlington, 1970) these are genetically identical, there is no genetic variance but only within family environmental variance. Thus:

$$\sigma^2 ITT = \sigma wt^2.$$

Subtracting this from equation (2) one has one of the unknowns:

$$\sigma^2 wg = \sigma^2 o - S^2 BFO - \sigma^2 ITTO.$$

Similarly $\sigma^2 SAO$ (the observed variance of siblings raised apart):

$$= \sigma wg^2 + \sigma wt^2 + \sigma bt^2.$$

This σbt^2 comes in because siblings raised apart yield the environmental difference of two distinct families. Subtracting this from equation (1) one can solve for σbg^2. Similarly by comparing all obtainable kinds of hereditary and environmental mixtures, other unknowns can be determined. Indeed, as Cattell (1971) points out these equations not only enable the four major unknown variances to be solved, but also the correlations and interactions of environmental and hereditary influences. These solutions are however more complex. Cattell (1950) has a detailed description of this algebra.

Cattell (1971) reports on two tentative research findings where this method was applied to crystallized and fluid ability measures. A somewhat simplified form of MAVA which forced certain assumptions to be made concerning the correlation of genetic and environmental effects, has probably inflated the within family variance. Nevertheless, in one study based on 647 subjects fluid intelligence had a genetic variance component of 77% of which 46% was attributable to within family genetic differences. For crystallized ability the genetic component was 73%, of which 66% was due to the within family genetic component. Even though these results are rough, what is striking is that they are in good agreement with the figures obtained by the twin study procedures—including those of Burt (Burt and Howard, 1956) which, Kamin has hinted, were heavily biased by Burt's prejudices, and are little different from those deriving from the MZ twin studies which cannot be impugned. However brilliant the MAVA method is, it is not in fact the most powerful analytic method available.

Biometric Genetic Methods

As Jinks and Fulker (1970) point out in their lucid discussion of these methods, they are ultimately derived from the work of Fisher (1918). Unlike twin studies and the MAVA, a brilliant one-man attempt to develop a statistics of genetic biometrics which were both principally developed for the study of human genetics, biometric methods have been mainly with animals. Jinks and Fulker (1970) however, demonstrate most clearly how they may be effectively used in human studies.

Biometric genetic methods, according to Jinks and Fulker, include both MAVA and twin studies as special cases but go beyond them in assessing the kinds of gene action and mating system in the population.

A considerable and important difference between the MAVA and the biometric genetic methods which both break down the total variance into between and within family variances lies in their methods of handling the interaction of genetic and environmental influences, the great weakness of the simple twin study approach where the variance is obtained from correlations. Thus while:

$$\sigma t^2 = \sigma w^2 + \sigma b^2 \text{ it also equals } \sigma G^2 + \sigma E^2 + f(G, E)$$

where σG^2 is the genetic variation, σE^2 is the environmental variation and $f(G, E)$ is some function of the genotypic and environmental contribution. What complicates matters is that this last term may represent two distinct sources of variation. If the genotypical and environmental contributions are correlated both as regards sign and size, $f(f, E) = 2 \text{cov}(G, E)$. However, if environmental deviations depend for their absolute size, regardless of sign, on the particular genotypic deviations paired with them, there is genotype-environment interaction and $f(G, E) = \sigma GE^2$. The effect of $2 \text{cov}(G, E)$ may be to increase or decrease apparent $\sigma G + \sigma E^2$; the effect of σGE^2 will always be to increase it.

Twin studies, as mentioned, have been unable "to specify, detect, estimate or correct for" the effects of this source of variation. MAVA and biometric genetic methods both recognize the effects of $f(G, E)$, specify them in their models, estimate their effects in analysis but do this in quite different ways. In the MAVA approach all possible contributions to $f(G, E)$ are allowed for but the decision to include them in the equation for any particular σ^2 depends on a subjective estimate of the likelihood that they will contribute to it. This is partly because when all possible sources of $f(G, E)$ are included the number of parameters in the models is raised so high that the necessary data are almost impossible to obtain. In the biometric genetic methods, on the other hand, there are invariable rules for deciding on the presence or absence of a particular item in the equation. However, even more important, the method poses the question whether the correlation or interaction terms are essential or redundant by means of scaling tests that specifically detest their presence.

Jinks and Fulker (1970) stress the significance of this ability in biometrical genetics to test the necessity and adequacy of models and regard the fact that MAVA fits complex models to its data as a risky procedure. Indeed they argue that to fit a complex model to inadequate data can lead to unfounded conclusions. Thus, they conclude that the chief value of these biometrical methods is that they can provide insight into gene action and the mating system of the population and test the adequacy of various models for accounting for the data.

Jinks' and Fulker's paper shows how biometrical methods test for the genotype-environment interaction, and for the presence of correlated environments. They also discuss how gene action can be examined. In this section they point out that the broad heritability of the population is not adequately measured by any of the older indices Holzinger's (1929) H, Nichol's (1965) HR, Vandenberg's (1966) F or Cattell's (1971) Nature/Nurture ratio. Furthermore, they show how these factors can be teased out when there is genetic-environment interaction and when there is not and when there is also a correlated environment.

Thus, Jinks and Fulker's (1970) paper is a brilliant expliquée of a statistical method of investigating the heritability of traits which appears to overcome all the difficulties associated with earlier procedures. This alone would be sufficient. However, even more valuable for a book such as this, concerned with the substantive findings from psychometrics, they report the results of applying these procedures to previously published data. These include the work of Shields (1962), Burt (1966), Newman *et al.* (1937) all discussed, as we have seen, by Kamin (1974), the studies of siblings reared together in 689 families of size greater than three (Reed and Reed, 1965), and the investigations of Japanese inbred children by Spuhler (1967).

Before examining these findings one small issue needs to be resolved. In a paper which is stated with great conviction by Feldman and Lewontin (1975), it is claimed that the analysis of variance cannot really separate variation that is the result of environmental fluctuation from variation that is a result of genetic segregation. However, in their attempts to demonstrate this point it is clear that the approach which they are attacking is not the one discussed by Jinks and Fulker (1970), whose work is not cited. Thus one of their arguments is that only broad heritability (H^2b) can be estimated, a parameter of little use in human population genetics. Jinks and Fulker (1970) however, arc able to compute both the broad and the narrow heritability, (see p. 316). Thus, Feldman's and Lewontin's (1975) arguments do not refute the biometric genetic analysis.

When one looks at the findings of the reanalyses of these experiments one finds that broadly the old-fashioned, more primitive methods are upheld. Thus the Shields' (1962) study was found to demonstrate that for the dominoes test and Mill-Hill Vocabulary, Hb was around 70%. There were no effects of correlated environment and only a suggestion in the case of the Mill-Hill that there was a phenotypic-genetic interaction. In the dominoes test a simple genetic model was adequate. Reed and Reed's study yielded no data on the heritability as such, but additive and dominant gene action was detected (dominance level 0·74). The Japanese WISC investigation showed dominance for high I.Q. and a clear polygeneity (about 100).

These reanalyses are a powerful demonstration of how psychometric tests given adequate statistical analysis can make substantive findings in the field of psychogenetics. It is a considerable contribution to have shown that (a) simple genetic models which ignore correlated environments and environmental genetic interaction are adequate to account for the data; (b) that around 70% of I.Q. is genetically determined, and (c) that there was polygenic dominance.

An interesting confirmation of these findings was made by Jensen (1972) who reanalysed data from Tenman's (1926) study of gifted children. Terman and his colleagues had obtained data from 1000 gifted adults and their children. Jensen utilized a formula from Crow (1970) to predict the mean I.Q. of the children of these gifted subjects. This formula is based on a model which is similar to that of Jinks and Fulker (1970). This formula which requires the population mean (100), the parental mean, 152 (Terman, 1926) and the HN 0·71, (Jinks and Fulker, 1971), predicted the children's mean as 127 while the observed value was 132·7. Jensen accounts for the five point discrepancy by assuming that there was an advantageous environment provided by these parents and using family income as an index of environmental advantage, the prediction can be improved to within 0·5 of the observed value. However, I am far from convinced by this latter part of the study since it seems generally agreed that environmental assessment is peculiarly difficult.

Actually as Eysenck (1973) points out, it is probably better to use Crow's (1970) equation to work out HN^2 putting in observed values for P, M and O (offspring intelligence). When this is done, one obtains a figure of 0·849. This is high, higher than anything suggested in the paper by Jinks and Fulker. However, as Eysenck points out, the same argument concerning the superior environment of this group, reduces the HN^2 to 0·71. Nevertheless, the fact that these models can be used to predict values close to those obtained is yet further support for the validity of these biometric genetic methods.

The conclusion, then from these studies is that Burt, despite his anomalous reporting of results and Cattell, despite the problems with the MAVA method, are in fact in good agreement with biometric genetic analysis and that the heritability of I.Q. in Great Britain and in U.S.A. is high, around 75% which is different from the conclusions of Kamin.

Before leaving the topic of heritability from which the biometric methods seem to have removed most of the speculative arguing points and to have provided firm and irrefutable evidence, a few further studies require brief commment. This is not because the results are in doubt, but that biometrical genetic methods have not always been properly understood by proponents of the environmental position, as seen in the paper by Feldman and Lewontin (1975), who did not even refer to them.

Jenks (1973) for example has reanalysed data on the heritability of I.Q. and claimed that in fact broad heritability is around 45%. His methods tended to demonstrate different degrees of heritability depending upon the relationship of the subjects from which the figures were estimated (which gives one little confidence in his methods of analysis). Furthermore, he postulated there was the possibility of positive correlation between genotypic and environmental variations—a factor which in simple statistical analysis, at any rate, produces inflated heritability indices.

However, Jinks and Eaves (1974) have convincingly pointed to a number of flaws in the methods used by Jenks (1973) which not only invalidates the results but also accounts for the low heritability estimate which he reports. For example, Jenks offers numerical solutions for H^2b some of which are genetically nonsensical: in genetical theory only solutions in which the relationship between parental and offspring genotype are equal to or less than half the heritability for parent-offspring covariation are genetically sensible (Jinks and Eaves, p. 287). If this is taken into account, together with the possibility of dominance and the amount of associative mating, the estimates rise, lying between 0·59 and 0·76 (instead of Jenks' 0·25 and 0·30). Jinks and Eaves also argue that much of the variation in estimates in Jenks' analyses is due to the fact that he fails to deal with dominance, and as shown above, this is clearly a non-additive source of genetic variation in I.Q.

Jinks and Eaves (1974) much as did Jinks and Fulker (1970), then submitted the data in Jenks (1973) to a full biometric genetic analysis. When this is done it is clear that the heritability for the I.Q. data is around 70%. The analysis showed too that there is no evidence for genotype-environment covariation when proper allowance is made for dominance. Indeed, even if such a parameter is added to the model there is no improvement in fit. The analysis, in brief, is in good agreement with the earlier ones, discussed in this section by Jinks and Fulker (1970). Jenks' results are clearly an under-estimate based upon inadequate statistical analysis.

Finally I turn to Eaves' paper (1973) on associative mating and intelligence which subjected data of great interest (Reed and Reed, 1965) to a biometric genetic analysis. The data consisted of the I.Q. scores of 3558 individuals with pedigrees known for at least five generations—in fact, the subjects are from 53 pairs of great, great grandparents. The I.Q. scores were those obtained at an age of 14 years old. In the pedigrees there was at least one instance of mental retardation, but the mean I.Q. of the sample was not subnormal.

These data which are clearly extensive yielded an estimate of narrow heritability of 0·60 for I.Q. and clear evidence of associative mating. This was not based upon marital correlation for I.Q. (this figure was used to check the evidence). In fact, using the heritability of 0·6 and A (associative mating) index of 0·27, the predicted μ (marital) correlation was 0·45. This is strikingly similar to the corrected observed correlation of 0·46. This again supports both the high figure for narrow heritability and the power of biometric genetic methods—that observed correlations can be predicted. Although dominance was not detected here, Eaves (1973) demonstrates that the experimental data were such that it was almost impossible to detect it in this investigation.

CONCLUSIONS

Taken together there seems little doubt that these biometric genetic studies yield clear conclusions that are not open to the objections which earlier less sophisticated studies were unable to refute:

(1) There is almost beyond question, a large genetical component in the development of intelligence. Certainly around 70% of the variance would be thus accounted for, in Great Britain and the U.S.A.

(2) Simple genetic models are adequate to fit the data: correlated environments and genetic environment interactions are not important.

(3) There is polygenic dominance for I.Q.

(4) Assortative mating is a factor that must not be ignored.

These clear results are striking evidence that psychometric data when subjected to proper statistical analysis can yield substantive psychological knowledge. Ideally I should like to see these biometric genetic analyses applied to all the factored variables that are discussed in later chapters.

THE NATURE OF INTELLIGENCE

The extensive examination of the factorial analysis of abilities enables me to state with far more precision than was possible at the beginning of the chapter, what intelligence, as generally conceived, turns out to be. The brief definition effectively summarizes much of the discussion. Intelligence is best regarded as a combination of two factors, fluid ability, our basic general reasoning ability which is employed in almost all problem-solving, and crystallized ability which constitutes the particular cognitive skills most important in the culture in which one happens to live. In the West there is considerable genetic component involved in the determination of fluid ability (around 75%), the heritability being polygenic and showing effects of dominance. A relatively simple genetic model accounts for findings in this area. Although it is clear that different national groups have characteristically different scores on tests of fluid ability, this may be attributable to the problems of adequately providing tests for such groups. Furthermore, the national confusion of race and culture makes the elucidation of the nature/nurture problem in the genetic determination of social differences in I.Q. scores difficult, a problem compounded by the fact that there can be no possible jump from the within race genetic variance to the between race genetic variance, tempting though this argument may be. The structure of abilities in the West as it has emerged from factor analysis confirms the importance of intelligence as a factor (strictly factors) in abilities but also makes clear that there are other important abilities, both at the primary and secondary factor level as demonstrated in Tables 4.1, 4.2 and 4.3. Finally, the pervasive nature and psychological importance of gf and gc was made clear by reference to work by Terman and Ghiselli who show that these g factors are highly predictive of educational and occupational success—see Chapter 9.

Aptitudes

A question that obviously springs to mind in the field of abilities concerns the meaning and nature of aptitudes. Certainly in the usage of normal English, individuals are described as having mechanical or clerical aptitude or in slightly different terminology, artistic or musical ability. Again one might consider two individuals to be equally intelligent, but clearly different in terms of aptitudes: a lawyer would probably be high on verbal ability, an engineer on numerical and spatial ability. These terms, however, aptitude, ability, are vague, and verbally defined and without precision or consistency. One must discuss the meaning and nature of aptitudes and abilities, having regard to the lists of primary and higher-order factors and the structures and models that attempt to order them.

    The first point to note is that aptitudes are not necessarily factorially pure. Aptitudes cannot exist *in vacuo*; our aptitudes are for some activity or other. Now this gives the clue to the nature of aptitudes. For any activities are culturally-bound (other than those few such as eating perhaps, which are biological in origin), especially those requiring skills. Hence aptitudes tend to refer to those constellations of skills which happen to be useful in a culture. The skills themselves may be psychologically disparate and independent, but it is to be noted that it is unlikely that the skills be negatively correlated. If they were by definition few would possess them. On the other hand, if the skill happens to demand only one ability factor for its successful execution, then it could be the case that the aptitude will be factorially pure. Possibly a skill such as interpreting might largely load on verbal ability. Thus aptitudes are in the main, constellations of skills that happen to be useful in a particular society. They are unlikely to be fundamental dimensions of human ability since they vary widely from culture to culture. In one sense aptitudes are equivalent to crystallized intelligence. For as gc reflects the crystallization of fluid ability in the particular set of cognitive reasoning skills used in a culture, so aptitudes reflect the particular set of abilities (not only gf) useful in the culture.

Thus clerical aptitude and computer programming aptitude are clearly culture bound. There can be no factor reflecting these constellations of abilities. In fact, therefore, aptitude tests are constructed empirically. Items tapping ability are administered to subjects and those discriminating the good programmer from the bad can be utilized in a programming aptitude test. If the criterion scores are reliable and valid, and if the sampling of subjects has been satisfactory, then an efficient test can be constructed. However, this analysis makes it clear that aptitudes in this sense, and aptitude tests are of little psychological interest.

Actually the construction of empirically-keyed aptitude tests, however efficient, for vocational selection or guidance is to be deplored. Test scores, thus factorially complex, tell us little about the abilities involved and give one no information that is psychologically insightful. If, however, one were to develop aptitude tests by regressing the major ability factors against the criterion of success, some aptitudes, thus defined, by regression weights on the major factors, could be psychologically meaningful. No such attempts have been made, however, to achieve this. However, this topic is discussed in Chapter 9.

Generally, therefore, aptitudes are to be conceived (to restrict this discussion to the ability sphere) as disparate constellations of ability that happen to be useful in a particular culture. Before leaving the topic of aptitudes for that of special abilities, one further point needs to be mentioned. This relates to the value of aptitude tests in the practical situation rather of guidance of selection. One of the best known aptitude tests, the DAT (Bennet *et al.*, 1971) described in Chapter 3 is simply not differential. As Quereshi (1972) points out, follow-up studies of 1700 subjects showed that occupational membership was best discriminated simply by the overall score on the DAT, not the separate sub-scales. Similarly in the test manual (Bennet *et al.*, 1972) one finds that the highest score on all tests is made by engineers. Engineers score at the 74th percentile on clerical aptitude, clerks at the 65th percentile, so that on this test one would not have advised clerks to be clerks. This is due, of course, to the pervasive nature and psychological significance of the g factors, as argued in the section on intelligence. The engineers were simply more intelligent than the clerks. Even if one takes account of the importance of "g" and does not use the absolute level of score, but the relative level of each scale, one finds the same difficulty, since clerical aptitude was not the clerk's best score.

From the discussion of the structure of abilities, one should expect gc, gf and V to account for most of the variance in a paper and pencil test such as the DAT. In fact, this is almost certainly the case since the manual indicates high correlations with the OTIS SAIQ test (loading on a combination of gf and gc) of all the DAT scales. Furthermore Quereshi (1972) reports an orthogonal varimax analysis of the DAT in which four factors effectively accounted for all the variance and an orthogonal analysis is unlikely to have obtained simple structure. In summary, therefore, the notion of aptitudes is not psychologically powerful: aptitudes represent syndromes of socially valuable traits. Atheoretical, criterion-keyed aptitude tests may select efficiently for a job but are highly dependent on the criterion and ideally new tests are needed for individual employers since no two jobs are identical. This is the difficulty with tests that have no psychological meaning. However, attempts to provide differential measures are usually defeated by the fact of correlation of such primary factors due to the pervasive influence of the g factors, as one would expect from the work on the structure of abilities. If one wants to discriminate jobs in terms of abilities, it is probably best to do so by developing regression weights for the most important ability factors. One must conclude, therefore, that the term aptitude both conceptually and practically is of little value. One obtains greater insight into the demands on cognitive skills of various tasks if they are defined in terms of primary abilities.

However, in the opening discussion of aptitudes mention was made to what is perhaps a separate category of abilities—sometimes referred to as aptitudes—musical and artistic ability. Since music and art are clearly not culture bound (perhaps indeed these two abilities are alone universal among different racial groups) they are not aptitudes as defined above. Perhaps they are best regarded as special abilities. However, they are clearly independent of intelligence. Many highly intelligent subjects find themselves unable to play music well (if at all) although they would much like to and the same applies to art. I shall now examine the evidence relating to these special abilities.

Music Ability

I shall begin with music ability partly because of all these special abilities music has attracted the most attention and research. This is probably because, as seen from Chapter 3, it is relatively easy to construct tests of musical ability because the skills involved are plain—keeping time, analysing chords, recognizing pitch and so on. It is all too obvious when subjects cannot do the test.

Shuter (1968) has summarized the main findings resulting from the application of psychometric tests of music ability and some reasonably clear results emerge, which can be regarded as substantive contributions to psychological knowledge.

(1) Music ability develops early in a large number of cases. Actually, this could be stated without reference to psychological testing. Grove's (1954) dictionary of music is ample witness. The child prodigy in music from Mozart onwards is well known. This is not the case in the other arts and sciences. However, amazing early gifts do not always flower into adult greatness as the studies of Areola by Richet (1900) and of Nyiregyhazy by Revesz (1925) demonstrate, the latter ending up as an orchestral musician.

(2) Similarly the earlier the training, the easier again learning seems to be. Again this arises from studies of musicians rather than from studies of

psychometric tests of music. Furthermore, Shuter (1968) argues that musical ability *per se* is not so important in becoming a virtuoso performer. Rather it is motivation (as measured by hours of practice) that counts. Her evidence from this, however, is anecdotal relying on the writings of Cortot (1935) who trained a large number of highly talented musicians.

These well-substantiated findings have emerged not from the study of musical tests, but the study of musicians. However, they relate to psychometric measurement of musical ability because it is clear that music ability tests do tap musical abilities, i.e. they are valid. For example, all members of the National Youth Orchestra scored grade A on the Wing test.

(3) Music ability is regarded by Shuter (1968) from her survey of the studies of musical tests as consisting of tonal sense (pitch discrimination), rhythm, and the ability to develop an inner ear for music. Studies indicate that among adults, musical ability is independent of intelligence, although it is related among children below the age of 12—because at this age music ability depends in part on understanding instructions, learning musical notation and similar non-musical problems. Thus, what tests there are indicate that musical ability is indeed a special ability independent of others. This is the one substantive finding that can be generally attributed to psychometrics.

I have not discussed in any detail the studies summarized by Shuter (1968) into the structure of musical ability because almost all of them are, by the standards of factor-analytic design (discussed in Chapter 2 and in Cattell and Kline (1977)), defective to such an extent that the results cannot really be trusted. Although many of these studies were completed before computing facilities were sufficient to enable adequate rotations to be carried out so that this is not a condemnation of the research, they are technically inadequate as regards rotation. No studies quoted by Shuter used any form of objective oblique rotation either topological or analytic so that it is unlikely that simple structure was obtained. One research, Holmstrom (1963), did make use of orthogonal Varimax analysis. However, *a priori* orthogonal rotation in the case of musical abilities would not appear sensible. Evidence for this failure to reach simple structure resides in the fact that these analyses did not give replicable results in different samples, although there may have been population differences.

What is really needed is a factor-analytic study with all possible measures of music ability, together with all the ability factors discussed earlier in this chapter. In addition since, as seen, Cortot has argued that personality and motivational factors become at the highest level more important than simple musical gifts, these temperamental and dynamic factors (as discussed in Chapters 5 and 6) should also be included. This would then demonstrate unequivocally the extent to which musical attainment depended on musical abilities or personality. The structure of musical ability would also be revealed as would its relation to other variables. Such an investigation would need to be carried out on subjects who were musicians as well as a normal sample.

One further point needs to be mentioned concerning the musical tests. Most of these were constructed through relatively primitive factorial analysis. As a result it is not clear whether the scales are factor pure. That they work at all derives from the musical and psychological insight of the test constructors not the statistical efficiency with which the tests were constructed. Shuter (1968) argues that statistical sophistication is unnecessary in the interpretation of factors. However, as shown in Chapter 2, this is not so. Shuter herself, for example, tries to make psychological inferences from the fact that the first unrotated factor was always general. Yet this is a statistical artefact of principal components and to a less extent of the centroid method which approximates it (Harman, 1964). Thus such an inference is unjustified and is due to lack of statistical acumen.

Indeed, in future studies of music ability it might be wise not to rely too greatly on the published musical tests (although these should be included because they have some validity and their factorial structure should be known). In addition measures would be required of all the basic musical skills.

So far psychometrics has not made the substantive contribution to the psychology of musical ability that is well within its grasp. As Shuter's survey demonstrates, there is now a considerable body of research but much of it is on too small a scale and inadequate technically.

Artistic Ability

In the case of artistic ability psychometrics has so far made no contribution of any value. The Meier Art Tests (1963) are the main instruments used in research, but these are measures which fall short on all psychometric criteria (Siegel, 1972).

However, research into artistic ability appears, relative to musical research, extremely difficult to carry out. This is because the performance itself cannot be broken down into constituent parts in a meaningful way. Furthermore, in musical ability one concentrates on performance which has no equivalent in art. The great artist creates his work and is thus analogous to the composer. Since many composers have most of the musical abilities possessed by performers (indeed most are good performers, if not virtuosi), the study of performance is not irrelevant to the study of composition. Composers could be compared with performers if these musical abilities had been properly defined. None of this obtains in the case of artistic activity however.

Furthermore, unlike music there are few fixed criteria in art. There is no real equivalent of harmony, counterpoint or fugue for example, all of which are reliable components of musical composition, and certainly no equivalents in art to accuracy of performance, in pitch, tempo rhythm, ornamentation or phrasing, most of which can be reliably judged by musicians.

In brief, I have no confidence that psychometrics is likely in the near future to be successful in elucidating the nature of artistic abilities. The only approach that would appear even vaguely hopeful is to compare artists with controls on all the personality, motivational and dynamic factors discussed in this book. In this way it may be possible to isolate the essence of artistic achievement. Such a differential approach would not be likely to be successful were it not the case, as has been argued, that factor-analytic variables represent fundamental dimensions of individual differences.

Motor Abilities

In Chapter 3 the ability factors found by Fleishmann (1966) were listed. What these factors represent is not clear since their criterion relations have not been clearly worked out. They may be as Cronbach (1970) suggests, little more than specific factors since there is no evidence, as yet, that they predict occupational performance. Certainly, at present this factor list cannot be regarded as a definitive picture of motor abilities. What is here required, however, is what was done early on in the sphere of cognitive abilities, by Thurstone (1938). One needs a large scale series of factorizations of motor skills, where simple structure is reached and the whole motor ability sphere is included. If this were done one would be able to present at best a list of the major primary factors. These could then be studied experimentally and knowledge could be built up.

SUMMARY

(1) The primary ability factors were set out. The large number of these required some kind of structure.

(2) Second-order and third-order factors were set out. Some writers have preferred to construct models of abilities based, purportedly, on the factorial findings.

(3) Guilford's model, Cattell's model and Hunt's and Carroll's models were evaluated and compared. It was found that Hunt's approach rooted in cognitive psychology did not reveal anything not found in factor analysis. A combination of the cognitive and factor-analytic approaches was suggested.

(4) The nature of intelligence was discussed in the light of the psychometric findings: the natures of crystallized and fluid ability were explored.

(5) The place of creativity was examined and its status found to be weak.

(6) The heritability of intelligence was discussed in the light of the biometric genetical analyses. Kamin's findings were shown to be false and, without Burt's data, the heritability of I.Q. in the West was shown to be high, around 75%; polygenic dominance and assortative mating was also demonstrated.

(7) Finally, aptitudes and special abilities were briefly discussed in the light of the factored results.

5

Human Temperament

In this chapter I set out reliable data which has been compiled from the application of psychological tests and the statistical analysis of the resulting data (individual differences) in the field of human temperament.

DEFINITION OF TEMPERAMENT

Temperament is defined by psychometrists in terms of traits. Temperamental traits are picked out to explain how we behave and to show the way we do the things we do. An obvious homely example can be seen in lawn-mowing. Some lawns are meticulously striped, weedless and perfect. Others are cut regularly but by rotary mowers which leave no lines and scatter mowings on the lawn. Others are left to grow wild as hay. In terms of traits the striped lawns might be held to reflect their owners' meticulousness, or obsessionality. Those not cut at all reflect carelessness or indifference, or untidiness. In this way temperamental traits can, in principle, be used to understand behaviour.

To complete the definition of temperament it is necessary to distinguish temperamental traits from dynamic traits and moods. Dynamic traits account for why we behave as we do. The dynamic traits that account for mowing or not mowing the lawn might be: self-assertion (my lawn is better than yours), and self-sentiment (every decent chap has a good lawn). From this example one can see how, again in principle, it must be stressed, that the knowledge of a subject's self-assertion and obsessionality might enable one to predict that the subject would mow the lawn in stripes. Of course I am not arguing that these are the only determinants of lawn-mowing. Obviously there is a bourgeois cultural influence that makes good lawns a point of self-assertion. However, given that these cultural factors are known and are common to large numbers of subjects, and hence could not account for differences in behaviour, our temperamental and dynamic traits come into play. This analysis takes no account of the ability traits discussed in Chapter 4. If these are added in to the predictive equations, yet more accurate results would be expected.

Finally, moods or states must be distinguished from both temperament and dynamics. Perhaps the most significant example of this is anxiety. Anxiety is unquestionably, one of the most important temperamental traits. To continue with the mowing example, the anxious person is worried whether the mower is set too low and ruining the grass or too high and not cutting it short enough. He scours the lawn for stones which may harm the mower and gets in an extra tin of petrol in case more is used than usual. To the non-anxious mower, all this is so much nonsense—straight on with the job and get it over. So much for the anxiety trait. The state of anxiety (e.g. Spielberger, 1972; Curran and Cattell, 1974) is the transient short-lived feeling that arises from some particular event, the impending examination, the dentist's treatment or the interview. Thus moods and states are to be distinguished from temperamental traits usually by their transience. Indeed, after repeated measurements the only distinction between states and traits may lie in the standard deviations.

The Findings from Questionnaires

The findings of the main researchers in the area of temperament have been set out in a series of tables. However, before examining them it is necessary to discuss the methodology that has been largely employed. This section is restricted to questionnaires because the rationale and consequent methodology are different from those where projective and objective tests are used although these results are examined in subsequent sections.

There can be no doubt that the early pioneering workers in the psychometric study of personality using factor analysis (Guilford and Guilford, 1934; Cattell, 1943) did so on account of the powerful results from this approach in the field of abilities, results which have been fully discussed in Chapter 4 (Cattell, 1946).

The rationale of factor analysis to clarify the structure of human temperament is simple and compelling, given a few basic psychological assumptions, the main one of these being that there are in fact, temperamental traits. A further assumption is that such traits are dimensions and are more or less normally distributed. Behaviour can then be seen as a function of these traits (together obviously with other variables). Such a viewpoint is not in any way arbitrary or capricious since literary and clinical approaches to personality which were the only ones before the advent of multivariate statistical techniques apart from common sense intuition, took this view implicitly or explicitly. Macbeth is portrayed, for example, as courageous yet unscrupulous, Falstaff is cowardly and unprincipled. Underlying these characterizations is the trait courageous versus cowardly. In the field of clinical psychology, Freudian theory postulates, *inter alia* (Freud, 1905) traits such as dependence, and orderliness arising from oral and anal fixation, respectively. In the analogous field of motivation MacDougall (1932) proposed a large number of dynamic traits. In an everyday view of personality one describes people in terms of traits. Given, then, the trait approach to temperament, psychometric assessment of traits, followed by factorial analysis of the correlations between traits, would inevitably reveal the structure of human temperament, as the description of factor analysis as a statistical technique in Chapter 2 makes clear. Since there is also, as the richness of descriptive vocabulary demonstrates, a large number of temperamental traits, factor analysis, by revealing the most important of these shows how the underlying source traits or dimensions would be essential in directing the attention of psychologists to what should be studied. If, therefore, trait X is found to account for considerable temperamental variance, as g in the field of abilities, then it follows that research into X, identifying factors influencing its genesis development and atrophy must reveal much about personality. In brief, the trait view of temperament demands psychometric assessment and multivariate analysis.

Recently, however, an attack has been launched on trait psychology, an assault led by Mischel (1973, 1977). His approach which can be described as situationalism, claims that traits such as dependence or sociability are determined by situations. In situation X subject A will be dependent, in situation Y he may not be. The factorial findings from questionnaires, according to this argument, show consistent results because they are consistent in regard to situation: where the subject is filling in questionnaires.

The obvious counter-argument that in fact people are seen to be consistent in everyday life, e.g. it makes sense to call Churchill brave and Bertrand Russell mercurial, is met by situationalists who claim that observations of such consistency are tainted by trait notions. One expects individuals to exhibit the traits one has previously observed which thus tends to confirm one's own observations. Furthermore Mischel argues that the concept of trait is itself otiose. One infers the traits from observed behaviours. It is, therefore, better, and this is the old behaviourist argument (e.g. Skinner, 1953) to study the determinants of the behaviour in the situation.

In my view this situationalist argument is refuted by the facts. This is not to say that there is perfect consistency between situations in subjects' behaviour or that the correlations between temperamental factors derived from psychometric tests and external criteria are as high as is desirable. Nevertheless as the results demonstrate, in this and following chapters, effective predictions can be made from trait scores to other behaviour which would be impossible if the situational argument were true. Thus the refutation of the case can only be made in the light of the results set out in this chapter and in the applied fields of educational, clinical and occupational psychology. The final refutation of this case is made in Chapter 11 when the full implications and conclusions to be drawn from psychometric testing are discussed.

The other point which is relevant to situationalism is the analogue of the argument against traits. If this case is correct, in any given situation one should expect identical behaviour. Not all the football crowd shouts abuse, not every driver obeys the traffic rules. To account for this individual differences have to be invoked. I would argue that the situation is important but that it interacts with individuals' traits of temperament, ability and motivation and that these must be known before predictions can be made.

This section presents the temperamental factors in the work of the leaders in the field—Cattell, Eysenck, Guilford and Comrey (although Cattell (1973) considers that Comrey's work is of dubious quality). In selecting their work, I have borne in mind the criteria for carrying out adequate factor analyses and the usual psychological experimental evaluatory principles of adequate sampling and replicated findings. One other important criterion has been used. As I pointed out in Chapter 2 on factor analysis, the identification of a factor is properly made *not* simply, in the case of personality inventories, fom the content of the items loading on the factor, rather some external referrents are needed. For example, an anxiety factor should discriminate anxiety neurotics from controls. Cattell and Eysenck are outstanding with regard to the vast amount of psychological data gathered which is relevant to their factors. The factors found by these researchers represent, from the rationale and nature of factor analysis, the major dimensions of personality. Actually these factors are the variables measured by the factor-analytic personality tests discussed in Chapter 3.

Recent work by Howarth and his colleagues at the University of Alberta (Howarth, in press and Browne and Howarth, 1977), has attempted to answer the questions posed in this chapter.

Browne and Howarth (1977) have carried out an extensive factor analysis of personality questionnaire items. Factor-analytic scales were searched and 1726 non-repeated items were selected. However, it must be noted that there were some significant omissions. The seven extra Cattell factors, the abnormal Cattell factors and the Grygier DPI scales for example, were not included. This item pool was reduced by postulating 20 hypothetical factors and selecting 20 items relevant to each. Items were then rewritten, to achieve scales balanced for "Yes" and "No" responses and to make the inventory linguistically homogeneous. These 400 items were administered to a large sample of whom 488 female and 515 male students satisfactorily completed the scales. The inter-item phi correlations (including sex) were subjected to both orthogonal and oblique solutions. The one preferred by Browne and Howarth was the orthogonal Orthomax (Hakstian, 1970). Twenty factors were rotated, less than the number of factors with eigenvalues greater than one, a criterion which Browne and Howarth regard as inapplicable in large matrices.

The factors emerging fell into five categories of robustness defined in terms of consistent patterns across the various solutions, Orthomax, Varimax and two oblique solutions using the Harris Kaiser method.

(1) Eleven factors were consistent across solutions and accounted for about 60% of the variance: social shyness, sociability, mood swings, emotionality, impulsiveness, persistence, hypochondriasis, dominance II, general activity, trust and super ego.

(2) Two factors, consistent other than in Varimax: social conversation and inferiority.

(3) Three factors which did not appear in all solutions: dominance I, cooperativeness and social responsibility.

(4) Three factors which could be given only tentative labels: frivolity, relaxed composure and optimal arousal.

(5) One factor which could well have been an attitudinal rather than a personality measure—sex and superego.

Although Browne and Howarth prefer the orthogonal solution, they attempted to locate higher-order factors from the oblique rotation. However, neither anxiety or extraversion clearly emerged and since the mean primary factor correlation was low (0·169), the higher-order factors were not thought to be worth pursuing.

From this description of this large-scale investigation, it is clear that Browne and Howarth have done empirically what psychometrists have attempted to do from an examination of previous results, i.e. by inference. However, I have refrained from utilizing their findings in Table 5.1 on account of a number of problems in the investigation which are briefly examined. These difficulties mean that the emerging factors must be validated against external criteria before they could be regarded as substantive findings. All the points mentioned have been examined in Chapter 2 on factor analysis.

(a) Not all factors were included in the study. Thus it could be the case that the results are far from complete.

(b) The rewriting of the items may have changed their psychological meaning. The phrasing of items in personality tests crucially affects (and in ways not fully understood) the variance (Guilford, 1959).

(c) As has already been discussed the use of phi coefficients can produce factors of item difficulty. Furthermore, the correlations are affected by the polarity of the items (Holley, 1973) and the proportion of subjects putting the keyed items. Item parcels (Cattell, 1973) may be more reliable as a basis for correlations.

(d) The original factor hypotheses which guided the item selection may have been faulty.

(e) In any case item selection in this way is little more than choosing items from their content. As I have argued, the face validity of items is not a good guide to their validity.

(f) The extraction of the factors for rotation was subjective. As I have argued, the number of factors rotated can affect the solution.

(g) Orthomax is an orthogonal solution. It is highly unlikely *a priori* that orthogonal factors are the best description of the personality sphere.

(h) The fact that both the oblique and orthogonal solutions were similar (in 11 cases they were considered to be the same) suggest that simple structure was not obtained.

(i) In fact no test of simple structure was made. A Maxplane topological rotation would have been highly interesting for comparative purposes. These nine technical problems all mean that no reliance can be placed upon the factors, without further evidence of their validity. However, in this paper Browne and Howarth use only item content to identify them. This is little more than face validity.

(j) This brings us to the severest objection to the results: the lack of external correlates for the factors. This makes them far less psychologically meaningful than those of Cattell and Eysenck, about which so much is known. Thus more research is necessary to identify these factors before they can be regarded as substantive findings.

That this objection to the method of factor identification is no idle point is attested by some of the factor descriptions given in the paper. For example, social conversation is admitted to be what Eysenck and Eysenck (1969) refer to as a tautological factor, that is, a bloated specific comprised of items all reflecting talkativeness. Such a factor can hardly be regarded as a substantive psychological finding. Since, in factor analyses, there is always the danger that such bloated specifics arise it is essential, as I have argued, that factors be shown to relate to external criteria. That is why these 20 factors have not been inserted into the table, which includes those factors whose psychological meaning has been, to some extent, explicated.

All this does not mean that this research by Browne and Howarth is not important. It represents an essential first step in synthesizing a huge variety of disparate results. It is unfortunate that there are so many technical problems involved. In fact, Howarth (in press) has further developed his studies of personality test items into three inventories, the HPQ (Howarth Personality Questionnaire), the Individuality Inventory and the APF. The HPQ seeks to measure what Howarth refers to as Mainstream Factor scales, essentially those emerging in the paper discussed above. The others measure adjunct factors, i.e. those not in the Harman and French list of personality factors (1973).

The factors in the HPQ are: sociability, anxiety, dominance, conscience, medical hypochondria, impulsiveness, cooperativeness, inferiority, persistence and suspicion. All are acceptably reliable. Factors in the Individuality Inventory are: future orientation, phlegmatic temperament, involvement with others, felt tension (state anxiety), self-regard, independence, psychoticism, fate control and dislikes-annoyances. APF factors are: fear of social unacceptability, hope, general activity, self-pride, existential realization, individual tolerance, "unusuality", self-actualizing, time anxiety and rigidity.

However, there is no evidence of validity for these factors, Howarth (in press). The location in factor space of the APF and individuality factors is not stated. No external validating correlations are given. Before these factors could be accepted, much further research is necessary. Consequently, important as this research could be, at present the results cannot be regarded as substantive.

DISCUSSION OF TABLE 5.1

If the previous discussion of factor analysis has been even approximately correct, then I should be able to state, with regard to Table 5.1, that the psychometric study of personality has revealed that there are 100 important dimensions of temperament. It is always claimed by the advocates of factor analysis that it is a simplifying procedure: 100 factors do not suggest that it has been highly successful. Secondly, each of these researchers claims (with the exception of Grygier, 1961), that his own set of factors is the best resolution of the problem of how many dimensions are needed to describe temperament.

Guilford (1975) argues strongly that the orthogonal rotations which he favours give the most simple description. Cattell (1973), Cattell and Kline, (1977) has argued consistently over the years (from 1946 onwards) that his set of factors both embrace the whole sweep of human temperament and represent the multivariate ideal of simple structure, a point equally strongly argued by Eysenck for his set (Eysenck and Eysenck, 1969, Eysenck, 1977). Comrey (1970) in the handbook to his personality inventory also makes it clear that his factors are the best description of temperament so far devised. Indeed, only Grygier and Grygier (1976) do not make this claim. These factors are a synthesis of factor analysis and clinical psychoanalytic theory. They are not entirely independent. The Grygier factors have been included because they are tied in with theory yet rest on a statistical basis. This, as I shall argue throughout this book, seems to be the ideal way to maximize what psychometrics can contribute to psychology. In conclusion, therefore, one cannot say that psychometric studies have demonstrated that there are 100 factors of human temperament.

Similarities of Factors

How are these studies to be integrated? First, an examination of the names and descriptions of the factors reveals obvious similarities. Thus Eysenck's extraversion is obviously similar to Cattell's Exvia, Guilford's T, F and S, Cattell's A, H and Q2, Comrey's E and Grygier's Ai. This is an example to demonstrate that there is some degree of overlap in the descriptions. However, this is not complete. Many of Grygier's scales have no counterparts in any of the other scales. There is no equivalent of Eysenck's P in Cattell's normal factors, and Comrey's empathy factor seems distinct. Thus an examination of the descriptions of the factors reveals some overlap. This, of course, is an empirical question which requires an empirical answer. I have examined those studies which attempt to determine the relationships between these factors in a later section.

The very similarities between the factors raise another important problem. How can it be that in some systems a factor appears at the first-order and in others at the second-order? This is certainly the case with extraversion and anxiety.

Clearly different factor-analytic researches have yielded different factors (despite some similarities). If this is the case how can one put any trust in any of them? Could it not be that as new researches are undertaken, yet more factors will appear? If so, then as a method for establishing findings of scientific worth, factor analysis is valueless.

Results in the Sections of Table 5.1

Cattell and Kline (1977) have devoted considerable attention to accounting for this plethora of factors. It was argued that two separate points of disagreement could be distinguished. There could be differences in the factor structures themselves—three factors or 23—and there could be differences in the *interpretation* of structures about which there was agreement. Indeed the latter can be seen in the case of the second-order factors. Cattell identifies QII as anxiety with no necessary pathological implications. Such differences in interpretation are by definition subjective: judgements have to be made in the light of evidence about the factors, often of a non-factorial kind.

In this discussion of the 100 factors, I shall have to refer to criterion evidence about the factors as I strive to identify them. The first point to examine is the differences in the factor structures. Cattell and Kline (1977) argued that there were three possible explanations for differences of this kind. It is possible that poor execution of the factor-analytic research methods has caused the solutions to be incorrect (in as much as they differ from a "true" solution). In Chapter 2 I mentioned various criteria for a satisfactory study. In many researches failures here could cause deviant results. There is also the possibility that the differences are true differences, that researchers in fact have sampled different populations. A third possibility is that the different investigations are using factor analysis for different purposes so that it is not meaningful to compare the results.

The discussion of poor research methodology will be longer than that of the other possibilities. It is unlikely that the differences in factor structure are real for two reasons. First, all the authors claim that their findings are applicable to the educated middle class European (I thereby include the U.S.A.). Furthermore, examination of the samples on which the studies have been done indicates considerable similarity. Finally, the cross-cultural studies of personality factors that have been conducted (e.g. Kline, 1967b in Ghana, Honess and Kline, 1974b in Uganda, Tsujioka and Cattell, 1965 in Japan) show that there are relatively few structural differences even in these distinctive cultures.

The second explanation that different methods (because of different purposes) create the different results carries more weight. Such differences can be reconciled without difficulty. A good example of this type can be seen in the work of Guilford and Cattell. Cattell prefers an oblique solution on the grounds that in the real world it is unlikely that the major temperamental factors would be independent (Cattell, 1973). Guilford on the other hand, maintains that orthogonality provides a cleaner solution (Guilford, 1975). Regardless of the merits of these two arguments, it is clear that there can never be complete agreement between orthogonal and oblique factors. Thus differences in the two systems are inevitable. However, this cannot account for all the differences between the systems, which introduces the third explanation—poor execution of the methodology.

Inadequate technical execution of factor-analytic studies is certainly a most important cause of differences in results among different investigators. In Chapter 2 the eight practical requirements for adequate factor analyses, as set out by Cattell (1973) were discussed. Vaughan (1974) has shown that more than half the published studies in the field of personality leave out at least two of these conditions and are thus invalidated. This, however, is a rigorous viewpoint.

TABLE 5.1
PERSONALITY FACTORS IN PERSONALITY INVENTORIES

Cattell factors (normal)	Cattell factors (abnormal)	Cattell second-order factors	Comrey factors
A Sizia: Reserved	D1 Hypochondriasis	1 Exvia	T Trust
C Low ego strength:	D2 Zestfulness	2 Anxiety	O Orderliness
Emotional	D3 Brooding discontent	3 Corteria	C Social conformity
D Insecure excitability	D4 Anxious depression	4 Independence	A Activity
E Submissiveness	D5 Euphoria	5 Discreteness	S Stability
F Desurgency: Sober	D6 Guilt and resentment	6 Subjectivity	E Extraversion
G Superego: Conscientious	D7 Bored depression	7 (Intelligence)	M Masculinity
H Threctia: Shy, timid	Pa Paranoia	8 Good upbringing	P Empathy
I Harria: Tough-minded	Pp Psychopathic deviation	9 Humanistic involvement	
J Coasthenia	Sc Schizophrenia	10 Tough stolidity	
K Mature socialization	As Psychasthenia	11 ⎫ not yet clearly	
L Alaxia: Trusting	Ps General psychosis	12 ⎭ identified	
M Praxernia: Practical			
N Naivety			
O Untroubled adequacy			
P Sanguine casualness			
Q1 Conservative			
Q2 Group dependent			
Q3 Low self-sentiment			

Q4 Low ergic tension: Relaxed
Q5 Group dedication and
   inadequacy
Q6 Social panache
Q7 Explicit self-expression

Eysenck factors		Grygier factors		Grygier factors confirmed		Guilford factors	
E	Extraversion	H	Hypocrisy	Pa	Icarus complex	G	General activity
N	Neuroticism	Wp	Passivity	Ph	Fascination by height	R	Restraint
P	Psychoticism	Ws	Seclusion	Pf	Fascination by fire	A	Ascendance
		O	Interest in food	Pi	Icarian exploits	S	Sociability
		Oa	Oral aggression	S	Sexuality	E	Emotional stability
		Od	Oral dependence	Tl	Interest in handcrafts	O	Objectivity
		Om	Independence	Cl	Creative interests	F	Friendliness
		Ou	Verbal aggression	M	Masculine identification	T	Thinking introversion
		Ah	Anal hoarding	Mf	Tendency to seek roles	P	Personal relations
		Ad	Attention to detail	Sa	Interest in social activities	M	Masculine emotions
		Ac	Rigidity	C	Interest in children		
		Aa	Submission to authority	Ep	Persistence		
		As	Emphasis on authority	Ei	Initiative		
		Ai	Reserve, mistrust				
		P	Interest in phallic symbols				
		Pn	Narcissism				
		Pe	Exhibitionism				

A less severe but still scientifically reputable approach to these requirements would allow one to examine research that is valuable but would otherwise be ignored. First it seems that not all the requirements are of equal importance. Violation of the first two, proper choice of variables and subject-sampling, is critical. If these are not well done, the worth of the results must be dubious. Similarly the maximizing of simple structure (for the reasons given in the section on simple structure) is essential. However, the omission of the Bargmann test of simple structure (1953) is not in the same category. What matters is not whether this test has been done but whether simple structure has been reached. A recent example from my own research into the oral personality will clarify this point. Kline and Storey (1978) subjected a large number of personality tests to an oblique Promax (Hendrickson and White, 1964) rotation. I am fully in agreement with Cattell (1966) when he argues that the topological rotations such as Maxplane (Cattell and Muerle, 1960) are superior in obtaining simple structure to analytic programmes such as Promax which suffers from the additional disadvantage that it begins its rotations not from the original principal components but from the orthogonal Varimax (Kaiser, 1958) position. However, I am confident that the Promax rotation did reach simple structure because the factors emerging from the 16 PF and EP1 tests were as expected from the technically superior researches already published. Since in any reputable factor-analytic research there are marker variables included in the data so that factors can be identified, there are often checks (of consistency and psychological meaningfulness) on simple structure. Oblique rotations, other than Maxplane, can reach simple structure, although they may not do so with such regularity. In conclusion, there is no doubt that the eight requirements ensure a sound factor analysis. Nevertheless certain conditions can remain unfulfilled and results can (if not always) be obtained which are perfectly satisfactory. Ultimately, however, the identification of factors rests upon experimental studies and replicability.

With the three sources of variation in mind, inadequate technical execution, different uses of factor analysis with different ends in view and, finally, different interpretation of what is essentially the same structure, we are now in a position to examine Table 5.1. If successful one should be able to emerge with a brief and scientifically potent new Table 5.2.

Reduction of Table 5.1

The amount of research carried out with these different sets of factors is not equally divided among them. The most concentrated research has been on the EP1 and 16 PF tests so these are the best understood factors. Since examination of Table 5.1 suggests that the Eysenck factors and the second-order Cattell factors have considerable overlap (so that the sets are themselves interrelated) I have scrutinized the relationship of the other scales to the Cattell set. Finally the Cattell and Eysenck scales have been related together.

GUILFORD'S FACTORS

Guilford is undoubtedly one of the pioneers in the factor-analytic study of personality. His first researches were carried out in the mid-1930s (Guilford and Guilford, 1934, 1936) and consisted of the factor analysis of face valid items. Technically, by modern standards, these factors which formed the basis of all the later work, have an inadequate base since the item inter-correlations were tetrachoric and the factor analysis of the centroid variety, both unlikely to allow of a simple structure solution. Perhaps even more serious was the fact that the resulting factors were identified only by the content of the items loading on them. In other words they had little more than face validity.

In fact, the list of Guilford's factors gradually grew as new studies were conducted. As Eysenck and Eysenck (1969) argue there is no definitive list and I have followed these two writers by using the factors described by Guilford and Zimmerman (1956) in Table 5.1.

Guilford's main research efforts have been in the field of abilities (e.g. Guilford, 1967, see Chapter 4). This has meant that the nature of Guilford's factors, their psychological meaning as determined by external criteria and experiment, remains largely unknown, despite the publication of a large number of collected studies by Guilford *et al.* (1976). The problem with this catalogue of research findings is that many of them are doctoral dissertations with inadequate samples. In addition, the authors make little attempt at psychological interpretation of the factor scores for different groups. Rather, one has to turn to studies where the relationship of the factors to other sets is investigated.

Guilford (e.g. 1959) is one of the few factor analysts of any repute who still prefers to use orthogonal factors, which he regards *per se* as more parsimonious than perhaps more clear oblique factors. For this reason his personality factors are othogonal which makes straightforward comparison with the oblique set of Cattell factors unsatisfactory.

Two important questions can, therefore, be posed in respect of the Guilford and Cattell factors. To what extent do they overlap if given oblique rotations? Is an orthogonal solution perhaps a more simple solution than the oblique? Cattell and Gibbons (1968) attempted to answer these questions in an investigation with 15 of the Guilford factors (five more than in Table 5.1) and 14 of the Cattell factors, which were administered to 320 undergraduate students. The technical details are set out below so that the investigation can be evaluated against the criteria for proper evaluation of factor-analytic studies.

Owing to the difficulties encountered in the correlation of items, 424 items from the Cattell and Guilford factors were parcelled in 68 personality variables (see p. 21 for the description of and rationale for parcelling) and administered to 302 students. A principal components analysis was subjected to two different rotations after the significant factors had been selected by the Scree Test (Cattell, 1968) With communalities in the diagonals, a Varimax orthogonal rotation was computed. This, however, did not reach simple structure against the criterion of the Bargmann test. A Maxplane oblique rotation was carried out which was hand-adjusted by Rotoplot (Cattell and Foster, 1963). This was shown to have reached simple structure by the same Bargmann test.

Since this study was designed to answer the same question which is posed in this section, and since Cattell laid down the technical criteria for evaluating factor analyses that I am following, although, with less rigour than he would probably advise, it is hardly surprising that this investigation cannot be faulted.

The results of this study clearly support the stability of the Cattell factors in the 16 PF test. Only Q4 ergic tension failed to emerge, although two of the important anxiety primaries C and O were intertwined. This finding demonstrates that the oblique factorings favoured by Cattell do produce, as would be expected from the discussion of simple structure, replicable factors. The argument that perhaps an orthogonal solution is better (Guilford's) is answered in the negative, because the orthogonal solution was not simple. Thus the data demand obliquity.

Given the oblique solution, one cannot expect the Guilford factors to emerge unscathed. Three of the Guilford factors are clearly identical with those of Cattell; 4 each split into 2 of the Cattell factors and simply loaded on 1 factor, as set out in Table 5.2 below.

TABLE 5.2

Guilford factors	Cattell factors	Guilford factors
M Masculinity =	I Tough-minded	G General activity
N Calmness =	O Guilt	R Restraint
S Sociability =	H Adventurousness	T Reflectiveness
D Depression		E Even mood
P Tolerance		
O Objectivity } load on	O Guilt	
F Lack of hostility		

Since one test of primary factor identification consists in examining the second-order factors underlying them, the second-order factors were extracted using a Rotoplot oblique analysis. The four main second-order factors were a good fit to those of Cattell (see Table 5.1) although Exvia loaded on G, O and Q1 which do not normally define it.

From this study by Cattell and Gibbons (1968) it seems that one can safely draw the following conclusion:

(a) The orthogonal position is not the simplest fit to the data. Thus Guilford's factors should be rotated to an oblique position.

(b) When the oblique rotation is carried out, the Guilford factors align themselves with those of Cattell. Some are identical, others load on two factors, i.e. the factors are bifactorial or mixed.

(c) It therefore follows that the Guilford factors do not provide any concepts or dimensions not provided by Cattell. This is also supported by the emergence of Cattell second-order factors.

(d) Therefore, the Cattell and Guilford factors are effectively equivalent.

(e) However, the Cattell factors are more rational as dimensions because they are the more simple structure and because they are unifactorial.

(f) There is, therefore, little point in further discussing the relation of the Guilford factors to our other sets.

(g) The Guilford factors can be removed from Table 5.1.

There would appear to be the inevitable conclusions from this technically impeccable study. Another investigation by Eysenck and Eysenck (1969) who put the Cattell, Eysenck and Guilford items into a large-scale research with 600 male and 600 female students, will be fully discussed in a later section of the chapter when the Cattell and Eysenck systems are related together. Here, only the results relevant to the Guilford factors are mentioned. Two analyses are of interest here: that of the combined items and that of the Guilford items on their own.

Analysis of Guilford Items

A Promax (Hendrickson and White, 1967) oblique rotation was carried out on these items. Naturally the match to Guilford's own orthogonal set could not be good but five factors were reasonably close to the Guilford models and 4 were a meaningful blend of 2 factors each. This is independent support for the Guilford factors. At the third-order two factors were extracted—neuroticism and extraversion. This again supports my previous argument that the Guilford factors are essentially those of Cattell rotated to a different position.

Analysis of the Combined Scales

The main interest of this study lies in the relation of the Cattell and Eysenck factors. However, at the primary factor level neither the Cattell nor the Guilford factors were clear. Furthermore the factors from both tests did not tend to form the sensible combined factors which one should hypothesize from the Cattell and Gibbon (1968) study. Thus, this result does not confirm the identity of the Cattell and Guilford factors; rather it casts some doubt on the stability of the Guilford factors (though not to the same extent as is the case with the Cattell factors).

At the third-order in this combined study two large factors turned up—extraversion and neuroticism—if one follows the identification made by

Eysenck and Eysenck (1969). This study of Eysenck and Eysenck (1969) does not support the finding that the Guilford factors overlap those of Cattell. Rather, it is the case that the Guilford factors do not properly cohere at all, while the Cattell factors fail to emerge. The reasons for the disparity between these results and those of Cattell and Gibbon (1968), lie most probably in technical differences, especially due to the fact that Eysenck correlated items. As pointed out in the discussion of test construction, dichotomous correlations have a considerable standard error and fluctuate not only when the proportions answering items differ but also according to the polarity of the item, i.e. whether it is keyed "Yes" or "No". These fluctuations tend to produce factors of small variance. In addition there were only 8 items in this study per Guilford factor so that these would have had to be most excellent for factors to have clearly emerged. There are further technical points demanding discussion for a proper evaluation of this research but they are included in the examination of the relation of the Eysenck and Cattell factors. I would still argue in view of the problems of correlating items that the Cattell and Gibbons (1968) result stands. Therefore, the Guilford factors from Table 5.1 can be removed.

THE COMREY FACTORS

The Comrey factors in the Comrey Personality Inventory (Comrey, 1970) are not based upon item inter-correlations, but upon the correlations among factored homogeneous item dimensions (FHID's). Despite the name "factored", FHID's are constructed by selecting items that appear to be homogeneous and grouping them together. Correlations between these groups of similar items are then factored, thus overcoming the problems of item unreliability. The rationale for actually putting an item in an FHID was effectively face validity with regard to Guilford's and Cattell's factors.

Examination of the Comrey factors in Table 5.1 suggests some overlap with the Cattell second-order factors—E and S being clearly similar to exvia and anxiety. M, too, may resemble Cattell's tough-mindedness. If, in fact, the Comrey factors were to be identified with the Cattell second-order factors, it would not be surprising. According to Cattell (1973) the use of FHID's as a basis of correlations is like using factors so that on analysis second-order factors, rather than first-order, emerge. Thus, there are good *a priori* reasons to expect that Comrey's factors are second-order, and that some of these are highly similar to those of Cattell.

The evidence is contained in two studies. Comrey and Duffy (1968), using FHID's and scales (not items) computed a factor analysis on a sample of 272 undergraduates using the Comrey factors, the EPI and the 16PF test. An oblique rotation was adjusted by hand to a psychologically meaningful position. The results from this study showed that there was a clear extraversion factor loading on Cattell's exvia primaries and the EPI E factor. Similarly an anxiety factor loaded on Eysenck's N and the Anxiety primaries in the Cattell test. The other factors were not good fits to any in the Cattell system.

The conclusions from this study can be but tentative because hand-rotation is unlikely to achieve simple structure. However, at least two of the factors are the same as the Cattell second-orders, although it is possible (but unlikely) that these would disappear with proper rotation. However, Barton (1973) carried out an oblique rotation of the Comrey scales and the 16 PF, where simple structure was in fact obtained. In this investigation which followed all the technical precepts previously advocated, it was found that the Comrey factors were essentially the Cattell second-orders.

Thus, as with the factors of Guilford, it appears that the Comrey factors are essentially those of Cattell. They are imprecise versions because hand-rotation, rather than objective procedures were used, and second-order rather than first- through the influence of the FHID's. The Comrey factors may, therefore, be removed from Table 5.1.

THE GRYGIER FACTORS

Kline (1972, 1973) has extensively reviewed the rationale of, and the research up to those dates with the Grygier factors in the DPI. This is an important test because it makes the bridge between multivariate analysis and personality theory, in this case of a psychoanalytic persuasion.

The test attempts to measure Freudian psychosexual variables, as an examination of Table 5.1 makes clear. If the factors there were correctly identified not only would these be highly interesting empirically, but they would provide powerful support for Freudian psychosexual theory and the notion of defence mechanisms. What evidence is there, therefore, that these factors are what they purport to be?

The three manuals to the test (Grygier, 1961, 1970; Grygier and Grygier, 1976) certainly fail to provide the necessary evidence for factor identification. There are some factor analyses but the results are far from definitive, although correlations with external criteria are given in the latest manual, because the DPI was not factored with other tests. As I have pointed out, identification of factors of this type demands this so that resulting factors can be related to markers in other systems. Indeed the best evidence which is at all relevant to the identification of the DPI factors in the manual consists of the comparison of different criterion groups. From this it can be argued that the factors make interesting discriminations as might be expected from their identification, so that it would appear useful to submit them to further analysis.

In a preliminary study, I (Kline, 1968) gave the DPI and my own test of anal character, Ai3Q (Kline, 1971) to a small sample of 70 training college students. Although the sample was small and although only Varimax analysis was carried out, the results clearly indicated one factor in accordance with the theoretical background of the test. This was the anal or obsessional personality factor which loaded up on Ai3Q and the majority of the Grygier anal scales. The other factors were not closely related to any that would be hypothesized from Freudian theory and some of these could not even be given tentative labels. The second factor was probably one of masculine interests and the third was feminine interests and attitudes. I should not like to make too much of the results of this study since the sample size was small and the rotation only orthogonal (at that time oblique rotation programmes were not available).

Stringer (1970) attempted to improve this investigation. He first subjected the original correlations to an oblique analysis and then replicated the study on a much larger sample. Again, however, his factors were difficult to interpret. Without doubt, however, they were not an obvious fit to Freudian theory.

Bromley and Lewis (1976) factored the DPI scores of subjects receiving psychiatric treatment. Although factor identification was difficult because no other factors were used to locate the DPI factors in personality space, an anal and oral factor were tentatively identified. However, clearly an investigation with marker variables is required.

Of course, all these studies of the DPI, apart from any technical imperfections, suffer from the design defect that no marker scales were included (with the exception of Ai3Q in my study (Kline, 1968)). What is needed is not just an indication of the factor structure of the test, although this is, of course, important, but an indication of what these factors are or, to put it into the phraseology of Cattell (e.g. Cattell and Kline, 1977) where these factors lie in the personality sphere.

As part of an extensive investigation of the oral character I and Storey (1978), have recently provided almost exactly the evidence needed in a research which meets most of the criteria of technical efficiency. The DPI was administered to 128 subjects (61 male) of whom the majority were students. In addition the 16 PF test and the EPI were given to enable the relation of the DPI factors to be elucidated against those which are best established. Further, since it was clear that some of the Grygier factors if valid would not load on the Cattell and Eysenck factors, all other psychosexual scales with any claim to validity were inserted into the study—the Gottheil oral scale (Gottheil, 1965), the Lazare oral scales (Lazare *et al.*, 1966), Ai3Q, the measure of the anal character (Kline, 1971) and OPQ and OOQ, two new scales to measure oral optimistic and oral pessimistic personalities (Kline and Storey, 1978c).

The correlations between all these factors were subjected to a Promax rotated factor analysis, in which there were 15 significant factors. Although the Promax (Hendrickson and White, 1967) rotation does not always reach simple structure, in this case the factor structure is unlikely to be awry since the Cattell and Eysenck factors load up as they normally do. Furthermore, as evidence of the stability of the results, the first factor closely resembles the first factor found in the previous study. Table 5.3 presents the 15 factors (only tests loading significantly >0.3 are shown).

DISCUSSION OF TABLE 5.3

With respect to the validity of the DPI from Table 5.3, two conclusions may be drawn. First the results do not support the validity of these factors as putative Freudian psychosexual variables—with the exception of the anal characteristics measures—on the other hand it does appear that some of the scales measure the traits which they are designed to test. Finally, and of great significance for this chapter, it is true to say that the Grygier scales are almost all entirely unrelated to the Eysenck and Cattell factors. In brief, it appears that the DPI scales cover variance unaccounted for by Eysenck and Cattell but with factors that are of small variance themselves and unrelated to psychoanalytic theory.

I shall now briefly identify each factor and clarify the points above. Factor 1 is clearly anal or obsessional. It loads on the DPI A factors and Ai3Q, all anal measures, and also on H, hypocrisy and negatively on Si, sexuality and Ou, unconventionality. As in the original study of the anal character (Kline, 1968), the anal factor loads also on G and Q3 among Cattell's factors. There can be no doubt that Factor 1 replicates previous findings (Kline, 1978) and can be considered as an anal or obsessional personality factor. Whether it should be added to my list of factors is, however, not so clear, since it is not factor pure.

Factor 2 with its large loading on Cattell's L, distrust, (Hendrickson and White (1964) point out that loadings can be greater than 1 with Promax rotation) must be regarded as essentially L—the defence by projection of inner tensions, a claim supported by the fact that OPQ, a measure of oral pessimistic traits (Kline and Storey, 1978) loads on it. From the viewpoint of the validity of DPI factors, there is little in this factor to confirm its validity, although Ou, verbal aggression loads on it.

Factor 3 is important. This is clearly the N of Eysenck or the anxiety factor of Cattell. No DPI factors load on it. This means that all DPI factors are independent of N. Grygier has constructed a scale which measures totally different personality variables from those related to what is generally accepted, as can be seen in Table 5.2, as one of the two most important personality factors. Factor 8, which is labelled as gregarious sociability, must also be considered in this context. This factor is the one associated with extraversion or exvia, the other large personality factor found in most studies of temperament. Examination of the DPI factors loading on 8 indicates that only 2 are related to extraversion, Sa, liking for social activities, which supports the validity of this scale and Pe, liking for admiration. This is an interesting loading in that it suggests that those who like mixing, like praise and admiration, i.e. this is their reinforcement. Factors 3 and 8 demonstrate that the DPI scales are largely independent of E and N which accounts for the fact that good predictions (e.g. Hamilton, 1970) in the field of academic performance can be made. Since many of the Cattell factors themselves load on E and N, the DPI factors must be different from the Cattell factors. On this line of argument, unlike the previous studies of the factors of Guilford and Comrey (previously discussed), the DPI factors should be retained for being independent.

However, as I mentioned in the introduction, the factors emerging from this investigation are of small variance so that one has to decide (a) whether they are sufficiently large to warrant inclusion in a definitive list and (b) whether the emerging factors actually support the validity of the DPI scales. One thing must be made clear: the DPI scales are not separate or factorially pure. The 15 rotated factors include several DPI scales in some cases. This implies in the vocabulary of Cattell that the DPI scales are surface traits. The factors, in my analyses were made up of several scales, but of small variance. Thus in the final table of factors, I shall not include *all* the DPI scales, although some factors consisting of several DPI scales may be inserted.

So far in the study of this factor analysis I have demonstrated a clear obsessional personality factor which supports the validity of the DPI "A" scales and the H and S scale. I have also shown the DPI to be essentially independent of E and N.

Factors 4 and 5 are Feminine and Masculine attitudes and interests respectively. These are highly interesting since feminine interests are related to food choices, dependence, liking for children and creativity, as well as oral dependence—an ideal portrait of the all-American Mum. It is noteworthy that no Cattell factors load on this factor. Masculine interests and attitudes are equally stereotyped with loadings on energy and drive, achievement, fascination with height and fires and a liking for adventure. Only N, shrewdness, of the Cattell factors loads on this. I would argue that, like Factor 1, Factors 4 and 5 are new and valuable factors.

Factor 6 with loading on Cattell 1 and Q2, tough-minded and self-reliant, is probably broadly the well-known tough versus tender-minded factor. Its loadings on DPI O and WP would fit this interpretation. There is nothing novel here. Factor 7 with its major loading on impulsivity and negative loading on Q3, self-control, together with minor loadings on various oral scales and negative loadings on anal scales (which again hints at the control involved) is probably an impulsivity factor. It is not stressed in Cattell's work but is clearly a rather small factor.

Factor 9 is not a personality factor but is general ability, loading only on B. Factor 10 loads only one DPI factor and would appear to a factor of down-to-earth practicality. Factor 11 loads on Ws, and introspection, and on scales of aggression, dependence and unconventionality. This is probably an introspection factor but of rather a specific kind. Otherwise a larger loading on Cattell's A and Eysenck's E would have been expected.

Factor 12 loads on persistence and one other scale, Q1. It cannot be regarded as of great importance. Factor 13 does not load on any DPI factor but must be interpreted as a Lazare factor, loading very highly on passivity, egocentricity and on pessimism. However, the DPI passivity factor does not load on it. This factor would appear to be a specific Lazare factor. Factor 14 seems to be a dependent factor loading on the DPI, E1 and M, planning and masculine interests. However, its largest loading is on Q4 and it is clearly nothing new.

Finally Factor 15, which, loading only on DPI scales, is of considerable interest. Apart from Factor 1, the obsessional personality, this is the only factor which supports psychoanalytic theory. Here one finds creative and tactile interests going together. This is the common sense basis of the factor which is probably best labelled—handling objects. However, loading on it are the variables Ah, anal hoarding and the phallic variables, PPh and Ph. This is powerful support for psychoanalytic claims concerning the genesis of such interests. Thus, according to Jones (1923), all object collectors are anal erotic—storing objects is storing faeces—the basis of the anal retentive character. Similarly creative interests in painting and pottery are sublimations of the desire to handle faeces. The loading on Ah confirms this hypothesis. Another source of interest in the arts, other than anal erotism, is the sexual symbolic function obvious in the creative and tactile arts. The phallic loadings point this out. Of course, this factor is small and it is probably not worth inserting it in a list of personality factors for this reason. However, there can be no doubt that this Factor 15 is in full accord with psychoanalytic theory.

In conclusion it would appear from this investigation that the DPI does in fact measure different factors from those in the Cattell and Eysenck tests. There is no rotational position which largely overlaps these well-known factors. There is also no doubt that the 33 scales can best be grouped into a smaller number of factors. However, despite the fact that DPI factors are a distinct set, only four of them would appear to be of broad enough interest to merit inclusion in any list—Factor 1, obsessional personality, which has regularly appeared in previous investigations (e.g. Sandler and Hazari, 1960), Factors 4 and 5, feminine and masculine interests and Factor 15, interest in handling objects. Of these factors, Factor 15 is too small accounting for less than 4% of the variance in this study, although of theoretical interest, to be inserted into a table of the *main* temperamental factors. Factor 1, although important, loads on other Cattell factors and is best regarded, not as a source trait, but a syndrome or surface trait, so that again it will not be included in my table. Factors 4 and 5, although still of small variance are independent of other factors and appear to make sound psychological sense. They would appear useful additions to a list of temperamental factors, such as is required for the purposes of this book.

Finally from the psychoanalytic theory viewpoint, the DPI is not completely successful since only Factors 1 and 15 are as expected—the obsessional (anal) factor and the factor relating to creative interests. Thus, one has two factors to add to the list of masculine and feminine interests in Table 5.3. Factors 1 and 15 will not be ignored but cannot be inserted as they stand.

It now remains to examine the relation of the Eysenck and Cattell factors. The first study is by Eysenck and Eysenck (1969), which has been mentioned in connection with the Guilford factors. The first part of this research was concerned with the factors in the Eysenck, Guilford and Cattell tests, where the

TABLE 5.3
FACTORS

Variable	1	2	3	4	5	6	7	8	9	10	11	12	13	14	15
O				0.3792		−0.5305				−0.3592					
Om	−0.6620														
Ou											0.3043				
Oa				0.3556							0.6363				
Od				0.5568							0.4075				
Oi					0.3284		0.9758								
Ov		−0.5087													
Ws						−0.6889					0.8012				
Wp											0.3356				
C				0.8885											
Ci				0.4192											−0.6039
Ah							−0.7399								−0.4346
Ad	0.6929														
Ac	0.3830														
As	0.8226														
Aa	0.9143														
Ai	0.5382			−0.3966											
Ti				0.5603											
H	0.6779														−0.6827
Ep								0.3382				0.8998			
Ei								0.8548						−0.5943	
S	−0.7796														
Sa															
Ph						−0.8060									
Pe		−0.3133						0.5181							
P					−0.8151										−0.7042
Pa					−0.4483										−0.3305
Ph					−0.3022										−0.5173
Pf					−0.8061		0.4263								
Pi															
F				0.8622											

DPl Variables

Factor loading matrix (varimax-rotated). Columns are headed by the percentage of variance accounted for by each factor; decimal points are printed as mid-dots in the original.

	5·47	3·35	4·51	2·70	2·85	2·69	3·01	4·45	2·03	2·17	2·29	2·05	1·99	2·38	2·53
16 PF Variables															
A								0·4820	−0·8926						
B															
C															
E		−0·6889	0·7844												
F	0·6236							0·6485							
G								0·6028							
H		−1·002		−0·5109											
L										−0·3567					
M					0·4943				0·4948	−0·8479					
N										0·4148					
O		−0·4155	−0·7478			−0·3380	−0·3888	−0·7610			−0·3059				
Q1			0·3024												
Q2			0·3055												
Q3			−0·8755												
Q4	0·4658														
Gottheil															
D		−0·3760					0·3391	0·3435							0·8339
Lazare															
E			−0·6184												
F			−0·3649											0·3662	
Pa			−0·3722												
Pe													0·9787		
Sd			−0·3323				−0·3274							−0·5163	−0·3034
OOQ			0·4271					0·6634							0·3008
OPQ		−0·5006	−0·4288												
Ai3Q	0·4350														
E						−0·3172		0·6033							
N		−0·8180													
Percentage variance accounted for	5·47	3·35	4·51	2·70	2·85	2·69	3·01	4·45	2·03	2·17	2·29	2·05	1·99	2·38	2·53

scales were the variables. The second part examined the factors underlying the inter-correlations between the items.

In the first investigation, 48N and 48E items from the EPI together with items from the 15 (no factor B) Cattell factors, 109 items from Guilford's 13 scales, and 18 lie scale items were subjected to a Promax rotated analysis. The samples were 600 males and 600 females, and a separate analysis was obtained from each. At the first order in both samples two factors, unambiguously extraversion and neuroticism, accounted for much of the variance, while the ten other factors seemed of little psychological interest. At the second-order factorization in the females three factors emerged, extraversion, neuroticism and a factor defined as acquiescence. Among the males four factors emerged, extraversion and neuroticism, a lie scale factor, presumably social desirability, and finally an unidentified factor loading on, A, G, 1 (Cattell) and negatively on R (Guilford). At the third-order among the males, extraversion and neuroticism finally emerge alone.

There is no need to look at these results with the Guilford factors since they have already been shown to be (Cattell and Gibbons, 1968) essentially those of Cattell's although it must be noted that this finding is not confirmed here. Instead, none of the primary factors clearly emerged. Cattell's factors seem, therefore, to be dubious, at least, so unreliable that they do not regularly appear. Only E and N are supported in Table 5.1. (Factor P, was not included in this study and this is discussed in the section on abnormal factors.)

However, this immediate and obvious interpretation of these results is not warranted. Eysenck and Eysenck expected E and N to emerge at the first-order and there were 48 item per factor. The Cattell factors had only 6 or 7 items per factor and the Guilford 8. If one accepts that any variable consists of true and specific variance plus error variance, a scale with 6 or 7 items could hardly be expected to emerge clear cut.

There are other curiosities about these results which Eysenck and Eysenck do not comment upon, the most notable being the fact that the solutions are different among males and females and that apparently the same factors emerge at different orders. Finally, in evaluating this first part of the study one must remember that the Promax rotation may not have reached simple structure, for which there was no test. All these points will be fully discussed when the results of the analysis of the *items* rather than the scales have been set out, before one jumps to the conclusion that the Cattell primary factors are not stable.

Factorization of Items in the EPI and 16 PF

The same sample and method was used as in the investigation of scales. The product-moment correlations between the items were subjected to an oblique Promax analysis. Twenty factors were rotated which was less than the number of factors with roots greater than one (the usual criterion when rotating factors, e.g. Guttman, 1954), but presumably sufficient on theoretical grounds to embrace all the factors that might be found in this investigation. However, it is less than the number of significant factors if one was to use the Scree test (Cattell, 1966b). As has been previously argued under-factoring can lead to the premature emergence of second-order factors at the first-order—a critical issue in the comparison of the Cattell and Eysenck factors. These factor analyses were computed for each test individually and finally with all items pooled. The analyses of the male and female samples were also separate.

Factors in the EPI Items

At the first-order, 8 factors emerged with good agreement between the male and female samples: sociability, impulsiveness, mood-swings, sleeplessness, jocularity, carefreeness, nervousness and sensitivity. Three further factors, different between the sexes and only tentatively labelled, also emerged. At the second-order there were 7 factors which differed among the sexes, and had in general very small loadings. For men, there appeared to be an E and N factor, but for women only E was even tentatively identified. At the third-order, however, there were two large factors, similar among the sexes and unequivocally identified as E and N. In the male sample, there was a small additional extraversion factor.

These results obviously support the claim that both Eysenck and Cattell make that extraversion and neuroticism are powerful higher order factors. The distinction, if any, between neuroticism and anxiety will be left to a later part of this chapter. However, the argument as to whether primary factors are important in the EPI items is not unequivocally answered. Many of these primary EPI factors are bloated specifics where items with different phraseology load on the factors, and there is the possibility that simple structure was not reached in the Promax rotation. In addition, there is the considerable problem of the stability of the item inter-correlations. Thus the product-moment correlation is numerically identical with phi and suffers from the same disadvantages. Further discussion will be delayed until the results with the Cattell scales and the combined analysis have been examined.

Factors in the Cattell Items

The first-order factors emerging from this analysis entirely failed to support the Cattell primary factor structure. Obviously 15 factors, identical for males and females would have been expected. In fact, 20 factors were put into the Promax rotation of which 10 showed agreement between the sexes. Even these, however, were hard to identify and the scale items did not load on the appropriate factors. At the second-order the factors were even more chaotic and these factors are not presented. At the third-order, however, clarity returned. Three factors emerged, similar in both sexes, extraversion, neuroticism and a third, possibly social extraversion. (Eysenck and Eysenck (1969) also analysed the Guilford factors which Cattell and Gibbons (1968) had shown to be essentially similar to those of Cattell. These results have been fully discussed in the section on Guilford's factors.) This leads on to the results of the combined analysis of the items.

Factors in the Item Pool (all tests combined)

It would have been curious if the combined analysis had produced results substantially different from those which have been described above. In fact, at the third-order two clear factors of extraversion and neuroticism emerged among both sexes. In the males there was a further third-order factor which could not be identified, while in the famales there were two equally dubious factors, consisting of Cattell and the other of Guilford items.

Conclusions concerning Second-order Factors

One clear fact emerges: there are unquestionably two important higher-order factors in these personality questionnaires—extraversion or exvia, neuroticism or anxiety. There can also be no doubt that in this investigation, the Cattell primary factors are not confirmed. However, the technical deficiencies of this study which I have frequently mentioned, may account for this. Cattell (1973) and Cattell and Kline (1977) not unnaturally take this view. Thus Cattell (1973) argues that the technical inadequacies of the study are just those which would influence the *primary factor structure*, which is, of course, the point at issue. These technical inadequacies, judged against the criteria advocated by Cattell (1973) are by no means gross errors which would render the results valueless. Rather they constitute a number of small points which in total may well influence the primary factors. These inadequacies are: Promax analysis, which may not have reached simple structure; small number of items representing the primary factors; no test for the number of factors when under-factoring can easily lead to the first-order emergence of second-order factors; unities rather than communalities in the diagonals: no check on the hyperplane count. All these indicate that the findings on primary factors cannot be accepted. Further work is needed. These same arguments apply to the replication of this work by Vagy and Hammond (1976) who almost certainly failed to obtain simple structure.

Other Researches into the 16 PF

Other studies have also failed to isolate the 16 PF factors. As early as 1961 Levonian demonstrated that the 16 PF scales were not homogeneous. Howarth and Browne (1971a,b) factored the 16 PF items and failed to reproduce the factors, utilizing however a hand-rotation, a method both notoriously subjective and highly unlikely to obtain simple structure. These researches indicate that the Cattell factors are elusive if nothing worse. However, Cattell (1973b) and Cattell and Vaughan (1973) on two samples totalling over 1000 subjects have shown that the items do load the factors as intended. This was the case both with items and item parcels as the basis of correlation. Their success is attributable to the technical correctness of their factor analyses.

Thus it would appear reasonable to argue that the Cattell Primaries are stable structures. Since, as we shall see later, they are highly valuable in the practice of psychology, and in theory building, hence there are no doubts in listing these 16 personality factors in the table. The 7 extra normal factors, although less well supported because they are newer would also seem worthy of inclusion based upon the studies of Cattell and Delhees (1973), De Voogdt and Cattell (1973) and Cattell and Marshall (1973).

It has sometimes been argued (e.g. Cattell, 1973) that the EPI factors are an example of pseudo-secondary factors or grounded secondaries. This can happen when too few factors are put into the rotation. However, while this may well be the case with the Comrey factors, although as I have argued the FHID's are themselves virtually primary factors, there is no need for this argument in the case of the Eysenck factors. The study by Eysenck and Eysenck (1969) demonstrates that E and N are genuine higher-order factors.

From this then I would argue that the 23 Cattell Primaries deserve mention in the table of substantive findings in the field of temperament as do the two second-order factors—extraversion and neuroticism. However, these two last raise a new issue. How many second-order factors are there, and what is their proper label?—a question relevant not to the structure itself but to the interpretation of an agreed structure. Therefore, we shall turn to a study of the higher-order factors that should be included in the table. However, for this purpose there is a bridging study by Saville and Blinkhorn (1976) which should be briefly discussed if only because a huge sample was used so that the results are likely to be reliable.

In all, more than 2000 undergraduates in their second year were tested with the 16 PF and EP1. In one part of the study the variance in each of the factors which was not attributable to Eysenck's E or N, was calculated, thus testing the position that the Cattell primaries contribute something over and above E and N. As regards the primaries O, C and Q4 (the main anxiety factors), the results do not support Cattell's claims. Thus only 16% of the variance of C is not accounted for by N, 4% of O and 9% of Q4. It would therefore appear that these factors add nothing to N. Examination of the correlations of these three factors with N shows that they are all around 0·7 and this is the correlation of the factors with each other. In addition the reliability of these scales is no higher. Saville and Blinkhorn (1976) therefore argue that the anxiety primaries add little information over and above N.

In the case of the factors contributing to the extraversion or exvia factor Cattell's case is supported because these primaries have considerable variance independent of E- the figures being A, 69% independent variance; E, 68%; H, 29%; G, 81%; and Q2 68%. In fact, only F has most of its variance accounted for by E.

As I have suggested, this is a bridging study for it also compares the Eysenck factors with the Cattell second-orders. These findings strongly support the position of Cattell in that E and N account for the exvia and anxiety variance almost completely. In other words the argument here is not about structure, but the interpretation of the agreed forms—extraversion or exvia, neuroticism or anxiety. Similarly, the other Cattell second-order factors—cortertia, independence, discreetness, prodigal subjectivity and superego—are not accounted for by E and N. This finding, of course, supports the value of the Cattell primaries loading on them.

Thus in conclusion one can argue that this study by Saville and Blinkhorn, demonstrates the value of the Cattell primaries, the Cattell second-order factors, and the identity of the two largest second-orders of Cattell with those of Eysenck. It throws into doubt however, the independence and worth of the anxiety primaries O, C and Q4. In this study they appear to be essentially identical.

Since this study is to be taken seriously because the numbers are large, if O, C and Q4 are to be retained in the list of factors, then one must try to account for these findings. Is there any explanation which would enable one to do this?

It seems that the correlations between C, O and Q4 in this investigation were exceptionally high. This coupled with the low reliability of the scales and the fact that, as intended, they load on the N factor, does effectively ensure that N covers all the reliable variance. In the investigation, for example, of Kline and Storey (1977) with 120 students the inter-correlations were between 0·5 and 0·6. Furthermore their loadings on the N factor were all high, thus demonstrating the scales had behaved in this investigation as they were intended. It must also be pointed out that in the Kline and Storey research O, C and Q4 did not behave as one test. Thus OPQ, our test of oral pessimism, had a significant correlation with Q4 and C, but not with O, for example. Finally, in the work on the contribution of psychometrics to clinical psychology (Chapter 9), one can see that there is practical value in the differentiations made by these three factors. I would argue, therefore, that the results of this investigation are due to the combination of low reliability of scales (which indeed must be improved) and the fact that the correlations were particularly high in this case. Other evidence, of a different type, suggests that this particular finding is not typical.

Second-order Factors

The fact that (other than exvia and anxiety) the second-order factors in the Cattell system are independent of E and N and the fact that their primaries are as well in this study by Saville and Blinkhorn, is good support for including them in my list of factors. It is interesting to note that cortertia resembles the well-known tough- versus tender-minded dimension discussed by James (1890) and invoked by Eysenck (1954) in his study of politics. The other second-order factors have no especially obvious characteristics to discuss here. This now leaves one with the proper identification of exvia and extraversion, and anxiety and neuroticism.

First there is no doubt both from this investigation by Saville and Blinkhorn and by numerous others, that extraversion, the E of the EPI and the exvia second-order factor of Cattell are identical. Cattell indeed prefers the name exvia because of the rag-bag connotations of extraversion (Cattell, 1973). There is no disagreement as to the interpretation of the factor.

Similarly there is no question that N and the second-order anxiety are essentially the same factor. Here, however, the different names do represent a different identification. Eysenck has argued that N is neuroticism, the essential personality factor underlying neurosis. Cattell on the other hand regards it as anxiety, only *one* of a number of differentiating factors between neurotics and normals. This distinction must be briefly examined.

Anxiety or Neuroticism

Cattell and Scheier (1961) have devoted considerable experimental attention to this second-order factor. Some of this work is considered in Chapter 9. It was pointed out that anxiety seemed a more accurate label than neuroticism simply because neurotics differed from normals on other factors, although this is a central component in neurosis.

Summary of the Normal Temperament Factors

The initial table (5.1) of factors can now, as has been seen, be drastically reduced. The Guilford, Comrey and the majority of the Grygier factors have been shown to be essentially similar to those of Cattell or bloated specifics. A few Grygier factors seem worth retaining. In addition one surface trait dimension—obsessionality—has been clearly defined by a number of psychometric tests. Eysenck's two main factors E and N are agreed to be most important but to be virtually identical with the second-order factors derived from Cattell's oblique primary factors. Recent work by Eysenck and Eysenck (1977) has broken extroversion down: there are now sociability factors. Guilford (1977) too insists on this point.

However, as can be seen from the list, Eysenck and Eysenck (1975) have recently introduced a new factor P or Psychoticism which is the factor that broadly distinguishes psychotics from normals. Although the EPQ is designed for use with normals, and P is seen as a dimension of normal personality, it is clear from the handbook to the test that P is a factor on which normals score low unlike the anxiety factor. It, therefore, seems appropriate to consider the status of P alongside the abnormal personality factors.

Abnormal Factors

The basis of Cattell's normal factors were ratings of actual behaviour on all non-tautologous words describing behaviour. A full description of this original basis can be found in Cattell (1946) and Cattell and Kline (1977). There it was argued that behaviour can only be said to occur if it has been described—i.e. that the world is a function of our conceptual framework. Since Cattell's factors embrace much of the variance in these ratings, he has persistently claimed that his factors must cover the totality of temperament— the personality sphere or from the way it has been defined, the semantic personality sphere.

It is clear that if there is discontinuity between normal and abnormal behaviour words (or factors) descriptive of one, it will not necessarily be applicable in the other. For example, if a group of abnormals were prone to barking and biting, those terms, unimportant normally, would be significant. It is, therefore, logically possible that abnormal factors might differ from normal. It follows that it is necessary to make a special study of abnormal behaviour. Cattell and his colleagues at Illinois and Eysenck at the Maudsley in London are the only factor analysts to have done this systematically. However, the MMPI item pool, based on criterion discrimination is also a useful source of psychometric data in this area.

Driven on, therefore, by the logical necessity to investigate the abnormal personality sphere and encouraged further by the fact that the normal factors were not good at discriminating psychotics (who are most obviously disturbed) from normal, Cattell and his colleagues have attacked the problem in three ways. Psychiatric texts have been searched for descriptions of abnormal behaviour; items have been specially written to tap factors as they appeared in ongoing clinical research and finally the MMPI items have been used, this last being the most important source.

I have already described the construction of the MMPI and the disadvantages inherent in test construction methods based upon criterion-keying. Thus the MMPI together with items derived from other sources was not used in the normal empirical discriminatory way. Rather, items were subjected to factor analysis in an effort to establish basic abnormal personality factors.

Unfortunately factoring the clinical scales of the MMPI is not likely to be useful for a number of reasons. The scales are not properly independent since some items contribute to more than one scale: response sets of acquiescence and social desirability indubitably influence some of the scales (see Jackson and Messick, 1961). Despite these difficulties, various investigations of the factor structure of the scale have been carried out: Finney (1961) found five factors, Orme (1965) argues that one factor of general emotionality can account for the results and while I was (1967) working with student subjects I found two factors very similar to exvia and anxiety.

Obviously item factoring is the best solution to these problems, or item parcel-factoring. Cattell and Bolton (1969) factored the correlations between the 16 PF factors and such MMPI item parcels—thus enabling them to see whether any resulting MMPI factors were independent of the 16 PF or not. In fact, all the 15 (no. B) Cattell factors emerged, plus four other abnormal factors.

These four MMPI based factors were then re-factored together with 16 PF items and abnormal items from the other sources mentioned previously. In all 750 items had to be used to cover the abnormal personality sphere. In fact, as one can see from Table 5.1, 12 *pathological* factors emerged, plus, of course, the first 16 normal factors.

As can be seen in Chapter 9, these 12 factors are of considerable practical and theoretical interest. Most striking is the fact of 7 depression factors—thus indicating the rag-bag nature of the psychiatric category of depression. However, the concern in this chapter turns on the relations of these factors to Eysenck's P.

The psychoticism factor P, is at last able to be measured by a published psychometric test, the EPQ (Eysenck and Eysenck, 1975). In the handbook to this test the nature of P is clarified as far as is possible with present results. Eysenck and Eysenck admit that at this stage the nature of the P factor "can only be guessed at". The high scorer is described as solitary, not caring for people, troublesome, a bad fit, cruel, inhumane, lacking in feeling and empathy, altogether insensitive, hostile even to his own kith and kin and aggressive even to loved ones. He likes the odd or unusual, disregards danger and enjoys making a fool of and upsetting people. All these traits are taken from the Handbook to the EPQ and apply largely to children as well as adults.

Such descriptions resemble, as the authors point out, the psychiatric syndromes measured by the MMPI such as schizoid, psychopathic and behaviour disorder patterns. Psychoticism is a concept which, of course, would include them all. However, it radically differs from these MMPI variables in that P is a dimension underlying normal behaviour and it becomes pathological only in extreme cases.

Psychoticism correlates with a number of objective tests, such as vigilance tasks and variability of reaction time which are capable of discriminating psychotics from normals and with social variables such as drug addiction and alcoholism—all of which is support for its validity. How then does this P factor relate to the abnormal factors of Cattell?

Examination of Cattell's abnormal factors in Table 5.1, comparing them with the descriptions of Eysenck's P factor, which is all that can be done at present since no empirical studies linking P to these factors have been carried out, shows similarity to two factors. Brooding discontent, D_3, the desire for something exciting (which incidentally is high on psychopaths (Cattell, 1973)) and Pp—psychopathic deviation, which resembles the typical psychopathic syndrome—immunity to criticism, amorality, little need for sleep. Another of Cattell's factors, Ps—general psychosis is also of interest. This is the best discriminator of psychotics yet it loads on feelings of inferiority and unworthiness. Thus it is quite unlike Eysenck's P.

From this it would appear that Eysenck's P may be a second-order factor underlying these abnormal factors. However, if this is the case it is curious that Ps should be so different from it. At present one must await further research to link P to these abnormal factors. However, there is no doubt that it must be included in the final list of personality factors. (The relevance of P to clinical psychology is discussed in Chapter 8.)

I have now discussed all the factors in the preliminary Table 5.1, and it has been seen that many could be removed as ill-defined duplicates of others. However, in the course of these arguments I have had to consider the claim not only of factors but in one case at least, of a personality syndrome or a surfact trait—the obsessional personality factor.

The standard MMPI clinical variables, which may be regarded as surface traits can be dismissed. The factor analyses which have been discussed clearly cover much of their variance, and the notorious unreliability of psychiatric diagnosis means that one should not be particularly anxious if the abnormal factors do not precisely pin-point the standard MMPI categories.

Indeed, if the temperamental factors were all-embracing there would be no need at all for the separate delineation of any surface traits. As it is, however, the obsessional personality is best measured by a separate multi-factor test. There are a few other such syndromes which I would argue psychometrics has been able to discriminate and which have proved useful research instruments.

The most well known of these is the "Authoritarian Personality" (Adorno *et al.*, 1950). Although there has been much justified criticism of the original F scale in terms of response sets such as social desirability and acquiescence (e.g. Bass, 1955), there seems to be a corpus of meaning left in the syndrome. This view is supported by the fact that similar syndromes have been isolated by Rokeach (1960)—called Dogmatism or rigidity—and by Wilson and Patterson (1970) where the variable is named conservatism. Although there are differences between these variables, a factor analysis by Knapp (1976) of most of the variants of these scales indicated that there were clusters of traits common to all. The authoritarian rigid, conservative dogmatist may be conceived of as, (not surprisingly) rigid, willing to be a subject to authority and exerting his authority on others, anti-scientific and intellectual, believing in traditional values, a lover of discipline and order and generally illiberal. Indeed the factor has been identified by Dixon (1976) as being responsible for military blunders (rather than sheer stupidity).

Brief mention must also be made of a variable which has recently attracted a considerable body of research—locus of control (e.g. Phares, 1976). This variable is derived from the work of Rotter (1966) where it is conceived as generalized expectancies of internal versus external control of reinforcement. Broadly, the internalizer considers that events are within his control; the externalizer that external forces are the most significant.

Although various reviews of the literature (e.g. Joe, 1971, Prosiuk and Lussier, 1975) demonstrate that locus of control correlates modestly with a wide range of variables and can be measured with a reasonable degree of reliability, it is clearly contaminated by social desirability. In addition, correlations with anxiety and dogmatism and the fact that the items themselves of the IE scale form two factors even on a Varimax analysis (Mirels, 1970) all suggest that locus of control is a multi-factorial scale and that it is best measured by the appropriate combination of source traits. The fact that the IE scale has not been located in the personality sphere means that the reported correlations with other variables cannot be given a meaningful psychological interpretation. Before continuing to use the IE variable, researchers should locate it relative to the major source traits. I suspect that if this were done, it would no longer be used.

This year myself and Storey (1978c) have been attempting to delineate two further psychosexual temperamental syndromes—oral pessimism and oral optimism—analagous to the Ai3Q measure of anal or obsessional personality developed in 1971 (Kline, 1971). Initial studies of these two tests, OPQ and OOQ, suggest that these are sensible and useful syndromes. Thus OOQ loads on E and negatively on N, indicating that the oral optimist is a stable extrovert. However, this test is not just a simple amalgam of the two E and N factors since correlations with these factors are low. Similarly, the oral pessimist may be seen as an unstable projecting, distrustful personality loading on N and Cattell's L. More research with these syndromes is required, however, before they could be reasonably added to the list of temperamental variables discovered through psychometrics.

I have now examined the major factors and syndromes of human temperament isolated by psychometrics. The revised and shortened list appears in Table 5.4.

TABLE 5.4
FACTORS AND SYNDROMES OF HUMAN TEMPERAMENT

23 Cattell normal factors $\Big\}$ Primary factors	$\Big\{$ M F	Grygier

or

Second-order factors
Eysenck's E, N and P
   +
Cattell second-orders
Syndromes
Obsessional personality
Authoritarian personality

CONCLUSIONS

These are the constructs that have emerged from the psychometric questionnaire study of human temperament. The meaning and implication of Table 5.4 are clear. These are the variables that account for the variance in human temperament. As such, it is these that must be used in the investigations of personality. If one understands the development and nature of these dimensions, *ipso facto* one understands temperament. These constructs have demonstrated importance. Their factorial status is evidence of this. Thus they stand in contrast to intuitive guesses of brilliant clinicians whose concepts have been, in the past, the building blocks of personality theory. Any personality theory of any value must take account first and foremost of the variables in Table 5.4. This then is the contribution to the psychology of temperament made by psychometrics: the significant variables are known. In later chapters of this book one can see this knowledge has yielded insights into occupational, educational and clinical psychology. In addition one sees how these and other factors bear upon various theories of personality and how they themselves may be woven into their own theory.

I do not set out here any factors derived from T tests or projective tests. This is because, as yet, no clearly established factors from these tests have been found. However, where they have been used with some effect in clinical psychology, despite the problem of identification, the results have been examined (see Chapter 9 on clinical applications of psychometric factors). Similarly some projective test results are scrutinized in the chapters on human dynamics and clinical psychology.

SUMMARY

(1) Temperament was defined in terms of traits and the objections of situationalism to traits were discussed.
(2) 100 factor-analytically defined traits of temperament were set out in Table 5.1.
(3) The similarities of these factors were discussed in the light of the technical problems of factor analysis.
(4) Studies were reviewed demonstrating similarities and differences between the Cattell, Eysenck, Comrey, Guilford and Grygier factors.
(5) Abnormal factors, including Eysenck's P factor were examined, together with a few other psychometrically defined syndromes of personality traits.
(6) The most well-established factors were finally set out in Table 5.4.

6

Human Dynamics

Chapter 5 has shown that the contribution of psychometrics to the knowledge of human temperament lies in the clear establishment of what are the most important temperamental dimensions and syndromes. Psychometrics clarified which variables merited research.

This chapter examines the substantive, psychometric findings in the even more complex field of human dynamics, an area of psychology which even now is largely the province of clinical speculation; speculation, however, of great interest.

THE DISTINCTION BETWEEN DYNAMICS
AND TEMPERAMENT

Temperamental dimensions account for the different ways we do things. Dynamic traits explain our reasons for doing them, a distinction discussed in the opening section of Chapter 5. The substantive contribution to the psychology of motivation from psychometrics is likely to lie in establishing what are the most important motivational traits or dimensions.

That this is an important task for a science of psychology can be seen from even a cursory glance at the confusion of contradictory claims made by motivational theorists, most of whom would regard themselves as thorough-going scientists despite failing to establish any set of measuring instruments, a *sine qua non* of scientific method. This, of course, is the reason that I have argued in the earlier chapters that the psychometric approach (with its implications of multivariate analysis) must yield fruit.

Examples of motivational theories make the need for a rigorous quantified approach obvious. Some hallucinatory behaviour used to be regarded as literally diabolical and exorcism was the cure. The Church of England, indeed, still uses exorcisory rites today to defeat possession. Freud (1940) postulated two motivational determinants, eros and thanatos, both of which are difficult to put to an empirical test. Earlier in psychoanalysis, Freud had put forward sex and aggression as being the most important determiners of human behaviour (Freud, 1933). Murray (1938) in his development of Personology listed a large number of human needs, along with corresponding environmental presses as underlying dynamics. In addition it is to be noted he did provide a measurment device: the Thematic Apperception Test (TAT). McDougall (1932) listed 15 propensities—virtually drives. Adler (1927) concentrated on one, "the upward striving for superiority", saying more, in all probability, about Adler than about human motivation, although this work has been recently revived by McClelland and colleagues (McClelland, 1961) under the title of "Need for Achievement". Indeed the work of Murray has also received psychometric attention from Edwards (1959) and Jackson (1967). The status of all these theories will be examined in Chapter 11 in the light of psychometric knowledge.

Experimental psychology under the influence of behaviourism has tended to regard the term "motivation" as redundant, based upon, as Skinner claims (Skinner, 1953), the primitive tendency at least as far as science is concerned, to create abstract entities from descriptive terms: intelligence to account for intelligent behaviour, agression for aggressive behaviour and so on. In this approach the dynamics of behaviour reside in the past pattern of reinforcement. We act because we have been previously reinforced. Our introspected reasons are epiphenomena. With this view, of course, it would appear at first sight that the psychometric, multivariate analysis of motivational traits is doomed to failure.

Furthermore if one adds in the classical conditioning of Dollard and Miller (1950) which they would adduce in understanding the dynamics of some behaviours then it does appear that the very search for traits in the area of motivation is scientifically mistaken. However, as I shall demonstrate in this chapter, the weakness of the multivariate trait analysis is more apparent than real. The dynamic traits themselves may be the result of the past patterns of experience. Furthermore the reinforcement approach implies some kind of instinctual drive, the reduction of which, according to Hull, is most essential to the dynamics of behaviour. In addition, the nature of reinforcers for man (as distinct from some lower organisms) is not well understood, due in part to the fact that men think and feel. Reinforcement, I would argue, depends in any particular subject, on his particular drives or needs.

So even if one can see that the operant approach to motivation does not really rule out the study of drives, it is evident from this brief summary of some of the claims made by psychologists who are not using adequate methodology, that all is chaos: sex, inferiority, aggression, eros, thanatos, 20 needs and presses, 15 propensities.

The matter is further complicated by introducing the work of ethologists, for example Lorenz (1966) and Tinbergen (1951). Their main contribution has been to stress the importance in behaviour of responses released by sign stimuli. In addition with the concept of imprinting, the importance of initial learning periods in infancy has been stressed although the significance for Man of these mechanisms has not been demonstrated.

Against this background of speculation, one has to see how the of behaviour have been approached in psychometrics.

In previous chapters I have stressed how the psychometric study of human temperament has resolved itself into the study of traits. It is therefore pertinent to ask what, in the dynamic field, the equivalent of traits might be. One answer is simple: states.

The Trait State Distinction

This is a distinction which has been much employed in the work of Cattell (1973) and by Cattell and Kline (1977). It is especially important in the discussion and understanding of anxiety (e.g. Cattell and Scheier, 1961, Spielberger, 1972). Both Cattell and Spielberger have produced separate measures of state and trait anxiety. Trait anxiety is the general anxiety level of an individual: his place on the second-order anxiety factor or Eysenck's N. However, the anxiety level at any given time reflects both trait anxiety (a stolid person is less moved by events than a highly excitable one) and state anxiety arising from some event. Thus state anxiety, if it can be separately measured, should fluctuate continually over time, whereas trait anxiety, by definition, should remain relatively stable. State anxiety can be a powerful dynamic influence on behaviour. For example, the student near examination time behaves differently from normal.

Indeed states, relatively transient in nature, as distinct from traits relatively stable over time, should, if everyday observation is correct, play important roles in motivation. Roused by anger, envy or fear, a man may behave in a manner unpredictable if we do not take into account his mood or state. Thus it would appear imperative in the study of motivation that psychometrics attempt to measure states. Previously, it will be noted I have used the word moods. Moods are everyday terms for what one calls states. Moods refer usually to feelings such as boredom, energy, elation or depression. It is normally used to refer to states of anxiety but this is almost certainly simply a matter of idiom.

This state trait distinction is also useful in understanding objections to trait personality questionnaires of the kind that have been discussed in relation to temperamental factors (see Chapter 5). Many subjects claim that sometimes they feel sociable, other times not (aggressively), so how can they fill in the questionnaires. In this case subjects are referring to the state, sociability, rather than the more enduring trait. This example makes it clear that ideally, as has been done with anxiety, all personality tests should contain both trait and state measures.

Thus, the psychometric study of motivation must concern itself not only with attempting to sort out the baffling claims about human drives but with the measurement of moods and states. With the latter I shall begin pointing out the psychometric contribution to the field. In fact, psychometrics has been able to delineate a number of important moods and states some of which have never been found in clinical studies.

Problems in the Study of Moods and States

In order to appreciate the methodology behind the substantive findings that appear in Table 6.1, it is necessary first to discuss some of the logical and practical problems which are inherent in the study of moods. Indeed their severity is such that relatively little work has been done in this area.

The first difficulty (which has not been appreciated by most investigators) concerns the correct factor-analytic procedure. Moods, by definition, change over time. Any procedure, therefore, which is going to reliably differentiate moods from traits must involve time: in other words there must be some retesting. This, of course, means that the standard regular factor-analytic technique, R technique, where correlations between tests are factored, cannot be used to measure states. Factors emerging, R factors, *could* be states but could equally well be traits. The logic of this argument (see Chapter 2) removes, at a stroke, most of the best known work on moods (e.g. the Clyde Mood Scale studies (Clyde, 1963) and the research of Nowlis (Nowlis and Green, 1957)).

Howarth (in press) contains a list of mood scales—The Howarth Mood Adjective Check List. However, no details of provenance, reliability or validity are given and without these, the scales cannot be regarded as measuring substantive, psychological dimensions. The moods are: aggression, scepticism, egotism, outgoingness, control, anxiety, cooperation, fatigue, concentration and sadness.

In the discussion of factor analysis in Chapter 2 it was pointed out that where repeated testing is necessary, which is the case with moods and states, the requisite method is P factor analysis where the correlations between occasions, on a number of variables, within each individual, are subjected to factor analysis. P factors are, therefore, the moods and states of the individual over the particular period of time of testing. P technique is undoubtedly the most suitable method for revealing moods but unfortunately it requires an enormous expenditure of time by subjects since it involves constant retesting. This, in any case, especially with psychometric test materials brings its own obvious difficulties—boredom with the items, memory of previous responses, and the fact that items change their meaning or lose it altogether (semantic saturation) after constant examination and scrutiny. A further practical problem lies in the fact that volunteers for a P technique research project, almost by definition, are exceptional and, in my experience (which we discuss later in this chapter), they are hard to come by.

Cattell (1973) and Cattell and Kline (1977) have proposed two substitute procedures for P technique simply because they overcome the practical problems of obtaining subjects since they require less time. In addition both avoid the limiting condition that P technique involves only one subject.

The first of these is known as dR technique, essentially an R analysis of the differences between scores of tests given on two occasions. dR factors must, therefore, reflect the dimensions underlying the differences in moods, on the two occasions. If therefore one gives subjects trait measures, dR analysis must indicate the factors accounting for changes in trait status, i.e. moods or states. This is the rationale of dR analysis. Obviously this method requires far less of the subject's time and can be used with a large number of subjects thereby improving sampling.

Cronbach (1970) has argued that analysis of difference scores (and this would be particularly true of factor analysis) is hazardous because of their large standard error. Indeed, he rejects their utility. However, this is an extreme view. If one splits this sample (Cattell and Kline, 1977) and obtains virtually identical results, there seems no reason not to trust them. These are the precautions adopted with other volatile statistics such as the beta weights in multiple correlation. There is another possible disadvantage of this technique which only further research can illuminate. If, as is possible, in different subjects different moods have the same effects and the same moods different effects on temperamental traits, dR analysis is not likely to be successful. At best it will be unclear, at worst positively misleading.

A further possibility is to try to combine the advantages of both methods as in chain P technique (Cattell, 1973). Here if one tests 10 subjects on 10 occasions, one can put the subjects in a series so that effectively one samples 100 occasions. This method overcomes the problem of the possibly idiosyncratic nature of moods revealed by P technique and of the weakness in dR technique that only two occasions are sampled. However, this method is a compromise. The best information is still to be obtained from P technique with a large number of subjects.

A final problem common to all methods of studying moods and states needs to be mentioned. This relates to the interval between testing sessions. Volatile moods need, by definition, frequent testing sessions if they are to be caught. Certainly many moods (indeed most) probably last for less time than a day which is the shortest interval used in retesting in this research.

Bearing these problems in mind one must now turn to the substantive results that have emerged fom the use of these methods in the field of moods and states. I must make it clear that the distinction of moods and states (themselves distinguished by their fluctuations to internal and external stimuli, from stable traits) from drives, is more for convenience than from conviction or from the clear-cut results of research. However, it does appear as Cattell and Child (1975) discuss that general moods and states (e.g. boredom) are different from rather specific drives such as hunger and thirst.

The mood and state factors set out in Table 6.1 have been discovered in various investigations.

TABLE 6.1
MOOD AND STATE FACTORS

State exvia State anxiety State cortertia State independence	Cattell and Schaier (1961) N = 95 9 months retest	dR Second-orders	16 PF factors
+ Depression Psychoticism	Cattell (1973) 185 normal and neurotics 3 months retest	dR Second-orders	16 PF and abnormal factors
+ Discreetness Subjectivity Intelligence Good upbringing	Cattell (1973) less systematic evidence for these	dR Second-orders	
Arousal fatigue Stress regression Guilt	(Barton, 1973b and Curran, 1968) in Cattell, (1973)	Chain P technique dR technique	
+ 3 depression factors (a) general (b) low energy (c) anxious Strong superego	Nesselroade and Cable (1974)	dR analysis	
+ Alpha Beta Gamma Delta	Barton and Curran in Cattell (1973)	Third-order factors	

DISCUSSION OF TABLE 6.1

Table 6.1 lists all the different state factors together with a key investigation, where they were clearly shown and a brief description of the method used in isolating the factors. These are not the only investigations where these factors have been found. Furthermore, each horizontal section of the table includes only the *new* factors discovered in the investigation. For example Cattell (1973) found the first four factors of Table 6.1 in addition to depression and psychoticism.

Before interpreting the factors it is necessary to examine more closely the distinction between traits and states: states being transient, traits enduring. In addition one has to examine the relation of dR and Chain P (and P) techniques: are their findings comparable?

Further Distinctions between Traits and States

The terms transient and stable are the root of the problem in making a proper distinction between traits and states. Some states are very brief: annoyance at missing a bus may be almost immediately changed if the individual then gets offered a lift. Other states however are perhaps ended only by death. Grief at death of a spouse can be an example of this. I have already mentioned the practical difficulty in psychometric testing of moods and states, a difficulty associated with the differing of duration of states, namely that a testing session is of finite length. Hence a mood more brief than this will not be captured.

However, if a state such as grief, lasts for a year or more, could it not really be said to be a trait? How long enduring must a state be to become a trait? From this it is clear that there is no absolute distinction between traits and states. If this is the case, one must now present the arguments for (not only using the two terms) but for making the distinction empirically, as has been done, thereby producing the state factors in Table 6.1. In effect one must try to justify the interpretation of dR and P factors as state factors.

Cattell (1973) has attempted an objective and neat definition of states and traits based upon differences in variance. This has been set out by Cattell and Kline (1977): if one measures people on several occasions for traits, the between people variance is greater than the variance between occasions. For states the position is reversed.

The first horizontal section of Table 6.1 is based on the work of Cattell and Scheier (1961). dR technique applied to the 16PF seems to demonstrate at the second-order at least that each trait has its corresponding state. Since this is work that has been extensively replicated (Cattell, 1973) one must make sense of it. With anxiety the result is fine: this has long been recognized as both state and trait. The other variables make little sense in the light of common sense or clinical theory. Logically it could be the case that R analysis has revealed not traits but states. However, in the analogous field of abilities this is manifestly not true. (Aristotle was always intelligent.) Furthermore, empirical studies of R personality factors indicate clearly that they are traits not states.

Since it is really not sensible to conceive of exvia and independence for example as states, Cattell has been forced to develop a new concept. These state factors are interpreted as trait change factors, an interpretation that would equally apply to the dR studies reported in the second and third horizontal sections of Table 6.1. Thus then dR studies have revealed a new construct—hitherto unnoticed by clinical psychology—the trait change factors. Before going on to interpret particular state-change factors, it is necessary to distinguish state or mood factors, trait-change factors and trait factors. One finding is clear, trait factors have corresponding trait-change factors.

Distinction between Trait, Trait-change and State Factors

A possible argument about dR factors, particularly in view of their large standard errors is that they are essentially statistical artifacts. However, Cattell (1966) in a complex statistical argument to which readers must refer, demonstrates that this explanation for trait-change factors can be dismissed.

If one supposes that personality growth is uniform then trait-change factors which represent changes in traits (growth and decline) by definition will resemble traits. Thus dR studies are bound to unearth some trait-change factors. State factors, however, do not necessarily resemble traits although anxiety most certainly does. Thus one can see that trait-change factors represent changes in traits while state factors are probably quite different from traits.

In terms of our factor-analytic research designs, we can also make a distinction. Traits can only appear in R analysis. States can appear in R, dR and P analysis and change factors in dR and P technique. Thus by a study of factors as they emerge from the three types of analysis, states, trait-change and trait factors can be clearly discriminated. Generally as we have said, trait-change factors mimic traits while state factors generally do not.

This distinction of trait-change and state factors, that the former represent the growth and decline of traits means that strictly they are not motivational factors at all. However, because they are so akin to state factors and can only be discussed in relation to state factors they have to be placed here. In the final list of motivational factors they will have no place.

Although anxiety mimics the trait anxiety it is clearly a state and not a trait-change factor. This can be shown because it appears in R analyses as well as dR and P technique. Whether there is also a trait-change factor that can be distinguished from state anxiety is problematic. Presumably there is, but up to this date, no studies have convincingly demonstrated such a factor.

If one examines the state factors listed in Table 6.1, again one can see that from the viewpoint of motivation, with the exception of anxiety and depression, they are not relevant, being trait-change factors which are not (either by clinical hypothesis or research) related to motivation. Indeed we can now leave the question of trait-change factors, content to note that, perhaps not unexpectedly because they resemble traits, they are a new concept unrecognized by clinical psychology and discovered through multivariate research.

The state factors isolated by chain P, P and dR technique, arousal, fatigue, stress, aggression, guilt, anxiety and the three depression factors make sound psychological sense, i.e. such states have been experienced by most people and most clinical theorizing on motivation makes use of such concepts. Given this, it is still pertinent to examine the factor-analytic basis for the factors. In brief can these mood and state factors be as confidently listed as the temperamental traits in Chapter 4?

So far the mood and state factors, mainly trait-change factors, have emerged from studies based upon sampling the personality sphere (traits) rather than sampling some kind of state sphere. However, work on moods and states based upon a more deliberate attempt to sample a specific state sphere was going on, based upon T or objective behaviour tests and psychological measures. Cattell and Rhymer (1947) conducted a 55 day study of questionnaire items, psychological measures and T tests, although in fact only trait-change factors emerged from this research. Cattell and Scheier (1961) in their study of anxiety combined the factor analytic with the traditional experimental method by introducing stress on certain testing sessions. Five factors from eight were identified as anxiety, pathemia, effort stress and two physiological factors, adrenergic system response and raised pulse rate and cholesterol level. The distinction between anxiety and effort stress was noteworthy and too the fact that anxiety was not linked to rises in cholesterol level.

Van Egeren (1963) utilized T data, physiological data and Q data including the abnormal depression factors in a study of moods where depression was implicated in both anxiety and regression. All these studies have been discussed briefly because, utilizing physiological indices strictly they are outside the sphere of psychometrics. However, they do support the factors discovered through the application of psychometric Q data.

Indeed, this work with physiological indices and T data has become exceedingly complex, as evinced by the work of Curran (1968) and Cattell and Nesselroade (1976). However, eight factors can be measured by questionnaire as in the "Eighth State Questionnaire" (Curran and Cattell, 1974). Exvia, anxiety, depression, arousal, fatigue, guilt depression and stress regression, are the factors appearing in Table 6.1.

Thus I would argue that further work strictly beyond the confines of psychometrics has tended to support the true state factors discovered through P, chain P and dR technique applied to questionnaire data. One problem with this additional work utilizing T factors is that these do not usually match well with Q factors. As fully discussed in Cattell and Kline (1977) T first-order factors resemble Q second-order factors. This has meant that higher-order factorings of these studies do not always give clear results. However, at the third-order three factors are found—alpha, loading on exvia and anxiety, beta, loading negatively on depression and guilt, positively on fatigue and gamma, loading on stress and regression. The proper identification of these factors is difficult but as Cattell and Kline (1977) have argued, beta resembles what Flugel (1945) has called a primitive kind of reparation—work hard and you feel good—the psychodynamics of the presbyterian ethic. It could be argued that all three factors are in fact environmental. Alpha may reflect situations that arouse social anxiety—such as having to perform in public; beta may be, as previously suggested, the reparation situation described in psycho-analytic theory while gamma may represent overwork. Much further research is, however, demanded before these factors can be properly labelled.

Thus to summarize these findings one can state that two kinds of mood or state factors are included—genuine state factors and trait-change factors. Trait-change factors represent growth and decline over time in traits and are thus not strictly motivational at all. These mimic traits and are found in P, R and dR analyses. The state or mood factors in Table 6.1 are genuinely implicated in motivation. Those found through psychometric work with questionnaires are: anxiety, cortertia, exvia, independence, general depression and psychoticism. Work with physiological and T measures supports these and finds also, stress, fatigue, arousal regression and some minor depression factors as measured in the eight state battery. All these moods and states discovered by psychometrics are set out in Table 6.2.

TABLE 6.2
FINAL LIST OF MOODS AND STATES

Anxiety	Independence	Stress	Regression
Exvia	Depression (general)	Fatigue	Depression
Cortertia	Psychoticism	Arousal	Depression

THE PSYCHOLOGICAL IMPLICATIONS OF TABLE 6.2

These are the moods and states discovered by the proper application of multivariate analysis to the state sphere for which R analysis will not do. Just as was the case with abilities in Chapter 4 and temperamental traits in Chapter 5, so it is that one can claim these are the fundamental dimensions of moods, the essential moods. This is the substantive contribution that psychometrics has made to this aspect of personality. What then are the implications of Table 6.2?

(1) Since one can assume that moods and states affect behaviour, one can now argue that it is these factors that must be considered when one tries to weave moods and states into the understanding of behaviour. By utilizing these factors one must (from the nature of factor analysis) account for a major part of the variance.

(2) The question then becomes one of how these states can be woven into the specification equation. In Cattell and Kline (1977) we have argued that a modulation model will be necessary to fit the data as they are presently known. For this purpose a state liability trait has to be postulated (corresponding to each state) on which each person differs. This liability value has to be modulated in accord with the average stimulation of a given stimulus for a given state.

(3) The measurement of all possible stimuli has to be taken. While the stimulus value of a hungry killer whale is not in much doubt, in other spheres measurement is more difficult. The average sexual arousal value of a beautiful young film star is not meaningful, if some men are attracted and others not.

(4) In brief there are practical and theoretical problems in working these state factors into the specification equation. These however are due largely to the novelty of this type of research.

Drives

Since drives are inferences from patterns of behaviour, just as the notion of intelligence is inferred from the patterns of cognitive activity which can be observed, it is likely that multivariate analysis of drive-associated behaviour will clarify the picture. In the case of abilities, it was obvious that the factorial analysis of problem-solving activities would structure the field. In the matter of human temperament, the semantic personality sphere enabled the structure of traits to be discerned. With states and moods, P and dR techniques have been useful. For drives, therefore, it is necessary to sample "driven" behaviour. How this is to be done, in effect how the motivational sphere can be defined, must now be considered.

Definition of the Motivational Sphere

Cattell and his colleagues are the only research group who have attempted the factorial analysis of human dynamics on the rationale that has been given above, i.e. essentially that adopted in the study of ability and temperament. It is therefore their work that is considered in this and related sections. However, there have been other psychometric approaches to motivation and these are examined in later sections of this chapter. At present, however, I am forced to restrict myself to the studies of dynamics stemming from Cattell. Two recent publications Cattell and Child (1975) and Cattell and Kline (1977) contain full discussions of the research that is briefly scrutinized in this section.

Cattell (Cattell and Child, 1975) follows McDougall in recognizing for purposes of motivational measurement, three aspects of driven behaviour. The first is the tendency to attend to certain stimuli (cathexis, in psychoanalytic terms) in preference to others. Each drive, further, has its own characteristic emotion, e.g. fear or sexual arousal. Finally there is an impulse to a particular course of action. Of course this approach to motivation means that it is imperative to establish the proper number of drives. If this is not done, it is obviously impossible to study either the emotions or the goals.

Motivational structures are revealed in the study of attitudes. Attitude strength reflects the strength of an impulse to action in response to a stimulus. As Cattell and Child (1975) put it, attitudes can be best understood thus: "In these circumstances (stimulus) I (organism) want (need) so much (of a certain intensity) to do this (specific goal, response) with that (relevant object)". This definition fits the concept of motivation, previously discussed advocated by McDougall. With this model, Cattell has subjected measures of attitudes to factorial analysis.

Observant readers will have noticed that this approach to attitudes heavily involves what are usually referred to as interests. In Chapter 2 we saw that interest measurement has long been a focus of criterion-keyed test construction, work which is discussed later in this chapter. However clearly Cattell's model of attitudes implies that interests have to be measured.

Interests

First we shall examine the meaning of interests. It is possible to aruge as Kline (1975) did in his "Psychology of Vocational Guidance" that the concept of interest is otiose. Thus we only say that a person is interested in something as an inference from a particular pattern of behaviour: he spends time voluntarily on the subject of his interest, he knows a lot about it and devotes perhaps all his spare money on it. He probably talks frequently about it. There are two points about this argument. First, if to say that a person has an interest in X is a brief way of describing a whole series of behaviours relevant to X, then it is in fact a useful term: one no longer has to set out the full list. Secondly, it gives us an excellent—virtually a criterion set of objective measures of interest. If one wants to validate a test of interest in gardening the test should load up on these objective measures in a factor analysis.

Yes but, runs the obvious objection to this argument, if criterion measures are so easy to obtain, does one need tests? The answer to this, of course, is that in the actual application of interest tests in occupational psychology (see Chapter 8), one may wish to measure future interests as for example in vocational guidance. Here one may need measures of a different kind since for example, potential engineers may have had little or no experience of engineering.

Since interest is but a shorthand term embracing a criterion set of behaviours, as I have indicated, one obviously must include these at some stage in the study of interest measures. However such tests have problems. A man with a private income may spend more time and money on an interest than another who has less of each to spare but yet is in reality more interested. To overcome problems of this sort all scores have to be ipsatized i.e. expressed as a deviation from the subject's own mean. In this way the penniless man who spends his meagre all on cricket can be seen, correctly, as more interested than say, the rich amateur who can afford to indulge himself on cricket but who spends far more time, effort and money on his real interests, say horse racing and exploring. Similarly this ipsatization applies in the field of information. From the viewpoint of interest what is important is not the absolute level of information but what a subject knows most about, relative to the rest of his knowledge. Thus, Bertrand Russell and Galton, through the pervasive influence of gc, as discussed in Chapter 4, may know more about most subjects than most people, without being at all interested in the subjects. Ipsatization effectively rids us of the influence of g. The factor of analysis of ipsatized scores is most unlikely to yield, therefore, a g factor.

With these viewpoints about the measuring of interest, the nature of some criterion variables and the importance of ipsatization of scores in the study of interests, one is in a better position to study more closely the work on interests by Cattell.

Interest Strength

As I have argued, information, amount of time and effort spent on a subject all indicate strength of interest. However these are only a few of the interest measures that might be used. In fact Cattell and his colleagues searched the literature, especially the clinical work, looking for what was thought to be evidence of motivated behaviour and found in all, 68 different expressions, as set out in Cattell and Child (1975). These include, high level of information, perceptual skill (LBW is more easily perceived by cricket enthusiasts than others) better memory for preferred material and physiological indices, GSR, muscle tension and blood pressure.

Cattell (1957) in what is still one of the best discussions of this aspect of the psychometry of dynamics, administered a battery of such objective T tests to almost 400 male subjects. The tests were aimed at attitudes towards jobs and hobbies, and attitudes that were likely to have moral and unconscious components. Later research summarized by Cattell and Child (1975) has yielded similar results. From these studies seven primary motivation factors have been identified, regarded as factors of motivational strength.

DISCUSSION OF TABLE 6.3

From Table 6.3 one can say that psychometrics has revealed five clear factors, determining our strength of motivation, which can be thought of, at the gross level, in terms of two second-orders. The psychological implications of these findings must now be examined.

The first implication of these results is that the level of interest in anything depends upon our position on seven dimensions, although for all practical purposes one can ignore zeta and eta. Thus in the prediction of motivational strength one must have scores on all these factors. The measurement of interest therefore, by a single score cannot be correct—an inference which bodes ill for the value of most interest inventories. A single score will inevitably consist of

TABLE 6.3
MOTIVATIONAL STRENGTH FACTORS

Alpha	"Conscious id." The component related to the satisfaction of personal desires, even when one knows this is unwise. The factor implicated in the purchase of an unsuitable car—the foundation indeed of many an economy. Factor loadings: stated preferences, fluency on cues and rapid decisions.
Beta	Realized, integrated interest. Factor loadings: High information content, capacity to learn in the apposite interest area. This is the factor that governs our replies to careful questions about attitude; our reasoned responses to reality. In Freudian terms, this is the ego component.
Gamma	"Superego." Factor loadings: fantasy, conscious preference for an activity, lack of relevant information. Cattell and Child (1975) argue that this is the moral component in interest, hence the name superego. It is this component that compels the middle class to pretend to aesthetic interests, and which fills Glyndebourne with hampers and champagne and "in the room the women come and go talking of Michelangelo".
Delta	A physiological factor loading on blood pressure and PGR. This is the factor reflecting the autonomic response to stimuli, the thrilling sensation, for example to the lowest registers of the flute, or the lump in the throat on reading Dido's reproach to Aeneas.
Epsilon	Here is the factor relating to conflict, loading on PGR and poor memory for material and poverty of reminiscence. Such a factor is presumably implicated in word-association and the fact that blocking reflects problems, as psychoanalysts have long maintained.
Zeta Eta	Not yet identified.

Second-order strength of motivation factors:

(1) Integrated component: loads on beta and gamma, reflects reality oriented, information-based experience.
(2) Unintegrated component: loads on alpha, delta and epsilon, reflects spontaneous interests, below the level of our awareness.
(3) Unidentified component.

only one of these factors, some of them or all but in a crude mixture with random weighting. None of these could be highly valid.

In addition this multifactorial approach enables us to understand better the psychological nature of interest. To take for example, an interest in cars, an interest shared by many men, I shall relate it to this factorial model, for simplicity dealing only with the first three factors, ego id and superego. The car fanatic in whom the alpha component is the most important, will like sports cars or cars of immense luxury and power. The phallic symbolism of sports cars (usually red) is obvious and the surge of speed and power is symbolically in

Freudian terms, sexual intercourse. The identification with cars so that huge cars confer prestige is also clear. Fortunate indeed for the car industry that alpha component of interest exist, otherwise there would be but one or two mundane simple models for efficient transportation.

The car fanatic in whom the beta component predominates is the expert on the rational aspect of cars, engineering and specifications. He uses this interest in all probability as a means of life. He will be the dedicated engineer, reality-based, seeking to make a car an efficient machine. Contrast him with our man in whom gamma is most important. His interest will be in the value of cars to society, the production of the cheapest, simplest and least polluting form of transport. The designer of the Deux Cheveux was a gamma and beta man. The Ferrari is a product of the alpha and beta interest.

From the speculative analysis, included to *illustrate* what the psychological implications of these motivational components are, rather than as a definitive statement about interest in cars, one can see that equal degrees of interest can represent motives which are very different in psychological terms. Actually experimental study of the motivations behind the interest in cars could give effective insight into the components. Thus one might postulate that an interest in fast and powerful cars is related to aggression, a claim supported by the work of Willet (1964) who found that a high proportion of drivers convicted of serious (i.e. dangerous) driving offences had been previously convicted for violent crimes. Thus aggression may be a further determinant of interest, a factor likely to be implicated in the epsilon component.

I have not yet scrutinized the identification of the factors of motivational strength as ego, id and superego, referring to them merely by their alphabetic labels.

Eysenck (1974) in discussing my claim that these factors provide some support for Freud's tripartite division of the mind (Kline, 1972, 1973) has objected to their psychoanalytic nomenclature because it is misleading. For example, he argues, the essence of id is that it is unconscious, thus conscious id is a nonsense. While this is true, there are undoubtedly id-like elements in the alpha factor especially the feeling of "I desire", the irrational urge that one knows is stupid but yet often gives in to. Beta and gamma do resemble more closely the ego and superego of psychoanalysis but neither is so compelling in its similarity that one would be forced to adopt these titles. The point is, rather, as Cattell (1957) and Cattell and Child (1975) put it, that psychoanalysis is the only current theory which can even loosely accommodate these findings in Table 6.3. Delta and epsilon about which far too little is known, again support the general notions of psychoanalytic theory in that they strongly implicate factors below the level of our awareness.

At the second-order the two largest factors, the integrated and unintegrated components, do resemble to some extent the psychoanalytic notion of conscious and unconscious. However with so few factors, second-order rotation is not as accurate as is desirable and without further research one would be rash to discuss further the possible psychological meaning of these second-order factors.

CONCLUSIONS

The contribution to the understanding of motivational strength from psychometrics, while not completed is still important. Table 6.3 demonstrates convincingly that strength of interest is complex not simple (not univariate). This in itself is useful and can explain why such crude measuring devices as Gallup polls composed of simple stated preferences are so often wrong, especially when there are only small differences in the interests of the groups being sampled. Furthermore the factors so far identified indicate that the clinical depth psychological approach to motivation even if not correct in detail is correct in principle. There are factors involved in interest strength that one does not know of and that cannot be understood and measured except through multivariate psychometric techniques. Table 6.3 while imperfect, demonstrates that psychometrics will be able to provide a solid measurement base for a proper theory, a theory which will in all probability resemble psychoanalytic approaches but will be identical to none of them.

STRUCTURE OF INTERESTS

Another important aspect of personality dynamics lies in the study of drives. As indicated in the opening sections of this chapter, there seems to be fundamental disagreement among clinicians themselves and between clinicians, biologists and learning theorists, concerning the number and nature of human drives. I now examine what psychometrics has had to say about this.

The multivariate approach obviously requires one to sample as many and as diverse variables as possible. However the problem here is knowing what variables will reveal goals and drives.

As in the previous aspects of dynamics discussed in this chapter, the main research effort into dynamic structure has come from Cattell and his colleagues at Illinois, and I shall first briefly discuss the assumptions behind their choice of variables.

The main assumption, derivable from almost any of the clinical theories of motivation such as those of McDougall (1932) or Murray (1938) as well as from psychoanalytic approaches is that our drives are reflected in our interests, that ultimately various behaviours can be traced back to certain goals (one piece of behaviour perhaps being related to several goals). Thus one may buy an expensive suit, to impress one's colleagues, to make one feel more impressive, to please one's aesthetic sense, to please one's girl friend and so on. Each of these sub-goals is different and itself relates to further yet more remote goals. Finally there comes a time when no further goals are possible. Such goals, "to get food", "to get water", to enjoy sexual activity, to be warm, are regarded by Cattell as our basic drives: in his terminology ergs. In addition he postulates that certain goals are learned in a culture—drives which he calls sentiments. Thus, for example in our culture, sartorial interest can be said ultimately to reflect narcistic, sexual, self-assertive and self-sentiment goals.

Given this assumption Cattell and colleagues have subjected interests to factor analysis, arguing that the resulting structures represent the major human drives. The clinical assumptions discussed above have been elaborated into the *dynamic* lattice, a concept which is discussed while evaluating the contribution to psychological knowledge arising from this psychometric work.

Only two other sets of researches, those of Edwards (1959) resulting in the Edwards Personal Preference Schedule and the more recent work of Jackson (1967) which has spawned the Personality Research Form, have produced motivational factors which cannot be dismissed on technical grounds.

The EPPS was designed in part to eliminate the response set of social desirability by pairing statements, of equal social desirability from which subjects had to chose one. However as Heilbrun (1972) justly argues, so much attention was devoted to the elimination of response sets that the validity of the test which purports to measure 15 of Murray's manifest needs has never been properly demonstrated. Since in addition ipsative scoring is used, despite the considerable research with the EPPS, there are no grounds for including any of its variables as a contribution by psychometrics to motivation. In fact, Edwards assumed the validity of the Murray needs and aimed to measure them. This is particularly disappointing since by 1972, there were in Buros (1972) well over 1000 references to this test.

More recently (1967) Edwards has produced a new inventory which has abandoned the old item style for items of a more conventional kind which do not furthermore involve ipsative scoring. However there is little evidence for the validity of this test and the putative variables (53) no longer seem relevant to motivation so I shall not discuss it further.

The Jackson (1968) Personality Research Form in many respects resembles the EPPS in that it aims to measure Murray's (1938) needs, the latest version providing scales for 20 of them. It has been constructed with considerable psychometric expertise, as Anastasi (1972) points out. Thus 3000 items were tried out on 1000 college students. Items were retained if they correlated highly with their scale total and low with other scales. Items were assigned to parallel scales on the basis of precise matching of frequency of item endorsements and correlations as well as item content. All this is most impressive. However our own development of Ai3Q (Kline, 1971) and OOQ and OPQ (Kline and Storey, 1978) has forced us to conclude from studies of split samples that item indices are not as stable as is necessary for Jackson's procedures, to be entirely effective. Nevertheless there is no doubt that psychometrically the PRF is a fine test. Needless to say, in the light of Jackson's extensive research into response sets (Jackson and Messick, 1961) these are carefully controlled.

Despite these technical qualities, however, the validity studies of the PRF in the test manual are based upon self and peer ratings, with which the correlations are respectable. However these cannot be regarded as good evidence for the validity of these test variables as constructs. What is needed is some kind of external support for these needs, for example that entrepreneurs compared with controls were higher on need achievement but not on other needs. Thus I am forced to conclude that far more evidence concerning the validity of these variables is needed before the PRF factors could be considered as a substantive contribution to psychology. Nevertheless there is also no doubt that this is a test which deserves research. The variables need to be located in the personality and motivational spheres.

Recently Nesselroade and Baltes (1975) have examined the relation of the Cattell temperamental factors (in the HSPQ) to the PRF factors on a large sample of 1662 adolescents. Despite the fact that the PRF was not constructed by factor-analytic methods, it fell into eight neat factors—conscientiousness, ascendance, independence, aggression, aesthetic-intellectual orientation, social contact and one nameless factor. Support for the identification of these factors was given in a small-scale study by Stricker (1974) with 71 subjects. He found six factors which were descriptively in good agreement with the first six in the investigation by Nesselroade and Baltes (1975).

As regards locating these factors in the personality sphere, the evidence from this investigation is clear. There was substantial overlap with the HSPQ factors. Since these are temperamental rather than dynamic, it suggests that PRF is not a measure of motivation alone. Thus of the HSPQ factors, only B (cognitive, intelligence), C, O and Q4 had no significant correlations with any of the PRF factors. Similarly, of the PRF scales only abasement, change, sentience, social recognition and understanding failed to correlate with the HSPQ. Of the factors, four of the PRF factors were substantially similar to those of Cattell—ascendence (to exvia), infantile control (to superego), aesthetic orientation (to cortertia) and independence (to avoidance of social contact).

Two conclusions can be drawn from this carefully conducted and adequately sampled investigation. First the PRF is not wholly a motivational test: to a large extent it clearly measures temperamental traits. Secondly it is essential that the PRF be factored with Cattell's dynamic test the MAT. If this were done one could then see what independent scales remained in the PRF. As it stands however, I should not be willing to put forward the PRF variables as substantive psychological constructs.

Finally to link up with the next section on standard interest tests a research by Siess and Jackson (1970) merits discussion. This research correlated the PRF factors to the occupational scores of the Strong Interest Blank. Generally the results were sensible, for example office workers' and accountants' scales were correlated with conscientiousness. Aggression was related to the Army officers' scale. This is some support for the identification of the PRF factors. However I must still conclude that the PRF unquestionably overlaps the temperamental sphere as mapped by Cattell and in all probability the motivational sphere as measured by the MAT.

Standard Interest Inventories

At this juncture I shall briefly mention what many psychologists still regard as the only psychometric approach to motivation—the standard interest tests used in vocational guidance and selection especially in America, namely the Strong Interest Blank (Strong, *et al.*, 1971) and the various Kuder Preference Tests (Kuder, 1970).

Where I discussed the various methods of test construction I pointed out that tests such as these two developed by the criterion-keyed method, even if apparently valuable practically, in as much as they could discriminate various occupational groups, had no necessary psychological meaning, unlike factored tests. Thus one group is likely to differ from another on a variety of variables, and criterion-keyed tests which discriminate well, will probably pick up a hodge-podge of these variables. Indeed a criterion-keyed test that happened to be factorially pure would not be highly discriminating. Work with factored tests indicates, as would be expected, that for good discrimination a profile of factor scores (i.e. from many factors) is best. Thus criterion-keyed tests will only provide substantive psychological knowledge (as distinct from pragmatic discrimination) by chance. Studies of interest inventories have failed to indicate that any important psychological variables are measured by them (see, for example, Dolliver, 1969).

Actually as Kline (1975) pointed out in an extended discussion of the value of interest tests in vocational guidance, the use of such criterion-keyed tests can be regarded as *hindering* psychological knowledge. Thus for a sound understanding of the determinants of occupational success and happiness, one ought to know what are the psychological characteristics important in various occupations. The use of factored tests with variables that had psychological meaning would enable this to be discovered. However, the use of the admittedly effective criterion-keyed tests prevents the accumulation of the necessary data.

These arguments mean that neither the Strong Interest Blank or the Kuder tests could provide substantive psychological knowledge. In reality they are not measures of interest: they are measures of how closely subjects resemble criterion groups in terms of responses to certain sets of items.

Holland has constructed an interest test, the Vocational Preference Inventory (Holland, 1965) which attempts to classify people into types, according to which of their interests are paramount. Six types can be classified—realistic, intellectual, social, conventional, enterprising and artistic. The items consist of job titles to which subjects have to indicate preference. Although there is some evidence that (as one would expect) scores are correlated with type of job, there is almost no support for the validity of these scores as basic interests which could correlate with a large number of external criteria. I have no reason to include these variables in any list of substantive findings about human motivation.

Owing to the demands of professional psychologists for tests of interests that can be used in vocational guidance and selection, a large number of interest tests have been developed. None of them, however, for reasons similar to those elaborated above, in relation to the Strong and Kuder tests, is capable of providing clear findings of psychological interest and I do not intend to discuss them further. Readers who desire to know more of the instruments should consult Buros (1972) for a full and up to date list or Kline (1975) where many of them are carefully examined.

From my scrutiny of the most important psychometric interest tests it appears to be the case that in principle only the work of Cattell and his colleagues is able to provide substantive knowledge about human motivation, and the structure of drives.

As I have previously indicated the rationale of Cattell's studies of dynamic structure rests upon the factorial analysis of objective T measures of interest. Objective T tests, as described in the compendium of Cattell and Warburton (1967) are usually brief samples of behaviour which can be objectively scored and of which the real purpose is hidden from the subject. However some forms of objective test are of the paper and pencil variety and thus fall entirely under the heading of psychometric tests. The results of the studies of dynamic structure set out in Table 6.4 are based on a large number of factor analyses which have been summarized in Cattell and Child (1975). Before discussing the psychological import of the factors, a few further points must be made.

An erg is defined (Cattell, 1957): "an innate reactive tendency, the behaviours of which are directed towards and cease at a particular consummatory goal activity". An erg, therefore, must resemble mammalian drives, as postulated in zoology. However, as shall be seen, other drive patterns have been identified in these factor analyses which are clearly different from ergs. These, Cattell (1957) has called sentiments, defined by Cattell and Child (1975): "Dynamic structures visible as common reaction-patterns to persons, objects or social institutions and upon which all people seem to have some degree of endowment". Sentiments may be thought of as culturally moulded drives: making money would be a European example. In the dynamic lattice sentiments take an intermediate position between attitude and final goal.

DISCUSSION OF TABLE 6.4

Section 4 of Table 6.4 which indicates that various interests form separate clusters merits little discussion. It fits the *a priori* interest categories of all the standard interest tests and demonstrates no more than that such interests in our culture reflect particular occupations and hobbies which tend to be separate for reasons of time, if nothing else. Clearly such interests are sentiments and culturally moulded by the particular environment. In the dynamic lattice they will be very close to the observed attitudes and will be subsumed by more fundamental sentiments and ergs. The practical value of such interest factors is probably best realized in the rather specific area of vocational guidance and selection.

Section 1 indicates that 10 basic ergs have been found to account for the motivation of man. The first point of interest here is the number. If psychometrists were followers of McDougall (1932) or Murray (1938) they should be surprised how few ergs have appeared. Both these writers have listed

TABLE 6.4
LIST OF ERGS AND SENTIMENTS

---

(1) Well-defined ergs with clear tests

Food-seeking	Escape to security
Mating	Self-assertion
Gregariousness	Narcistic sex
Parental pity	Pugnacity
Exploration	Acquistiveness

(2) Factors where more evidence is needed

Appeal	Rest-seeking
Constructiveness	Self-abasement
Laughter	Disgust

(3) Sentiments

Career	Parental family	Wife or sweetheart
Self-sentiment	Superego	Religion

(4) Sentiments (interests), isolated by factor analysis:
Sport, mechanical, scientific, business, clerical, aesthetic, outdoor, thinking, philosophical, patriotic, sedentary, travel, education, home decorating, domestic news, clothes, pets, alcohol and hobbies

---

far more. Freudians on the other hand, would consider the list too long: eros and thanatos, or in an earlier formulation, sex and aggression, with the sexual factor as the more important, would have been expected. Thus in respect of the number of drives, or dynamic traits, factorial analysis makes it plain that these early clinical theorists were wrong.

If one examines the factor loadings of some of these ergs, some theoretical positions are confirmed. Thus the sex erg loads on sexual satisfaction, smoking, drinking and music. This is striking confirmation for the Freudian concept of sexuality which of course embraces (Freud, 1905) the wider concept of pregenital erotism. Thus smoking and drinking would be examples of oral erotism while music, "the food of love" is considered to be a sublimation of the sexual drive. Similarly the narcism factor, self-directed sexuality or sensuality, is also stressed on psychoanalysis where narcism is the infantile precursor of object-directed love, and one which is never entirely abandoned. This factor is negatively correlated with superego which again fits the Freudian theory since such primitive aspects of sexuality would be expected to be accompanied by guilt.

Study of section 3, wherein are found the most important cultural sub-goals—the sentiments—is interesting for two reasons. First the fact that wife and sweetheart sentiment is different from the sex drive, is one that makes it reasonable that the restriction of sex to marriage is universally so difficult. The superego and self-sentiment factors are important also, first because these have been so strongly emphasized in the work of McDougall (1932) and also because it is to be noted that these dynamic factors also appear as temperamental traits (see Table 5.1). These last two points will be fully discussed below when I come to evaluate the contribution made by this table to substantive psychological knowledge.

In summarizing the discussion of Table 6.4, first, this is a full list of factors but there exists only good measuring instruments for sections 1 and 3. These are the factors about which one can feel confident. The ten ergs and six sentiments demonstrate that as regards number of drives, the clinical theorists were wrong. Qualitatively their emphasis on and description of the sex drive, and of the self-sentiment and superego is supported. There are more tendentious problems of the empirical relationships between these factors and their validity to be examined. The theoretical implications of the findings will be discussed in Chapter 11. These comments will be restricted to the best known factors in sections 1 and 3 of Table 6.4.

Since it is not self-evident that the analysis of attitudes will reveal drives as distinct from traits, one must first consider the evidence for the validity of these scores. In assessing validity, the distinction between P and R factor analysis needs to be borne in mind. R analysis refers to the factoring of variables so that the factors represent dimensions accounting for correlations between these. P analysis refers to the factoring of an individual's scores across occasions. Resulting factors, therefore, represent dimensions idiosyncratic to him. The importance of this distinction in respect to the validity of ergs and sentiments resides in a possibility that I have already mentioned in the brief introduction to Cattell's work on dynamic structure. Thus there is the possibility that for some individuals the sex drive, for example, might be expressed through dancing, while for others it could be expressed through attending poetry recitals. Certainly such individual differences in the expression of factors have been noted in the realm of physiological psychology, in the case of physiological indices of autonomic activity (Lacey, 1967). Such differences might well present problems in the R analysis of variables with a large number of subjects. P analysis, where each individual is separately scrutinized, overcomes this difficulty. Comparison of P and R factors quickly reveals whether such a problem exists.

Cattell and Cross (1952) in a much quoted study gave objective tests of ergs and sentiments every day to one student over a period of approx. 80 days. This student also kept a diary, and the peaks and troughs of the various scores were related to diary events. This investigation produced good evidence for the validity of some of the factors. Thus during the period when the student was taking part in a play, there was a large upsurge in the Narcism sentiment, the rise in the sex erg was related to an increase in dating noted in the diary and the protective erg rose when his father had an accident. This evidence certainly confirms the validity of the scales although obviously data from one subject (an inherent disadvantage with P techniques, as essentially this study is) cannot be conclusive. A further point that should be noted about this study is that it made use of individual, objective T tests, many of which require a psychological laboratory for administration.

Cattell *et al.* (1970) have developed for group testing a paper and pencil set of dynamic trait tests known as the Motivational Analysis Test (MAT) with its correspondingly high school version, the SMAT and junior version, CSMAT. Five ergs and five sentiments are measured—sex, assertion, fear, narcism and pugnacity (the ergs) together with self-sentiment, career, sweetheart–spouse, home–parental and superego sentiments. From this the integrated and unintegrated components of interest strength can be measured. Two studies using P technique have investigated the validity of the factors as measured by the MAT. The first by Kline and Grindley (1974) examined the daily responses to the MAT together with a diary of one female student over the month of February. As it turned out, this subject was highly volatile and there were large swings on almost all variables, which were remarkably related to the diary. Incidentally the test was not scored until the whole study was complete to avoid contamination of the diary by the scores.

Every weekend the fear erg rose. Every weekend the subject used to go off on a car journey with her boyfriend—a dangerous driver of an unsafe car. Regularly on Tuesdays the subject's self-assertion rose—when she attended a weekly seminar when students had to argue a case against fierce opposition. Two further ergs deserve comment. The career erg was flat and low all the month except on one day when the subject was interviewed for a further course in teacher training. Finally a wonderful confirmation of the Oedipus complex. As our subject's sexual drive was reaching its highest point, she went out and purchased a jar of pickled eels as a present for her father.

As with the investigation by Cattell and Cross (1952) this research powerfully supports the validity of the ergs and sentiments, as measured by the MAT in this case. There are, however, obvious objections to this study. First it has to be admitted that the diary was unquantified. Possibly another investigator might not have made these apparently clear links between diary and scores. Perhaps more importantly, it can be argued that this was an isolated instance of a subject with great insight and literary ability. That among a gifted minority, such results are possible. Notice however that this argument by no means invalidates the results as confirmatory of the MAT ergs and sentiments. It rather attacks the methods of this research as being generally unsuitable. A final objection is that the results were a statistical fluke.

I (Kline, 1978b) therefore carried out a further similar study using two more subjects, one male and one female over a 40 day period, to counteract these plausible objections. In neither case were the fluctuations in factor scores related to diary events. However in this experiment the diaries were far less interesting as personal documents and the scores fluctuated far less. For each individual separately the diary was objectively scored. For example, if feelings for their girl- or boyfriend were mentioned, a score of one for that day on the sweetheart sentiment was registered. Total scores for each factor based on the diary, were thus obtained. The MAT scores, and the MAT conflict scores derived from the difference between integrated and unintegrated components were subjected (separately for each subject) to a P factor analysis. In each individual the relation of the P factors to the objective indices from the diary was examined, but no significant findings emerged. However if I took a more subjective approach to the diary the P factors made sense. Thus in the case of the male subject, the first conflict P factor was the sex factor. At this time he was engaged but unable to have a full sexual relationship. The second home factor was also interesting because both parents of the subject had recently died. In the diary there were 12 references to home and it was obvious that the subject (not unexpectedly) mourned his parents and missed his home.

In the case of the second subject, the conflict factors again related well to the diary used subjectively. Here the home factor was important and the subject was from a family of ancient lineage which was proud of its background. Similarly the sweetheart-spouse conflict score reflected the disturbance, evident in the diary, caused by this second subject having recently broken off just such an intense relationship.

In conclusion this study generally supported the validity of the MAT, especially the conflict scores judged against diary records of life events, although in a far less spectacular manner than in the first study by Kline and Grindley (1974). It also supports the commonsense notion that in psychological research, diaries are only useful if written with considerable literary skill and insight.

There is some other evidence for the validity of the ergs and sentiments as measured by the MAT which has been extensively discussed by Cattell and Child (1975) and Cattell and Kline (1977) which I shall deal with briefly here. In the manual to the test Cattell *et al.* (1970) demonstrate test validity from correlations with the ergs and sentiments in the original basic research. This only demonstrates, of course, that the MAT works as intended by its authors—by no means evidence of validity. Furthermore all depends on the validity of these original investigations.

However as Cattell and Child (1975) make clear in their review, this original work (Cattell *et al.*, 1967, Cattell and Horn, 1963) demonstrated a clear and replicable factor structure of ergs and sentiments. There was no external evidence for their validity. Recently a number of studies have used experimental techniques to manipulate erg level, and it has been shown that ergic tension levels change as predicted. Thus fasting students showed changes in hunger measures (similar tests to those in the MAT) in a study by Cattell *et al.* (1972) and pornographic films produced differential changes in the integrated and unintegrated scores on the sex erg (Cattell *et al.*, 1972). This last finding is particularly interesting in the context of the tentative suggestion that the U and I components were the conscious and unconscious aspects (in the psychoanalytic sense) of motivation. These experimental studies do support the validity of the relevant ergs and taken in conjunction with the individual studies it is a reasonable case that Cattell has managed to define factorially some of the most important human drives. Yet further evidence for the validity of these ergs and sentiments can be derived from the scores of various occupational groups on the MAT. However, this evidence which is by no means clear cut (in respect of validity) is best discussed in the chapter on occupational psychology.

In conclusion although the evidence is by no means complete, these ergs and sentiments, in sections 1 and 3 of Table 6.4 can be regarded as valid. This means that psychometrics has been able to state what the main motivational drives are. This is in clear contradistruction to the descriptive, intuitive schemes of clinicians, among whom there was no agreement. However this achievement is not all that psychometrics can offer. The relation between the ergs and sentiments has been examined and in addition a theoretical account of the findings has been drawn up. These two aspects of the psychometric contribution to motivation will now be examined.

The Relation of Ergs and Sentiments

So far there is a paucity of data on the correlations between ergs and sentiments, and the higher-order factors derived from them. Cattell (1957) took subject mean values from three investigations of primary dynamic factors to higher-order analysis. Since this research has not been replicated and since the factors have not been externally validated (unlike the temperamental factors in Chapter 5) one has to be careful in assessing the psychological impact of the results. Six factors emerged; the largest, loading on fear, narcism self- and religious sentiment at one pole, and sex and self-assertion at the other, was interpreted as ergic inhibition versus ergic expression. The other factors were of less interest, two contrasted sports with mechanical interests, three could not be interpreted, four was related to career, five contrasted gregariousness and rest-seeking with curiosity and self-assertion, while six was concerned with fear and self-sentiment. This preliminary research is not particularly helpful in classifying what is obviously a highly complex field. Certainly no substantive implications can be drawn from the results.

Burdsall (1975) has provided some relevant evidence. He investigated second-order factors in the MAT in a sample of night students and airforce men. He also found six factors which however, bore little relation to those discussed above or to the hypotheses implicit in the nature of these ergs and sentiments. The factors, which were identified only from their loadings on the MAT variables and which had, therefore, no external referents, were: long-term growth, social values, masculinity, orientation to people, egocentricity and realized materialism.

Clearly there is considerable need for further investigations with large samples and utilizing factorial procedures in accord with the technical demands which are listed in Chapter 2, so that one can have confidence in the attainment of simple structure and the consequent psychological import of the results. As it stands I am forced to the position that the proper higher-order structure of dynamic traits is not known.

The Dynamic Lattice

Whereas the empirical structure of dynamic traits await full explication, in the dynamic lattice (Cattell, 1957) which has been previously mentioned, Cattell has hypothesized how these factors interrelate. The dynamic lattice is the complex network of paths by which we attain our goals. In effect the lattice is a flow chart from behaviour to near and more remote goals, from ergs to attitudes.

Indeed the dynamic lattice is only the explicit description in terms of operationally defined factors (ergs and sentiments) of the intuitive perceptions of clinical psychology. Many of the networks in the dynamic lattice would be unconscious, as of course psychoanalysis has stressed. What, hopefully, empirical work must do, is unravel the dynamic lattice. The kind of studies which have already been discussed, P technique work in conjunction with diaries (Kline and Grindley, 1974, Kline, 1977) needs to be carried out over longer periods, with more sophisticated analysis, and a wide variety of subjects. Then the dynamic lattice might take on an empirical rather than a speculative shape.

As can be seen the dynamic lattice is a formal attempt to relate attitudes to goals and sub-goals in advance of the evidence, although the observed dynamic structure of ergs and sentiments, the fact that it is as it is, supports the dynamic lattice in principle.

The next important issue with respect to the nature of ergs and sentiments is their relation to temperament—specifically those temperamental factors shown in Chapter 5 which were the most important dimensions of personality. From the *a priori* analysis of individual differences which I have adopted in this book, involving separate but not unconnected personality motivation and ability spheres, it is obvious that I should not expect high correlations between dynamic and temperamental traits.

However, consideration of the nature of dynamic and temperamental traits enables one to see that *some* correlations might be expected. Generally temperamental traits are broad. They are temperamental because they show themselves in a wide variety of situations. Dynamic factors are in the main more narrow or specific; an interest in moles or birds' eggs for example. Some dynamic factors however, such as self-sentiment or superego should also, like temperamental traits, be widely manifest. Indeed a truly broad dynamic factor such as self-sentiment might be effectively a temperamental trait. Thus not only might a few very broad dynamic traits perhaps manifest themselves as factors but in addition since temperamental traits are broad, there should be low correlations between a wide variety of dynamic and temperamental traits. One should not expect substantial correlations between one or two specific factors.

Cattell and Child (1975) have summarized all reputable results in their detailed survey of motivational factors. The results indicate that the arguments above are sound since virtually three-quarters of the correlations are non-significant. Furthermore almost all the significant correlations are small, except for those between the temperamental and dynamic factors, superego and self-sentiment. Indeed Cattell and Child (1975) argue that if one takes into account the fact that the MAT and I6PF are different types of test (objective test and questionnaire) the variables are probably identical.

Of course this finding is particularly interesting because it supports McDougall's (1932) concept of self-sentiment as the master sentiment around which the personality is organized. Generally however one can conclude that the temperamental and dynamic factors are indeed distinct, although two of them are so pervasive that they are temperamental traits as well—self-sentiment and superego.

Cattell (1957) and Cattell and Child (1975) have gone far beyond these factual results and their interpretation, which I would argue is the main contribution of psychometrics to the psychology of motivation. They have elaborated a dynamic calculus and specification equation in an attempt to predict behaviour quantitatively and in detail. However since these are to a large extent speculative and because they involve the integration of motivation, personality and ability factors, this topic is best left to the final chapter which examines future applications and theoretical implications.

Apart from the speculative theoretical aspects of the dynamic calculus (which is discussed later), the contribution to the psychology of motivation arising from the work of Cattell and his colleagues has been fully explored. This can be briefly summarized by pointing out that factors contributing to strength of interest and factors representing basic drives have been identified, factors moreover which have some evidence for validity and which relate satisfactorily to the temperamental factors previously discussed. Sections 1 and 3 therefore of Table 6.4 contain the variables that need to be investigated in the study of motivation.

As I have indicated the main contribution to the psychology of motivation (as regards psychometrics) has come from the work of Cattell. However there are some other findings of substantive value which must be examined. The first of these concerns the variable, Nach, need achievement. McClelland (1961) has carried out considerable research into achievement motivation, the need to achieve. Nach was originally utilized by Murray (1938) based upon the TAT responses of his Harvard undergraduate population in "Explorations in Personality". McClelland and his co-workers have even argued that achievement motivation is a major drive in high achieving societies. Their evidence was obtained from the analysis of art and literature at various periods of time in various cultures. More recently questionnaires have been developed to give a more objective measure of the variable (e.g. Lynn, 1969). Studies of this kind often compare entrepreneurs and executives and even in such non-Western cultures as India, need achievement would appear an important determinant of business behaviour (Hundal, 1970).

Given then, that need achievement is a variable of some discriminating power it is pertinent to enquire its fate in the Cattell system of ergs and sentiments, where it does not obviously appear. However achievement motivation is essentially a surface trait, ergs and sentiments are source traits. In other words Nach is a multifactorial variable loading on a mixture of ergs and sentiments of which, self-assertion, career, and self-sentiment are the most important. Need achievement in terms of the dynamic lattice enables us to express these drives and sentiments. Indeed this factorial complexity of Nach is implied in the recent paper by Fineman (1977) who showed that there is little agreement among currently used questionnaire measures of this variable—as is to be expected where there is a lack of factor homogeneity.

McClelland and his colleagues (McClelland *et al.*, 1953) have demonstrated how need achievement is fostered by particular social and family environment, but as Cattell and Kline (1977) argue, this fails to explain which of the source traits is in fact affected and by what. In other words, by using a surface trait such as need achievement, which is multifactorial, a great deal of precision is lost in the research. Certainly it is meaningful to talk of need achievement but far more precise to talk of its weighted components. I need hardly point out that need achievement is little more than a variant of an older concept: Adler's inferiority complex (e.g. 1929), the upward striving for superiority. In conclusion I should prefer to deal with need achievement in its component form, i.e. its basic ergic loadings (as described in Cattell and Child, 1975).

Finally there is G analysis, an approach especially suited to the statistical analysis of projective tests. Although there were no clear results to put in the table, as has been possible with the questionnaire and objective tests, there is much promise in the preliminary results.

G Analysis

In principle G analysis consists of the correlation between persons using dichotomous data by means of the G index (Holley and Guilford, 1964), Q factoring of the matrices of G indices to isolate groups, followed by the application of D estimates (Holley, 1973) to identify the variables discriminating the groups.

There are several reasons for advocating this method of G analysis. First there is now a large number of studies where validity figures in assigning subjects to groups approach 1, i.e. perfection. This has led Holley to argue that much of the failure to demonstrate the validity of projective tests can be attributed not to the tests but to the methods (i.e. not using G analysis), (Holley and Kline, 1976b). In fact G analysis has provided impressive discriminations, as set out in Table 6.5. This is not a complete list but a sample of some recent studies with different samples and tests (fully discussed in Chapter 9).

So far G analysis has not been relevant to motivation. However there is little doubt that its capabilities for handling dichotomous data and thus projective tests gives it a powerful capability. What would be required would be G analysis of the motivation relevant signs of the Rorschach and TAT for a first research probe. In my view G analysis must be a major line of approach in this field. It is pertinent to note that G analysis has been extended in scope, by Vegelius (1966) who has explored its mathematical qualities and proposed modified forms of it, and by Holley and Kline (1976a) in a version which allows trichotomous data to be handled. Furthermore various weighting systems have been developed to compare discrimination. A combination of projective tests, G analysis and MAT marker variables could prove powerful in elucidating human motivation.

TABLE 6.5

Author	Groups	Tests	Comments
Holley (1973)	Schizophrenics and depressives	Rorschach	3 separate studies
Hampson and Kline (1977)	Various offenders	TAT, HTP, family relations	Not all factors identical
Vegelius (1976)	Diabetic children	Rorschach (Penetration scores)	31 out of 32 correct in cross-validation
Schubo *et al.* (1975)	Schizophrenics, depressives, paranoids	Items from rating scales	83% correct placement on cross-validation

CONCLUSIONS

What are the substantive psychometric contributions to a knowledge of motivation? All answers are available in Tables 6.1–6.4. The most significant mood and state factors have been identified. A new concept of state-change factors has been discovered. The most important factors influencing strength of interest have been identified. The most important dynamic structure factors of ergs and sentiments have been discovered. Altogether these factors, once inserted into a specification equation with temperament and ability factors, can play an important part in predicting behaviour. These substantive findings as shown later, can be built into a theory of behaviour which is based upon replicable public observation. Finally a new and useful method of data analysis, G analysis, has been briefly introduced. If used in conjunction with the previous findings, G analysis could prove highly useful on the elaboration of knowledge of motivation.

SUMMARY

(1) Discussion of temperament and dynamics illustrated their differences and the distinction between them. Psychological theories of motivation were examined.
(2) The distinction between states and traits was discussed. Moods were scrutinized and logical measurement problems were examined relative to them.
(3) Mood and state factors were set out in Table 6.1. The new concept of state-change factors was introduced, and disctinctions between all these kinds of factors were elaborated. A final list of moods and states was set out in Table 6.2.
(4) Drives and the motivational sphere, were discussed. Interests were examined and the meaning of interest carefully analysed.
(5) The factored analyses of interest strength were discussed. Strength of interest factors were set out in Table 6.3 and their psychological implications were extended.

(6) Dynamic structure was discussed. Conventional motivation and interest tests were scrutinized.

(7) Cattell's work was then examined. In Table 6.4 a full list of ergs and sentiments (drives) is set out. These are discussed and their validity examined, together with their measuring instrument, the MAT.

(8) The relation of ergs and sentiments was discussed and the dynamic lattice was described in the context of motivational theories.

(9) The relation of Nach to Cattell's factors was described.

(10) Finally G analysis was described and put forward as a promising method for further psychometric study of motivation.

(11) Conclusions were drawn: Psychometrics has contributed to the knowledge of human motivation:

by setting out the most important mood and state factors and introducing the notion of state-change factors, see Tables 6.1 and 6.2.

by setting out the motivational strength factors, see Table 6.3.

by setting out the dynamic structure factors, see Table 6.4.

by developing a possible method, G analysis, especially suited to the study of motivation.

7

Psychometrics and Theories of Learning

THEORETICAL CONTRIBUTIONS

At first sight the contribution of psychometrics to theories of learning has been so slight that it is probably most accurately described as nil. However, recently Cattell and his colleagues have attempted to integrate into a theory of learning some of the factor-analytic findings which have been discussed in the previous chapters (Cattell and Child, 1975, Cattell and Kline, 1977). Eysenck (Eysenck, 1967b) has also made use of contributions from psychometric findings and theories of learning in his personality theory. In this chapter I shall discuss as the contribution to learning theory from psychometrics, two sets of hypotheses, concerning some mechanisms of learning. Unlike the contributions of the previous chapters, therefore, which were essentially empirical and factual, this contribution is theoretical.

Before examining these two sets of hypotheses which mainly arise from psychometric results, one further point needs expansion. It is sad that no greater efforts have been made, especially by the learning theorists themselves, to integrate psychometric findings into their work, for it is an obvious weakness that theories of learning essentially ignore individual differences. That is to say, the question of why one reinforcer is effective in one case and not another and why, in some, certain responses quickly extinguish and not in others, has not been clearly answered. Neither is it enough to argue with neat circularity that a reinforcer is only a reinforcer when it *does* increase the probability of response: this begs the question. From this it is obvious, I hope, that the two theoretical contributions are of considerable importance to psychological theory.

The Work of Cattell

Cattell (e.g. Cattell and Child, 1975) attempts to blend his factors into a special theory of learning—structured learning theory. This has been developed to account for the kind of learning which Cattell regards as most important in human affairs—integration learning—a topic which has not been much discussed in standard texts on learning.

What is integration learning? Cattell recognizes four different kinds of learning, of which two have been carefully researched especially among animals—classical conditioning (in Cattell's terminology, co-excitation learning) and operant conditioning (means–end learning). These are too well known even to the introductory student of psychology to demand further discussions. However, two further kinds of learning are distinguished and these are of the highest importance in understanding human behaviour.

There are integrative or integration learning, and ergic goal modification which refers to the acceptance of a modified goal or aim. This is the kind of learning referred to in psychoanalysis as sublimation: a girl through sublimated penis envy becomes a sculptor renowned for phallic-like creations.

Integration learning, however, aims to maximize satisfaction in terms of reduction in ergic tension. The point at issue here really concerns the nature of reinforcement. Cattell has never attempted to deny the importance of reinforcement as conceived in standard learning theory. Furthermore, reinforcement is seen, as Hull saw it, as drive reduction—ergic tension reduction. However, as I have demonstrated, we have more than one erg to be satisfied. Sometimes a response can satisfy not one but two ergs—in which case we should expect its rapid acquisition. Often however a response can satisfy one erg but frustrate another. Masturbation would be a good example of this since although it manifestly satisfies the sex erg it does so at the expense of the self-sentiment, in some young people at least. Thus if one were to work out the total ergic satisfaction to be derived from masturbation it would not be as great as might be expected. Integration learning is concerned with learning behaviours such that over all ergs, there is the maximum satisfaction, i.e. release of tension.

To ensure such maximal satisfaction over all ergs means, inevitably, that at some stage, a satisfaction of one drive has to be given up or inhibited for the sake of others—delayed gratification. The way this is done is through the development of two sentiments which are discussed in Chapter 6—the superego and self-sentiment. Through the satisfaction of these drives one can usually ensure maximum satisfaction of the other ergs and sentiments. It is noteworthy that the superego and self-sentiment are correlated because satisfaction of the superego is essential for maintaining the self-sentiment and similarly satisfying the self-sentiment is important for maintaining the superego.

What Erickson (1950) has referred to as the adolescent search for identity, is in the terms of this ergic tension, integration learning model, the attempt to fulfill the demands of the self-sentiment and superego. The young person has to discover for himself how, in the particular environment he finds himself in, he may best satisfy the master sentiment, by scholarship or by sport or both, or by financial success. For example, the good highly motivated student (I am ignoring for purposes of this example what is meant in ergic tension terms by highly motivated) works hard at his syllabus, thereby missing out on much social activity, sport and other youthful pursuits. This is because in part he sees himself as a successful academic performer. Therefore, not to study would damage his self-sentiment. The white faces of those who learned that they had failed the 11 + (Pedley, 1955) and the well-known phenomenon quoted by Freud (1900) of the examination dream, bear evidence of this. Ultimately however by successfully completing his studies, this student will then feel in a position to gratify these ergic drives that he has so long postponed.

This example, example, however, now raises another important point to which integration learning is highly relevant. Freud (1933) claimed that the purpose of psychoanalytic theory was to strengthen the ego. In that redolent phrase "where id was, there shall ego be" the therapeutic aim of psychoanalysis was encapsulated. However, as Fenichel (1945) makes clear in many cases of neurosis, the problem lies in the domination of the superego which is far too strict. The patient feels riddled with guilt. Thus in psychoanalytic theory, the superego does not merely delay gratification of ergic tension (notice that Freud was largely concerned with the sex and pugnacity ergs), it prevents it altogether or produces such strong feelings of guilt and anxiety if tension is released, that effectively no release is enjoyed. Here then integration learning seems to have occurred but such that the maximal release permitted by the self-sentiment and the superego is too small; the individual suffers. There is probably less ergic satisfaction than the simplistic satisfaction of one erg, regardless of all others. Even if one does not wish to accept the psychoanalytic interpretation of patients' behaviour, it is manifest in the clinic that patients are restricted in expression (e.g. the clinical descriptions of obsessionality and anxiety neurosis in Mayer-Gross *et al.*, 1967). Indeed the behaviour therapists who above all are opposed to psychoanalytic theory argue that patients' symptoms are learned maladaptive responses, although they make no use of the concept of integration learning relying rather on conditioning. The question, therefore, arises of how, not in detail but in principle, can the notion of integration learning account for these clinical behaviours which, as has been seen, almost all schools of therapy would agree, indicate some kind of maladaptive learning process.

Cattell (1965b) has attempted to answer this question of how integration learning can actually work to produce its various outcomes by developing *adjustment process analysis*. This, ultimately, may be quantified into the dynamic calculus. Adjustment process analysis supposes that a person X is stimulated with respect to drive A (sex). At the first decision point, (called a chiasm) he can either satisfy the drive, or see a way to a satisfaction that is currently barred, or remain unsatisfied. At the second chiasm he can break the barrier, fail to break the barrier or remain unsatisfied by retreat into fantasy (a procedure which presumably supports in this instance a huge pornography industry). If one follows to chiasm 3, the behaviour that has failed to break the barrier, this can be resolved by a decision to control the drive. This leads in turn to conflict and anxiety which in turn, leads to repression, which leads to symptom formation. At chiasm 3, however, instead of renunciation, the individual may lapse into pugnacity persistent because it will not lead to ergic satisfaction or he may give way to despair—the grief of unrequited love.

This adjustment process analysis is, of course, nothing more than an illustration of how the stimulation of a drive can lead to a variety of behaviours depending upon one's choice at any given time. However, its relevance to integration learning is that the influence of the superego and self-sentiment determines our choices.

Thus for example the young man with a very strong superego and a self-sentiment as a moral, loyal, God-fearing, pure person, on meeting a girl to whom he was powerfully attracted but who was engaged to his best friend would undergo a powerful frustration of his aroused sex drive. However, one can feel certain that he would not woo her away: he would try to control the drive and this would be likely to happen in similar instances with this particular individual. Thus, well-adapted integration learning depends upon what kind of superego and self-sentiment has been developed.

Although, as the chart depicting various adjustment processes in Cattell (1965) indicates, it is possible to illustrate a number of typical resolutions of drive conflict by this system, one must be aware that it is nothing more than an illustration. However, Cattell and Child (1975) have attempted to reduce the model to quantitative terms—with the multidimensional learning matrix calculation. This assumes that any given activity directed to a goal is likely to produce small changes in various personality trait factors. If, therefore, one knows how often an individual involves himself in such an activity (and if the effects are additive) then it is possible by matrix algebra to calculate all the learning changes. Since actual personality trait values can be experimentally supplied for various conditions this matrix algebra can set out the power of a given experience or condition to produce personality changes (different indeed from the intuitive guesses made on the basis of data from the psychoanalytic couch). The learning summary matrix model, as it has been called by Cattell and Child (1975) enables us to examine the effects of real-life events on personality. The example given in Cattell and Child (1975) shows the effects of different therapies and different drugs on two important personality factors, C and O, ego strength and guilt processes.

The summative learning effect of such experiences is easily recognized in everyday life. Thus the Oxford scholar has been made by regular examination success so confident in intellectual argument and debate, that he sometimes ends up talking nonsense on subjects on which he is entirely ignorant. Notice, too, that this summary matrix model enables simultaneous changes on many personality dimensions to be measured as in fact occurs in human behaviour. In this respect it is superior to simple reinforcement models where the frequency of a particular response is measured.

The kind of learning measured in the summary matrix model reflects changes in personality trait scores. If however one thinks of a human being developmentally, one can see that such learning procedures themselves produce the personality and motivational traits which have been discussed in previous chapters. This is to say that such factors are in part at least the product of our experiences.

This learning summary matrix model however can do more than explain changes in personality trait scores alone; as a function of learning it is also able to encompass the fact that learning experiences affect the way in which individuals combine their capacities (abilities, personality and motivational traits) in any given behaviour. This appears to be clearly the case, especially in the field of motivation and it is relevant to the Allportian notion (Allport, 1937) of functional autonomy. Thus for example Ernest Jones (1923) claimed that all collectors were anal erotic, i.e. what they collected were symbolic faeces. A child's interest in birds' eggs would be a clear illustration. The notion of functional autonomy, however, suggests that while the first inclination to collect may have been symptomatic of anality, once a good collection has been obtained, this becomes interesting *per se*, i.e. biological or scientific or even aesthetic interests maintain egg collecting. Since some readers may distruct both these explanations thus casting doubt on the claim that capacities are differently combined in the identical behaviours, an everyday example from school can be used. At the early stages bright children enjoy Latin or Greek because of the problem-solving aspects of the subject. However later, although these are still important (I remember having to render into Greek a letter to "The Times" beginning: "Sir, the sale of varnished kippers...") the literary and philosophical delights of the classics become more important. In terms of the tension reduction approach to reinforcement the examples illustrate how the same behaviours on the two occasions, reduce tension on different ergs.

Structured learning theory, however, (based upon the learning summary matrix model) does attempt not only to account for changes in trait scores but for the changes in the way the traits are combined as in the examples in the previous paragraph. To do this three vectors are employed in the model.

(1) The trait vector: T. This represents the changes in ability, personality and motivation factor scores. These are the changes in scores (and behaviour) which most learning theories seek to explain.

(2) The bearing vector: B. This represents the change in the bearing of traits upon any given action.

(3) The situation vector: S. This represents the changes in the emotive meaning of the situation, for the individual.

The trait vector T can be clearly quantified from the scores on the trait measures involved in the studies of ability, personality and motivation factors. The bearing and situation vectors however, are more difficult to assess. The B vector is measured by testing on two occasions, for example, before and after psychotherapy. The T vector is obviously reflected in the changes in scores between the two occasions. The B vector is measured by changes in factor loadings for each variable on the two occasions. Thus Cattell and Child (1975) cite an example where attitudes to psychology were examined in relation to a ten week psychology course. The fear erg increased its loading significantly on the second occasion, thus showing that fear of failure was playing a different part in organizing the behaviour compared with its original role. In studies of psychotherapeutic effectiveness one should hope to see C, ego strength loading more highly on our criterion behaviours and O rather more low than previously, thus indicating that the subjects were indeed combining their capacities differently—which is what the B vector is supposed to measure.

As regards the situation S vector, measurement here is more complex. Cattell and Child (1975) break down situations into two sets of stimuli—focal stimuli and ambient stimuli. The focal stimulus, as the name suggests, is what the individual concentrates his attention on while the ambient stimulus is its context. Thus, if a beautiful girl presents herself to a (masculine) gaze she can be said to be a focal stimulus. The ambient stimuli in this instance would be the place, the time and the relationship with the girl and so on.

Now the ambient stimulus modulates the level of states and dynamic traits and, as has been discussed in Chapters 5 and 6, each situation has a modulation index (which is the average excitatory power for an erg of any stimulus) and each person has a specific liability to a given emotion. Thus the situation or S vector describes how the ambient situation affects the psychological readiness of the individual.

Learning, therefore, in its widest sense, as conceptualized in structural learning theory involves changes in these three vectors, the bearing vector, the trait vector (which can be represented by L, the liability vector—for liability is a function of traits) and the situation vector. Structural learning theory is, therefore, a tri-vector description of the learning process.

This breakdown of the situation vector into the focal and ambient stimulus and the liability index for each individual, raises a practical problem which must be briefly discussed. How are these S vector values measured? What is needed is repeated measurement of traits under various specific conditions. When this is done both the L indices for subjects and the modulator values for each condition can be worked out. However, as must be obvious this would involve testing under an infinity of conditions. This would certainly require an enormous testing programme, even if by studies similar to those in the field of temperamental and dynamic traits one was able to utilize a properly sampled situational sphere. However this is simply a practical problem. With time, a huge collection of modulating indices for different stimuli could be collated.

It may have been noticed that the quantification of the S vector is highly relevant to the work of Mischel (1971) who has argued that personality is far more a function of the conditions we find ourselves in than of particular temperamental and dynamic traits which we may possess. If it turns out that the S vector is by much the most important of the three in understanding learning, the situationalist position will be vindicated. If, however, as I have argued and, as this tri-vector formulation of structural learning indicates, the other vectors are clearly important then situationalism will have to be abandoned.

The tri-vector structural learning theory attempts to explain in detail how integration learning, defined as learning aimed at maximizing reduction in ergic tension, comes about, and as I have argued, Cattell's operationally defined concept of integration learning is perhaps the main contribution of psychometrics to theories of learning.

In fact, Cattell and Child (1975) have set out what they call the ergic tension equation which states for a given individual what his ergic tension level is. By implication, of course, this leads us to see how it may be modified. This equation, therefore, can be regarded as the precise formulation of our discussion so far. It reads:

$$E_K = (S)[L] = (S_K + Z)[=(C + H + 1) + \{P_K - aG_K) + (N_K - b\overline{G}_K)\}]$$

$$\text{Appetitive state strength}$$
$$\text{Need strength}$$
$$\text{Resultant ergic tension}$$

The ergic tension is clearly the result of the provocation level of the ambient stimulus situation and the liability level of the particular person: thus $E_K = S.L$. However, as the equation indicates, both S and L being highly complex, can be further broken down. S_K is the stimulus strength of the ambient situation. Z is added on because if S_K falls to zero, ergic tension does not drop entirely away. A monk in his cell still experiences sexual tension. C represents the constitutional genetic component of a need, H, its modification through experience (patterns of reinforcement in terms of operant learning theories) and I, the special effects of the investment of the drive in the particular attitudes by which it is measured. Thus, as Cattell and Child (1975) point out, there will probably be differences if a similar quantum of ergic tension is invested in an attitude, in two people, one young, the other senile. The C is a constant to allow the possibility that appetitive and non-appetitive need strengths are differently affected by the ambient stimuli.

C has to be measured using the multiple analysis of variance techniques developed by Cattell (1970) for behavioural genetics or the methods in the Fisherian tradition, as described by Mather and Jinks (1971). H refers to the effect of environment on drive, hypotheses which psychoanalytic theories have made much of albeit in an unquantified way. At present studies of the effects of the environment on drives are not sufficiently advanced for any precise account to be given. However Bowlby's work on the infant–mother attachment (1969) certainly indicates that in *some* cases at least, interference with this relationship has powerful effects on the parental erg (virtually destroying it entirely). Later work both with young monkeys and human infants by Hinde in Cambridge (e.g. Hinde and Spencer-Booth, 1970) actually begins to point up the key feature in these results—the more disrupted the relationship, the more influential the effects, a finding which can accommodate the many contradictory results in this area (Rutter, 1972).

So far I have discussed the trait strength as it can be decomposed into its parts. However, as the ergic tension equation makes clear there is a second portion referring to appetitive state strength. P represents the physiological, hormonal state of the organism; low blood sugar, high adrenalin, low testosterone, K indicating the point P has reached since its last discharge. G is a statement of the amount of gratification in the same K period. The constant a is a scaling factor.

As the chapter on motivation clarifies, not all drives are basically biological in origin (as in hunger, thirst or sex). Some such as curiosity and gregariousness have a different biological basis. These are catered for in the ergic tension equation by N, a neural need which has to be from time to time discharged. G is written $\bar{G}$ because it refers to consummatory behaviour rather than physiological reduction.

Cattell and Child (1975) raise the question concerning this equation of whether increases in external stimulation act equally on the two components of need strength. As they point out this is unlikely. A highly sexed man will have his sex erg tension increased more by a beautiful woman than will a eunuch (whose sex drive has been rendered very low).

Again, as discussed in the chapter on motivation there is some empirical research evidence that in fact ergic tension is raised and lowered in ways suggested by the model. This means that integration learning, as I have argued, is a useful way of conceptualizing the effects of reinforcement; this is surely a worthy contribution to learning theory from psychometrics.

Work of Eysenck

In the "Biological Basis of Personality" Eysenck (1967), has dealt in the greatest detail with the psychology of, and hence to some extent the implication in learning, of the two factors which among normals are recognized in all systems (see Chapter 4) as the most important—extraversion and neuroticism or in the Cattell terminology, exvia and anxiety.

Consideration of the influences of these two factors on learning leaves the theorizing inevitably incomplete. There are more than two second-order factors, and the existence of the primary factors cannot be ignored. Furthermore, the Eysenckian formulation ignores, except in a general notion of drive, the motivational dynamic aspects of personality which, having regard to the previous description of integration learning and the ergic tension equation, is considered to be highly important.

However, since Eysenck and his colleagues have made enormous research efforts to tie these factors into orthodox, Hullian, classical learning theory of a Pavlovian rather than a Skinnerian kind, I shall examine the essentials of their theory.

In his study of learning theory and abnormal behaviour Jones (1960) argues that N, being essentially vulnerability to neurosis, carries with it the implication of low stress tolerance both physical and psychological. The high N scorer therefore would "be characterized by a high level of drive in avoidance situations". Furthermore, the old Yerkes-Dodson law of the curvilinear relation between N and achievement is invoked by Eysenck (1967) and Jones (1960): too little N, low drive produces poor performance as does high drive. The results of experimentation in this area, as Eysenck (1967) points out, are highly equivocal and many anomalous results demanding *post hoc* explanations have been noted. "Most of the studies are positive, many of them quite strikingly so; but there are always other studies which give negative results or which are at best inconclusive" (Eysenck, 1967, p. 49). Nevertheless Eysenck feels that the following points can be safely made. (1) It does appear that broadly emotion acts as a drive. (2) N, the personality factor, refers to the dimension of greater emotional arousability. (3) High emotionality produces high drive in emotive situations and (4) the emotions acting as drives can facilitate or hinder performance depending upon an interaction of: drive strength, task difficulty, stress experience, intelligence and extroversion etc. (5) As Eysenck argues, prediction cannot yet be made in the individual case without proper quantification which does not yet exist.

Before going on to see how extraversion is woven into a theoretical model of learning, a few comments on this use of the N factor are necessary.

First, the concept as N as a general drive is not supported by the factor-analytic evidence. In this connection one has to remember that Eysenck has not specifically factored the motivational sphere, N being a temperamental not a dynamic trait. In the analyses of dynamic traits, no general drive factor in fact appeared, as is suggested by Hull's work and by Eysenck's approach which is avowedly influenced by it. Indeed the only erg which descriptively at all resembled N as a drive was the fear erg. This, of course, is not necessarily to deny the importance of N or anxiety in learning, because as can be seen in the ergic tension equation, important for structural learning theory, temperamental traits do play a part, in the trait vector and in certain situations (perhaps indeed all) some may be highly important.

Since both Cattell and Eysenck are in full agreement as to the importance of this N factor (their disagreement concerns only its identification, see Chapter 5), it is interesting that it did not appear as one of the factors in both the dynamic and temperamental spheres, as did the self-sentiment and superego factors. To this extent, therefore, I am forced to argue that the factor-analytic evidence does not support this formulation of N as a drive factor.

The other closely related issue concerns the nature of reinforcement. One of the most neat aspects of structural learning theory was its conception of reinforcement in terms of total ergic reduction, on specific ergs and sentiments integrated by the self-sentiment and superego. Jones (1960) in his postulation of N as threat avoidance has considerably restricted the scope of reinforcement and in so doing has produced some extremely awkward problems. For the restriction of reinforcement to N tension reduction makes certain symptoms (such as phobias) and their resistance to extinction, difficut to account for, although recently Eysenck (1976) has attempted this with his somewhat *ad hoc* incubation theory (which is discussed in Chapter 9).

Conclusions, therefore, on this aspect of Eysenck's attempt to implicate N into a theory of learning are that the psychometric evidence does not support its conceptualization as a drive. However, this is not to doubt its influence on learning: of this there is little doubt. It would appear, however, that there is no need to postulate N as a drive. It can still be important as a personality trait, as indeed is the other great higher-order factor extraversion.

Extraversion and Learning

To understand clearly how Eysenck has implicated extraversion into learning (and indeed a huge variety of other behaviours) I first discuss two other concepts which in various forms have long been embedded in the history of psychology—excitation and inhibition.

Excitation. This is regarded by Eysenck (1967) as referring to cortical processes which facilitate learning, conditioning, memory, perception, discrimination, thinking and mental processes generally.

Inhibition. This has the opposite effect, reducing the efficiency of the cortex. These definitions are somewhat general, and much effort has been expended by psychologists in the pursuit of more precision. Eysenck (1967) tends to follow Hull's (1943) claims that reactive inhibition is dependent upon direct physiological inhibition of responses; he therefore subsumes under the notion of inhibition what is usually referred to as satiation.

Eysenck (1957) has tied in these two terms to personality in the following way. Individual differences can be found in the speed of the dissipation of inhibition. This was the individual differences postulate. In addition there was a typological postulate which claimed that subjects of slow excitatory potential and whose excitatory potentials are weak, are predisposed to develop extraverted behaviour patterns and hysterical neurotic disorders. Similarly subjects of quick excitatory potential which is strong are predisposed to introversion and dysthymia. A classification is also possible based upon reactive inhibition. Subjects whose inhibition is developed quickly, which is strong and which dissipates slowly, show the extroverted pattern: if inhibiion is slow to develop, is weak and dissipates quickly, the introverted pattern is evident.

As shown in the case of neuroticism, this fundamental dimension of personality was related to the experimental concept of emotion and drive. In the two postulates described above, the dimension extraversion–introversion is related to fatigue. Emotion is vague, too vague to be scientifically satisfactory but fatigue, as Eysenck (1967) argues, is if anything worse, since the fatigue to which extraversion is referred is *psychical* not physical fatigue. What this means in terms of psychology is that, just as the high N scorer seems highly emotional and is in specified circumstances of high drive compared with the low N scorer, so the high E scorer, the extravert, behaves as a fatigued person, vis-à-vis, the introverted low scorer.

Given this theoretical underpinning, it is obvious that performance of extraverts and introverts on tasks of any duration and requiring vigilance, for example, would be expected to differ, as inhibition and excitation builds up and dissipates. There would be differences at the beginning, in the middle and at the end, and there is much experimental support of these contentions summarized in Eysenck (1967 and 1970). Gray (1964, 1967) in work that is still more speculative than factual has attempted to identify the E factor with the strong–weak nervous system dimension of Teplov (itself derived ultimately from Pavlov) and in Gray (1967), with the equilibrium dynamism dimension of Neblytsyn. Frigon (1976) too presents evidence that the dimension of extraversion–introversion can be identified with the Russian concept of strength of the nervous system. Given then that the extraversion–introversion factor seems to subsume behaviours which previously have been seen by different investigators as related to excitation–inhibition of the C.N.S. (albeit under different names), it is clearly implicated in learning. The question to be considered is in what way this involvement occurs.

Eysenck (1957) argued that a good test of this theoretical position discussed above, lies in conditioning. Introverts would be expected to condition more quickly (and the responses would be more resistant to extinction) than extraverts—a prediction based upon Pavlov's work. Eysenck is thus allowing an identity between his and the Pavlovian concept. Utilizing the postulates concerned with inhibition Eysenck argued that the extravert–introvert difference would be most sharp when the experimental conditions were designed to maximize the build-up of inhibition. In summarizing the results of empirical studies of this issue, Eysenck (1967) argues that it is well supported where the experiments were properly designed to produce inhibition. Where this is not the case the extravert–introvert differences disappear. Even if this is so the objection to this aspect of theory that was first made by Vernon (1964) still holds—namely, that to be confirmed, this theory demands that conditionability be shown to be unitary. Thus the experimental evidence concerns mainly only three responses—verbal conditioning, GSR and eyeblink conditioning. It could be the case that some conditioned responses are affected by inhibitory processes as the theory, demands, but not all. Until a factor analysis of conditioned responses indicates a general conditionability factor, the theory remains weak. This is particularly so in the light of the work done on autonomic nervous system indices—GSR, heart rate and the like— by Lacey (1967) who found that some individuals responded on one index, others on another. It may be so with conditional responses.

At best I can argue, although even here there is some dispute, that, conditioning (one form of learning) some response is tied in to the psychometric dimension of extraversion (and it should be noted that subjects for the theoretical experimental studies are selected by psychometric measures of extraversion). However, work has been carried out on other forms of learning and this must be briefly discussed.

Extraversion and Learning

This is a brief discussion because as Eysenck (1967) claims, the results of the research into this topic, although demonstrating *some* kind of link between extraversion and learning are equivocal. As was the case with the studies of conditioning examined in the previous section, it is evident that the precise experimental conditions are highly important, powerfully affecting the results. This makes clear statements of the relationship between extraversion and learning impossible. Furthermore, and of greater significance for this subject, it makes generalization from the laboratory experiments to real life learning situations hazardous. However, by remarkable agility and considerable *post hoc* explanations of the results (techniques which Eysenck (1967) does not seek to disguise) the results can be fitted into the theoretical framework linking poor learning to cortical inhibition. However, such theorizing is tenuous and so far even now there is no rigorous experimental evidence to support these hypotheses.

One study quoted by Eysenck (1967), i.e. Jensen (1964) is of especial interest, because the work has recently been followed up in part, thus casting light on the interpretation of the original findings. In this research Jensen submitted to rotated factor analysis, measures of learning and scores on the Maudsley and Eysenck Personality Inventories. At the third-order a factor emerged loading on rapid completion of Raven's Matrices (a performance task) and good performance on learning tasks such as freedom from error in trigram learning and delayed digit span. Several points about this study are necessary. First, the learning tasks are very different from those in real life, so that generalizing to other learning may be inappropriate. Secondly, to what extent the factor is one of performance rather than learning is arguable, although the loading on the retroactive interference scores probably support its identification as learning. Finally it could be argued, for power is highly correlated with speed (Vernon, 1950) on the matrices that this third-order factor is nothing but an intelligence factor, the ubiquitous g. This interpretation would fit both the learning task and the Raven's Matrices loadings. However, as has been seen extraversion is independent of g, and it must be the case that the matrices loading represents speed in performance. However, as Eysenck (1967) fairly argues not all learning tasks loaded on this factor, although at the fourth-order there was a more general learning factor which loaded on extraversion. The evidence so far adduced would lead to the conclusion that extraversion was related to speed of completing tasks and short-term memory.

However, recently, Mohan and Kumar (1976) working in the University of Chandigarh have put this Eysenckian hypothesis of the build-up of inhibition differentially among introverts and extraverts to the test in a research that is relevant to the work of Jensen. Utilizing the Punjabi version of the EPI to select extravert and introvert groups, Mohan and Kumar (1976) examined their performance on the Raven's Matrices. It was found that extraverts started better than introverts but their performance gradually declined, whereas the introverts improved over the course of the test. Of course this research is relevant to performance rather than learning. Since, however, the earlier study by Jensen (1962) had indicated that matrices performance was related to the learning factor, it is possible to extrapolate these Indian results to learning tasks, of the kind examined by Jensen (and thus they are not necessarily relevant to real life learning). It would therefore appear that extraverts begin well but decline whereas introverts can keep relentlessly ploughing on, gradually improving.

Such findings as these are likely, at least in part, to account for small but significant correlation almost always found between academic success and introversion, research which is fully discussed in Chapter 8 on the contribution of psychometrics to educational psychology. In addition of course they would suggest that introverts and extraverts should adopt very different strategies when they require to learn material. The extraverts should utilize spaced practice of rather brief duration, while the introvert is best advised to work for long periods using massed practice. There would seem little doubt that the old-fashioned studies of the learning strategies as summarized by McGeoch (1942) for example, would yield far sharper results if subjects were classified along the extravert–introvert continuum. Furthermore, it is also possible to classify the materials to be learned into what is likely to produce inhibition, nonsense syllables and typical rote-learning tasks on the one hand, contrasted with meaningful and interesting passages. However, one does not want to make too much of this point since it should be obvious from the previous discussion on integration learning that motivational factors are highly important (the traits that make us feel some things are interesting, others not) in learning as are ability factors. No matter how long he perseveres the dim introvert will not master calculus. Some of these findings are relevant to occupational psychology, job selection and satisfaction, to say nothing of efficiency and safety which are examined further in Chapter 8.

Unfortunately most results in this area are confused both theoretically and empirically by a feature of learning discussed by Eysenck under the term consolidation theory (Eysenck, 1966), which attempts to describe the results of the inevitable interaction between the arousal produced by the stimuli to be learned and the consolidation of the memory trace. That there is such an interaction is strongly confirmed by the work of Kleinsmith and Kaplan (1963, 1964), both with words and nonsense syllables. They found that high arousal words were poorly recalled at first but after a week there was improvement, whereas the opposite was the case with low arousal stimuli.

Eysenck tries to tie in these results for predicting outcomes with extraverts and introverts in the learning situation. He writes "Stimulus produced arousal may be hypothesized to have similar effects to personality-associated states of excitation/arousal..." (Eysenck, 1967, p. 130). However, this statement is indicative of the problems and confusion of this aspect of Eysenck's theorizing. The critical words are excitation/arousal. As the theory has been developed up to this point excitation and arousal have been *separate*. Excitation–inhibition refers to the CNS and extraversion–introversion is the manifest behaviour claimed to be subsumed by it. Arousal refers to the ANS and neuroticism (emotionality) is the factor implicated here. These factors are orthogonal, as we have seen. Thus this linking of excitation and arousal is not permissible within the theory.

Indeed the invocation of consolidation theory, inhibition, arousal and the Yerkes-Dodson law makes the theorizing so complex that any given experimental results, as with Freudian theory, can be fitted in *post hoc*. So far the theory has been examined in some detail, that the theoretical difficulties and the problems of acquiring data that could refute it can be seen. Thus, attractive as Eysenck's approach to learning is, utilizing the concepts of N and E, it cannot be considered a truly useful theory. What is established however is that N and E do not affect learning in some way, a conclusion which could be certainly drawn from commonsense observation.

In fact, Reid (1960) in a study of the concepts of inhibition as utilized in the work of Pavlov, Hull and Eysenck has pointed out some even more fundamental problems in the theorizing of all these writers, difficulties, however, which most psychologists have chosen to ignore. A major problem lies in attempting to understand how conditioned inhibition can build up in the first place. For example, it was postulated that when involuntary rest pauses occur, reinforcement due to resting would generate conditioned inhibition. However, in eyeblink conditioning experiments such as Frank's there was no time for involuntary rest pauses so that it is not clear when and therefore how extinction could take place. Even worse, as Reid points out, Eysenck talks of Ir (Reactive Inhibition) being unreinforced and therefore being extinguished, where no involuntary rest pauses occur. However, since sIr (Conditioned Inhibition) is not a response in terms of the theory it can neither be extinguished or reinforced.

Two further points about the learning theory involved by Eysenck should be made. In the first place extinction can be thought of as learning the response of not responding. In which case inhibition would be expected to reach a point such that extinction never takes place. A more important argument has been made before in another context, namely, that it has never been demonstrated that conditionability is a unitary trait, as this theorizing demands: if the eyeblink conditions quickly in a subject, do all his responses thus condition? This seems to limit (until demonstrated) the theorizing: extrapolations should not be made as Eysenck has done to smoking (1965), crime (1964), politics (1954) or neurosis (1957). Reid makes the converse point. If Eysenck's theory were true one should expect far *greater* differences in learning than in fact appears to be the case between extraverts and introverts. Indeed it would affect all learning.

All these considerations force psychometrists to argue that this attempt by Eysenck to weave extraversion and neuroticism into a theory of learning is simply unsuccessful. To account for the experimental results which, as he admits, are closely bound up with the parameters of the experiment, the theorizing has become so complex that almost any result can be accounted for and in places, as Reid has shown, the theory has become incoherent.

CONCLUSIONS

In this chapter I have looked at two attempts to integrate the findings of psychometrics into theories of learning. In one respect there is complete agreement. There is no doubt that both have demonstrated the importance in human learning of the two largest second-order temperamental factors, N and E, exvia and anxiety.

Neither theory is entirely successful. Cattell's theory is more broad than Eysenck's and attempts to account for reinforcement, embracing both the dynamic and temperamental aspects of personality. However, in doing this it has avowedly become speculative and far in advance of experimental work. Eysenck's theory, as has been shown, does attempt to account for the evidence but nevertheless is not able to do so with consistency and simplicity. Both workers, however, have clearly demonstrated that an adequate theory of human learning must take into account individual differences of temperament and dynamics.

SUMMARY

(1) Two theories of learning which are based upon psychometric findings have been scrutinized—those of Cattell and Eysenck.

(2) Integration learning and its relation to reinforcement in the theory of Cattell, structured learning theory—was discussed.

(3) The APA chart, the multidimension learning matrix calculation, and a tri-vector learning model were all described.

(4) Finally a specification equation was outlined which quantifies the Cattellian structured learning theory.

(5) The learning theoretic approach of Eysenck was also examined and described.

(6) Various difficulties were discovered which tended to infirm its value: (a) there was no evidence that conditionability was a unitary trait, (b) basic inconsistencies within the theory itself were found, as discussed by Reid (1960).

(7) It was concluded that as yet more theoretical work is needed.

8

Psychometrics and Educational Psychology

In this chapter the term educational psychology refers to the whole gamut of psychological problems affecting education so that to some extent there will be an overlap with both clinical and industrial psychology. Indeed it would perhaps have been more logical to devote a single chapter to the contribution of psychometrics to applied psychology. However, this would have had to have been broken down into subsections on clinical educational and industrial psychology for reasons of length and because the core of these subjects is sufficiently separate to make the discussion possible. Nevertheless the scope of educational psychology is wide.

THE SCOPE OF EDUCATIONAL PSYCHOLOGY

For the purposes of assessing the contribution of psychometrics the discussions are confined to five areas within educational psychology, of which one impinges strongly on the industrial field.

Diagnosis and Treatment of Educational Difficulties

Children presenting behavioural and/or learning difficulties in the classroom are referred to educational psychologists. These omniscients are expected to diagnose the problems and treat them. Although learning difficulties and behaviour problems are frequently interlinked, it is a reasonable categorization to separate the two. Some children have learning problems due to low intelligence or brain damage without necessarily being a nuisance to teachers. Some very bright children disrupt classrooms. Thus, it is reasonable to argue that educational psychology is concerned with (a) behavioural problems and (b) learning problems, both in their exact description (diagnosis) and far more important, their treatment. The contribution of psychometrics to these two areas of educational psychology forms one section of this chapter. It should be noted that this aspect of educational psychology is hard to distinguish, in essence, from clinical psychology.

Allocation of Children to their Proper Educational Level: Assessment of abilities

This is the side of educational psychology which was once the whole. While it often forms part of the diagnostic procedures of the educational psychologist it is sufficiently complex and large to be a virtually separate category. Assessment of abilities is obviously essential in all educational selection procedures and often in vocational guidance. This is clearly the province of psychometrics and is indeed the field where many psychometric tests and methods were developed. The first section of this chapter is concerned with this aspect of educational psychology.

Vocational Guidance and Counselling

Although, in practice, this may be carried out by specialists rather than educational psychologists, it is clearly a branch of educational psychology. Here, in essence, as Rodger (1952) pointed out, one assesses people (far more than abilities) and jobs. This is an aspect of educational psychology which owes much to psychometrics and one which has much in common with industrial psychology.

Counselling is sometimes separated from vocational guidance referring to problems other than specifically vocational. As such it includes aspects of the first category of problems. Usually, however, counselling is devoted to the solution of children's personal problems and is, effectively, a part of clinical psychology.

Educational Psychology: Theory

This is the side of educational psychology which is the least developed. What is needed is a theoretical account of learning, as applied to school subjects and typical human learning processes. This, as has been seen in Chapter 7 on the contribution to learning theory of psychometrics, classical learning theories, derived in the main from experimental work with animals, are ill-equiped to do.

It is also necessary to develop a theory of instruction which would effectively enable psychologists to train teachers. Although efforts have been made in this area (Gagné, 1962 and Ausubel, 1963) this is a field in which far more research and theory construction is needed.

In this chapter the impact of psychometrics on learning and teaching theory is examined. This will largely consist of working out the implications of structured learning theory and certain parts of Eysenck's theorizing for educational psychology.

Developmental Theory

Psychological developmental theories are implicit in almost all educational practices. Curricula are designed putatively suited to children of particular age groups. Implicit in this is a theory that at such an age material of such and such a difficulty and of such and such a content is appropriate, whereas at both younger and older ages different materials are needed. In fact often obeisance (like most religious practices ritualistic rather than practical) is made to Piaget.

Obviously, a section of this chapter must be devoted to seeing to what extent psychometric tests have been able to help educational psychologists, set out at useful stages of development (a) of intellectual problem solving power, and (b) of interest which itself is likely (as seen in the chapters on personality and motivation) to be related to personality development.

These five areas do not necessarily represent the whole of educational psychology. However, there is little doubt that these categories embrace the most important aspects of it.

ASSESSMENT OF ABILITIES

This is *the* province of psychometrics. Much of the factual side of the subject has been fully covered in Chapter 4 on abilities which is of especial importance. Further factual material can be found in Chapters 5 and 6 on temperament and dynamics.

In this section I shall take the final lists of factors in the relevant chapters. There is no attempt to justify them. This is simply to try to show how tests of such factors can be used in educational psychology for educational selection purposes.

Educational Selection

The principles of educational selection which underlie this discusion are as follows. One assumes that for the various educational objectives certain psychological qualities are ideal or at least necessary. For example, for success in the sciences, I would argue, *a priori*, that high general ability and numerical ability together with reasonably high verbal ability were essential. In terms of personality an introverted, rather schizoid, independent but stable and non-psychotic temperament would be likely to be important. In respect of dynamic traits one should expect high self-sentiment and superego. The reasoning behind these claims is quite straightforward. Without high g and N and V it is simply impossible to do the work of a scientist. As Cattell and Kline (1977) have argued, for too long psychology has been the convalescent home for refugees from the rigours of the natural sciences. Good, if not outstanding, verbal ability is important if reports are to be adequately written. Prolixity and jargon are the mark of low V. Pascal once apologized for the length of one of his papers to the French Academy: he had not had time to make it short.

A scientist normally has to spend long periods alone in his laboratory or sitting in his office wrestling with models for encapsulating the results. This is not the work for extraverts and convivial cyclothymes, they like the noise and bustle of the market place. Independence is necessary because creative scientists need to hold their beliefs against current beliefs and opinions if they really think them false: witness Galileo. Stability is important because scientific endeavour may be long and unrewarding. Similarly psychotic tendencies may mean that theorizing gets out of control, by losing touch with data or reality. This point has been made by Storr (1976) in a study of creativity where he points out that had Newton or Einstein been psychotic their work would have been valueless. Finally, as has been pointed out in the discussion of integration learning, self-sentiment and superego are important in the maintenance of behaviour without immediate tension reducing characteristics. Furthermore, they ensure the high standards of honesty without which science would collapse. From this, therefore, it can be seen that it is possible (theoretically if not in practice) to specify the characteristics needed for educational success of various kinds.

The second principle related to this, and implicit in this approach, is the simple notion that psychological variables are most efficiently measured by tests unless there is clear evidence that this is not the case. Certainly all the research on interviewing has always demonstrated this simple but unpalatable fact. Vernon and Parry (1949), in their account of British War Office selection procedures make it quite clear that interviews are only of value in the assessment of variables for which no tests exist. By definition virtually no interview will be able to compete with the psychometric tests in the assessment of individuals for educational courses.

Finally there is a third principle which apparently contradicts the first, namely that in practice empirical findings should replace hypotheses concerning the psychological characteristics required for educational success. Thus scientists should be chosen according to the weighted variables that best predict success in science. The contradiction to the first principle is only apparent because this third constitutes its practical application.

From this discussion of the implicit assumptions behind the psychometric assessment of individuals for educational selection, the methods and hence the kind of substantive findings should become obvious. The contribution to this branch of educational psychology from psychometrics will essentially be a number of correlations or beta weights between predictions (psychological characteristics of individuals) and various kinds of academic success. Since this work is empirical and since over the years there have been countless investigations, a problem of interpreting the results arises. What, for example, should one make of the finding that H significantly correlated with French but not German 'O' level success (ro.21) as found by Rushton (1966)? In setting out the findings some integrating approach must be used or otherwise there will be an overwhelming confusion of atheoretical correlates of virtually no psychological significance. This is especially true since this branch of psychology has been the favourite area for research for generations of Ph.D. students in Education.

Table 8.1

This table sets out some typical findings which are the result of considerable selection from, and interpretation of this mass of research. The huge number of studies have overall employed an even larger number of predictor variables. However, from the analysis of the salient variables in ability, temperament and motivation it was demonstrated that most of the variance could be accounted for in terms of relatively few variables—the main factors can be found in the relevant tables of the chapters. Only results with these variables—which are of some psychological significance, will be considered.

A further problem resides in the statistical naivety of many of the published studies. Thus in many examples of this research there is earnest discussion of the meaning and implications of a significant correlation of 0·19. This ignores the distinction between statistical and psychological significance. Such a correlation leaves more than 96 % of the variance unexplained. Suppose the result had been reversed and only 4 % had been left unpredicted, this would have been abandoned as trivial.

A related difficulty with multivariate studies of this kind concerns the huge number of correlations. From so many, by definition, some will reach significance by chance. This again makes interpretation of small, albeit significant, correlations hazardous.

In evaluating investigations of selection for academic achievement where evidence of pass rates is presented, the base rate for the population must also be stated. If it is not, the meaning of the pass rate in respect of validity is uncertain. Brown (1976) has a good example, since the suicide rate among the general population is only around 0·05 %, any selection system must be better than 99·95 % accurate. Clearly this is highly unlikely, and any attempt to screen out potential suicides could worsen the situation.

Finally, a comment about the actual size of the correlations must be made. There is a tendency for correlations to shrink as the range of each variable is restricted. Indeed the correlation among children between height and age would be quite nullified if one computed the coefficient, using children born at 1700 hours on a certain Monday and 2200 hours that same evening. In many studies of academic achievement at a relatively high level, there is considerable homogeneity of intelligence thus leading to small correlations between intelligence and University degree class. If however the whole spread of intelligence test scores had been included in the research (which is in practice impossible, since few with low I.Q. attend university, at least in Great Britain, although the position may be different in the polytechnics), the correlation would be far larger. This attenuation of correlations through homogeneity of variance will occur with those variables which played explicitly or implicitly, some part of the constitution of the particular group.

Yet another factor reducing the size of obtained correlations, is the unreliability of most academic examinations, at least in Great Britain. Most public examinations consist of essays which are notoriously difficult to mark reliably, as was known at least forty years ago (Hartog and Rhodes, 1935), and fail to cover the whole curriculum. On another occasion the results could be different with different questions. All these points are elementary notions in educational measurement and have been fully discussed by Vernon (1950). Their relevance to Table 8 is that such unreliability reduces all correlations with academic success.

Attempts to correct correlations for both unreliability of variables and homogeneity of variance are not altogether trusted. It is one thing to know that an observed correlation is low due to essentially artefactual reasons which deserve pointing out in discussion, it is another to correct the figure and present that as the result. This is misleading.

Provenance of Table 8.1

Since there is so large a number of studies of which many are unsatisfactory, both in design and analysis, not to say interpretation, a simple averaging of all coefficients between two variables would be misleading. Ten bad studies should not be taken into account against one good one, although Ghiselli (1966) chose this method when trying to assess the best predictors of occupational success (work which is fully discussed in the section on the contribution of psychometrics to industrial psychology). Thus, I have simply quoted what seems to be the typical finding (except in the case of E and N where an average figure seemed useful). Where this has proved difficult as with some personality variables, where there are divergent results, it is brought out in the discussion of the table. In all cases the citations have depended on the *judgement* of what constitutes a typical *result* from well-conducted investigations. This table is therefore simply an illustration of the findings in this area. It sets out the correlations between academic success and the most important psychometric test variables.

Discussion of Table 8.1 and other Relevant Indices

The first horizontal row of the table is devoted to the most important ability variables. This is because (see Chapter 4) ability tests are essentially

TABLE 8.1

RELATION OF ACADEMIC SUCCESS TO PSYCHOMETRIC TEST VARIABLES

Variable	Primary school	Correlations and/or beta weights — Secondary school						Higher education	Source of research and comments
		Language		Maths		Stanford			
		r	β	r	β	r	β		
Ability sphere									Secondary School: 278 children in Cattell and Butcher's study (1968).
gc (including g)		0·40	0·09	0·45	0·13	0·43	0·08	235	
gf		0·37	0·11	0·45	0·19	0·44	0·14	181 (estimated)	
V		0·54	0·30	0·46	0·14	0·64	0·44		
N		0·35	0·08	0·50	0·30	0·39	0·10		
Fluency		0·46	0·19	0·38	0·05	0·41	0·06		
K		0·26	0·03	0·33	0·08	0·34	0·08		
Multiple correlation	0·60	0·64				0·68			

Variable	Pass/Fail	School achievement			Source of research and comments
		r	β	β	
Personality sphere					Secondary School: 310 children. From HSPQ manual. Only largest correlations shown. N.B. The high multiple r. Beta weights in the second column are from Cattell (1971). Results for E and N: These are averages from a large number of studies reported by Entwistle (1972) and Cattell (1973).
Anxiety Q₁ or N	−147	0·25			
	138 (U.S.A.)	−0·25			
Exvia Q₂, E		0·3	0·24	0·25	
Cattell's tests		0·35			
16 PF G	132				
HSPQ A		0·15	0·15	0·15	
CPQ F					
Q₂		0·30	0·21	0·20	
Multiple correlation		0·53	(without B)		

Personality sphere	As	0·185
Other	Om	0·173
tests	H	−159

DPI results from Hamilton (1970).

		Maths		Reading	
		I[a]	T[b]	I	T
Motivational sphere	Self-sentiment	32	24	41	24
	Superego	23	04	42	25
MAT	Self-assertion	27	23	27	15
	Fear	13	22	16	32
	Pugnacity	28	19	28	00
	Sex	42	30	43	22
	Narcism	24	18	31	22

Secondary school: 13-year-old students. Figures from Cattell et al. (1972), a decimal point should be inserted before all these figures.

[a] I is integrated.
[b] T is total.

constructed and validated (and the ability factors are certainly thus identified) against the very criterion of academic success. This part of the table is almost tautologous. If an intelligence test did not correlate with academic success, one should not regard it as a test of intelligence.

In terms of psychological knowledge, this section is of interest. The importance of the g factors is evident from the results. High general ability is useful for anything as the early studies by Terman and colleagues (1926) indicated. Indeed, the psychological implications of this section of Table 8.1 (namely the general significance of g) seem to have been recognized and taken into account in the education systems at school level of almost every country other than England and Wales. Only in these is specialization forced upon pupils, sometimes from the age of 15 years. Scotland, in common with the European continent, insists on a wider spread of studies.

It is also interesting to note the tendency for gf to be more important at the primary school age than later (Cattell, 1973), although this is not shown in this table. This is simply because in the early years learning basic literary and numeracy involves one's basic intellectual abilities. Later progress at school and in university depends partly on this gf but more on gc. If, for example, one has not invested fluid ability into French and German knowledge, performance at the school subjects will not be good. Raw intelligence can get one some way relying on contextual clues and on philological similarities between the languages and English, but clearly gc, in this example, becomes the more important.

Again as befits intuition and common sense, V, verbal ability, is important in verbal subjects, as N is in the sciences. These correlations between academic success and the main ability factors demonstrate (a) that to be highly proficient in the whole range of academic subjects, good endowment on g, V and N is essential, a finding that is not unexpected, and that (b) important as such endowment is, it is by no means the guarantee of academic success. As Warburton showed (1965) in his study of vicious criminals in Chicago, a high proportion were gifted intellectually, although of low academic attainment. In any case all teachers at every level know the bright student who achieves little and the relatively dim one who, by weary plodding, succeeds in the end.

It should be noted that any specialized ability factors have been omitted from the table because in this context they are not of great psychological interest. For example, to be told that high musical ability contributes to high performance in music (especially when musical tests are samples of musical skill) is not revealing. If it did not, it would have been included in the table. A similar argument applies to a whole variety of minor almost specific ability factors.

Although some of these correlations, especially at the tertiary level of education, may be lowered through homogeneity of variance, as the teaching example makes clear, the main reason why the correlations with ability are not higher is that factors of temperament and dynamics are also important in the determination of academic success. This, of course, has also been recognized by educators and they refer to the phenomenon as character. Having the right character, being a good chap, could do much, in the view of Britain's public schools, to compensate for possible intellectual deficits. Indeed many of these schools attempted to train character. Such a recognition of the influence of character or personality on performance is an example of what Cattell and Kline (1977) have referred to as pre-scientific notions of personality.

However, psychometrics has been able to identify what are the most important dimensions of individual differences in these two fields, and in the second and third rows of Table 8.1, the main results of the study of temperament, motivation and academic success, are set out. I shall examine the second row of the table, devoted to temperamental factors.

As demonstrated in Chapter 5 on temperament, the Cattell Personality factors, as quantified in the 16 PF represent most of the variance measured in other putatively different systems (notably, Eysenck, Guilford and Comrey). The miscellaneous personality factors at the bottom of this row are included so that factors, which are demonstratively different from those of Cattell, as are those in the DPI for example (Kline and Storey, 1978), but still correlate with academic success and which can be taken into account.

Before looking at the psychological significance of these results one further point must be remembered. It was argued in Chapter 5 that the two Eysenck factors, extraversion and neuroticism, were identical with the first orders of Cattell, exvia and anxiety. The findings in the table for anxiety and exvia are held to apply to Eysenck's E and N, without alteration. The difference between these factors, is one of nomenclature and interpretation, and not identification.

One of the problems in assessing the psychological significance of the results, and hence the psychometric contribution to knowledge, is that to some extent the results in the U.S.A. and Great Britian have been different. While this is not *a priori* evidence that the findings are trivial for the two educational systems *are* different, it is nevertheless surprising, especially since similar work in India, Uganda and Ghana, produces results consonant with those in Great Britain.

However, one set of results with young children at the primary school can be discussed because in this case the U.S. and British findings are in broad agreement. In second-order terms (these are the factors in the EPI) at the primary school, the extraverted, stable child does best.

Although the correlations with extraversion and stability at this level are not large, being in the order of 0·2 to 0·3, almost no results run contrary in either country to this result. Furthermore one of the surveys, by Eysenck and Cookson (1969), used a large sample (4000) so that the statistical reliability of the findings is well assured.

In the U.S.A., Sarason *et al.* (1960) found that anxiety produced poorer performance in school work as clinically oriented educational psychologists have always maintained. Schonell (1944) regarded anxiety as the main factor in educational backwardness. This claim has generally been supported by all this work although, in a small-scale study with primary school children, Savage (1966) reported a curvilinear relation between neuroticism and academic performance. As with the Yerkes-Dodson law there was an optimum level of neuroticism for academic success at the primary school: too little and the child did not worry about bad marks and trouble from teachers; too much, and anxiety crippled his performance.

In conclusion, with respect to the two most important second-order temperamental factors, it is possible to state clearly and unequivocally that the stable extravert is best in the primary school. To interpret the result seems relatively straightforward. Modern primary school methods encourage the active cheerful and sociable child. He flourishes in the lively atmosphere of a good primary school, especially where he can change his activity when he wishes, rather than at the end of a pre-set period. To be stable is, as common sense suggests, an advantage when performing difficult tasks. To be constantly worrying simply distracts the child from learning. These comments are designed to put the findings into a possible psychological perspective one may also conclude from these investigations that these temperamental factors are not highly important in academic achievement on their own.

As has been pointed out in Chapter 5 on human temperament, the second-order factors favoured on grounds of reliability by Eysenck hardly give sufficient information for any kind of psychological insights into these findings. It is therefore instructive to turn to the researches carried out with the Cattell tests, the CPQ, HSPQ and 16 PF. The question to be examined concerns the utility of the extra information from the CPQ.

Firstly, there is complete agreement at the second-order level, between the Eysenck and Cattell tests. Of the primary factors, G, conscientious, has the highest correlation, although this is small, around 0·2 and less than the correlation between academic success and fluid ability, gf (Cattell and Butcher, 1968, Barton *et al.*, 1971). Warburton (1968) in his survey of researchers with the Cattell factors supports these findings. In relation to E and N, the Cattell primaries do not yield any useful further information over and above the EPI. However, they do indicate that the persevering conscientious child is more successful.

At the primary school therefore the conclusions remain: the stable extravert has the advantage.

At the secondary school level, there is a problem. In Great Britian the results indicate that the neurotic introvert performs best, although, again, the correlations are small, about 0·2, meaning that only about 5 % of the variance has been explained. As the survey by Warburton (1968) shows, this change-over from the primary school pattern of stable extraversion seems to occur at 15-years-old.

In the U.S.A. the stable introvert is always better in academic performance at the secondary school level. Furthermore, as Cattell and Kline (1977) have argued when the Cattell HSPQ test is utilized in these studies, the extraversion primary factors act differently since $F+$ and Q_2+ are associated with good performance, as is $A-$. This means in the case of extraversion that the HSPQ is probably better in prediction than the simple second-order extraversion factors. This claim is substantiated by the results of Cattell and Butcher (1968) who found a multiple correlation between secondary school achievement and the HSPQ of 0·462. Thus the HSPQ at the secondary school level is a better predictor than the JEPI.

In the case of anxiety, the HSPQ and the JEPI produce very similar results and all the anxiety primaries act in the same direction so that as regards this factor there is no advantage with the somewhat cumbrous Cattell test.

Thus at the secondary school level there are two problems. First, one has to account for the different correlations with personality factors at the primary and secondary level. Secondly, one has to account for the differences in the results in the U.S.A. and Great Britain. Finally, however, one must bear in mind that these correlations are small.

Before attempting to answer these two questions one must first examine the results at the higher education level. Obviously, the answers would be different if it was found that at this age the correlations resembled those at the primary school, from what they would be if the correlations were quite unlike those at either primary or secondary level.

In the case of higher education once again one finds different results in the U.S.A. and Great Britain, although the discrepancy is not so large as it was at the secondary level. In the U.S.A. virtually all studies show that the successful student is the stable introvert but again the correlations are small, accounting for about 5 and 10% of the variance. In Great Britain introverts are always superior, although the largest correlation noted by Entwistle (1972) in his survey was only 0·26. As regards anxiety the findings are more equivocal: in some studies anxious students are better, in others, stable, although again correlations are small. This was especially so in the work of Saville and Blinkhorn (1976). Entwistle (1972) suggests that subject differences account for this. The stable introvert, the evidence indicates, is best at history and the natural sciences. The neurotic introvert at engineering and languages. Perhaps, as some confirmation of this interpretation, the findings of Kline and Gale (1971), which show that there was no correlation between performance in psychology and either E or N, as measured by the EPI are relevant because psychology is a social science. However this interpretation is not convincing. What do engineering and languages have in common, or history and natural sciences? An *a priori* analysis of these subjects would not have grouped them together.

One further set of results deserves mention before attempting to interpret the whole set of findings relating the main dimensions of temperament to academic success. These are the cross-cultural studies of this same phenomenon. It appears that in cultures quite different from the U.S.A. and Great Britain the same broad pattern can be found. Thus in Ghana, academic success (first year Science in the University) was correlated with neuroticism and introversion (Kline, 1966). Similar results are frequently found in India (e.g. Madan, 1967). In the case of secondary school pupils, I have obtained results in Uganda (Honess and Kline, 1974a) as in Great Britain. It should be pointed out in connection with the research in Ghana and Uganda that great care was taken to demonstrate that the tests were still valid in those cultures, the items being subjected to item analysis (Kline, 1967b, Honess and Kline, 1974b).

With all these results in mind, how can one answer the two questions which have been raised, and give some psychological coherence to the findings?

Changes in Results from Age-group to Age-group

Since there is no clear evidence that would enable one to avoid speculation in accounting for these changes, the discussion is brief. It does appear sensible to attribute the difference to the teaching methods employed in the primary school which would seem likely to encourage the outgoing, sociable and extraverted child. In contradistinction, the secondary schools and especially higher education utilize teaching methods much more suited to the introvert, with great reliance on books and on concentrated working sessions. At the secondary and higher levels the material and content dealt with is inevitably more detailed than earlier, again appealing to the introvert rather than the extravert.

Actually this analysis supports the Eysenckian notion (Eysenck, 1967) of extraversion being related to arousal and inhibition in the central nervous system. Thus the primary school child is allowed to work at his own pace and to change subjects, as he pleases. This is necessary for the stimulus hungry extravert if he is to avoid error. Similarly, the long lessons and lectures at the higher stages of education are fine for introverts but bad for extraverts (see Chapter 7). If this hypothesis is correct it follows that there are optimal strategies for teaching different kinds (in terms of the major personality dimensions) of pupils. An experiment is needed to examine the effects of different teaching procedures on extraverted and introverted pupils—at all age levels. Clearly interaction studies of classroom teacher pupil interaction are required here. If such hypotheses are supported this would explain why it has proved so difficult to describe any one ideal teaching method. There are serious implications for both teacher-training and, more important, for the education of pupils in these findings, if this interpretation of them is correct.

Differences in Results: U.S.A. and Great Britain

The most important difference here was at the secondary school level: in the U.S.A. the stable student was always best, in Great Britain the neurotic. Obviously the difference might be attributable to some educational or social factors (as yet unidentified). This possibility is made less likely by the cross-cultural results where a pattern similar to that of Britain was found in cultures far less like that of Britain and the U.S.A. In fact there does not appear to be a satisfactory explanation for this discrepancy.

Since the American results are consonant with the clinical appraisal of the effects of anxiety on performance and learning this discrepancy might be better termed, the pecularity of the British results. One possible explanation lies in the notion that anxiety causes individuals to work hard, unless it is so great as to be crippling. This hypothesis fails to explain the differences between the two cultures. Furthermore it predicts a U-shaped relation between anxiety and performance which is not generally found. In brief, there is no satisfactory account of this discrepancy.

Differences between the Correlation with Different Subjects in Higher Education

Here again psychometrists must admit defeat. Although as we shall see in the later section on the contribution of psychometrics to industrial psychology, it is clear that vocation and occupation are closely related to personality patterns, so that one should not be surprised that different personality variables are related to success in different disciplines. Any more precise statement than this cannot be made. For example, Cattell has shown that leading physicists are highly introverted (Cattell *et al.* 1970). However, as shown, introversion goes with all the university disciplines so that this is not useful. However, engineers are neurotic and physicists are not. This, as has been argued, was not and could not be predicted. *Post hoc* explanations are not convincing. This therefore is a subject which demands far more research, again of an observational kind to see, if it is possible, what elements in various subjects (characteristic teaching methods, content, laboratory hours) might appeal to those with the relevant temperamental endowment. Until the necessary research is carried out, it must be admitted that the differences between the correlations with different disciplines cannot be accounted for except speculatively.

CONCLUSIONS

Since this chapter is concerned with the substantive contribution from psychometrics to educational psychology, a few brief concluding comments will be useful:

(1) The first conclusion that can be drawn is that temperamental variables (at least those which are the most important in personality) contribute only a little to academic success. However this small contribution is the more valuable because it is distinct from that of the ability and motivational variables, (see later sections of Table 8.1).

(2) Despite the slight predictive power of these temperamental variables, a few clear psychological statements can be made.

(2a) Among younger, primary school children, it is advantageous to be extravert. This is most possibly due to modern primary teaching methods. Should primary school methods change and come to resemble more current secondary school practice, this slight advantage could be nullified or even reversed.

(2b) Among younger, primary school, children it is advantageous to be stable.

(2c) At the secondary and higher education level, the introverted student holds a slight advantage. This is almost a universal finding, even in non-western cultures. There would appear to be some common factor in the nature and content of secondary and higher education, depending on lectures, books and written examinations which give a slight advantage to introverts. As with finding 2b, this fits well with common sense.

(2d) At the higher and secondary stage of education the role of anxiety is still not clear. Most often it appears to hinder academic success, although some studies in Great Britian indicate that anxiety is an advantage. Careful observational studies of learning are needed to resolve this anomaly, to discover under what conditions it is advantageous to be neurotic and when not. More than classroom interaction studies are required here, although these are valuable. It will be necessary to find out just what anxious students do when they study on their own. Do they adopt more efficient learning procedures (see Howe, 1977) or do they just spend more time on their work.

(3) A final question is obviously raised by the conclusions outlined above. If the arguments are correct concerning the fundamental nature of the temperamental traits in Table 8.1, is it not surprising that the correlations with academic achievement are so small? The answer to this highly important point, for the value of the factor-analytically derived variables was claimed to be in their pervasive influence in many of behaviour is, complex. It is best left until the results in other sections of Table 8.1 (which will be implicated in the answer) have been scrutinized. However, it is admitted that the correlations are smaller than would be expected from the nature of these temperamental variables.

The other temperamental factors which have been shown to play some part in academic success, factors which are outside the dimensional systems of Cattell and Eysenck must now be examined.

Hamilton (1970) has reported an investigation of student success at University utilizing the DPI (Grygier, 1961), a test discussed in Chapter 5. Kline and Storey (1978) have demonstrated that the DPI factors are in the main, independent of those in the 16 PF test and the EPI, so that Hamilton's results demonstrate that yet further temperamental factors are associated with academic success. This claim that the DPI is useful (albeit in a small way) in the prediction of academic success at the tertiary level is further supported by the recent study by Stringer *et al.* (1977). However the correlations were difficult to interpret and were small but significant.

Unfortunately insufficient external evidence concerning the DPI factors is available to be able to identify what they measure (as distinct from what they do not) with any confidence. The research by Kline and Storey (1978) above atempts to validate the nature of these factors. As discussed on p. 145 the following factors could be identified in this test: an obsessional or anal factor, a masculine interest factor and a feminine interest factor. The other scales loaded on factors that could not be confidently labelled. This means that only those correlations with identified factors in Hamilton's study, can be interpreted.

Examination of the results in these investigations shows that as with the previous factors all obtained correlations were small although it should be noted that they were as large as that with AH5, the well-known intelligence test discussed in Chapter 4 on abilities. However, as was the case with the Cattell primary factors, there is no clear argument to account for the findings. Furthermore most of the discriminating scales were not those which loaded on the identified factors—making interpretation even more difficult. For example, successful students could be discriminated from failures in the investigation described in Hamilton (1968) on O_I, oral impulsivity and C_I, creative interests. Only *ad hoc* explanations could make psychological sense of this, especially since creative interests might be thought of as a disadvantage in typical university examinations. What is especially odd here is that this was true only of the Science faculty, not the Letters. The only conclusion therefore, that can be drawn from the DPI data is that here is yet further evidence for the implication (albeit a slight implication) of temperamental factors in academic performance.

To turn to the bottom row of Table 8.1, which is concerned with the relation of dynamic factors to academic success. Again, the discussion is restricted to the dimensions of most importance in Chapter 6. These are the ergs and sentiments, the dynamic motivational factors of the Cattell system. All the work, therefore, inevitably concerns the relation of the MAT and the SMAT to academic achievement.

Motivational Variables

In this area the amount of research is far less than was the case with the temperamental factors. The most important single study is by Cattell and Butcher (1968). The other researches have been fully described in Cattell and Child (1975) and this discussion is based upon these.

The first conclusion to be drawn from Cattell and Butcher's work is that among 13- and 14-year-old high school samples, motivational variables had little influence on academic attainment. The multiple correlation of the SMAT scales and success was only 0·164—less than 4% of the variance has been explained. This is not impressive and the only argument in favour of the SMAT as a predictor of academic attainment is that its predictive power is quite separate from that of the temperamental and ability variables. Thus the multiple r with MAT and HSPQ is 0·449 and with I.Q. added in is 0·650.

However, more recent investigations have shown increased predictive power with the correlations reaching the 0·25 region. This is still very low and one must be wary of the claims made by Cattell and Child (1975) who argue that the motivational variables account for 25% of the variance. These figures are obtained after correcting the observed correlations for the unreliability of tests and criteria. These correcting formulae make assumptions about the nature of the test variance that are not always met in the practical research setting, and the psychological meaningfulness of corrected figures is always open to wide interpretation.

Some of these more recent investigations of Barton *et al.* and Cattell (e.g. Cattell *et al.*, 1972) have analysed separately the SMAT unintegrated and integrated component scores as well as their total score. The results of all this detailed work show that the academic achiever is high on curiosity (total), self-sentiment (1) and superego (1) but low on pugnacity (total) gregariousness (1) and narcism (total).

Since all these relationships are small the discussion is limited to noting that superego and self-sentiment were shown in Chapter 6 on motivation to be the master sentiments by which much behaviour is organized, and the sentiments responsible for integration learning. Essentially, it was argued, they contribute to delaying gratification. Since to undergo education inevitably involves such postponement of pleasure, the relationship of superego and the self-sentiment to educational success most certainly makes sense. So too does the finding with curiosity.

In respect of the motivational variables on which the academic achiever is low, there is certainly intuitive common sense to support the findings. A gregarious person most probably spends too little time studying alone, an argument which was used in support of the related finding that extraversion is inversely related to academic success. Narcism is defined in the MAT as a liking for warmth and luxury, the fear of work, which it is claimed by Conservatives, runs high on those in the dole queue. As defined thus, the negative correlation would appear correct, supporting the validity of the MAT narcism scale. However, Cattell and Kline (1977) have pointed out that this is too simplistic an argument. In some families where academic prowess is greatly valued, part of a child's narcism could be involved in such prowess. Hence a positive relationship might be hypothesized. Cattell and Kline, in connection with this evidence have raised the possibility that this MAT narcism is only a part of what is referred to under that name in psychoanalysis. It could be the case that the psychoanalytic concept—narcism—comprises both self-sentiment, which as seen, is positively correlated with academic success and indeed to later achievement in life. The sensual aspects of narcism, those embodied in the narcism scale, could still be negatively correlated. This is a research topic which demands research by those who combine both psychometric and psychoanalytic expertise.

The negative correlation with pugnacity is also interesting. It would be difficult to see any obvious reason why pugnacity should play any part in poor academic performance. However this could be, for correlations are *not* necessarily causal, the result of poor performance. There has long been evidence (see Dollard *et al.*, 1939) that pugnacity or aggression is the response to frustration. Thus poor academic achievement may create the high pugnacity drive itself.

Finally, the list of motivational variables in the last section of Table 8.1 includes the sex erg. As discussed in Chapter 6 on motivation, this variable, while clearly highly important, does not appear to possess the overwhelming importance attached to it by psychoanalysts. However, as might be expected, it does affect academic performance. Cattell *et al.* (1972) and Cattell and Butcher (1968) both confirmed this point. Both researchers showed that there was a negative correlation between performance and scores on the unintegrated sex erg. However, with the integrated component the correlation was positive.

As argued previously (Cattell and Kline, 1977), these contrary findings are in fact consonant with Freudian formulations. Since, in Freudian theory, any activity is regarded as a substitute for sexual activity, these who work exceedingly hard should have less energy for the real thing. This would suggest that there should be a negative correlation between the unintegrated sex erg component and achievement in almost everything (not only academic matters). Since sexual activity is also time-consuming, this alone leads one to postulate a negative correlation. All these arguments, therefore, support the negative correlation which has been noted.

One argument, however, implies a positive correlation. There is little doubt that lack of satisfactory sex drive discharge leads to considerable preoccupation with sex, to the detriment of academic work. However this would not seem as strong an argument as those previously advanced and generally, the hypothesis would be a negative correlation between academic performance and the sex erg.

Conclusions concerning the Main Motivational Variables

Although there is far less work in this area than with temperament, some fairly clear conclusions can be drawn:

(1) The motivational variables are only slightly related to academic success. All correlations are small and account for little variance.

(2) In the complete specification equation for academic achievement, motivational variables are of some value because they account for different aspects of the educational variance from either temperamental or ability variables.

(3) The most important motivational variables for the prediction of academic achievement are self-sentiment and superego, the master sentiments which, as shown, are so pervasive as to emerge as temperamental traits.

Contribution to Future Research

One may now attempt to answer the question which was posed as arising from the final conclusions to be drawn from the results with the major temperamental factors: why are their correlations with academic performance so small?

From the discussion so far one should point out that the largest temperamental factors, certain ability factors and some motivational factors, each account for a small portion of the variance in academic achievement. However if this is the case whence arises the remaining variance?

As I pointed out (Kline, 1975b) in a discussion of some of the correlations between personality variables and academic performance, what is needed is not more research on even larger samples as carried out recently on thousands of postgraduates by Saville and Blinkhorne (1976). What is needed is research to identify what might be called uncontrolled factors in educational success. By this I mean that research should be directed at answering the following questions: the differential classroom behaviour of extraverts and introverts; the differential teacher–pupil interaction of introverts and extraverts: the different learning procedures of introverts and extraverts: all these same questions could be asked with respect to neurotics and, in more complex designs, with both factors adequately quantified.

In addition, longitudinal, detailed studies of children are needed to identify the environmental reinforcers which (chance events) modify their academic performance. These are likely to be different for introverts and extraverts, just as a crude example of personality variables, as shown in Chapter 7, by Eysenck's attempt to mould his findings into theories of learning. Do those children who enjoy mathematics have different experiences in the classroom early on in their education from those who fear it?

Cyril Burt (1937) always argued that teaching reading was hampered because no distinction was made between audiles and visiles, those with predominantly auditory or visual memory. For the one, phonetic methods would be likely to be better, for the other the look and say. This is a clear example of what interaction studies of classroom behaviour could reveal if measurement of all the main variables in Table 8.1, both in pupils and teachers, were carried out and taken into account in analysis of the data. In this way efficient teaching methods for different subjects and different types of pupil might receive an empirical rather than an intuitive basis. The highly intelligent, neurotic introvert needs quite different teaching procedures from a dim, stable extravert, if there is any value at all in psychometrically defined individual differences. To teach them in the same way is professional lunacy.

Finally reference must be made once again to Eysenck's personality theory (see Chapter 7). Despite its flaws and internal inconsistencies, the basic differences between extraverts and introverts in performance, even if the theoretical basis of inhibition is not correct are well established. Such differences, of course, imply that quite different teaching methods are likely to be successful with these groups.

Summary of the Psychometric Contribution

In conclusion, therefore, I argue that the psychometric contribution to the knowledge of the determinants of educational success is both factual and implicative. Factually it has been demonstrated that small correlations with academic performance can be obtained from the main ability factors, temperamental factors and motivational factors. Together a moderate multiple correlation is found. Generally however, all findings indicate that the relationships are small. At the primary school the stable extravert is superior, at the secondary school and later, the introvert is superior. These results however, have important implications for educational research and teaching methods. That the correlations are small suggests that apparently chance factors are affecting pupils' performance, events which could be studied longitudinally and in interaction classroom studies. If all the psychometric variables are measured, it would be possible to discover the teaching procedures and learning strategies which were most efficient for different kinds of pupils. Thus psychometric studies clearly point the way research into this aspect of educational psychology should go. The results are bound to be theoretically illuminating and of great practical value.

VOCATIONAL GUIDANCE AND COUNSELLING

This is a branch of educational psychology to which the contribution of psychometrics has been considerable and should be much larger. The assumptions upon which this section are based will be made clear and the psychometric contribution can then be evaluated.

As pointed out at the start of this chapter, the psychometric approach to vocational guidance and counselling is broadly that of Rodger (1962), renowned in Great Britain, at least, for his seven-point plan for fitting men to jobs. However, this approach which seems logically impeccable (that the sum total of an individual's abilities, temperament dynamics and moods best fit him for a particular set of jobs) has been considerably expanded in "The Psychology of Vocational Guidance" (Kline, 1975). Here I set out the two vital aspect of Rodger's plan which are only mentioned in it: how are individuals to be assessed and how are jobs to be measured. These appear to be the critical ingredients of vocational guidance and counselling.

Person Assessment

The assessment of people which is advocated here is the measurement of the most important psychometric variables of ability, personality, mood and motivation, those set out as being the best established, most clearly identified and most psychologically meaningful, in the relevant tables of the chapters in this book. In every case these psychometric factors, the main dimensions of the area, have their own validated measuring instruments. I argue, therefore, that the assessment of people is relatively straightforward.

Job Evaluation

What is required is to evaluate jobs in terms of their psychological demands. This is the aspect of vocational guidance which is not well developed. Ideally, one could characterize jobs in terms of the psychological traits necessary for their proper performance. One might postulate, for example, that airline pilots need to be reasonably intelligent, stable, with high ego strength, so that should an emergency arise they will deal rationally with it and not collapse in panic or make disastrous decisions. Moreover, they ought to be high on g, superego, conscientious, in other words, so that they carry out all the numerous checks which *most* of the time are redundant. This example has been chosen because clearly it raises all the difficulties inherent in job evaluation, problems which must be discussed before the contribution of psychometrics to vocational guidance and counselling can be appreciated. Two problems emerge: first, how is a job to be evaluated in psychological terms? My analysis was purely *a priori*, intuitive. Another psychologist might well disagree; the second problem concerns the nature of job demands. Are they really so constant as this example implies? Might it not be that in most jobs, workers can make them what they will?

Basically there are two distinct approaches to the evaluation of jobs, each of which has their adherents and some special disadvantages.

Jobs Defined by Psychological Characteristics

This is the method utilized, as shown in Chapter 6, by the constructors of the most well-known and widely administered interest tests, the Strong Vocational Interest Blank (Strong *et al.*, 1971) and the Kuder set of tests (Kuder, 1970). Items are given to the occupants of various jobs and the discriminatory items are held to complete a particular interest test. In the discussion of criterion-keyed tests I pointed out the weakness of this method of test construction—such scales have no necessary psychological meaning because there may be a wide variety of differences between the occupants of different jobs. As used by Strong and Kuder, jobs are not in fact evaluated in terms of psychological characteristics (although this may appear to be the case) but in terms of discriminating items; a blind empiricism.

Cattell (e.g. Cattell *et al.*, 1970) advocates this method, defining jobs in terms of the basic personality and ability dimensions of their holders. This is similar to the procedures discussed above, except that as I have persistently argued throughout this book, these basic, factor-analytically defined variables do have psychological meaning. The advantage of this method where meaningful variables are used is that it enables vocational guidance and counselling to be rational. A client's profile of scores can be compared with the profile for various occupational groups. In addition since the variables are meaningful even if the mean scores for an occupation are not known, it is possible to make cautious extrapolation. For example, there are likely to be some similarities between solicitors and barristers. For the latter verbal brilliance is probably more important, for the former a certain sociability (as with doctors), for solicitors have to be able to get on with the public.

However, this method does have certain disadvantages which have persuaded some psychologists to abandon it. First, there is no guarantee that the most suitable people are in post. The administrative Civil Service, (see Cattell and Kline, 1977), used to favour applicants with a classical education, without firm evidence that this indeed was the best training for the job. Thus the profile of civil servants would have been, perhaps, misleading. A second point is that a job demands change. Thus fitting clients to a mean group profile could be selecting people with the wrong attributes. Finally, some job demands are necessary but for the wrong reasons. To work in the steel or textile industry one needs people who are able to withstand considerable noise. Is it more sensible to select such persons or to quieten the machinery? These problems, especially the first, mean that this method of job evaluation has severe limitations. The second approach is job description.

Task Analysis

The difficulty with job description is a simple one: how is it to be done. The principle of job description is obvious and the National Institute for Industrial Psychology has long had such descriptions although intuitively based, as can be seen in Oakley et al. (1937), and indeed in their natural successor the Rodger (1952) seven-point plan, which in intelligent hands can be exceedingly useful.

However, modern specialists in ergonomics, especially systems analysis, consider these commonsense attempts to describe jobs as worthless. Gagné (1965) and Miller (1965, 1966), make the point that only systematic job description with agreed terminology is of value for psychological insight, and this they argue can only be done within systems analysis.

Since the only aim in discussing task analysis is to see how it may be related to psychological test scores, thus enabling one to evaluate the psychometric contribution to vocational guidance and counselling, the examination will be brief. For greater detail readers are referred to Gagné (1965), Miller (1965, 1966) or Kline (1975).

As indicated, task description and analysis are conceived as part of a systems analysis. To take an example of what is meant by a system, one can consider a pen. Now a pen is not just an instrument for writing. It is part of a communication system, the writing has to be easily written and read. Thus a fault with many old-fashioned copying systems was that excellent as they were, the smell and feel of the copies made reading unpleasant. Similarly a pen that wrote superbly but only on newspaper or with noxious ink would not be a good pen in system analytic terms.

As part of a system analysis task, analysis entails the construction of a highly detailed set of instructions for performing a job. When this precise analysis is carried out, it illustrates clearly all the weaknesses of the general job descriptions based upon common sense and intuition. First general job descriptions may lead to the insistence on unnecessary skills. For example, is it necessary for a psychiatrist to have a sound knowledge of anatomy and materia medicica? At present this is demanded by the general job description for psychiatry. Clearly, profile matching techniques might be misleading, if in fact a task analysis of what a psychiatrist actually does demonstrates that he never utilizes these skills.

Such detailed description of what is done in a job, as is forced on us by task analysis, also reveals another weakness in general job description. The task analysis demonstrates clearly also what is not done. For example, it might show that psychiatrists do not spend much time in keeping numerical records suitable for statistical analysis. If one thought the research aspect a desirable feature of psychiatry, one could write this into the task analysis. This would lead one, perhaps, to exchange anatomy and materia medicica for statistics and computer programming.

Miller demonstrates in his papers that the commonsense job description can easily underestimate what is required for any job. Where for example, sequence of operations may vary, it is not sufficient simply to know the operations. A further problem in job description is concerned with emergency procedures. It is often the case that such descriptions fail to recognize the crisis points in any tasks and so take no note of emergency procedures but identify false crises. The example given by Miller is highly pertinent. A lorry driver should be able to diagnose and correct, simple faults on his lorry such as starting difficulties, hydraulic problems and lights so that he does not have to waste time immobilized, awaiting repairs. On the other hand the professional flute player who learns sets of diabolically difficult and faulty pitched alternative fingerings in case a key fails is wasting his time. This event is unlikely and if it occurs he should stop or replace the flute.

Task analysis overcomes these problems and reveals what has to be done. This task analysis is then combined with task description which is the minutely detailed statement of what is involved in a job for which, Miller claims, an algorithm can be developed. One is required to state the function of the job, its context and the other concomitant skills. The professional flautist illustrates the method. Thus an orchestral player must be able to play in large orchestras, be familiar with nineteenth and twentieth century music, able to play with little rehearsal and double up on the piccolo. The contextual aspect of the description indicates that he must be able to get on well with a large group of musicians (the orchestra), be prepared to be away from home and stand the strains of constant travel. These requirements are mainfestly different from those of a jazz flautist or a solo or small group player.

From this it is clear that the combination of task description and analysis (and the examples are by no means wrought in the necessary fine detail) enables one to obtain an insight into what a job involves such that an estimate of the psychological characteristics demanded by it can be based upon behaviour, and is thus likely to be accurate. All such estimates have to be validated against real life criteria of occupational success and occupational group differences, but job analysis and description give a proper behavioural basis for psychological evaluation. Thus task analysis followed by psychometric evaluation of individuals on the variables discussed in this book should *a priori*, lead to highly effective vocational guidance and counselling. In Platonic terms mere πιστις, belief, can be replaced by reason, ἐπιστημη.

Two points remain before examining the contribution of psychometrics to this area of educational psychology. First, it is possible to describe jobs accurately and in sufficient detail without task analysis and systems analysis. However, it is far more difficult to do and, as most general descriptions indicate (see Oakley *et al.*, 1937), they fail in these respects. The methods of task analysis and description virtually compel the investigator to produce a description which is correct and adequate for evaluating the psychological demands of the job. A second advantage is that task analysis and description can be applied to new changed jobs, thus obviating the objection to the first method of measuring the psychological characteristics of job occupants. Actually this is even more important for the ergonomics of large-scale industrial planning where totally new jobs can be designed taking into account psychological and physiological characteristics of workers, thus making far more pleasant and efficiently conducted work routines (in theory).

Task analysis and description also quickly point up what characteristics happen to be necessary in a particular job (finger dexterity with poorly designed machines) and which are simply intrinsic, lifting sacks, for example, in coal delivery. From this discussion one can conclude that careful task analysis and description is likely to enable psychometrists to estimate the psychological characteristics necessary to do a job successfully. However one can also argue that such inferences of necessary traits *are* only inferences. They must always be checked against the first method. Do occupants of the job possess the characteristics that one expects from our job analysis? In addition, and this is perhaps even more important, the findings must be checked against job success.

Criteria of Success

Mention of job success leads to a further issue which must be examined before the contribution of psychometrics to vocational guidance and counselling can be assessed. Ideally prediction of job success would be perfect. The table would therefore show a set of beta weights or correlations with success for various jobs for each of the main factor analytic dimensions. Since there must be ideal sets of characteristics for doing various jobs, these should be specifiable.

In reality the imperfection of the test instruments and the problem of measuring job success makes predictions far from perfect. The imperfections of these tests have been fully discussed in the previous chapters. Here one must discuss why job success is so hard to measure in an attempt to utilize only the best criteria. The problem of the criterion, as in all studies of test validity, is particularly acute in the evaluation of job success. Indeed this is a subject which deserves lengthy treatment. However Ghiselli (1966) contains an excellent discussion and the brief summary depends much on his work.

The first difficulty lies in the fact that a vast number of diverse methods have been used in the evaluation, as Ghiselli (1966) found in his survey of 10 000 investigations. The most frequently utilized was rating by a supervisor (the problems of ratings have been fully discussed). However, output, errors, wastage, sales volume and number of new accounts are often used. It is noticeable that not all these indices are applicable to all jobs. Thus teaching would be difficult to evaluate other than by ratings. Judges could be evaluated by errors (although these are difficult to determine) and possibly by opening of new accounts (although this could never be made public). The most sound method is to use as many criteria as possible unless, of course, these are very highly correlated.

Difficulties abound. Many of these criteria are unreliable which limits their predictive power. Some of the ratings and figures are often obtained during training. Now it is possible that skill acquisition requires different psychological characteristics from its maintenance. There is a further problem in establishing useful criteria for job success—namely that the qualities required at an early stage of the job may be different from those required in a senior capacity. Indeed, as Dixon (1976) has convincingly demonstrated in the case of army officers, the qualities of a junior officer are actually antithetical to those required of a general. It should be noted that job analysis and description would reveal this: to obey orders is psychologically different from giving them. Some indices may be reliable—income and number of accidents, for example, although these are imperfect criteria on their own. From this brief discussion, therefore, it is clear that all the findings with respect to job success have to be interpreted cautiously, showing regard to problems of criteria—both their reliability and validity. Clearly the more criteria that can be used in any one study, the better.

So far in the argument, the contribution of psychometrics to vocational guidance will arise from fitting the scores on the major factorial dimensions to three sets of scores: those derived from criterion occupational groups, scores derived from estimates based upon task analysis and description and scores on indices of occupational success.

Table 8.2

This table sets out a sample of results obtained from administering factor-analytic variables to occupational groups. The findings are discussed in the light of the examination of the problems in the previous paragraphs. However, to fully group the import of the results in Table 8.2 one must look at some of the ways in which the findings have been obtained.

In the field of abilities, especially intelligence, Ghiselli (1966) has surveyed 10 000 studies up to 1966. His survey provides a sound basis for any statement on the significance of the ability sphere in occupational success. In the field of personality and motivation, Cattell and his colleagues have been very active in relating their factorial variables to occupational performance. Since this is, in

TABLE 8.2

PERSONALITY AND MOTIVATIONAL VARIABLES AND OCCUPATION

	Variables	Occupations									
		Army officers (or cadets)	Executives	Air pilots	Artists	Theology students	Physicians	Physicists	Engineers	Teachers	Writers
		$\bar{X}$	$\bar{X}$	$\bar{X}$	$\bar{X}$	$\bar{X}$	$\bar{X}$	$\bar{X}$	$\bar{X}$	$\bar{X}$	$\bar{X}$
Personality sphere	A	5·4	7·8	5·1	3·1	5·9	5·4	2·9	5·9	5·6	4·1
	B	6·0	7·5	7·2	8·8	6·6	6·2	9·6	6·3	6·5	9·7
	C	6·1	5·7	7·8	7·7	6·5	5·4	7·3	4·3	5·0	6·6
	E	5·6	5·8	6·0	6·8	5·7	4·8	6·2	5·3	5·5	8·1
	F	5·9	5·3	6·7	3·4	5·8	5·6	3·1	1·6	5·5	4·6
	G	6·4	5·5	7·2	3·7	5·2	5·1	3·9	4·8	5·7	3·2
	H	5·7	6·6	6·9	7·0	5·8	5·4	6·1	4·4	5·6	7·0
	I	5·0	5·6	3·8	9·2	6·8	5·7	6·8	5·4	5·9	7·9
	L	5·2	5·4	3·7	5·0	4·7	5·4	3·8	6·4	5·0	5·3
	M	5·4	5·7	4·1	8·9	5·7	5·5	4·8	6·8	5·4	7·3
	N	6·1	6·2	5·7	4·4	4·3	5·8	5·6	5·3	5·8	5·1
	O	4·6	5·5	3·5	4·8	4·6	5·5	3·7	6·3	5·1	5·4
	Q_1	5·5	6·4	5·8	6·4	4·9	5·6	5·6	6·8	5·5	6·9
	Q_2	5·4	5·5	5·1	7·0	5·3	6·4	6·3	7·0	5·7	7·2
	Q_3	6·3	5·6	7·5	6·3	5·4	6·1	7·2	6·4	6·0	5·9
	Q_4	5·2	5·3	3·0	6·3	5·8	5·0	5·1	6·7	5·3	6·7
Dynamic sphere	Career	6	6			5	6		7	5	
	Home	4	3			4	3		5	3	
	Fear	5	5			4	6		5	5	
	Narcism	8	10			6	8		5	3	
	Superego	4	1			6	6		5	5	
	Self-sentiment	5	10			6	7		5	7	
	Mating	6	8			5	5		5	6	
	Pugnacity	7	4			5	6		5	5	
	Assertion	5	5			4	5		6	5	
	Sweetheart	6	6			6	4		6	6	

fact, extremely difficult to do, one must first look at their methods before trying to interpret the results.

Firstly, it must be realized that there is a huge body of work relating the temperamental 16 PF scales alone, to occupational criteria (nearly 100 pages in the 16 PF Handbook), so that the account here will be brief, but enough to grasp the essence of the approach, which can, of course, in principle, be used with any set of variables. Two complementary methods have been employed. There is the Adjustment or Type placement method and the effectiveness or performance approach. The merits and disadvantages of each will now be scrutinized.

The Adjustment Method

This involves fitting an individual to a type, in the case of vocational guidance matching a client's scores to an occupational profile. Since such a profile is derived usually from a study of the occupants of a job, this suffers from all the difficulties of such group measurement. One difficulty still remains even if one can fit subject to profile. In some ways this is not the best model since the overall profile of abilities, personality and motivational factors may be the critical feature, the total configuration of the subject, abundance of one quality not really compensating for lack of another. For example, not all the perseverance in the world will make up for lack of good pitch perception in playing the French Horn.

Despite the problem of profile similarity which is perhaps the all important feature (and there are statistical methods for just such comparisons, e.g. rp, the pattern profile similarity coefficient, Cattell, 1949), essentially the adjustment method involves matching scores. Everything depends on the adequacy of the criterion data, and there are grave doubts arising from such data. To overcome them, Cattell and colleagues have developed another procedure, the Effectiveness or Fitness by Performance Method. This consists essentially of maximizing the beta weights, correlations or discriminant functions with the criterion scores for actual performance in the job itself.

In the Handbook to the 16 PF test, Cattell *et al.* (1970) set out the weights for the 16 PF factors for different occupations so that fitness scores for individuals for each occupation can be worked out. This method obviously depends for its efficiency on how well each occupational group has been sampled and on how reliable and valid the performance scores are, which has been discussed in the section on the problems of establishing an adequate criterion.

Discussion of Table 8.2 and Related Results

Table 8.2 differs from Table 8.1 in one highly important respect. In examining educational success there were only three target results to be accounted for (Primary, Secondary and Higher education, in as much as each was different). In occupational success there are, obviously, a far greater number of results, although not, hopefully, as many as there are occupations. Thus Table 8.1, illustrated and in part summarized the psychometric contribution to the field, whereas Table 8.2 simply illustrates it. It is necessarily a selection from a large body of results. Despite this, the illustrations have been chosen with an eye to the most psychologically significant results.

Abilities

These do not appear in the table for they defy simple illustration. As to be expected from the theoretical account of the nature of the g factor, it emerges that g correlates on average 0·3 with success in any job. This means that if one had a number of different positions to fill and if one based advice on an intelligence test score, one would be significantly correct in one's choices (although the correlation is modest). This is the clear implication from the work of Ghiselli (1966).

However, this is the least powerful inference that may be obtained from these findings, the mechanical allocation of subjects to jobs based only on test scores on g. Further study of Ghiselli's results indicates that correlations with g are in the case of some jobs around 0·6 or 0·7. Thus, in jobs where intelligence is an important attribute, intelligence test scores are, not surprisingly, good predictors of success. Again, in jobs where intelligence can play little part, as in repetitive production line work, or in jobs where personal decision-making is at a minimum as in the lower echelons of the army, intelligence is not a positive advantage. These results are a powerful contribution to vocational guidance and counselling, as is set out below. (For further details Kline, 1975.)

If, instead of using test scores mechanically, one tempers the scores with other information about the individual and about the occupation, it is obvious that gc as measured by most of the investigations in Ghiselli (1966) is going to be highly useful to the counsellor. Thus, one statement that can be made with confidence and which must be regarded as a psychometric contribution to knowledge is: high intelligence is advantageous for success in all jobs. For certain jobs it is a highly positive advantage. The practical corollary from the viewpoint of vocational guidance is that it is almost always useful to assess a client's intelligence. Of course, it is true that such a contribution is somewhat obvious not to say banal. However, it must not be forgotten that in Great Britain today, recent legislation has made it illegal for local education authorities to offer selective education at the secondary level, because as one former education minister put it, all intellectual differences are attributable to environmental differences.

The group ability factors play their part in occupational success much as might be expected. Thus, in jobs where verbal ability is obviously important such as journalism or writing, verbal ability has small but significant correlations with success. Similar results obtain for the other factors, numerical and spatial ability. The point of interest here for the vocational guidance worker is that in some jobs these group factors are better predictors than general intelligence. Generally, however, the work of Ghiselli indicates that the psychometric study of abilities other than intelligence, has not provided much new information relevant to guidance and counselling. Indeed it can be argued that its main contribution has been to give empirical support to commonsense notions.

Personality Variables

The first row in Table 8.2 shows mean differences between various occupational groups. These are simply a small but representative section of the tables of results in the Handbook to the 16 PF test. These illustrate the findings from which I shall try to draw some more general conclusions.

Scanning the mean scores of the different occupational groups (the first approach discussed in the study of the methods) is interesting and useful although it must be stressed that the whole configuration of scores, the profile, really needs to be considered rather than mean scores—exceedingly difficult to do since it involves holding so much information simultaneously. This difficulty brings home clearly why Cattell and his colleagues advise counsellors in the practical situation to employ some kind of statistical profile matching technique so that the resemblance of a client to any occupational profile can be expressed numerically. Finally, before scrutinizing this table it must be stressed again that the profiles are psychologically meaningful (since the variables are factor-analytically derived) and thus extrapolations can be made from the results to other similar occupations in contradistinction to the entirely atheoretical discriminating tests such as the Strong and Kuder (see p. 179–180).

In examining the mean scores one should remember that these are scores with means of 5·5 and standard deviations of 1·5 so that scores of 7 and above, and below 4 are likely to be of some psychological interest. The factors on which groups do not differ from the normal population can also be of psychological significance especially where they are contrary to common sense. For example, if writers were shown to be of only average intelligence (factor B) we would be very keen to see their verbal ability scores which ought to be phenomenal. A more likely explanation (in this quite hypothetical example) would be that the test was invalid since a knowledge of the writing abilities of the normal man based upon letters to the papers, and letters in the course of business and life, strongly suggests that writing is not his forte, and writing ability would appear likely to be linked to intelligence.

The accountants (American) are a useful group to scrutinize first since they demonstrate both the weakness and the power of these temperamental factors to contribute to a knowledge of vocational psychology. If one disregards B, intelligence, which is not truly a temperamental factor and on which they score moderately high, it is noteworthy that only in one factor, A, do they differ beyond the standard deviation limits from the general population. This indicates that in respect of personality the accountant is an anonymous grey figure with little memorable about him except a certain sociability, which is probably important to get on with clients. It is relevant that business executives have similar scores on factor A. This certainly makes sound psychological sense. A flamboyant, daring accountant might advise his clients well for a few years only to lead to a spectacular and probably illegal disaster. From the viewpoint of guidance this profile leads one to suppose that accountancy will fit clients whose personality pattern is close to average (other than A). Unusual and powerful or striking personalities are unlikely to be happy in the profession. Thus, the first example shows how the findings mirror the common experience of accountants as somewhat uninteresting people. They support the power of variables in occupational prediction but except for factor A they give little help for counsellors towards more positive advice. What is needed for accountancy, therefore, are ability scores and possibly motivation scores.

Airline pilots present a profile that demonstrates the contribution which temperamental factors can make in the understanding of occupational success. Thus they are high on C, ego strength, G, conscientiousness and Q_3, controlled, exacting will power; they are low on L, projection, suspiciousness, O, guilt proneness and Q_4, tension. The picture here is of a decisive, conscientious and stable person of above average intelligence, who is obviously capable in handling difficulties. It is interesting to note how similar a picture is presented by the air-hostess. As with accountants, this profile strongly supports what one would *a priori* think should be the case.

Finally, in examining this section of Table 8.2, it is worth comparing the artists, physicists and writers. Artists have 9 of their scores beyond a standard deviation from the mean, physicists 8 scores and writers 7 scores. This alone means if these factors play any part in their skills, that there are bound statistically to be few such people. By definition most people will have the majority of their scores at the mean level. Compared with accountants these three groups are necessarily composed of highly unusual (and therefore interesting) people. It also means that whereas one can easily find suitable people (in terms of temperamental factors) to be accountants, should it be necessary to increase the supply of physicists, one would find it difficult. Certainly the new physicists would not resemble those in post.

Some of the actual scores are revealing. Artists are withdrawn, tender-minded, Bohemian and unconventional. Physicists on the other hand are withdrawn but with high ego strength. Actually the artists high score on M is in strong contrast with the low score on this variable of the airline pilots and it is of especial significance in the light of the evidence in the Handbook to the 16 PF test that high M is associated with accident-proneness.

Before drawing conclusions from these findings vis-à-vis the psychometric contribution to vocational guidance, we must turn to findings derived from the fitness of performance approach—the beta weights and other functions which do not appear in the table.

Hammond (1970) carried out a study of policemen (although only 53 subjects were used) and regressed the temperament scores against success as a patrolman. Low A, realism, F, sobriety and L, paranoid defensive projection were the most important predictive factors. This method is superior to the first approach because one knows from the regression coefficients that these variables are actually related to success in the job.

Two studies of salesmen, quoted by Cattell *et al.* (1970), are particularly interesting in that the regression weights indicate that A, sociability, H, adventurousness, L (negatively), trustingness and Q_2, self-sufficiency, were the most important variables. The point here is that the tests have improved upon common sense because while the extravert factors of A and H are important, the *introverted* Q_2 self-sufficiency is also implicated, thus demonstrating that the second-order introversion factor is too broad as has now been admitted by Eysenck and Eysenck (1977) in their study of impulsivity (see also Eysenck and Eysenck, 1963). Note also that the E of extraversion, dominance, is also missing, as a predictor of salesmanship.

Owing to the difficulties of obtaining adequate criteria of success, such regression studies as have been quoted are far less numerous than those comparing the mean scores of different occupational groups. Nevertheless they provide an indication of what can be achieved utilizing this approach. Cattell *et al.* (1970) present an ingenious method of deriving regression weights for success from the occupational profiles which have been discussed, a method developed by Tatsuoka and Cattell (1970). However brilliant this mathematics is, in my opinion, there is no substitute for empirical data about success or failure in occupations. Indeed the interpretations that can be made of these specification equation weights are *necessarily* no different from the interpretations of the profiles.

What conclusions, therefore, can one draw about the substantive contribution of the temperamental factors to vocational guidance and counselling. First, these investigations demonstrate that in accordance with clinical theory and common sense, there are personality differences between members of different occupational groups. Furthermore the genuine regression studies demonstrate that certain of these factors are positively related to success. Most of the findings themselves are not surprising, e.g. that pilots are stable and calm or that artists are Bohemian. However, such results are not to be despised because many commonplace intuitions about behaviour turn out to be false or to be totally misconceived. Thus, from the viewpoint of understanding the psychological nature of occupational success and being able to put vocational guidance and counselling on a rational basis (matching men to jobs) these temperamental factors have made and with further investigations will continue to make a useful contribution. However, so far no more general theoretical statement about temperament and occupation can be made from these results. It must be described as a modest but practically useful contribution to knowledge.

Temperamental Factors, other than those of Cattell and Eysenck

While the few factorially derived temperamental scales (e.g. Grygier, 1961), which were clearly independent of the Cattell and Eysenck systems did prove of some value in the prediction of educational achievement, there is far less relevant evidence for their value in vocational guidance and counselling. Certainly the most recent DPI manual (Grygier and Grygier, 1976) provides no support for its use here. Nor do the scales developed by Kline (1971), Ai3Q, measuring obsessional traits, and OOQ and OPQ (Kline and Storey, 1978) measuring oral optimistic and pessimistic traits respectively appear to be useful in occupational discrimination or prediction.

Motivational Variables

This is the last horizontal section of Table 8.2, concerned with motivational variables. As pointed out in the chapter on dynamic factors, the only attempt to submit this area of psychology to multivariate analysis is that of Cattell and his colleagues in Illinois (see Cattell and Child, 1975). Most other workers, being content to rely on *a priori* analyses (e.g. Jackson (1967) and Edwards (1959) who both draw upon Murray, (1938)) or on purely empirical analyses, of whom Strong is the outstanding example, fail to provide variables which are psychologically meaningful. In this section of the table we are therefore restricted to those investigations which have utilized the MAT (Cattell *et al.*, 1970) or its school version, the SMAT (Sweney *et al.*, 1970) tests which in the occupational field have not been as extensively used as the corresponding temperament scales.

Before attempting to interpret the figures in this section of the table one should briefly recall the relation of interest to the ergs and sentiments of the MAT. In Chapter 6 it was agreed that the interest in a task reflected, in part, the number of ergic drives (the amount of ergic tension) it allowed expression. Thus, one should expect job satisfaction (and hence ultimately success, provided that the requisite abilities were present) to be related to the power of the job in respect to drive satisfaction.

Cattell and Child (1975) have collected together the occupational studies so far carried out with the MAT and the examples in Table 8.2 are extracted from that source. As can be seen these interpretations have to be extremely cautious because most of the samples are small. Presidents of insurance companies were high on narcism and self-sentiment but low on superego. Curiously, as Cattell and Child (1975) argue, their career sentiment was not high. Possibly the eminence grise, having arrived, can sit back in comfort. This picture of the pleasure loving, ruthless without conscience, striving to achieve, President fits in well with left-wing stereotypes of the tycoon. Cattell and Kline (1977) have also pointed out that this group scored low on home-parental attachment. In other words these highly successful men were truly independent of their parents.

Successful business men were also described by Cattell and Child (1975). Again, as is to be expected, they did not greatly differ from the Presidents except that for them (who were yet to reach the top) assertiveness and career were high, while the sweetheart-spouse sentiment was low. For these then the great upward striving (Adler, 1930) is still going on hence the high scores relative to the Presidents. As for the low sweetheart-spouse sentiment, work replaces the wife, a widely observed phenomenon in the professional middle classes who sometimes claim in defence of their salary structure that their work does not stop at five.

So much for these results obtained with the dynamic factor variables in discriminating occupational groups. Further perusal of Table 8.2 suggests that one or two tentative generalizations can be made which could be useful for vocational guidance and counselling. Highly educated occupational groups can be distinguished by their low home-parental sentiments and high self-sentiment. High status groups also tend to have high narcism scores. As Cattell and Kline (1977) have argued in relation to these scores it does appear that education makes people more independent, more able to break away from the cultural bondage of the home—a positive view of education and a hopeful one if social change is held desirable. This would account for the low scores on the home parental sentiment factor. The high self-sentiment is not perhaps so strong an advocate for American education. The implication here is education promotes confidence and feelings of personal value, epitomized in Great Britain by the Public School Oxbridge elite, whose only virtues are in some cases, the fact of their attendance at those institutions, persons not egregious for achievement. The narcism score is also interesting. This suggests that once the physical comforts and pleasures of life have been tasted, they are hard to abandon: the essence in this result of Acton's claim that absolute power corrupts.

What, therefore, can be regarded as the contribution to psychology from this branch of psychometrics? First, as was the case with the temperamental variables, the findings in the main fit in well with commonsense notions of what is likely to be important for jobs. Some of the findings, indeed, go beyond this and are not wholly expected, for example the fact that the career drive is not high in Presidents of companies. Such results enable the vocational guidance officer to make rational judgements about the suitability of clients for various occupations. However, as yet, few powerful generalizations (in effect theories) concerning the role of these factors in occupational factors can be made. At the moment what results we have and others to be collected, resemble a gazeteer or encyclopaedia of job specifications which can be looked up.

At present this dictionary is not very full or particularly accurate, owing to the paucity of studies with adequate samples and the relative unreliability of tests. However, this can be improved and here the contribution of psychometrics must be in the future in this area of psychology.

The Future Contribution of Psychometrics to Vocational Guidance and Counselling: An encylopaedia of job specifications

In fact what psychometrics could contribute to vocational guidance and counselling would be an encyclopaedia of job specifications with regression weights for all the major variables, ability, temperament and motivation against job success, the results of researches carried out on large, properly representative samples. In addition, mean scores of occupational groups could be given. This would enable the vocational guidance officer to match any chart with any job, especially since simple algorithms can be utilized for accurate matching. This encyclopaedia could be, therefore, the rational basis of a vocational guidance system. Ultimately as tests improve and the most fundamental variables are reached multiple correlations could approach unity. Until they do this the encyclopaedia could form the basis of a vocational guidance interview; it would not be used as a mechanical selection device. A final point deserves to be made concerning our proposed encyclopaedia of regression weights. When all these data were assembled it might be possible to develop a theory that would account for them, thus making such a dictionary otiose. Just as one no longer needs a detailed description of the motion of the planets because one has a theory by which their position at any moment can be predicted, so it is hoped a theory may be developed to account for the facts of occupational success. Thus ultimately the encyclopaedia I propose, may have theoretical ramifications far more important than its practical utility. More certainly it can be said that until the facts of occupational success are known, no adequate theory can be developed.

The implicit notion of such an encyclopaedia—namely that prediction of occupational success could approach or reach unity—has been attacked when previously proposed by Kline (1976), e.g. by Valentine (1977). The argument against it is, of course, that apparently random factors such as whether you get on with a particular individual in your particular job play an important part in success. This is to misunderstand completely the nature of the multivariate prediction. This is actuarial in nature and obviously may not apply to any given person. Such random factors can be assumed in large samples to cancel themselves out, thus still allowing very high regression weights and predictions.

This concludes the section on vocational guidance as an aspect of educational psychology. However, as mentioned at the beginning of this section, the study of the contribution of psychometrics to vocational guidance would also constitute what I wanted to say about industrial or occupational psychology, although this last is, of course, far wider than vocational guidance.

A few further brief points therefore need to be made. Although there are differences between vocational guidance and selection, the same psychometric information is relevant to both. All the profiles, beta weights and regression equations, together with the proposed encyclopaedia of job specifications are thus equally useful for vocational selection. The contribution of psychometrics to vocational guidance is therefore a contribution to selection.

Another aspect of industrial psychology to which psychometrics could make a contribution is consumer psychology. However, the findings are of insufficient generality for a book of this sort.

DIAGNOSIS AND TREATMENT OF LEARNING AND BEHAVIOUR PROBLEMS

Leaving the two aspects of educational psychology and the allied occupational psychology in which psychometrics has made its greatest contribution, we must now examine its place in the diagnosis and treatment of problems in learning and behaviour, i.e. in the practice of educational psychology.

There can be little doubt that in the past educational psychology as practised in the clinic placed great emphasis on psychological testing, especially on tests of intelligence. Educational psychologists were indeed often given the name of Binet-Bashers. In fact it was a common and justified complaint of teachers who had referred to the educational psychologists a somewhat dim and difficult child, that they received back a report saying that X was below average in intelligence and inclined to show difficult behaviour. More recently, however, there has been a change of professional emphasis to diagnosis and especially treatment, due in part to the stress on behaviour modification. The question essentially that this section of the chapter is concerned with is this: what part can psychometrics usefully play in practical educational psychology?

Diagnosis

Although both in psychology itself and in society beyond, testing and the classification of individual differences are considered to be the practices of Fascists, it still seems to us that in many cases of learning and behavioural problems, psychometric testing of the major variables discussed in earlier sections of this book is highly useful. This will be illustrated in arguments by examining two hypothetical cases, one of learning difficulties, the other behavioural. It is intended only to discuss a rationale for testing and some possible outcomes, the practicalities of testing, which are irrelevant to the purposes of this chapter, will not be discussed.

Suppose a child after one year at the secondary school is referred to the educational psychologists because he is performing extremely poorly in all subjects. It is not unreasonable to attempt a diagnosis: what are the reasons for failure? To answer this question one must know the child's intelligence test score. Without this one has no basis to presuppose how a child should perform at school. It is not sufficient that a child is not below average—suppose he were as bright as Russell or Newton. Thus the intelligence test score enables us to evaluate whether or not the child is reaching his potential. If a child is in the top 2% for I.Q. but in the bottom half of an unstreamed form, one must then attempt to find out the reasons for his poor performance. If his I.Q. is 75 and he is finding difficulty with Latin and geometry, one can feel confident in attempting to find an easier syllabus for him.

If the I.Q. is low one must ensure that the expectations of the child's performance are not unrealistic, if high one must seek out the cause of the disparity. It would appear essential in all problems of learning that an assessment of intelligence be made. Thus the I.Q. test is an essential for both diagnosis and hence treatment of learning difficulties.

Once the level of general ability (gf and gc) has been established depending on the result it may be worthwhile to investigate the pattern of abilities in greater detail by means of aptitude tests. In fact it would appear useful to do this only if the intelligence test score is well above average, say 120 +, about the equivalent of the standard for Grammar School entrance, when such schools existed. If this child is of average intelligence or below, the bias of his abilities is not so important in selecting the correct set of courses. For a bright child with a capability for any subject, there is considerable value in seeing where this capability is most likely to be employed successfully—hence, the suggestion for utilizing an aptitude test battery.

It will be remembered, it is hoped, from the chapter on the analysis of abilities that the presence of the important general factors, gf and gc, considerably diminished the usefulness of aptitude tests, both practically and theoretically, since all the scores tend to be correlated. Hence there is little differential information to be obtained from aptitude test batteries. However, despite this unfortunate fact, it was still possible to argue that at least aptitude batteries could reveal a verbal or numerical bias. With a bright child this additional information can be useful in guiding him to the right courses at school. In this diagnostic case, it may reveal that there is a mismatch of abilities and curriculum—a factor possibly implicated in the problems. Again, therefore, one would argue that in some cases at least, diagnosis of learning and behaviour problems at school can be aided by the administration of aptitude test batteries.

Given then that the pattern of abilities in this child have been measured one has to turn to personality and motivation tests. As is clear from the preceding sections of this chapter, there seems little doubt that the major personality and motivation factors each account for about as much variance in educational success as do ability factors, and furthermore, as Cattell and Kline (1977) have shown, this variance is distinct from that arising from the ability factors. Furthermore, as discussed in the chapter on the application of psychometric findings to clinical and abnormal psychology, some personality factors are important in disturbed behaviour in any setting.

For all these reasons therefore it would seem sensible to measure in cases of learning disorders and problems, the major temperamental and motivational factors, as set out in the chapters on temperament and motivation. It would clearly be wise to include measures of the abnormal factors in addition.

A serious objection, especially from practising educators, to the diagnostic use of tests as so far advocated, is that it is unhelpful. What follows, they ask, if one knows that a child is of low intelligence? It encourages teachers to write off children, to regard their case as hopeless. There is little doubt that such abuse of tests does occur, that some children are abandoned as thick. However, this is not intended. Ideally, one tailors the course to fit more closely the child's potential. This problem is seen in even greater clarity in the case of personality tests. Suppose one finds that the subject is low on the variables related to academic performance, what is the psychologist supposed to do?

In diagnostic terms such a finding is valuable. Essentially, it can be interpreted that the poor performance of the subject is explicable as a function of his temperament and dynamics. This does not mean, of course, that the psychologist should wash his hands and feel that hope is lost. On the contrary, as argued in the section on the relation of these variables to academic success, the observed relationship is itself a function of the educational institution, the kinds of teacher and the methods used. The correlations are not immutable. Thus one would in this case, try to fix this child up with different teachers and regimes, as far as was possible. Advise a fifth-former to continue his studies at the local sixth-form college, if the scores indicate that with standard methods, this subject is not likely to fulfill his potential.

If, however, this subject has his extreme scores on variables that are not related to academic success, then one has no reason to assume that personality problems are implicated in his difficulties. Rather, the root of the matter may lie in external events to a large extent beyond the subject's control, unfortunate quarreling at home, active discouragement from work, pressure to look after younger members of the family, or even more simply, nowhere quiet at home to study or work.

Of course such problems can be present in children who have low ability and are low on the variables important for academic success, thus having their problems made considerably worse. This is mentioned, obvious though it be, simply to make the point that regardless of psychometric test scores, the psychologist dealing with any educational learning difficulty, must always investigate the personal problems, if any, of the children.

The discussion up to this point has made it clear that the application of psychometric tests of ability, personality and motivation has considerable diagnostic value in learning problems and difficulties. Furthermore, it is hoped that it has shown that such diagnosis is useful and not a mere academic matter (i.e. useless).

Readers will note that utilizing any of the standard interest tests in the diagnosis of learning problems has not been suggested. This is because, as argued in the discussion of these tests, their variables have little psychological significance and thus practical power, such as it is, lies only in the field of vocational guidance and selection.

The first case, therefore, of a child referred to an educational psychologist demonstrates in principle how psychometric tests can aid diagnosis, provided they are measuring the fundamental dimensions of ability, temperament and dynamics which have been isolated by multivariate analysis. Essentially the tests seek to discover to what extent the problem arises from the nature of the child himself without of course assuming that no difficulties stem from his environment. In the case of learning difficulties, a rough diagnosis at least is possible because the variables implicated in academic success have been identified.

Before turning to the part psychometrics has to play in the treatment of these learning problems, one should examine a second example, albeit far more briefly for the principles of psychometric diagnosis are similar, this time of behavioural difficulties—the case of an aggressive child.

As argued, teachers hostile to educational psychology claim that if they refer an aggressive child to the educational psychologist, they receive a report telling them that the child is aggressive with I.Q. *X*. Such a report could be one result of using psychological tests in the diagnosis of treatment of behavioural problems and at the outset one would agree that in this form it is valueless. However, I shall still argue that there is a diagnostic and ultimately a therapeutic value in using psychometrics even in the case of aggression, an example chosen because it is particularly awkward. This is so because the psychological study of aggression has failed to reveal any one clear cause (hardly surprising of course, in view of the diffuse nature of the response—ranging from verbal abuse to murder). Realistically it appears that there is a large number of factors implicated in aggression. Just for example, it may be a response to frustration (Dollard *et al.*, 1939), learned by modelling a highly prestigious person (Bandura and Walters, 1963) or in the case of psychopathic aggression related to imperfect maternal attachment (Bowlby, 1944) and there are many other hypotheses. What then can psychometric tests do in so complex a phenomenon?

First, one would apply the same battery of ability, temperament and motivation tests as with the previous case. However, the use of the results would be different. The intelligence test score can be valuable in two ways. A very high score might indicate that the child was bored by his school work: the aggression was frustration. A similar interpretation could be made of a low score for a child in a high achieving form. This would be an example of utilizing the I.Q. score to test the Dollard and Miller hypothesis. A change of curriculum would be an obvious suggestion in this case. It should be pointed out that a further test of this hypothesis would be to examine the extraversion or E score. An acting-out aggressive child would be expected to be extraverted rather than introverted.

It is unlikely in the present state of knowledge that psychometric tests could be useful in elucidating the modelling hypothesis of the origins of aggression. For this, considerable knowledge of the child's family and friends is needed. However, one point deserves note, although this is theoretical rather than practical. If the psychometric study of large samples of children were carried out with other social psychological data added in to aid interpretation, it might well be possible to discover the individual differences implicated in modelling: presumably some children are more likely to copy aggression than others. If so, which children and what determines their modelling? Psychometric investigation could enable such questions to be answered.

In the study of dynamic structure as revealed by psychometrics (Chapter 6) it will be recalled, a pugnacity erg was isolated which is obviously closely related to aggression in most of its forms. Furthermore, the temperamental factor E, dominance, to some extent overlaps aggression as does the other erg important in this area—self-assertion. If one were to apply this test battery and find the child high on these factors and also on P and N (of the Eysenck system) one might easily hypothesize that one had a person who, given the circumstances, could display psychopathic aggression. With such a set of scores the psychologist would have clear suggestions to make to teachers: every effort must be made to avoid arousing this child's aggression; try to put him in situations where there is a retreat or a way out. Avoid confrontation because, if the tests are valid, the child has a control problem. The high N indicates the rapid lability of the autonomic nervous system, the rapid flushing of the features, the bristling of the hair, the preparation for fight. The high P indicates the pleasure the child may get from the sensation of fighting and the lack of touch with reality, the love of cruelty (Eysenck and Eysenck, 1976).

It must be observed that this diagnosis is far more than just a description. I am not saying that the child is aggressive. Rather, the tests demonstrate that by his nature the child has a problem over aggression being easily aroused. What the educator has to do, therefore, is (a) avoid arousing the aggression as far as possible and (b) teach the child to control it. This can be done by reinforcing the child when he does manage to control himself. Thus a psychometric analysis and description does far more than repeat what a harassed teacher knows only too well. Rather, because the psychometric variables are, as we have seen, the fundamental dimensions of personality, scores on them have psychological meaning and hence as it has been argued, the diagnosis has therapeutic implications.

These two examples, one straightforward, the other difficult, illustrate, it seems, the value of psychometry for diagnostic purposes in educational psychology. By locating individuals on psychologically meaningful variables, one is bound to get psychological insights. Having thus shown the place of psychometrics in diagnosis, I shall now examine its value in therapy.

Psychometrics and the Treatment of Educational Problems

At the outset it must be stated, as should be obvious, that in the treatment of disorders, psychometry plays a far less important role than in diagnosis. However, in as much as treatment in some cases at least is dependent itself on diagnosis, psychometry is highly implicated in treatment. In addition there is the important function of monitoring treatments that has to be discussed and in this, psychometrics is essential. In short, therefore, one can see that this second section will be more brief than the first and more concerned with principles, notably those concerned with evaluating treatment.

As has been made clear in the section on diagnosis, sometimes the diagnosis implies a treatment. In all those cases where one finds from testing, that one of the problems is the unsuitability of the course for the abilities and interests of the child, the procedure is obvious: efforts must be made to change the curriculum. In these relatively simple cases, it is fair to argue that psychometrics is implicated in the treatment because this is based so closely on the diagnosis.

Perhaps at this point one should briefly mention a category of tests which have not been discussed so far—diagnostic tests. Such tests, basically specially devised attainment tests, can be used in the diagnosis and treatment of educational disability in reading and mathematics, particularly at the early stages of learning. Schonell (1944) constructed an ingenious set of diagnostic reading tests which serve as an excellent example of this type of test. In these tests items were devised such that all the common reading errors made by young children were specifically tested. Thus letter reversals are common. Items were therefore written testing bp, bd, pd, pq, etc. In this way the psychologist was able to discover the precise errors made by the child. Treatment therefore, can be directed to these specific reading problems. Similar tests were developed for arithmetic where failure can often be due to one small error that can easily escape detection by a teacher in a large class of children. An example here might be multiplication where an o is involved. Treatment again is obviously implicit in the diagnosis.

In the case of the behavioural problem of aggression, any therapeutic procedures are far less dependent on the diagnostic results of psychometric testing. Thus one may decide if one thinks a child has an aggressive disposition that one should take care not to arouse his aggression. However, an intelligent educator would do this without the psychometric test results.

In this case, however, the monitoring function of psychometry in treatment is important. Its value can be easily seen. Thus if one decides that a child must learn to control his aggression one can assess the success of the treatment by comparing his scores during and after therapy with his original set. If a child is high on pugnacity, dominance, E, N (neuroticism) and low on C, ego strength, scores which one would regard as demonstrative of an aggressive disposition, successful therapy, of whatever kind, would be expected to result in scores lower on these variables. In principle, as I shall argue in the chapter on the use of psychometric tests in clinical psychology, this rationale is applicable to the treatment of all psychological disorders. In other words the argument is that successful therapy, by definition, should send back to the population mean, those scores which characterize the particular mental disorder. So, for example, if depressives are high on the D abnormal factors, treatment should lower these scores. It is to be noted that rationale does not attempt to make all people the same or turn them to contented cows. It is concerned to return not all scores to the population mean but those which are related to the particular disorder. A more detailed discussion of this topic can be found in Chapter 9.

This method of monitoring treatment is one of the few rational approaches to the problem of the assessment of psychotherapy. Such a method effectively indicates whether, as treatment continues, there is improvement, deterioration or no change. Properly used with a wide variety of subjects, the whole range of disorders and the whole gamut of different therapies, this method would allow the effectiveness of different therapies to be assessed. It is likely that different methods would be effective with characteristic groups and thus ultimately psychometrics could be a powerful way of improving treatment.

Educational Theory

Enough has been said now concerning the contribution of psychometrics to the diagnosis of educational problems and their treatment. One must turn now to a further aspect of educational psychology—educational theory. As indicated in the introduction, what is needed, but has been generally neglected, is a theory which would embrace the findings concerning educational attainment. What theory of learning, for example, can successfully account for and predict academic success. There is a similar need for a theory to account for instructional success. Thus if one had a proper theoretical account of the teaching and learning process as it occurs in institutions of learning not only should one be better able to train teachers but one should also be able to improve the academic performance of the students.

This is not the place for a study of those factors influencing human learning and school performance, for this is a text designed to establish the contribution of psychometrics to psychological knowledge. I shall therefore not attempt to cover all aspects of the topic. Rather, I shall restrict this to an examination of how Eysenck and Cattell have attempted to apply their theories to the field of education. Their theories, structured learning theory in the case of Cattell and a welding of factor-analytic findings to Hullian drive theory in the case of Eysenck, are fully described and examined in Chapter 7. Here I shall scrutinize how each may be applied in the educational field.

Unfortunately, structured learning theory, as Cattell and Child (1975) make clear, is too new to have been used in educational theory to any effect. This is true only in relation to any specific predictions which can be put to a quantified test. In more general terms, however, structured learning theory does have important and interesting implications for understanding the motivation of students—ideas which if shown to be correct empirically should have a useful influence in the training of teachers. Indeed they would give teaching a genuine theoretical rationale.

As pointed out in the discussion of structured learning theory, one of its most distinctive characteristics compared with orthodox theories of learning lies in its treatment of reinforcement. Generally, as in Hull (1943), reinforcement, if subjected to any kind of theoretical analysis, is seen as drive reduction. In structured learning theory, however, reinforcement is more precisely defined as tension reduction of the ergs and sentiments. Integration learning aims to maximize this tension reduction by taking into account all ergs and sentiments, rather than gratifying the one immediately pressing, perhaps at the expense of the others. Integration learning, of course, implying as it does the delay of gratification, typically is most commonly found among the middle classes: indeed it probably accurately describes the protestant ethic. It is this notion of reinforcement in terms of ergic tension reduction that is relevant to motivation in school.

From structured learning theory it would appear that where tension reduction is greatest, learning will be maximized. Thus one has to ask oneself as educators what tension reduction is taking place for each subject in the curriculum. If none it is hardly surprising that learning is so difficult for the students who are manifestly bored, and that teaching is thereby rendered aversive. Incidentally, of course, when learning is conceptualized in terms of structured learning theory, as changes in three vectors, the trait vector, the bearing vector and the modulation change vector, the futility of a common curriculum can be seen since trait scores are different for each individual. The point relevant to the motivation of students is simple. How great a tension reduction on each erg and sentiment is produced by learning the Ionic form of the optative of οἶδα? Although the answer to this question must be empirically determined, it is arguable that to the very bright scholastic child for whom the glories of Greece are a reality, it can be considerable. For the child of average I.Q. to whom Greece is but another land without a good football team, tension reduction from academic subjects will be quite different, thus structured learning theory allows an operational definition of such terms as relevance, salience and interest to be made. Teachers, therefore, can find out how to make their teaching interesting, i.e. tension reducing and, more important, curricula can be properly designed for pupils of various kinds. Individual differences can be respected.

Cattell and Child (1975) also argue that structured learning theory clarifies the aims of education. Thus, as the example from the classics showed, tension reduction from academic subjects would appear to be limited although where they impinge on life, via career, for example, their ergic importance is obviously greater. However, many of the ideals of education go beyond academic success. The Platonic aim is a knowledge of the good το αγαθον which once known profoundly affects behaviour. Plutarch with his "Lives of the Great" hoped to hold out models for the young. Many of our famous public schools aim to produce British gentlemen. In other words, the aim of education is to produce a specified set of scores on the T vectors, the trait vector. Thus the rulers of the Hindus and Moslems of India were to be high on C, ego strength, high on G, superego, low on O, guilt-proneness, and hopefully high on g, ability, certainly gc. Empirically one can now test to what extent the educational institutions produce the desired changes in the T vector.

Enough has now been said about the implications of structured learning theory for obtaining a rationale for teaching. All is speculation, however, until the necessary empirical work is carried out. This is an area of research which educationalists must pursue. I shall now examine the theoretical value for education of Eysenck's theory of personality.

As pointed out in the discussion of Eysenck's theory, there are several difficulties which make it somewhat unlikely that, as it stands, the theory will adequately account for the research results: the main problems being the doubt over the unitary nature of conditionability, and the diffuseness of concepts such as arousal and inhibition. Nevertheless it does appear that, even if the theoretical rationale is inadequate, very different strategies of work and learning are required if extraverts and introverts are to perform optimally. Extraverts quickly get bored and make errors, introverts work steadily through their tasks. Analysis of Raven's Matrices protocols item by item by

Mohan and Kumar (1976) strongly confirms this claim. These and similar findings in other fields concerning vigilance among extraverts and introverts (reported in Eysenck, 1967) for example, mean that effective teaching methods should be different for the two personality groups. For the extraverts, frequent changes of work, plenty of activity, spaced learning, working co-operatively together, all these are teaching strategies likely to pay off. For the introvert, quiet steady working for long periods utilizing books with the minimum of teacher interference, is likely to prove the most successful. For the majority, however, who score around the mean on this variable, a virtually standard lesson mixing both extreme procedures should be good. One interesting point that would test the teaching rationale is the size of the correlations between academic success and introversion–extraversion under this teaching regime. My guess is that it would be negligible.

From this discussion it is clear that some first steps towards a theory of teaching can be made from the psychometric work discussed in this book. Clearly far more educational research directly aimed at testing the utility of these psychometrically based theories is required. This is a proposition more exacting than collecting correlations between personality and dynamic variables and academic success, and as yet in Great Britain at least, there is little sign that this is about to be done.

Developmental Theory

Developmental theory is probably too grand a title for what is properly intended in this, the last division of educational psychology. More precisely it would be called developmental knowledge. Psychometric tests should be able to contribute heavily to this aspect of psychology. It is to be noted, in this respect, that what was laid down in Chapter 3 as one of the essentials of a good psychological test—namely, norms—in the case of tests designed for children of varying ages, provides this basic developmental information (provided that the norms are derived from standardization groups of sufficient size and quality).

The Different Requirements of Norms and Developmental Psychology

Unfortunately the requirements of good normative data and developmental data are not identical. For this reason, therefore, one cannot simply regard all norms as developmental data (of any value) derived from psychometric testing, although ideal norms would not always be different. In real life all one can expect of norms is that they provide a sound basis for comparing the scores of the subjects one tests. For reliable, valid developmental data, the samples must be large and fully representative of their parent populations. Norms, the careful tester uses as a guide: he knows the samples are unlikely to be ideal. Developmental data *must* be accurate. A rough guide is of no value. With developmental data, one wants to know accurately both the mean and the variance of the variables. For in my view, the point of such developmental data is that one has a yardstick by which psychological progress may be measured.

This distinction between developmental data and useful norms is clearly illustrated in the case of vocabularly tests. A vocabulary test with well-attested validity could have the most excellent norms for various age-groups. Yet, especially at the earliest levels of development of speech (exactly where developmental data are likely to be most useful) as developmental data, the norms are at their weakest. For a small child's vocabulary is highly dependent especially before reading and school, on its particular environment. Is a tractor for the country child, equivalent to the urban child's bulldozer. What in town parallels oats, corn, barley and wheat? Furthermore, even if one utilizes word counts as data, whether different types of word are equivalent is dubious. Of course this discussion has avoided as irrelevant, the more profound question as the criteria for accepting a word as understood: the child responds appropriately, uses it accurately or can define it. All these would give different sets of scores.

This distinction between norms and developmental data means that only in those cases where the test is measuring some fundamental variable (of the kind isolated by factor analysis) do norms overlap developmental data. Thus to use again the example of the vocabularly test, good norms will enable one to rank subjects accurately against the relevant population and thus make judgements about their progress in the acquisition of vocabulary. They do not enable one to make general statements about vocabulary at certain ages. Scores on a test of extraversion are different. Here it is possible to plot age differences in scores and this has a genuine psychological meaning since the extraversion test is the operational definition of extraversion. In other words, extraversion as a factor is defined by the test score and thus good norms do represent developmental data, although even in this case the particular test, whether the JEPI or the CPQ for example, needs to be specified.

So one may conclude this discussion by arguing that where tests represent the operational definition of the factor as is the case in factored tests, the age norms do have a genuine psychological developmental meaning. Where however the test simply samples a domain of knowledge or interest, this is not the case. This argument, of course, assumes that the tests are perfectly valid, are complete measures of the factor. The lower the validity of the test, i.e. the smaller its loading on the factor, the further away from useful developmental data are the test norms.

Despite this the norms of the two best established intelligence tests, the Stanford-Binet and the Wechsler are tacitly at least regarded as developmental data. Decisions on the basis of a comparison of scores with children of various ages, are made about intellectual competence. Similarly with the new British Intelligence Scale normative data (i.e. developmental) will be established relating to various of the Piagetian developmental stages.

So far, except perhaps in the case of intelligence tests, although even here the norms are far from ideal for use as developmental data, this aspect of psychometric testing has been ignored. What is needed, therefore, are extensive norms for the various populations comprising a culture. Thus in Great Britain, one should want the following properly and extensively sampled groups, at say six month intervals: male, urban, social class 1 and 2: female, urban, social class 1 and 2, and so on through the social classes and for rural children as well. Possibly even more fine grained groups would be necessary. If this were carried out for all the fundamental psychological variables discussed in the early chapters of this book, it would provide one with a baseline for estimating factors influencing development on these variables and the Orlansky (1966) claim that so far child-rearing had not been shown to affect adult personality, would, if indeed there is an effect, no longer obtain.

Sound data on the developmental course of the factorial variables combined with a detailed study of the life events of groups on the extremes of the dimensions (as carried out by Brown (e.g. 1974) in his study of depression among Camberwell housewives) would inevitably yield a rich harvest of psychological knowledge. Such developmental studies especially in the field of motivation and personality are an area in which psychometrics must surely advance. In the sphere of abilities, as seen in the discussion of the most important ability factors, some knowledge already exists. All that is needed is more refined replication. With data of this type, developmental theories could be constructed. It must be noted that some developmental theories e.g. those of Piaget, make the child different from rather than a miniature adult. However, psychometric developmental data of the kind I am advocating, can recognize this as, for example, when new factors emerge or disappear at certain ages or when relations between factors changes, or when what is clearly the same factor has different loadings among different age-groups.

SUMMARY

The length of this chapter is a reflection of how psychometrics has, in Great Britain at least, found a home more in education than psychology, demands a brief summary.
(1) Educational psychology was categorized into: (a) diagnosis and treatment of educational difficulties; (b) allocation of children to their proper educational level; (c) vocational guidance and counselling; (d) educational psychology theory and (e) developmental theory.
(2) The power of the factorially defined psychometric variables of ability, personality and motivation, in predicting academic success was examined. It was concluded that the *overall* prediction from all three spheres was moderate and that the correlations between extraversion and academic success were due largely to teaching methods. Differences in results among various sub-groups were discussed.
(3) The value of psychometrics in vocational guidance was demonstrated from scrutinizing the beta weights, correlations, and mean score differences of all the variables in relation to criteria of success in a variety of occupations. The construction of an encyclopaedia of job specifications in terms of factor scores was suggested.
(4) In the diagnosis and treatment of learning and behaviour problems the value of psychometrics in diagnosis and in monitoring treatment was emphasized.

Psychometrics provided insights into the problems and a rationale and check on treatment.

(5) Education theory had not yet been much aided by psychometrics, although structured learning theory seemed to offer some possibilities in this direction.

(6) Developmental theory was at the present state of knowledge, defined as developmental data to which psychometric tests of factored variables could add much. This data should form the basis of a proper developmental theory.

This brief summary makes it clear that in educational psychology there has already been a considerable contribution from psychometrics. What is also apparent is that there is far more to come especially in the establishment of developmental data and in the construction of an encyclopaedia of job specifications. In the prediction of educational success, correlations are about as high as they are likely to be and these studies need to be combined with interaction studies of the teaching process. In brief, psychometrics still has much to offer to educational psychology.

9

Psychometrics in Clinical Psychology

It is clear that clinical psychology to some extent overlaps educational psychology, especially, in the diagnosis and treatment of learning problems and difficulties.

In this chapter the term clinical psychology will be used to refer to the psychological problems arising from the diagnosis and treatment of mental illness, which includes neurosis and psychosis, as described by Mayer-Gross *et al.* (1967). There are really three fields of clinical psychology (a) diagnosis, (b) therapy and (c) theory which are related, but nevertheless each with their own distinctive problems so that it is convenient to examine the contribution of psychometrics to each separately, as well as giving an overall assessment of its value in clinical psychology.

DIAGNOSIS

The value of diagnosis in clinical psychology does not lie in mere labelling, as many of its detractors have argued, e.g. Laing (1960). Laing has claimed that psychiatrists and psychologists have been content to name a mental illness and thus categorize a patient as schizophrenic or depressed, and feel that there is a job well done. In fact, diagnosis is an aid, a first step in answering a set of questions that are fundamental to mental illness. For example, what are the causes of different mental illnesses (and surely even the most convinced phenomenological humanist is not going to argue that typical obsessional rituals are the same as or caused by similar factors to those related to depression?) An hypothesis which is so unlikely demands powerful supporting evidence. Are all or some mental disorders qualitatively or quantitatively different from normal mental states? For example, is the obsessional behaviour an exaggeration of the careful tidiness valued by housewives and accountants? Is clinical depression, similarly, an exaggeration of the depression that most people at times experience? It is to be noted that such research can also show that the notion of cause in these instances is not useful (as opponents of the medical model have argued, e.g. Foulds, 1976).

To answer such questions, accurate diagnosis is important. If one is investigating the antecedents in family life of depression and schizophrenia one must be sure that the samples really are depressed and schizophrenic. Again, if one is investigating the abnormal–normal continuum in obsessionality, one must examine obsessionals. Of course it may well be that these states are not distinct or that they have similar causes. However, without attempts at accurate diagnosis such "negative" findings could not be established. In other words it is important to have clear diagnostic criteria.

THERAPY

The value of therapy in clinical psychology is obvious. It is the point of the business to make people better. As Eysenck (1952) made clear in his attack on the efficacy of psychoanalytic therapy, there is considerable difficulty in trying to evaluate the success of any therapy. Despite this, within the area of psychotherapy there is a set of problems: does any therapy alleviate any disorder (the most fundamental question of all)? Are some therapies successful with some disorders and others with others? If one considers the earliest psychoanalytic papers from which the whole fabric of psychoanalytic theory stems, it might be possible to argue that psychoanalytic therapy was good for hysterical illness but not for other disorders. Similarly, on theoretical grounds alone one should expect behavioural therapeutic techniques to be at their best with phobias, especially specific phobias, although Eysenck's (1976) notions of incubation disturb the confidence with which clear hypotheses can be made. Such techniques, however, would apparently find the greatest difficulty with depressive symptoms, especially where these were pervasive and severe. Again the possibility arises that more important than the type of therapy is the interaction of patient and therapist and here clearly the personality, especially the temperament, of both individuals is likely to be critical.

THEORY

So far in clinical psychology there has been an abundance of theories although almost all are of the clinical variety based upon evidence (if at all) that is unquantified and lacks the essential replicability demanded of science. They are, as Cattell and Kline (1977) have pointed out, pre-scientific. Behaviour therapy is (see Breger and McGaugh, 1965) derived from learning theory and certainly overtly subscribes to Pavlovian and Skinnerian principles of learning. However this is the only current theory of any scientific repute of any applicability to clinical psychology. What is needed is a sound theoretical basis for treatment.

For reasons which have been fully explicated in the relevant chapters, we shall look at the fundamental variables of personality and motivation as they bear on the problems in the three main branches of clinical psychology, with specific reference to these two sets of factors because they are the focus of most of the work.

In addition, we shall examine carefully the specific contribution of criterion-keyed tests to diagnostic procedures in clinical psychology, although as I have argued, they tend to yield variables of little psychological meaning. This is simply because the MMPI has been so extensively used. We shall also consider the contribution to knowledge from projective tests especially where the results have been treated with psychometric statistical techniques and where objective scoring has minimized the low reliability of most of these methods.

CONTRIBUTION OF PSYCHOMETRICS TO DIAGNOSTIC PROBLEMS

Pre-scientific, clinically based theories of abnormal behaviour as traditionally exemplified in the work of the psychoanalyst (almost all schools agree here), in the writing of McDougal and the brilliant observational studies of Kretschmer (1925) have one feature in common. Psychiatric disturbance is seen as disturbance of temperament and dynamics. The sphere of abilities is not considered to be especially important. Indeed the fact that one can observe mentally defective patients of relatively normal personality suggests that in respect of abilities, in the diagnostic problems of clinical psychology, the most that could be expected would be an interaction with personality and motivational variables. For this reason in this section the main emphasis is on the impact of these variables rather than ability, on diagnostic problems.

As previously indicated, I shall discuss not only factored variables but also other psychometric and projective devices which have been specifically developed for use in clinical psychology. However, for reasons which have been consistently proposed throughout this book, the concentration is on the examination of personality and motivational dimensions isolated by factor analysis because these have psychological meaning. All results can be interpreted in the light of the knowledge of these variables (which have been fully described in the relevant chapters of this book).

The first question to be answered is: in what way do neurotics and psychotics differ from normals and among themselves? Four sets of results are examined—differences on Q factors, differences on abnormal Q factors and differences on T factors based upon objective tests. The work with projective tests and criterion-keyed tests is then scrutinized.

Differences between Normals, Psychotics and Neurotics on Cattell 16 PF Factors

I am attempting to establish the contribution of psychometrics to psychological knowledge. This involves setting out the findings, having given the rationale for the choice of variables and the factor analytic approach in general, in previous chapters. The danger of apparently dogmatic assertion is nowhere higher than in this part of the book where the results have to be the quintessence of a huge number of studies carried out over almost forty years. The number of investigations is so large that a proper discussion of all the problems of methodology is simply impossible. For a brief discussion readers are referred to Cattell and Kline (1977). All one can do is set out a typical sample of findings concerning neurotics, psychotics and normals, findings quoted in the technical manual to the 16 PF and indicate the psychological significance of the results. While discussing the findings, the more severe of the methodological problems are briefly examined.

In Table 9.1 one can see the 16 PF scores of various abnormal groups. A number of important diagnostic points can be made, points which clearly support the utility and meaningfulness of factorially derived dimensions. Compared with normals the neurotic patient has low ego strength (C−), is submissive (E−), divergent (F), of low superego strength (G−), is timid (H−) and anxious and guilty (O and Q4). This picture of the neurotic is not a bad fit to clinical descriptions as shown in psychiatric textbooks, e.g. Henderson and Gillespie (1956) or Mayer-Gross et al. (1967).

As Cattell and Kline (1977) argued in relation to these findings, they are of special interest to psychoanalytic theory which predicts that neurotics would be low on ego strength. However, the prediction of high superego is not supported; the mean of 4·6 is not significantly lower than the general population mean of 5·5. Indeed this result does not fit the claims of Mowrer (1950) either, who had proposed that the neurotic feels guilty because he is guilty because his superego is too low, a doctrine which is strikingly reminiscent of certain kinds of christianity "Peccavi, Domine ...".

The second-order factors clearly confirm the findings of Eysenck (e.g. 1967) and the claims as to the essential identity of the Cattell second-orders and Eysenck's E and N. According to the Cattell factors in Table 9.1, at the second-order the neurotic is an anxious introvert. So much then for the picture of the neurotic in general, as timid, submissive, guilty and indecisive. The psychological significance of these findings is discussed in more detail when some of the differences on the Cattell dimensions between the abnormal groups have been examined.

As we scan the different groups in Table 9.1, one fact stands out. All groups of neurotics are low on ego strength, factor C. In psychoanalytic terms the weakness of the ego allows the id or superego to dominate the individual. What is particularly interesting is the fact that psychopaths are not low on factor C together with the paranoids. In psychoanalytic terms the psychopath suffers not from lack of ego control but from lack of guilt (no superego), an

TABLE 9.1
SCORES OF ABNORMAL GROUPS ON THE 16 PF TEST

Group	N																					
Anxiety reaction	80	M	5.9	6.9	2.8	3.7	3.5	4.3	7.1	7.5	6.4	5.2	8.5	5.4	6.1	4.5	7.8	3.8	8.3	3.4	5.0
		σ	2.1	2.0	2.3	2.1	2.1	2.4	1.9	2.3	2.3	2.1	2.6	1.5	1.9	2.3	2.5				
Conversion reaction	31	M	4.9	6.5	4.2	5.7	4.1	5.2	5.2	6.1	5.2	5.7	6.9	4.7	6.2	5.0	7.7	4.4	7.2	5.5	5.1
		σ	1.9	2.4	2.0	2.6	1.8	2.1	2.6	2.8	2.4	2.3	2.3	1.9	2.0	2.3	2.2				
Depressive reaction	70	M	5.4	5.4	2.7	3.9	3.5	4.5	4.9	7.4	7.0	5.5	7.5	5.2	6.2	4.5	8.1	4.0	8.0	4.1	5.3
		σ	2.1	1.8	2.2	2.1	1.9	1.5	1.8	2.2	1.8	1.9	2.1	1.5	1.3	1.5	2.0				
Obsessive compulsive	29	M	5.9	6.1	4.8	3.7	3.8	4.9	3.7	5.3	6.0	4.8	7.7	4.4	5.4	4.4	7.7	4.1	7.5	3.5	4.0
		σ	2.3	1.8	1.9	2.0	2.4	2.0	2.2	2.5	1.7	2.3	2.3	1.3	1.6	2.1	2.2				
Inadequate personality	54	M	5.9	5.1	3.8	5.1	5.4	4.8	6.3	7.0	7.3	5.5	7.7	5.9	6.7	5.2	7.4	4.6	7.5	4.6	6.0
		σ	1.9	2.0	3.1	3.0	2.7	2.6	2.1	1.8	2.0	2.8	1.9	1.8	2.7	2.5	2.6				
Psychosomatic	76	M	5.2	6.9	4.9	5.3	4.8	5.0	5.1	5.5	4.7	5.6	6.4	4.2	6.2	5.1	6.8	4.9	6.5	5.6	4.8
		σ	1.9	2.6	2.0	2.1	1.7	2.8	1.2	2.3	2.4	2.3	3.4	2.1	2.1	2.2	2.0				
General schizophrenic	334	M	5.4	4.6	4.4	4.9	4.4	5.1	5.8	5.8	5.6	5.0	6.3	5.0	6.1	5.9	5.7	4.5	6.2	4.8	5.2
		σ	1.9	2.1	2.1	1.9	2.0	2.0	1.9	2.0	1.9	2.2	2.3	2.0	1.9	2.6	2.2				
Catatonic	30	M	5.2	4.9	4.1	5.1	4.7	5.0	5.6	6.4	5.2	5.0	6.7	5.2	6.4	5.5	6.3	4.4	6.7	5.1	5.3
		σ	1.5	2.0	1.8	2.0	1.8	2.0	1.8	2.0	2.0	2.1	1.9	2.2	1.9	1.5	2.2				
Paranoid	68	M	4.8	5.2	5.2	4.8	4.3	5.6	5.3	6.3	5.7	5.4	5.2	5.3	6.0	6.8	5.1	4.5	5.2	5.5	5.4
		σ	2.2	1.9	1.9	1.8	2.2	2.1	1.5	2.5	1.7	2.0	1.8	1.9	2.1	2.0	1.8				
Acute undifferentiated	41	M	5.6	5.1	4.0	5.8	5.4	4.5	6.1	5.9	5.8	5.1	7.3	5.4	5.9	5.0	6.2	5.1	6.8	5.0	5.7
		σ	2.1	2.5	2.5	1.7	1.7	2.1	1.7	2.0	2.2	2.3	2.8	1.9	1.8	2.8	2.6				
Chronic undifferentiated	74	M	5.3	4.7	4.1	4.8	4.5	4.6	5.9	5.6	5.4	5.2	6.8	4.8	6.2	5.8	5.7	4.2	6.4	4.6	5.0
		σ	1.5	2.1	2.2	1.9	1.6	1.9	2.0	1.7	1.8	2.4	2.2	1.9	1.7	2.0	2.1				
Schizo-affective	27	M	6.2	4.9	3.6	4.7	5.1	4.8	5.9	5.4	4.1	4.1	7.1	4.3	5.9	5.2	6.6	4.9	7.0	4.4	4.9
		σ	2.1	1.9	1.8	1.6	1.5	1.3	2.0	1.8	1.5	2.0	2.2	1.6	1.7	2.2	1.8				
Manic-depressive (Manic type)	20	M	5.7	5.1	4.5	6.0	6.1	5.0	5.5	5.7	5.3	4.7	6.2	5.0	6.0	5.9	6.0	5.9	6.1	5.9	5.7
		σ	2.1	2.1	2.2	2.0	1.6	1.8	1.9	1.8	1.8	1.7	1.9	1.9	1.8	1.6	1.9				
Manic-depressive (Depressed type)	53	M	5.4	4.5	3.4	4.2	4.2	5.6	4.3	6.6	6.3	5.3	8.0	5.1	6.4	4.9	7.4	4.1	7.8	4.1	4.8
		σ	1.9	2.2	2.3	2.2	2.2	2.3	2.2	2.4	2.4	1.9	2.5	1.8	2.1	2.2	2.7				

These figures are taken with permission of IPAT from the 16 PF Handbook.

hypothesis supported by the psychopathic group's scores on O and G in the table. Thus this pattern of scores confirms one aspect of Freudian theory. However, all interpretations with so small a sample must be extremely cautious. Finally, the paranoids' C score is also interesting, for this psychotic group in Freudian theory are characterized by their utilization of two particular defences—projection and reaction-formation—against homosexuality. Since defences are a product of the ego the high C score in this particular group is not unexpected.

The primarily psychoanalytic discussion of these results may offend some readers of a book which purports to be scientific. However, it should be noted that factor C, ego strength, although empirically derived, is a psychoanalytic construct and more "scientific" theories do not use the term.

Although the 16 PF factors distinguish neurotics from normals among neurotic groups, factor C is about the best discriminator, providing differences, as we have seen, consonant with psychoanalytic theory. The other factors which discriminate neurotics from normals however do not show nearly as great a differentiation among the different psychiatric categories. Thus all are high on O guilt. Perhaps after C, Q4, tension, is the most discriminating. The neuroses, rather than the psychoses, show elevated scores, and the highest groups are those where the symptoms are often held in clinical theory to reflect tension, to be an acting out of problems, as in the instance of alcoholics, exhibitionists and homosexuals.

One objection to the study of personality differences between clinical groups is the point previously made in the discussion of the MMPI and other criterion-keyed tests, an objection which might be held to weaken all the arguments in this chapter. It concerns the universal problem of establishing adequate criterion groups, a difficulty which is particularly acute in clinical psychology. There is much work to demonstrate that psychiatric classification is highly unreliable, typefied for example, by the work of Beck (1962). However this objection if anything strengthens rather than weakens the results. For the error, unless systematic, would tend to misplace patients at random so that any observed differences would be likely to be smaller than their real values if diagnosis had been more reliable. Of course it could be that error was systematic. However systematic error, while lowering the validity of diagnostic classification, actually increases the reliability. Furthermore, the error would have to be such that it was consonant with predicted hypotheses. Thus the argument against psychiatric classification, while fully accepted, is not held to infirm the differences between groups discussed above nor those that are examined later in the chapter.

As we have seen, at the second-order the Cattell factors provide a similar picture to that obtained from the first-orders. Compared with normals, neurotic groups are high on anxiety introversion and subdued dependence. This is precisely the picture which emerges from the EPI and EPQ, although there, there is no independence factor and here there is no psychoticism. It is also noteworthy that the rather gross second-orders cannot make such fine discriminations among these psychiatric groups as the primaries. This supports the utility of the primary factors despite their unreliability.

Results with the Abnormal, Pathological Factors

It will be obvious from Table 9.1 that the 16 PF primary factors seem efficient at distinguishing neurotic and disturbed groups such as alcoholics, from normals. However, psychotic groups such as schizophrenics and manic depressives are not much different from normal. Thus a weakness of the normal standard personality dimensions for clinical psychology is that they fail to discriminate the most strikingly disturbed groups.

As has been fully described in the major dimensions of personality (Chapter 5), for this very reason Cattell and his colleagues were forced to develop new tests to measure new factors or dimensions that were clearly important in abnormal behaviour. A list and description of these factors can be found on page 156, and the results achieved with this set of abnormal factors among clinical groups will be considered here. The test incorporating these factors is the CAQ (Delhees and Cattell, 1971a, b) which also allows measurement of the 16 normal factors. The differences between scores of various psychiatric groups on the 12 abnormal factors are set out in Table 9.2.

From Table 9.2 a clear fact emerges: all groups are distinguished from normals on all scales other than the As scale, which is both psychotic and neurotic. One can therefore argue that in terms of fundamental dimensions of personality, neurotics are distinguished from normals on both normal and abnormal factors, psychotics on abnormal factors alone. This fits in with the psychiatric claim (e.g. Mayer-Gross *et al.*, 1967) that in the psychoses, behaviours are seen which are qualitatively different from normal. It also fits other psychometric work by Foulds (1976) which is discussed later.

In the previous description of these abnormal factors I drew attention to the fact that there were seven primary depression factors with three second-orders, arising from their rather large correlations. Even though the psychiatric categories used here are not normally held to be characterized by depression, they can be discriminated from each other by the depressive factors. This is a finding of great interest but of a psychological significance that remains to be elucidated.

As discussed in Cattell and Kline (1977), a discriminate function analysis of these data indicated that the groups could be separated along three dimensions: (a) pathological/normal, (b) psychotic/neurotic and (c) brain-damaged and personality disorders versus the rest. Such findings in view of the small samples demand replication before too much reliance can be placed upon them.

These diagnostic results have some clear psychological implications which represent a significant contribution to knowledge in clinical psychology:

(1) Psychosis is not on a continuum with neurosis and mental health.

(2) Neurosis is on a continuum with mental health.

TABLE 9.2
DIFFERENCES BETWEEN ABNORMAL GROUPS[a]

Two groups[b] examined for differences	D_1	D_2	D_3	D_4	D_5	D_6	D_7	Pa	Pp	As	Ps	Sc
1-5		*										
	—											
1-6		**					**				**	
	—											
1-7	**	**	**	**	**	**	**	**	**		**	**
	+	+	+	+	+	+	+	+	+		+	+
2-5				*		**			**			
	—					—	—		—			
2-6		**				**	*		*		*	
	—	—				—	—		—		—	
2-7	**	**	**	**	**	**	**	**	**		**	**
	+	+	+	+	+	+	+	+	+		+	+
3-5									**			
									—			
3-6											*	
3-7	**	**	**	**	**	**	**	**	**		**	**
	+	+	+	+	+	+	+	+	+		+	+
4-5		*					*		**		*	
	—					—	—		—		—	
4-6		**					**		*		**	
	—					—	—		—		—	
4-7	**	**	**	**	**	**	**	**	**		**	**
	+	+	+	+	+	+	+	+	+		+	+
5-7	**	**	**	**	**	**	**	**	**		**	**
	+	+	+	+	+	+	+	+	+		+	+
6-7	**	**	**	**	**	**	**	**	**	*	**	**
	+	+	+	+	+	+	+	+	+	—	+	+

[a] Each row examines differences of each pathological syndrome group in turn from the normal group—7 (see paired numbers on left). A plus shows the group on the left is higher and a minus lower. The degree of significance of the difference is shown by an asterisk ($p < 0.05$) or two asterisks ($p < 0.01$) (by Tukey's HSD test). Data from May (1971).

[b] (1) paranoid schizophrenics, (2) chronic schizophrenics, (3) organic brain damage, (4) personality disorders, (5) neurotics, (6) affective disorders, (7) normal controls.

Reprinted from "Personality and Mood by Questionnaire" by R. B. Cattell with permission of Jossey-Bass.

This means of course that it is mistaken to conceive of psychosis as in some sense worse than or more extreme than neurosis. It is qualitatively different, as indeed has long been argued in the psychiatric textbooks. The neuroses can be seen, however, as a disturbance of the normal structure of temperament. This implies, therefore, that the neuroses and psychoses are likely to be different in respect of treatment and outcome, not to say cause. Both may reflect, however, the results of severe psychological trauma (the psychotic factors being indicative of physiological genetic influences) as the work of Laing (1960) clearly demonstrates.

Mention of the influence of Cattell's abnormal factors leads on to an examination of the significance for diagnosis of Eysenck's three main factors, E, N and P.

Significance of the Eysenck Factors

It has always been claimed by adherents of the Maudsley factorial approach to clinical psychology (e.g. Eysenck and Eysenck, 1975), that a major advantage of the Eysenck system vis-à-vis the Cattell system, is its simplicity: three factors instead of 23, and reliable factors rather than ephemeral primaries. However, to those psychologists who are prepared to recognize the complexity of human behaviour, an explanation in terms of three variables seems inevitably inadequate. As has been quoted before in this case, from a review of Ayer's "Language, Truth and Logic": "... nothing can be that simple, let alone everything". Indeed it is instructive to note, before evaluating the work of Eysenck, that over the years the signal simplicity of his system has been gradually lessened by the introduction of new factors, and this trend is increasing. Within a few years perhaps there will be less apparent disagreement between the work of Cattell and Eysenck in respect of the number of factors. As has been discussed, P has been formally inserted into a published psychometric test, the EPQ (Eysenck and Eysenck, 1975), and the evidence relevant to P has been collected into book form (Eysenck and Eysenck, 1976). Even more recently, two new factors of impulsivity have been adduced (Eysenck and Eysenck, 1977) which would certainly appear likely to be related to Q4 and possibly F, among the Cattell primaries. In addition, Eysenck (as in the "Psychology of Politics", Eysenck, 1954) has made some use of the factors of tough–tender-mindedness and radicalism–conservatism, both, of course, are present in the Cattell set but are regarded by Eysenck as attitudinal factors. It can be argued, therefore, that Eysenck's system is not much less complex than that of Cattell. Nevertheless, I am mainly concerned with P, E and N in this section, because that is where the largest mass of evidence has accumulated.

Of E and N there is little to add to what has already been written. All that is applicable to the Cattell second-order factors applies to these, for they are essentially identical. Whether the N factor best be labelled anxiety or neuroticism is not perhaps as important as first appears, because both Cattell and Eysenck have collected so much information about these factors that their psychological significance can be understood without the need of a label. Nevertheless two points about this identification have to be mentioned.

First, since, as Table 9.1 shows, neurotics differ from normals on other factors as well as N, therefore, to call N neuroticism, is misleading. Secondly, as pointed out in the discussion of learning theories, the concept of N, as reactivity to threat, dependent on the lability of the autonomic nervous system (Jones, 1961), is fully consonant with an interpretation of N as anxiety. Finally, in the EPQ and EPI handbooks the high N scorer is always regarded as a typically highly anxious individual.

Study of the manuals to the EPI and the EPQ, which set out the scores of different psychiatric groups on the two tests, needs little comment as regards E and N. The results are similar to Cattell's and generally in accord with Eysenck's theorizing. Most psychotic and neurotic groups score highly on N and the most extraverted of the neurotic groups are hysterics. However, these are still introverted compared with non-psychiatric samples.

According to Eysenckian theory (fully discussed in Chapter 7) criminals should be extraverted (having failed to learn the mores of society). However, this is only true of the female sample of prisoners in the manual. Indeed as Cochrane (1973) has demonstrated from a review of studies with the EPI, only about half of them show that prisoners arc more extraverted than controls. In fact as Waldo and Dinitz (1967) argued, and no data have been obtained which renders their conclusions oudated, personality questionnaires in general have been highly unsuccessful in discriminating differences between criminals and controls. If studies where discriminations have been made, are compared, it is often found that the mean scores of the criminal groups are so different that if the contrast groups in the studies had been exchanged there would have been no significant findings.

All this suggests what an even cursory examination of the nature of crimes would confirm, that the term criminal embraces a large variety of human behaviour. Hence, one should not expect *all* criminals, even if there were substance in the Eysenckian theory, to be the same. Indeed, since it can be argued that some offenders become criminals through learning the mores of a delinquent sub-culture: these on Eysenckian theory, would be introverted.

Mention of criminals, however, leads on to an examination of the P factor in the diagnosis of neurotic and psychotic groups, because this is particularly powerful in the discrimination of certain criminal groups. Since, the results with the P factor are important for a proper understanding of the nature of certain disorders, the results are examined in greater detail than with E and N, which are largely covered, in any case, by the Cattell second-order factors, of anxiety and exvia.

The nature of psychoticism has already been fully described in Chapter 5 on temperamental traits; here we are first concerned with the scores of different psychiatric groups on the P factor. One must bear in mind the description of the high P scorer as: "non-cooperative, to have poor vigilance, to preserve 'set' poorly, to have high creativity or originality ... and to have difficulties in attending ... they (the high P scores) undervalue people, particularly people in authority ..." (Eysenck and Eysenck, 1976, p. 202)—while considering the psychological significance of the results.

TABLE 9.3
ABNORMAL GROUPS: MEANS AND STANDARD DEVIATIONS

Males	n	Age	P	E	N	L
Psychotics	104	35·1	5·66 ± 4·02	10·67 ± 5·22	13·39 ± 6·06	9·62 ± 5·12
Neurotics	216	34·7	4·19 ± 2·96	9·42 ± 5·37	16·56 ± 4·64	8·01 ± 4·60
Endogenous depressives	58	43·6	4·10 ± 2·82	9·98 ± 5·44	15·92 ± 5·48	9·72 ± 4·61
Prisoners	1023	25·9	5·72 ± 3·56	13·62 ± 4·69	13·13 ± 5·23	6·78 ± 4·29
Drug addicts	8	27·2	6·94 ± 5·75	8·88 ± 6·98	17·88 ± 3·94	8·62 ± 3·20
Personality disorders	56	30·6	5·78 ± 3·44	10·09 ± 6·31	15·71 ± 4·74	7·06 ± 4·45
Sex problems	23	35·7	4·87 ± 3·24	11·91 ± 5·53	12·43 ± 6·05	7·07 ± 4·05
Alcoholics	14	33·9	5·93 ± 2·16	9·79 ± 5·13	19·64 ± 2·13	4·14 ± 3·37
Normal comparison	2312	27·5	3·78 ± 3·09	13·19 ± 4·91	9·83 ± 5·18	6·80 ± 4·14
Females	n	Age	P	E	N	L
Psychotics	72	39·3	4·08 ± 3·19	10·58 ± 4·66	14·56 ± 5·23	11·59 ± 5·14
Neurotics	332	34·9	3·25 ± 2·71	9·46 ± 5·43	17·88 ± 3·94	9·58 ± 4·51
Endogenous depressives	68	43·7	3·48 ± 2·47	10·24 ± 5·76	16·54 ± 4·36	12·01 ± 4·04
Prisoners	71	27·1	6·41 ± 4·07	12·32 ± 5·19	14·60 ± 5·58	9·01 ± 4·89
Drug addicts	4	32·5	6·25 ± 3·20	9·25 ± 4·86	20·00 ± 1·15	3·25 ± 2·50
Personality disorders	75	31·0	5·75 ± 3·51	10·19 ± 5·99	18·35 ± 4·64	7·17 ± 4·30
Sex problems	25	30·6	3·58 ± 3·16	9·96 ± 4·27	16·32 ± 4·18	9·44 ± 4·59
Alcoholics	5	44·0	5·50 ± 3·39	10·50 ± 4·56	18·50 ± 2·50	8·80 ± 2·02
Normal comparison	3262	27·0	2·63 ± 2·36	12·60 ± 4·83	12·74 ± 5·20	7·73 ± 4·18

Reprinted from "Psychoticism as a Dimension of Personality" by H. J. Eysenck and S. B. G. Eysenck with permission of Hodder and Stoughton.

Table 9.3: Personality Test Scores of Various Psychiatric Groups

From Table 9.3 it is clear that psychotics (in the main, schizophrenics) and prisoners have the highest scores. Drug addicts, patients with personality disorders, individuals with sex problems are all elevated compared with normals. Thus, clearly the P factor discriminates psychiatric groups from normals. Among the psychiatric groups there was one interesting finding, namely that the endogenous depressives, although their P score was elevated, had a lower score than the others.

Further examination of Table 9.3 reveals however, that N was equally successful at discriminating these abnormal groups. It could be argued therefore, as Davis does (1974), that P is just another somewhat unreliable measure of emotionality, a finding he made in a sample of abnormal offenders of low intelligence. Eysenck and Eysenck (1976) commenting on Davis' results, impugn the whole investigation on the grounds that the subjects probably failed to understand the questions. The only way therefore, to answer this question of the identity of P and N precisely, is to obtain the correlations. Eysenck and Eysenck set these out for all their abnormal groups and it is clear P and N are to all intents and purposes orthogonal. This orthogonality of P and N is highly important diagnostically and theoretically. It means that neuroses and psychoses are not on the same continuum. Psychoses are not just bad neuroses. They are *qualitatively* different from neuroses, not quantitatively different. In addition, it does appear that both P and N are continua with normals at the low scoring poles.

P, however, is more closely related to diagnostic criteria than is evident from its power to discriminate psychiatric groups from normals, and to rank psychiatric groups. In addition, as Eysenck and Eysenck (1976) point out, several investigations make clear that P is able to discriminate among patients with differing severity of psychotic symptoms despite the fact that P is manifestly not directly related, as the MMPI is, to symptomatology. Thus McPherson *et al.* (1974) found that P scores were positively correlated among a group of 27 schizophrenic patients with psychotic signs and symptoms. This was not so for E or N. Similarly, Slade (1975) found that P could discriminate schizophrenics with auditory hallucinations from those without such delusions. These small-scale studies all confirm a previous investigation by Verma and Eysenck (1973) who found, using the earlier PEN scale on which the EPQ is based, that P was related to severity of symptomatology among psychotic patients. The data from this investigation which is reported in great detail by Eysenck and Eysenck (1976) were treated to highly complex statistical analyses, and from the test-retest scores on the P factor, it appears possible that patients with a low P score are more amenable to psychotherapy. The general conclusion from all these studies, therefore, from the viewpoint of this section on the contribution of psychometrics to diagnosis in clinical psychology is both clear and significant. Indeed, one can set the conclusions out separately:

(1) Psychotics score more highly than neurotics on P, who in turn score more highly than normals.

(2) The greater the severity of the psychosis the higher the P score.

(3) Psychotics have a lower N score than neurotics, thus aiding the diagnosis if taken in conjunction with the P score.

These conclusions need expansion. As Eysenck and Eysenck (1976) rightly argue, although N, E and P are independent it is clear from the results that taken together, diagnosis is superior to that based on any one factor alone. A discriminant function analysis, reported by the Eysencks for each sex separately, effectively does this and it indicates how the psychiatric groups can be discriminated by both N and P. The sex difference in the results for prisoners was of great interest. The female prisoners were high on the P component, indicating that these tended to be psychotic. The results clearly contrasted psychotic and neurotic disorders with endogenous depressives classified as psychotic, the reactives as neurotic, results which fit in, to some extent, with the work with the Cattell abnormal factors.

Although Eysenck and Eysenck (1976) make no great claims for this investigation since it is modest in scope and of an exploratory nature, it well illustrates the thesis of this book that psychometrics can make, when properly used, a significant contribution to psychological knowledge. Here one clearly sees how clinical, pre-scientific classification systems, despite their problems of unreliability and conceptualization, can be illuminated by work utilizing variables demonstrated by factor analysis as the fundamental variables of personality. I have already pointed out the significance of these findings for diagnosis. In a later section of this chapter their significance for both psychotherapy and clinical theory is discussed. Here, suffice to say that this is clear evidence that psychosis and neurosis are qualitatively different.

As previously indicated, N and E have been implicated in criminal behaviour. Similarly, P is able to discriminate criminals from contrast groups. Eysenck and Eysenck (1976) devote considerable space to a study of psychoticism and criminality, and since it appears that P has made a significant contribution to criminological knowledge one needs to summarize and discuss their findings. It should also be noted that Eves and Eysenck (1976) have shown an important genetic component in the inheritance of P (as well as N and E) using the biometric methods discussed in Chapter 4.

PSYCHOTICISM AND CRIMINAL BEHAVIOUR

In Eysenck's original two factor theory of criminality the criminal was conceived of as the extraverted neurotic. His extraversion means that he is slow to learn the mores of his society and to develop a conscience. His neuroticism amplifies the extraversion by acting as a drive. Eysenck and Eysenck (1976) agree that this is clearly too simplistic. Although in some cases of criminality and psychopathy the formula $E \times N$ does fit the findings, it is not all inclusive, and since genetic studies of P seem to link it with criminality, it is considered reasonable to investigate the role of psychoticism in criminal behaviour.

Before examining this role one correction needs to be made: the formula $E \times N$ can explain nothing since if the values x and y for E and N were interchanged, the psychological meaning but not the product would be totally different; this was an error of reasoning first made by Burgess (1972) in connection with this theory.

Studies of the P score of prisoners show that they are significantly higher than married men, students or industrial apprentices. This is interesting but as Eysenck and Eysenck (1976) argue, there should be differences between different offender groups. Gang leaders should be high on E and violent and aggressive criminals should be high P scorers, for example. Eysenck *et al.* (1977) carried out a cluster analysis of five different types of criminal— "con-men", inadequates, those guilty of violent crimes, those convicted of crimes against property and a group guilty of miscellaneous offences. Here they found that "con-men" differed from the others in having a low P score, the rest being high. Inadequates and others had a high N score (compared with violent and property offenders). Indeed, a mixed N, E and P scale, the C scale, was formed of the most criminally discriminating items.

While not wishing to impugn this study I must point out several features. First, as our own studies of criminals indicated (Hampson and Kline, 1977a,b), single crime offenders are not common. Many criminals have committed quite a variety of crimes. Again the picture of a "con-man" as low P is not altogether convincing, especially if the offences involved, as is frequently the case, playing on sentimental and affectionate feelings in order to steal a lifetime's savings. Thus, the finding that "con-men" are low on P must be treated with some caution although it has been found elsewhere (Eysenck and Eysenck, 1976).

What other differences have been found on P among criminal groups? Eysenck and Eysenck (1976) report a study of 264 female prisoners compared with a variety of controls. The results here were clear: the female prisoners score more highly on P than the female control groups who were all very similar; they score more highly than male prisoners who in turn are higher than the control groups of either sex among whom, as is usual, the males score more highly. Thus the rank order on P is female prisoners, male prisoners, male controls and female controls. This reversal of rank on P among prisoners is most probably due to the fact that prison sentencing is more rare for women than men so that female and male prisoners are not equivalent in terms of criminality. Or again it could be the case that crime is so unusual an activity for women that only extreme P scorers can break the social barriers against it and achieve the longed-for equality with men.

As the Eysencks demonstrate, there are now a number of studies confirming these findings, that P is related to criminal activity (and not only in the West); other relationships documented can be summarized. Among Borstal boys who were followed up three years after release, neuroticism was not related to P (although there was a small difference in extraversion) (Eysenck and Eysenck, 1974). Teasdale *et al.* (1971) showed that high P was related to illegal drug usage (even when the P items actually relating to drugs were removed) and N, too, discriminated three of the groups. Similar results have been reported from Czechoslovakia (Capelak, 1973).

This summary of the evidence quoted by the Eysencks, together with the paper by Eysenck *et al.* (1977) indicates clearly that psychoticism is implicated in criminality. This finding makes good psychological sense on the descriptive level, when one recalls the description of the high P scorer: cruel, callous, hostile and sensation seeking. However, it is far more significant than this when one takes into account the psychological meaning of P, the nature of the psychoticism factor, as a genetically determined dimension of personality related physiologically to maleness. The evidence will be briefly examined, on which this claim is based—that maleness underlies psychoticism. If true, however, it would account for the huge preponderance of male prisoners in prisons all over the world. It would also explain the divergent finding reported above that female prisoners are actually higher than male prisoners on P— they are the extremes in terms of maleness of the female population.

Gray (1973) has pointed out that schizophrenia and being male are linked. Thus, the onset of the disease is often at that time when the male subject becomes fully sexually mature, whereas in the case of women, schizophrenic breakdowns tend to occur after menopause as if being sexually female offers protection. Since P, which is clearly implicated in schizophrenia, declines with age (as does virility) and is higher in males than females, it could be the case that P is itself related to maleness. This is the rationale for postulating the relationship.

Gray (1973) has argued that psychoticism is associated with intra-specific aggressive behaviour, which is itself linked into a physiological mechanism— the flight–fight system of which the physiological substrate is in the amygdala. The question, therefore, becomes one of finding evidence that the amygdala is involved in psychosis. The best Eysenck and Eysenck (1976) can do is to link up the temporal lobe (in which the amygdala is buried) with psychosis. Obviously a more precise test of the relation of maleness to psychoticism would be in studies of the relevant oestrogen androgen levels as well as with other hormones. This work, however, remains to be done.

From this it is clear that the evidence linking P with maleness is speculative although there is a rationale for doing so. Nevertheless this implication of a basic and fundamental personality dimension in criminal behaviour is an important and significant addition to knowledge. Furthermore, it is knowledge that, as other information about psychoticism increases, is likely to become more and more meaningful. P must be intensively studied together with the Cattell abnormal factors: these are factors of great potential usefulness both for theory and treatment.

We have now seen the contribution to diagnosis in clinical psychology that has been made by the questionnaire factors of temperament. Much clinical work has been carried out with them which is important because their psychological meaning has been explored. However, we shall now examine the contribution from objective T factors.

OBJECTIVE FACTORS IN DIAGNOSIS

It will be remembered from the previous discussion that objective tests have generally yielded factors that have proven in the main, more difficult to identify with certainty, than those from questionnaires. This is partly due to the fact that, by virtue of their construction these tests have low face validity.

Factors therefore have to be identified by reference to criteria other than the tests on which they load. This has always proven tricky.

Another general difficulty with objective factors is that some seem to resemble the second-order questionnaire factors, implying that they are broader than the primary questionnaire factors, yet there are far more than second-order Q factors. Thus, then status relative to Q factors is not entirely clear. Consequently, the meaning of results obtained from objective T tests is equivocal and any interpretations must be correspondingly cautious.

One study by Cattell *et al.* (1972) however, goes a long way in elucidating the diagnostic contribution of objective tests for clinical psychology. In this research a battery of objective tests measuring the most important T factors was administered to involutional psychotics, manic depressives, reactive depressives, anxiety reactives, schizophrenics, manics and controls—a total of 114 subjects—on two occasions. Both states, by dR analysis and traits could be examined.

In this monograph the data were subjected to considerable and fine-grained statistical analysis so that full details cannot be given here. A statement and brief discussion of the main findings follows:

(1) A discriminant function analysis showed that five factors were concerned in discriminating psychiatric groups from normals. In order of importance these are: (a) UI 19, independence, (b) UI 21, exuberance, (c) UI 23, mobilization of energy and (d) UI 28, asthenia.

(2) Regression weights to determine the special characteristics of each group gave the following results:

Involutional depressives 21 −, 19 −, 20 (conformity) and 28

Other psychotic depressives 21 −, 19 −, 23 − (regression) and 25 (tensinflexia)

Depressive neurotics 19 −, 23 −, 21 − and 25 −

Schizophrenics 23 −, 19 −, 25 −, 33 (dismay) and an unidentified factor

Manics 23 −, 19 −, 25 −. In addition, compared with other clinical groups they are distinguished by 30 − (disofrustance), 24 − (low anxiety), 17 − (trusting) and 28 − (self-assured).

The patients in these groups had been specially selected such that in almost all cases there was complete agreement among the different psychiatrists classifying them. These classifications are probably about as reliable as they could be, accounting for the fact that the beta weights allowed a 75 % correct classification which, if state and trait change factors were included, rose to 98 %.

If such diagnostic accuracy could be regularly obtained with these factors, which have been collected together by means of the tests most highly loaded on them as a clinical test battery by Schuerger and Cattell (1975), the objective-analytic test battery diagnoses could be automatic: a test administrator rather than psychologist or psychiatrist would be sufficient. However, these were special groups, clear examples free at the time of testing from the effects of medication. As with criterion-keyed tests, such as the MMPI or diagnostic atheoretical exercises, such as with the Rorschach, (important work which is discussed in a later section of this chapter), with different samples classified by different workers, results are not necessarily so impressive. As I have stressed throughout this book, there is a further distinction between results with factored tests and results from purely empirically based criterion-keyed work—namely one of psychological meaning. The true significance of the results of this study in principle, lies not in these impressive discriminations but in the fact that they have been achieved with variables with psychological meaning so that hypotheses can be meaningfully developed about the nature of these psychiatric abnormalities (hypotheses, need one say, that have to be put to the experimental verification). Thus the psychological contribution of this psychometric work depends on what is known about the objective T factors.

As I have already argued, these T factors are by no means clearly identified so only a brief delineation is necessary to enable us to see what insights these objective factors give us, into psychiatric classification, over and above that from questionnaire factors. In respect of the differentiation of normals from abnormals, the factors concerned seem to make sound psychological sense. UI 19 has been labelled independence and is a broader form of independence than Witkin's well-known field independence (Witkin, 1962). Thus, psychiatric groups compared with their controls are dependent. UI 19 is a factor high in creative people and leaders. This result makes not only good descriptive sense for neurotics especially those who are manifestly dependent (they have come for help), but is consonant with psychoanalytic theory, for this assumes that the neurotic is characterized by poor ego development of which dependence would be an important sign. UI 21, exuberance, is a factor not well worked out. Cattell (1975) argues that it might represent high vitality or low inhibition of output. In either case the subdued nature of the neurotic, other than the manic who is probably psychotic, fits the loading on this factor.

UI 23, regression, or capacity to mobilize energy, has long been known as an important factor clinically. It loads on tasks requiring accuracy, speed and freedom from rigidity. These loadings have led Cattell and his colleagues to identify UI 23 as regression. It is associated with neurosis (as in the study here), poor school performance, debility, a diagnosis of psychosis and with poor resistance to stress. Descriptively, the typical abnormal subject makes errors, is slow and rigid in his work, not through lack of ability, but failure to apply the skills which he does possess. This is why neurotics tend to work poorly under stressful conditions.

As Cattell and Kline (1977) have pointed out in connection with UI 23, Eysenck and colleagues in the Maudsley have long worked with this factor which they call neuroticism. The position of Eysenck's and Cattell's groups on the nature of these factors has become exceedingly confused but it may be clarified as follows. The factor pattern of three factors called by Cattell, UI 23, 25 and 32, is fully agreed upon by both groups, only the identification differs. Cattell has shown that there is good alignment between the T and Q second-order factors so that he has adopted these terms:

UI 23 Regression:	No Q equivalent	UI 23 Neuroticism	
UI 24 Anxiety:	Q2 Cattell's	UI 24 No equivalent	Q2 Neuroticism,
UI 32 Exvia:	Q1 *Titles*	in Eysenck's system	and N
UI 25 Psychoticism:	Q5	UI 25 Psychoticism	P and Q5
		Eysenck's Titles	

The point at issue which has not yet been settled empirically is whether UI 23 really does correlate with N as it should in Eysenck's nomenclature or whether in fact UI 24 is the true N factor, as appears from the work of Cattell and Scheier (1961).

The other T factors clearly implicated in the diagnosis of neurotics and psychotics are UI 20, 25 and 28. In the discussion of 23, it was necessary to introduce the psychoticism factor, UI 25, of which the questionnaire measurement has been fully discussed. The objective T factor is identified by loadings on Gestalt completion, alternating perspective, writing size, reasoning with numbers and mirror drawing. As stated, there is full agreement here between the findings of Eysenck (1967) and of Cattell (Cattell and Tatro, 1966). There is no doubt that this UI 25 measures the P factor in questionnaires. However, it must be pointed out that Cattell (e.g. Cattell and Kline, 1977) does not like the title "psychoticism" on the grounds that psychotics can be discriminated on other factors than P—hence the terms realism and tensinflexia in the work of Cattell *et al.* (1972), as outlined above. However, the recent study of psychoticism (which has been fully discussed) by Eysenck and Eysenck (1976) convincingly demonstrates that P seems to measure what is essentially psychotic in psychotics, as does Eysenck's N factor among neurotics. However, while it is psychologically meaningful to regard this latter factor as anxiety, the equivalent for psychosis has no non-factorial name (because it was not previously clinically identified) so that psychoticism does not seem inappropriate, and I do not favour neologisms such as tensinflexia.

UI 20 does not seem to have been studied as extensively as some of the other T factors but its loadings on agreeing with generalizations and respecting authority suggest, as Cattell and Warburton (1967) point out, that it is a factor of social conformity. UI 28 is not so well documented as the larger factors and its label of asthenia must be regarded as tentative only.

One further factor clearly needs to be discussed—a factor which curiously, was only implicated in the manics—UI 24, which, as we have seen, is claimed by Cattell to be the objective test equivalent of Q2, anxiety and N, neuroticism. The objective tests loading on this factor are, admission of common frailties, susceptability to annoyance and rigidity, and the questionnaire loadings are *inter alia*, O, Q4 and C−. These last make it clear that UI 24 is essentially similar to the anxiety factor.

With these brief descriptions of the T factors which were shown to be the most clinically useful in the investigation by Cattell *et al.* (1972) we are now in a position to evaluate the contribution from objective testing to this aspect of clinical psychology. Three factors seem obviously implicated in psychiatric abnormality—UI 19, 23 and 25. Descriptively the abnormals are dependent, regressed and psychotic. From these objective test studies one fact is therefore confirmed—the importance of the psychoticism factor, UI 25. It does appear both from questionnaire and T data investigations that this personality factor is heavily implicated in psychiatric breakdown. This factor of cruelty, sensation-seeking, lacking empathy and sympathy, and coldness, must be studied further. The following questions (to which the beginnings of answers are now emerging, Eysenck and Eysenck, 1976) must be answered. What is the interaction on its development of heredity and environment? Certainly there is a considerable hereditary determination as Eysenck and Eysenck (1976) show.

Even so, some environments are likely to encourage rather than depress its development, thus resulting in psychiatric breakdown. What kinds of psychotherapy are most effective with patients high on this factor? It is clear that personality factors are likely to influence such effectiveness. Clinical studies by Truax and colleagues (e.g. Truax, 1963) have shown that empathy, warmth and insight are important variables. Therapeutic success is measured by increases in these scores. Yet it is on these traits that the pychotic is low. Thus, techniques of therapy very different from those of the non-directive school are likely to be necessary for the high P scorer. So here one can conclude that objective tests and questionnaires are in agreement regarding the importance of psychoticism, which is a clearly identified, fundamental dimension of personality, significant in psychiatric breakdown.

UI 19 dependence is diagnostically powerful in discriminating normal and abnormal groups. This dependence is interpreted as a symptom of ego weakness—the inability to take decisions, to need help, to lean on people. Whether in fact this factor does reflect such lack of ego strength needs to be determined by further research. However, it is important to note from the viewpoint of understanding the development of mental abnormality, that this factor is sex-linked (males being more independent), and substantially inherited. This may mean, therefore, that being prone to mental breakdown is largely beyond environmental control.

The third factor which is clearly important in the diagnosis of mental abnormality is UI 23, regression, but regarded by Eysenck as neuroticism. As I have indicated, this factor seems to tap the capacity to realize in any given situation, the skills which one possesses. It can be hypothesized, for example, that UI 23 is an important component in high level sporting performance or indeed any of the performing arts. We can all think of fine players or musicians whose skill is infinite but who never quite reach the top. Cattell and Scheier (1961) have demonstrated that UI 23 rises in the face of difficulties. This has important implications for clinical treatment and therapy. It suggests the possibility that highly supportive techniques do nothing to help, and may even exacerbate the patient's problems in as much as these stem from UI 23. It may be advantageous to utilize harsh regimes, to compel the patient to face his problems.

From this description there seems little doubt that these objective test descriptions do clearly illuminate the essential personality difficulties faced by patients. They indicate too that there is a considerable genetic component in the development of mental disorders. One point must be stressed. The fact that a trait is largely genetically determined, by no means implies that nothing can be done about it. There is no reason why any behaviour should not be modified, given the requisite environment, i.e. reinforcement patterns. Essentially this still means that certain intra-family experiences are likely to encourage or inhibit the development of these factors. For example, eating is largely genetically determined. What we eat and how much we eat, is largely a product of our culture. If these results are verified by further research and if, as it now appears, there is a considerable hereditary component in the development of psychiatric abnormality, even though, as I have argued, this does not mean that the effects of experience are set at nought, a great burden of guilt can be lifted from the families of patients, which may in its turn produce a family environment less likely to exacerbate genetically determined tendencies to breakdown. In some instances clinical evidence does point to the importance of what may be referred to as psychotogenic family environments (see Scott and Ashworth, 1969). One further point must be mentioned— namely that UI 24 (the questionnaire anxiety factor), was not one of the discriminating variables. This is certainly surprising.

To summarize the contribution to psychological knowledge concerning the nature of mental abnormalities from objective testing, it can be argued that there seems little doubt that basic normal personality traits are involved, especially UI 19, 23 and 25. Some of these are strongly genetically determined and the nature of one, UI 25 (psychoticism), carries with it the implication that current treatments are unlikely to be successful. It would have been pleasant to be able to set out a more spectacular list of findings as the contribution to knowledge from these T tests, but, and this must now be apparent, there is a lack of sound knowledge about them in the clinical field, due to the fact that practising clinicians have been loth to use them. This lack springs from a natural reluctance to use tests based upon complex statistics, and measuring concepts which are often new in the clinical field. Perhaps more significant is the fact that until recently, no battery of objective tests was easily available.

Having discriminated normals from the mentally ill, we must now examine the differences between groups. Here however, as reference to the results of the study by Cattell *et al.* (1972) make clear, these objective tests are not so impressive: generally the groups are not clearly differentiated from each other by different T factors, although the beta weights do enable one to discriminate between groups. Indeed, if one takes different factors into account, as distinct from different weights, the only distinctive group is the manic one. This, of course, makes descriptive sense, especially on the low anxiety score.

In summary however the contribution to knowledge about differentiation among groups of abnormals from this study is not great. Its main force lies in the diagnosis of abnormality.

MOTIVATIONAL FACTORS IN CLINICAL DIAGNOSIS

In the field of motivation, Cattell and his colleagues have been almost alone in applying multivariate analysis. In fact this has resulted in the isolation of ergs and sentiments, conceived of as the main human drives, and in a number of factors related to strength of interest. Ergs and sentiments can be measured by published, group administered tests, the MAT and SMAT, from the age of about 12 years upwards (see Chapter 6 for descriptions).

Since, in many instances, much clinical theory, as in psychoanalysis and behavioural therapeutic approaches, has been concerned with the dynamics of behaviour, it would be reasonable to assume that the study of ergs and sentiments had been useful in diagnosis and clinical theory. As regards diagnosis, however, the survey by Cattell and Child (1975) makes it clear that there is remarkably little information. Caffelt and Sweney (1965) found that eleven criminals convicted for violence were conflicted (difference between integrated and unintegrated score on the MAT), on career, self-sentiment, sex and security. Among thieves, however, there were conflict scores on self-sentiment, fear and especially narcism. The conflict scores are so named because they are thought to indicate the presence of conflict. If this is the case what psychological sense do these results show? Although they are amenable to *post hoc* speculation there is little about these findings which suggests any new or powerful hypotheses concerning the motivation of crimes. It will not do, as Cattell and Child (1975) try to argue, to claim that the narcism conflict score for thieves suggests that rich living is the motive. This is hardly likely if one looks into the financial background of thieves and others. There is some correlation with material welfare, but by no means sufficient to support the hypothesis put forward.

The only other relevant study cited by Cattell and Child with the MAT, was carried out by May and Sweney (1965) who administered the test to 30 schizophrenics. Conflict scores on career and home and parental sentiments were high as was the overall sex erg score. Since the family environment has been closely linked with schizophrenia by Laing (1960), utilizing the concept of the schizogenic family, and Bateson *et al.* (1956), who suggested that the schizophrenic was put into a confusing double-bind, hypotheses which *may* account for some cases but almost certainly not all, as the genetic studies of schizophrenia indicate (see Mayer-Gross *et al.*, 1967), this finding of high family parental conflict is of considerable interest, although its precise significance cannot be estimated. Similarly the career sentiment conflict is probably associated with the tendency for schizophrenics, before the illness becomes fully manifest, to lose their jobs and descend the social scale. In both these instances, of course, one must note that conflict scores on these variables are not truly diagnostic since any individual could score high on both these measures without being schizophrenic or likely to become so. Similar comments apply to the high score on the sex drive which is not contrary to clinical impressions and descriptions, but is obviously a score not restricted to schizophrenics. Thus this study, while descriptively sensible, cannot be held to contribute much to psychological knowledge.

To conclude this section on the diagnostic potential of these motivational factors, I shall point out the weaknesses of the work cited and suggest the research that obviously needs to be done. First, all these studies are but pilots: the samples are far too small to be able to make firm generalizations. Indeed the idea of one "schizophrenic" sample is dubious in view of the heterogeneity of the category (e.g. Holley, 1973). However, the results indicate that the MAT could be valuable in diagnostic work. This is particularly true if one recalls the studies in the educational field by Cattell and Butcher (1957) which have been fully discussed above (see Chapter 8), where it was found that while the correlation with the criterion of academic success and the MAT was small on its own, when added in with the personality and ability variables, the multiple correlation was much improved. Thus, I would argue that if clinical diagnosis is to be put onto a scientific non-intuitive basis, which will be of value for both clinical theory and treatment, then one needs the intensive testing of different psychiatric groups with the MAT, such as has been carried out with the temperamental variables of both Cattell and Eysenck. As we shall see in the discussions of the theoretical and therapeutic import of psychometrics, such diagnostic precision will be extremely valuable. At present, however, one must conclude that the MAT has yet to contribute to the psychological knowledge in respect to clinical diagnosis.

We have now seen the contribution to clinical diagnosis that has arisen from factored tests. In the following section of this chapter I examine the implications of these findings for therapy and theory. I shall then conclude the chapter with an account of the contribution from atheoretical, psychometric, criterion-keyed tests as well as work from certain projective techniques.

CONTRIBUTION TO TREATMENT

Certainly since Eysenck's (1952) attack on the efficacy of psychoanalytic theory, the complacent assumption that clinical psychotherapy was effective has had to be abandoned. The notion of spontaneous remission has laid upon therapists the necessity to demonstrate that their therapy is successful. However, since it is by no means simple to show that any therapy or treatment is effective (and the same problems occur in the field of educational psychology with regard to evidence for one teaching method rather than another), a brief discussion of these difficulties will enable us to see what the contribution of psychometrics is.

PROBLEMS IN THE RESEARCH DESIGN OF STUDIES EVALUATING PSYCHOTHERAPEUTIC SUCCESS

Rachman (1973) has summarized the work on the effects of psychotherapy up to 1973 and he has argued that almost no studies convincingly demonstrate positive results. He writes off most studies as being badly designed. The difficulties can be described under the following headings:

Patient Variables

Kiesler (1966) argued that many studies considered patients to be homogeneous. This is manifestly not the case if terms such as "abnormal", "neurotic" or "psychotic" are used, hence treatments which may be effective with an unknown sub-group are masked by lack of improvements with other groups or by actual deterioration.

   One must note that the diagnostic use of factored tests as discussed in the previous section overcomes the first problem. If psychiatric labels are used, then individual differences in terms of ability, temperament and dynamics can be taken into account when analysing the results. If such nosological labels are considered to be unsatisfactory, patients can be described in terms of their psychometric test scores. Whichever method is preferred, there can be no doubt that this first objection by Kiesler (1966) to the research design of studies into the effectiveness of psychotherapy can be answered by psychometric methods.

Therapist Variables

Meehl (1955) argued that therapists of the same school may not be particularly homogeneous. Thus, if one is to study the efficacy of a particular therapeutic method, one should use a reasonable sample of practitioners of this method. Again, in overcoming this problem, psychometric tests will be helpful. One might find it useful to use variables in this analysis which are some of the major psychometric factors. Thus, it could be that far more important in therapeutic success than being, for example, a psychoanalyst is being an intelligent introvert or, that (an interaction) intelligent introvert psychoanalysts are successful but not extravert, and so on. In other words psychometric evaluation of therapists is essential for good research.

Criterion for Success

As I have pointed out in "Fact and Fantasy in Freudian Theory" (Kline, 1972) in the chapter on the scientific evidence for the efficacy of psychoanalytic theory, and this problem is common to investigations of all kinds of therapies, establishing an adequate criterion of therapeutic success is a major difficulty. In effect, the question of what is meant by recovery of the patient is raised. In physical medicine there is far less disagreement. It is clear when a patient has recovered from typhoid. The reliability of the diagnosis among competent practitioners is virtually perfect. For mental illness this is not the case, indeed the aims of different therapies are so different that a meaningful comparison appears not to be possible. For example, in behaviour therapy the treatment is aimed at the symptoms: in psychoanalysis where id was, there shall ego be.

This difficulty was so great that in my earlier work I suggested (Kline, 1972) that studies of therapeutic outcome were probably not a viable means of putting the efficacy of most psychotherapies to the test. Instead, I proposed that studies of the therapeutic process itself be instituted, as in the case of psychoanalysis by Bellak (1961), Bellak and Smith (1956) and more generally in the study of Rogerian therapy by Truax and colleagues (e.g. Truax, 1963).

In studies of the therapeutic processes, the interactions of the therapist and patient and the immediate consequences can be studied and matched to theoretical predictions, or as in studies of Rogerian therapy, the specific qualities of therapists are observed vis-à-vis improvements in specific personality measures, by patients. Even these brief descriptions make it clear that in investigations of psychotherapeutic processes, psychometrics must have an important part to play. Thus, instead of the somewhat arbitrary and unsatisfactory measures used in the Truax studies—such as positive regard, empathy and congruence—one can measure what has been demonstrated earlier in this book, to be the most important temperamental and dynamic variables.

A weakness of these studies by Truax and colleagues, not only for practising clinical psychologists but also for academic psychologists lay in the nature of the criterion test scores—scales from the TAT and MMPI—tests of notoriously low reliability and dubious validity for this particular purpose. However, if my contention is correct, that factor analysis in particular and multivariate analysis generally, lays bare fundamental dimensions in ability temperament and dynamics, then it can be argued that recovery can be measured. On those variables which distinguish a patient's nosological category, recovery is defined by the scores returning to the population norm. This will show real personality change and change of the kind intended by the therapist. It is important to realize that with this criterion of recovery, the return of the psychiatrically significant scores to the population norm, there is no blueprint for "making everybody the same" or turning people into contented citizens in a bad society. Only those high or low scores implicated in the mental disorder are expected to change. A patient can be extreme on any other variables.

From this brief discussion of the criteria of recovery it is clear that psychometry can give us psychologically meaningful and objective measures of therapeutic success. This measurement of patients on the most important factorial variables enables psychometrists to monitor the progress of psychotherapy and compare different kinds of therapy. This must be regarded as a significant contribution to therapy.

The Use of Control Groups

Most researchers into the effects of psychotherapy agree that a control group is essential for all properly designed investigations. Without controls who do not receive the experimental treatment, it is clearly difficult to attribute any improvement or deterioration to that treatment. Needless to say, the problems of producing a control group matched by diagnosis are acute, especially if the unreliability of psychiatric diagnosis is taken into account. This ignores the ethical problem of not treating patients (rather naively assuming that treatment is or can be beneficial).

With this problem psychometrics can be helpful in as much as patients can be matched in terms of their factor scores, which should be easier than matching by diagnosis (although this would be a different design and matched diagnoses would still be useful). Obviously psychometrics cannot be highly valuable in this particular difficulty.

Spontaneous Remission

Since control groups are difficult to obtain, Eysenck (1952, 1960, 1965b) has utilized the spontaneous remission rate as a baseline of recovery above which successful psychotherapy must rise. Even Rachman (1973) admits that data yielded by investigations using spontaneous remission inevitably lack precision because the nature and severity of the illness and standards of recovery are rarely described in sufficient detail. It is important to note that Eysenck and Rachman (1965) do not claim that time alone produces improvements in neurotic disorders. They agree that certain events in time are responsible for the effect, e.g. promotion, love affairs, financial windfalls, significant life events, in fact, an argument which disposes of the objection to spontaneous remission that it is not spontaneous (e.g. Kiesler, 1966). All the term implies is that there is no deliberate therapeutic procedure involved in the remission—as in the case of a successful love affair.

A second argument presented by Bergin (1971), also argues that the 70% remission rate quoted by Eysenck and his Maudsley colleagues is too high: 30% is the figure he prefers on his examination of the evidence. Rachman (1973) has examined the data utilized by Bergin in great detail and is forced to conclude that the lower figure is an underestimate of the true remission rate. However, he does admit that more refined investigations and accurate data are needed and that remission rates vary for different disorders. The importance of this last conclusion cannot be over-stressed for the study of therapeutic efficiency. It means that in evaluating treatments, one should take the results *within* and not across diagnoses if one intends to use the spontaneous remission rate as a baseline.

These are the main problems which have emerged in the investigation of the effects of psychotherapy. Kiesler (1966) proposed a solution of great elegance using analyses of variance. Main factors in this design are types of patient and schools of therapy including some under the heading of spontaneous remission. In this analysis of variance approach, individual difference among patients and therapists of each school can be accommodated. Interactions between therapy and type of patient would also be measured. As I have previously argued (Kline, 1972) the problem with this design is the difficulty of obtaining adequate measures of improvement. Analyses of variance of ratings of improvement, for example, which are usually unreliable and invalid are not impressive. Here however the role of psychometrics in the evaluation of psychotherapy and its contribution to this aspect of clinical psychology becomes clear. If one were to adopt the type of research design suggested by Kiesler and combine it with the best measures derived from the factorial analysis of ability temperament and dynamics, the following research design could be easily implemented, a design which would yield results not only of practical but also of theoretical value. The criterion of success would be changes on meaningful psychological factors.

In a design, therefore, of this type one would obtain patients clearly classified into nosological categories by their psychiatrists. They would be administered the major ability temperament and dynamic measures, described in the relevant chapters of this book, on entry into the investigation and for example, at three month intervals during the study. One would obtain from their therapists, who would each be of known persuasion, scores on these same variables, just once. Into the analysis of variance would go the change or difference scores of these patients, the main factors being type of therapy (including if possible, none) and type of patient, who could also be divided in terms of some of the main factors, e.g. intelligence, extraversion and psychoticism, as would be the therapists. Such an investigation would reveal some of the major determinants of therapeutic efficiency, if indeed any improvements were observed.

From this brief outline of the kind of investigation suggested by Kiesler (1966) it is clear that psychometric tests can make a valuable contribution. Furthermore, from the fundamental nature of the factor-analytic variables the results are likely to give us psychological insight into the nature of therapy. Indeed, if the results are at first sight baffling this means that a new theoretical approach to psychotherapy is needed, as was the case with the factor-analytic studies of mood described in Chapter 6. Thus, the theoretical contribution is inevitably considerable. This is so even if no improvement in patients is observed. In this case with such an experimental design which essentially covers all possibilities of interaction it is possible to claim that therapy of the schools used in the study, is ineffective.

One important point must now be discussed. In fact this experimental design, advocated by Kiesler (1966) although elegant and powerful, is not ideal. The weakness lies, as this description hints implicitly, in the limitation of the analysis of variance technique such that patients and therapists can be categorized on only a limited number of variables, e.g. intelligence, neuroticism and psychoticism. As I discussed in Chapter 2 on the special statistical procedures adopted in psychometrics, the great advantage of truly multivariate statistics (and this is their utility for psychometrics) is that they can handle a large number of variables. Thus, a more appropriate and even more powerful research design would be just such a multivariate technique.

The difficulty with multivariate analysis, however, is that the interaction of therapist and patient is hard to capture. One possible solution is to take each patient separately and subject his scores before, during and after therapy to P analysis. In such a study the therapist's scores could be included. In this way it should be possible to see how the critical variables fluctuate and how the therapist variables load on the factors. This would certainly show up interactions. Yet another multivariate approach would be to Q factor patients, i.e. use people rather than test scores as variables and subject these to factor analysis. If each patient's therapist's scores went into the analysis, interactions of patient and therapist personality could be revealed in a study of the variables separating each Q factor group, if in fact a group of improved patients was revealed. Similarly, multivariate techniques such as discriminant functions might be used to separate a "successful" group.

Such methods are not considered to be ideal for they have problems in assessing the interaction effects. Perhaps an ideal approach would be to factor or regress, against the criterion of success, patient's scores to find important patient variables and then use these in a more limited analysis of variance.

So far I have attempted to classify what psychometrics *could* contribute in respect of the problems of assessing the value of psychotherapy. However, a small number of investigators have begun to put these research designs to the practical test, and this work is briefly discussed below, briefly because definitive results have yet to be reached.

Cattell (1970) has shown that taking into account how scores on the abnormal second-order factors are composed in terms of primary factors, can affect the outcome of treatment. He therefore advocates that these scores should be scrutinized in the therapy of each individual. This whole procedure is called depth psychometry. Vidal (1972) has also made use of these ideas in the study of temperamental traits. Freedman and Kaplan (1970) also suggest that different treatments and aims should be undertaken depending upon the primary factorial composition of the second-order factors. This field of depth psychometry is too new and speculative to deserve further discussion at this point. However, it would appear to be a promising area for psychometrics to enter.

To assess the relevance to clinical theory of all these results, both the results concerned with diagnosis and those with the multivariate study of psychotherapy using factored tests, one has to look at the contribution to clinical theoretical knowledge.

PSYCHOMETRIC CONTRIBUTION TO CLINICAL THEORY

This contribution makes reference to issues which have been fully examined elsewhere in this book, for example, the nature of anxiety as a trait and a state and psychoticism.

First, it must be stated that the contribution to clinical theory from factored tests is as yet small. The reasons for the relative paucity of the clinical theoretical contribution are simple. As we have seen, the empirical observations which any theory must subsume are only being collected now, so that any theorizing may turn out to be wrong, simply because new facts are unearthed which it was not designed to account for. Eysenck's psychoticism (Eysenck and Eysenck, 1976) and his two impulsiveness factors (Eysenck and Eysenck, 1977), and Cattell's abnormal personality sphere factors, are cases in point.

Despite the fact that clinical theorizing is probably premature in the light of the knowledge of abnormal factors, more basic and descriptive research being necessary, both Eysenck and Cattell have adumbrated clinical theories which I shall briefly discuss. This brevity is on account of the fact that neither theoretical position is properly justifiable.

Eysenck's theorizing in the clinical field is now so well known as to merit the briefest description, especially since it is not essentially psychometric. Eysenck and Rachman (1965) probably contains the clearest summary of his position although an important addendum was made by Eysenck (1976). Briefly, Eysenck adopts the learning theoretic approach to abnormal behaviour which he considers arises from maladaptive learning, i.e. as a result of conditioning. The importance of this approach is, of course, that it has implicit within it, a method of treatment—causing the unwanted behaviour to extinguish to relearn more appropriate responses. How this is done has become the science or (*pace* Eysenck) the art of behaviour therapy. This theory which is an application of learning theory to abnormal behaviour involves psychometrics in as much as a subject's status on extraversion and neuroticism determines the likelihood of his being conditioned or not, and of conditioned responses extinguishing or not, in a given environment. Thus it can be argued that the psychometric contribution to this clinical theory is important because it gives one understanding of some of the determinants of neurosis, and if one involves the newer P, psychoticism, it is equally full of insight in respect of the likelihood of behaviour-therapeutic success. Unfortunately, however, as we have seen in the discussion of this learning theory in Chapter 7, the theory is inconsistent and not wholly coherent. It cannot fully explain the experimental findings. Thus, one cannot regard it as an adequate account of the genesis of psychological abnormalities, although in certain instances it may well be correct. However, what one must be careful to note is the fact that the questionable aspects of the theoretical structure are Eysenck's own attempts to tie extraversion and neuroticism into theories of learning. The effective parts, such as the notion of phobias as maladaptive conditioned responses are simply applied learning theory. Consequently, as I argued in the detailed analysis of Eysenck's general theoretical position, of which his clinical theorizing is a part, the theory cannot be accepted although it is arguably the last grand theoretical essay in psychology.

Before leaving this theory and turning to examine Cattell's attempts at clinical theorizing, Eysenck's (1976) paper on incubation theory should be mentioned which constitutes an attempt to account for the commonplace observations of the clinic which are manifestly contrary to theories of learning even when interpreted with Talmudical ingenuity and brilliance. An obvious example cited by Eysenck is that while snake and insect phobias are relatively common despite the fact that most people have had no unpleasant experiences, electric plug phobias are rare (with which, incidentally, a Freudian would be thoroughly at home, especially if of the three-pin variety). The explanation provided in the paper is the Chomskian one, that we are set to be especially reactive to some stimuli (e.g. snakes) and not others, a programming which is presumably of some evolutionary significance. In addition, in the case of such stimuli the rarity of the reinforcement in actual life does not lead, as it would normally, to extinction, but on the contrary, the opposite occurs. This incubation theory robs the original learning theory based approach of much of its elegance and precision. One now has the almost psychoanalytic position that both X and its opposite (reinforcement and non-reinforcement) can lead to the same symptoms.

Despite this recent addition one must still conclude that, impressive as Eysenck's attempt has been to embrace abnormal psychology within a learning theory which takes account of psychometrically defined individual differences, it has not been successful. One cannot regard it as a psychometric contribution to psychological knowledge.

Similarly, the clinical theorizing of Cattell is embedded within his structured learning theory which has been fully discussed in Chapter 7. Cattell's clinical theorizing differs from Eysenck in concentrating, in the tradition of the great clinical psychologists of personality, on motivation. Since structured learning theory has been fully described, and since I have also delineated in some detail the ergs and sentiments resulting from the factor analysis of motivation together with the specification equations that can be derived from them, they are not discussed here. I shall examine how they are utilized for clinical theory, or more accurately in the light of results how they may be utilized.

The Specification Equation in Clinical Theory

The specification equation, as Cattell and Kline (1977) argue, quantifies the dynamics of any given piece of behaviour in terms of weights on ergic and sentiment tension factors. The difficulty with this relatively simple notion lies in establishing the beta weights. However, P factor analysis (see Chapter 2 for an assessment of its potential) involving repeated measures of a subject can do precisely this. Consequently P analysis can demonstrate the dynamics of any behaviours one includes in the P analysis. This should be vital for clinical theory.

In the scrutiny of the validity of the MAT motivational test, I examined a study by Kline and Grindley (1974) in which our subject completed the test and a diary each day, for 28 days. This was a pilot study in which little more than a logical connection was made between test scores and diary. A better investigation would have included daily behavioural measures. These could then have been inserted together with the daily test scores into a P factor analysis. The P factors emerging would have inevitably implicated the dynamics of the behaviours tested, the factor loadings of the ergs and sentiments being the actual weights. The implications of this design for clinical theorizing are so obvious that there is no need for further examples. Nevertheless, an illustration of P factor analysis in the study of observed behaviour will convince even sceptical clinicians suspicious of statistical techniques. If one measures each day the various manifestations of obsessional disorder, the rituals, the handwashing, the repeated and anxiety provoking thoughts, the P factor analysis will show their ergic tension reducing qualities. Does handwashing reflect feelings of guilt and superego? Are sexual drives defended by certain repetitive thoughts? All these questions can be answered by a P factor analysis of these measures together with tests of dynamics and temperaments.

P factor analysis of behaviour and motivational variables is the technique especially suited to investigations of psychodynamics and since this is the aspect of psychology in which psychoanalysis is most concerned, P factor analysis could be powerful in the elucidation of general psychoanalytic concepts, especially defence mechanisms, which are peculiarly important to clinical psychological theory. If one measures musical, artistic and scientific behaviour among musicians, measuring artists and scientists with motivational and temperamental variables, the P analysis would reveal whether these activities reduced drives, especially sexual ones (as Freud (1916) claimed with his concept of sublimation), thus testing simultaneously psychoanalytic theories created for clinical psychology, and more general theories of aesthetics. In this way such studies could be described with propriety, as quantified psychoanalyses. Of course, since P technique is concerned with individuals, Freudian theories can be put to a highly specific test. If the writer expresses aggression vicariously in his writing, there should be a relation between this type of writing and MAT pugnacity scores. In view of the obvious power of P technique for clinical theory, it is sad to be forced to write that up to this date, there are virtually no researches where it has been thus utilized. The contribution therefore, of the specification equation to clinical theory remains potential rather than actual. This is an aspect of psychometrics which must be explored.

Cattell and Child (1975) have attempted to develop the dynamic calculus to account for the integrative action of the ego which is clearly highly important in clinical psychology, since as we have seen in the discussion of ergs and sentiments and in the examination of structured learning theory, this integration is essential for efficient functioning. However, their quantified description is highly speculative (for lack of research) and can by no means be regarded as a contribution to knowledge (see Chapters 7 and 11).

Cattell (1965) has attempted to illustrate the dynamic calculus in clinical psychology by his APA chart, the adjustment process analysis chart. It suggests ways in which different outcomes from the stimulation of ergic tensions are reached. Each route produces a variety of different symptoms and behaviours, thus accounting for the variety of the symptomatology observed in neurosis and psychosis. However, although the APA chart is referred to as a model, it is effectively a speculative attempt to accommodate some of the observations of clinical psychology within ergic tension theory. However, far more careful P technique research is needed before an APA chart could be compiled with any confidence for any individual. A study by Cattell and Sweney (1964) factored, in a group of children, indices of conflict in three separate conflict situations. They found some common conflict factors across situations—cognitive disturbance relating to suppression, perceptual vigilance, fantasy and muscle tension.

While these findings are by no means disconfirmatory of the APA chart, far more research is needed to lift it beyond the realms of clinical speculation which fits the known factors in the motivational sphere and the clinical observations of abnormal psychology. Again, therefore, as was the case with the P factor analyses of motivational and behavioural variables, the contribution of psychometrics to clinical psychological theory remains, potential rather than actual.

In conclusion, therefore, I must argue that in respect of theory, there are enormous possibilities in psychometrics that have yet to be realized. As Cattell and Kline (1977) have suggested, the necessary research is unlikely to be carried out until clinical psychologists are trained in multivariate analysis so that they are as at ease with it as with other clinical techniques. The statistical methods, the tests and some highly important variables are all sufficiently developed in order to make theoretical contributions. It remains only for the research to be done.

Psychometric Findings with Non-factored Tests

It should follow from the inherent nature of the construction of factored tests, that when tests are properly carried out, they provide results with psychological meaning—a meaning which has been explicated area by area. This has been facourably contrasted with the older but still utilized approach to test construction via criterion-keying, of which the MMPI is by far the. best example. However, because the MMPI constitutes a pool of items which in terms of content, at least, appears highly useful in clinical psychology and because clinical psychologists deal with subjects who have been previously categorized by psychiatrists into various abnormal groups, the pragmatic blindly empirical approach of trying to discriminate between them has been very widely adopted. This has resulted in a huge body of research findings most of which are valuable in clinical practice, to the extent that patients can be reliably categorized, and are therefore useful as screening procedures. However, their psychological meaning is dubious and I would argue that ultimately it is far more clinically valuable to describe psychiatric syndromes, if indeed these are psychological realities, in terms of meaningful factored variables. Nevertheless, from this huge if misguided research endeavour some valuable contribution to psychological knowledge has been made. In this section I shall deal with all aspects of clinical psychology, for in this approach diagnostic and therapeutic implications are inextricably intertwined. Naturally the theoretical contribution of the findings is not considerable.

G ANALYSIS

G analysis, which has been fully described by Holley (1973) and developed further by Holley and his colleagues (mainly in Scandinavia), especially by Vegilius (1976), is a set of statistical techniques peculiarly suited to the investigation of clinical diagnostic problems and one which has yielded results of considerable psychological importance. I shall first describe the techniques and then set out some of the most significant findings. As with much of the psychometric work in clinical psychology, the main contribution to knowledge is yet to come.

Description of G Analysis

In basic G analysis, dichotomous variables are correlated using the G index, Holley and Guilford (1964). The resulting correlation matrix between subjects is then subjected to Q factor analysis, thus forming groups. D estimates are then calculated which give the discrimination index between each item and membership of the groups. The formulae are:

G index is $G = 2Pc - 1$ where Pc is equal to the sum of $a + d$ in fourfold contingency table, and the linear transformation simply ensures the coefficient runs from -1 to $+1$.

D estimate is $D = \dfrac{a}{a + b} - \dfrac{c}{c + d}$ where a, b, c, d are the frequencies or proportions in a contingency table.

Thus the items which separate out the subjects are used to identify the psychological nature of the group. This has been referred to as basic G analysis because in the last few years, certain sophisticated statistical modifications have been added which will be described after the claims for the basic G analysis have been examined.

Holley (1973) has argued that G analysis is a technique of considerable power which has several advantages compared with other procedures. These are:

(1) Dichotomized data can be used. This means that one can use a huge variety of tests and other information including items from questionnaires, interview data and projective tests, the last two of which can be searched for the presence or absence of certain variables determined by content analysis. This means that projective tests can be reliably and objectively scored, as Holley (1973) demonstrated with the Rorschach test.

(2) Unlike most other indices of correlation between dichotomous variables such as the tetrachoric correlation coefficient or phi, G is unaffected by item polarity (whether the item is scored "yes" or "no") and by the evenness of the dichotomy. This makes it a far more suitable coefficient of correlation for factor analysis than other similar ones.

(3) Q factors based upon G indices have equivalent R factors in the data. Basic G analysis has been used in, and is especially suited to the study of, nosological groups. Do the groups fall into Q factor groups or do they break up? Are the new factor groups identifiable from the items discriminating them? These are the questions which G analysis has been set to answer. Holley (1975) has also demonstrated that where conventional analysis of variance can show no mean differences between subjects, G analysis can reveal perfect separation.

As indicated above, Holley and his colleagues have, over the years, improved the system so as to produce better replicability of findings and to take into account other forms of data. The most important modifications are listed below. An index G_0, has been developed for use with ordinal data, thus extending the scope of G analysis (Holley and Kline, 1976a). A method has been found enabling delegate scores (Sandler, 1956) to be used as marker variables in the research (Meyer and Kline, 1978), which is an extremely useful procedure in the replication of research findings, an absolute necessity in exploratory researches of this kind. Apropos of the rotational problem which is particularly acute in Q factor analysis because the psychological implications of oblique groups are not always clear (although oblique solutions often give the clearest and most easily replicable solutions), a number of solutions have been put forward. Holley and Kline (1976b) have proposed the symmetrical square root method for the alignment of reference axes with marker vectors, while Meyer *et al.* (1976) have yet another technique.

Essentially, therefore, G analysis is a set of multivariate statistical techniques especially devised for the isolation of groups and working with dichotomous or ordinal data. Its particular value in clinical research resides in the fact that its ability to handle such data enables research to be undertaken with interviews and projective tests, data sources which in the past have defied precise analysis. Indeed all the rich data from clinical sessions can be subjected to G analysis. Another advantage in clinical research is that it involves the study of people not variables. G analysis, as I have described, utilizes Q factor analysis, not R analysis. Indeed as Levy (1966) has shown, R analysis of G indices is likely to reveal only clusters of items with similar response sets so that the G index is a coefficient that is only really suited for Q factor analysis. However, it has been demonstrated by Holley (1964) that the Q factors resulting from the double-centred matrices of G analysis have their R equivalents; an important point when it comes to the interpretation of the groups isolated by the technique.

Before examining the substantive findings that have emerged from G analysis and before outlining its potential for research into clinical psychological problems, one further set of developments must be mentioned—those of Vegilius (1976). Vegilius has demonstrated that the G index is only one of a whole family of correlational coefficients—E correlation coefficients defined by the fact that they satisfy the demands of a normalized scalar product in a Euclidean space and are thus suitable for component analysis. At this point Vegilius suggests certain variants of G and even introduces the J index for nominal scales which is also an E correlation although only running from 1 to 0 (with no negative values). Readers must be referred for such mathematical developments of G to the papers, especially Janson and Vegilius (in press); for these purposes it is sufficient to note that G has been shown to be mathematically suitable for component analysis and that other coefficients could be substituted for it, in certain cases.

The Findings from G Analysis

Holley (1973) summarizes the results from a number of his investigations of the Rorschach test. In this work the Rorschach was used to discriminate depressives, schizophrenics and normals as the beginning of a series of studies aimed at providing a factorial description of the clinical domain. Three samples were used and very high placement accuracies (into diagnostic categories) were achieved: 18 from 20, 40 from 42 and 11 from 12. It is to be noted that this is a degree of accuracy not normally attainable with factored tests. It has two substantive psychological implications. First, it is clear that the Rorschach is, as its followers, e.g. Klopfer *et al.* (1956) have long maintained, a powerful diagnostic instrument, Holley accounts for the typical research study with the Rorschach failing to show results (see Eysenck, 1959) in terms of poor, orthodox, statistical methods. Secondly, it is clear that accurate classification into depressive, schizophrenic and normal, despite many of the studies objecting to them, is possible. These three investigations therefore confirm the validity both of the Rorschach and psychiatric classifications.

Both these findings were surprising and further confirmatory studies with the Rorschach were undertaken by Holley and colleagues at Lund and Gottenberg. Again these results were confirmed and what was particularly interesting was the fact that perfect placement resulted (12 of 12) and that the schizophrenic group broke down into two sub-groups, thus demonstrating that schizophrenia is not a homogeneous classification. What must be noted about all these results is that the differences are not mean differences which are significant but with considerable overlap between the distributions of scores. In these studies the differences are absolute: every schizophrenic scores higher than the others on the schizophrenia items as does every depressive on the depressive items. This is the kind of discriminatory power that can lead to completely accurate classification. It further implies a strong psychological meaning to the psychiatric classifications and a very high validity for the Rorschach test in respect of these clinical psychiatric criteria.

Hampson and Kline (1977a, b) adopted G analysis in a series of studies of prisoners who had been sent to hospital for treatment rather than prison. Their aim was to attempt to isolate criminal personality traits since the claims by Waldo and Dinitz (1967) based upon surveys of all studies using personality questionnaires, that no such criminal personality traits existed, did not seem *a priori* reasonable. The sadism of the Moors' murderer, Bradley, and his associate, Myra Hindley, who lured young people to a brutal death (whereof the agonies were tape-recorded), and buried them on the Yorkshire Moors seems, for example, redolent of a personality different from that of Menhuin or Cassals, who are gifted in the Arts and dedicated to Man's improvement. If personality questionnaires could detect no differences, so much the worse for them.

In the investigations, therefore, a battery of tests and interviews was used. The psychological tests included certain cards from the TAT, the FRI (Family Relations Indicator, Howells and Likorish, 1962), the HTP test (House, Tree, Person, Buck, 1948), the Porteus Mazes (Porteus, 1952) as the projective tests, and two personality questionnaires, the Dynamic Personality Inventory, (Grygier, 1961) which have been fully discussed in Chapter 2 and the Cattell 16 PF test, which is regarded as covering the most important personality variables. This test would, one hopes, help locate in personality space, any factors that were powerful in the discrimination of criminal groups.

Three samples of offenders were used: two groups from a local hospital with a ward for the treatment of offenders referred to it from the courts; the third group came from Broadmoor, the hospital to which serious criminals who are found to be criminally insane are sent. This third group differed in severity of crime from our first two groups who were, in the main, petty offenders convicted of a variety of crimes and offences including theft, aggression and sex offences.

Three contrast groups were used in this investigation with which all the offenders were compared, although each contrast group was chosen to match well with one of the experimental groups. These were students (only cynics would argue that these were a satisfactory control for criminals), a sub-normal group to control for the low intelligence of the offenders and Marines, who were similar to offenders in terms of social class and institutionalization. Finally a further control group was used for the Broadmoor sample alone, who were by definition psychiatrically disturbed—a hospitalized schizophrenic group.

The results again demonstrated that G analysis was able to discriminate groups with high efficiency, given obviously that the data were capable of so doing, thus confirming Holley's (1973) argument that weak statistical analysis was responsible for many of the poor outcomes of validity studies with the Rorschach and other projective tests.

Contrary to the claims of Waldo and Dinitz (1967) who had found projective tests the weakest method of discriminating offenders from controls, the projective test data, objectively scored, together with interview data, isolated in the first two criminal samples, four groups of offenders: a socially inadequate, authoritarian group, an insecure and aggressive group, a psychosexually immature group and a group characterized by egocentric rebelliousness. Among the psychiatrically disturbed Broadmoor criminals, two groups were again found, one characterized by psychopathic impulsivity and inadequacy and another which was anxious and pessimistic. It must be pointed out here that the interview data used was never such as would *ipso facto* discriminate offenders from controls, e.g. "have you been convicted of criminal offences?".

The identification of these factors was highly subjective, being dependent on interpreting the interview data and projective test responses which best discriminated the groups utilizing the D estimates, although subjects' factor scores were correlated with the questionnaire scales in an attempt to obtain more objective identification. Since, too, the samples were small—in all, only 40 offenders were examined, the findings could not be regarded, unless replicated, as substantive contributions to the psychology of criminals. What can be considered to be a useful contribution to the field is however, the method itself. There can be no doubt that the G analysis of projective test data, which has been objectively scored, can discriminate criminals from offenders in terms of personality. Here then one has a powerful method especially if resulting equivalent R factors are located in personality space, to reveal the underlying psychology of criminality.

Although, in this book which is directed to delineating the psychometric contribution to psychology, the significance of these findings lies in the method, the fact that discriminations were made, rather than the details of the discriminations, one set of results was of sufficient interest to demand further discussion here, because it illustrates the potential of this method: not just the efficiency of G analysis but rather the power of objectively scored projective tests. Indeed, one would modify Holley's claims in the light of this research. The power of G analysis is not its statistical efficiency, although it is efficient, but its ability to handle the rich data of projective testing which, before the advent of G analysis were in the hands of intuitive clinicians and beyond the scope of multivariate analysis. The bearing of the results on this point will also be discussed.

The Broadmoor patients fell into two groups using G analysis, tentatively labelled as psychopathic impulsives and anxious pessimists. The impulsive group (N = 5) were convicted of assault (2), attempted murder, manslaughter and murder. All but one had previous convictions for assaults, arson and thefts. Three were classified as paranoid schizophrenic, two as schizophrenic and their ages ranged from 28–35 years. A closer examination of the offences of this group (isolated, it must be remembered, by projective test and interview data), is revealing. Three of the group chose strangers or casual acquaintances to assault but fell short of actually killing them. Two of the offenders killed their victims who were well known (and in one case was related) to them.

A brief examination of the variables discriminating this group and on which, in part, this identification of it as impulsive and psychopathic depends, is highly relevant to the claim that projective tests properly scored and analysed can contribute to psychological knowledge. The HTP test was by far the most illuminating and I shall concentrate on these data. The tree was drawn by this group, without leaves or foliage. This was a statistically significant finding. According to Buck (1970) the tree represents the subject's subconscious picture of himself in relation to his psychological field. Jolles (1964) argues that leaves indicate ways of contacting the environment (only connect) and that absence could indicate feelings of inadequacy and failure in dealing with the environment. These interpretations based on clinical impressions (and precisely fitting Eysenck's (1959) perjorative description of projective tests as vehicles for the clinical imagination) do fit, it has to be admitted, the group of offenders which they discriminate.

Their drawings of a person also discriminated them from controls and the other offenders. Their drawings were characterized by being incomplete, none of them, indeed, drew a complete person; one of the group drew a pinman very rapidly, a response interpreted by Jolles (1964) as psychopathic; this subject was, indeed, a killer. The fact that this group produced pictures of heads or heads and shoulders only, is interpreted by Jolles (1964) as indicative of a denial of the body and its anxiety producing drives. One of these offenders drew the head in profile but the body from the front, a response claimed by Buck (1970) to be indicative of extreme conflict. Furthermore, the arms and hands were stunted features, which were associated according to Jolles (1964) with feelings of inadequacy.

All in all, therefore, it can be argued, as Hampson (1975) does, that these offenders seem to have feelings of helplessness and inadequacy, and are psychopathically unable to examine themselves too closely. In view of the crimes committed by this group this description is by no means wide of the mark. It is interesting to note the apparent accuracy of the clinical impressions of Buck and Jolles with the HTP.

If these results were to be replicated, then the value of projective tests would be unchallengeable. Certainly these results with this first psychopathic group are strong support for G analysis as a method of analysing projective test data, and even more so, for the HTP. All the results, indeed, from this series of investigations were highly interesting in relation to the value of projective tests, and readers must refer to Hampson and Kline (1977a, b) for more details.

At present G analysis studies of the clinical domain are restricted to four laboratories, Lund and Uppsala in Sweden, the Max Planck Institute in Munich and the University of Exeter, under myself. Consequently, this promising method has yet to reveal its full potential. However a few further substantive findings have been made despite the fact that inevitably and properly, much research effort has had to be expended in technical matters—exploring the mathematical properties of G indices and related coefficients, which has been done in Uppsala, and improving Q factoring techniques in Lund and to some extent in Exeter.

Jonsonn (1975) carried out a G analysis of 35 schizophrenics which was cross-validated using split samples. The test responses consisted of items reflecting psychotic symptoms and four objective personality tests developed at Lund: the meta-contrast technique (Kragh and Smith, 1970), the serial colour-word test (Smith and Klein, 1953), the spiral after-effect test (Anderson *et al.*, 1972) and the serial rod and frame test (Eberhard, 1964). Since this was a small sample of schizophrenics, so that any sub-classes would be necessarily smaller and hence possibly of low stability in further investigations, the results must be treated with caution and regarded not as substantive psychometric contributions to clinical psychological knowledge but rather as illustrations of what the contribution from G analysis could be, given more extensive sampling of both tests and subjects. For it must be made clear that, as I argued the case for multivariate techniques in general (see Chapter 2), G analysis depends upon complete sampling of variables and subjects, if it is to be used for comprehensive categorization. In fact, in this study four schizophrenic categories emerged of which two could not be confidently interpreted either from the subjects comprising them or from their discriminating variables. Two factors were recognizable: one included the paranoid group, the other those with early symptoms of schizophrenia as described by Chapman (1966). The first group, of course, is hardly surprising and as Jonsonn points out, has been isolated in previous Q factor analysis, e.g. Guertin (1952) and Lorr (1968). This research clearly indicates that in the study of schizophrenia G analysis could play an important part.

This study, discussed above, actually had a precursor in which twelve schizophrenics were investigated using G analysis of the same battery of tests (Holley and Nillson, 1973). In this two factors emerged, highly disturbed psychotic subjects and a group who seemed to show neurotic symptoms with only a few psychotic reactions, and who were also named pseudo-neurotic schizophrenics. This earlier research again demonstrates the value of G analysis in the area and the need for proper sampling.

Finally one should mention a replication of this study on eighteen new patients by Jonsson and Franzen (1976). The results were not entirely consistent with the previous work, a problem which was also found in the studies of criminals by Hampson and Kline (1977a, b) and as in this case attributed to the heterogeneity of the categories, criminal and schizophrenic, and the small size of the samples. However while the "neurotic" schizophrenic factor was found, the typical and commonly described paranoid factor failed to emerge in this study.

Rothstein (in press) investigated fear among a group of students scoring high on the Wolpe fear inventory, the items of which comprised the data for a G analysis. Six groups emerged, of which five could be interpreted, the sixth being one individual. As with the studies of schizophrenia discussed above, all findings must be regarded until replication with other and different samples, as illustrative rather than definitive.

One group was labelled masculine bravery of whom nine of the ten were men. They denied almost all fears other than being teased. Group two represented feminine fears—dead animals, uncanny things, social performances and being ostracized—which was composed only of women. Factor three (only two women) seemed to reflect anxiety. Here there was an extensive list of fears including elevators, a lull in conversation, being ignored, medical odours, for example. Factor four comprised three women who had no social fears nor fear of losing control or going mad, but were afraid of smaller animals, death, surgery and parting from friends. Finally factor 6 included those with special social fears such as losing status and aggression. It is an interesting fact that in this sample of fearful students, one does not find subjects with special fears, e.g. animal, medical or social. This G analysis would be highly interesting with genuinely phobic patients. Certainly, it is more pertinent than the R analysis of items usually undertaken, and would go a long way to testing the claims put forward by Marks (1970) as to the symptomatic features of severe phobias and the prevalence and nature of normal fears.

Finally, as a demonstration of the powers of G analysis in clinical diagnosis I examine two papers from the Max Planck Institute (Schubo *et al.*, 1975 and Hentschel *et al.*, 1976) which report different aspects of the same investigation. In these studies paranoid schizophrenics, unspecified schizophrenics, psychotic depressives and neurotic depressives were compared on two scales, the IMPS (Inpatient Multidimensional Psychotic Scale, Lorr and Klett, 1967) and on the AMP documentation system (Angst *et al.*, 1969). These four groups of patients, the most commonly occurring among the 454 rated on the two scales, were then randomly divided into two samples, an analysis sample and a cross-validation sample. A G analysis of the items in these scales which included a criterion weighted rotation produced on the cross-validation sample an 83% correct placement. This compared favourably with discriminant function analysis (77%), simple selection based on IMPS scores (73%) and selection from AMP scores (79%). These results are particularly interesting because they indicate that G analysis *per se* is a powerful technique and significantly better than comparable methods. It also demonstrates the previously argued point that strength of G analysis lies in its ability to handle the awkward but clinically rich data from projective tests.

A final example from the research with G analysis (in its broadest form) which should convince all but the most sceptical, of its actually realized rather than potential power, can be found in the work of Vegelius (1976). Strictly, this is not G analysis at all. Instead Vegilius (1976) utilized what he refers to as WHIDD analysis (the weighted H index Delegate Discriminant Analysis). This utilizes, as the index of similarity, not G indices but the weighted H index which is an E correlation, thus indicating that it satisfies the requirements of normalized vectors in Euclidean spaces, and is a generalization of the G index for interval scales. Instead of G factor analysis, the cosine theorem is applied (permissible for the H index is an E coefficient and thus a normalized scalar product) computing the Euclidian distance between two vectors and their scalar product.

Fallstrom and Vegilius (1976) applied this WHIDD analysis to data on diabetic children collected by Fallstrom (1974) consisting of Rorschach responses of 32 diabetic girls and their controls. The samples were each split such that validation groups were formed of 16 diabetics and their controls. Since the results were promising Vegelius (1976) replicated the study using a further 32 diabetic girls and controls.

The results of the WHIDD analysis based upon responses previously selected not, it must be remembered, responses which maximally discriminate the two groups, were spectacular. There were 31 out of 32 correct placements; one diabetic only was out of place. Particularly interesting was the fact that the most discriminating item was the Rorschach Penetration score, which according to Fisher and Cleveland (1958) is symptomatic of a disturbed body image. Vegelius (1976) argues that this makes sound psychological sense in that such disturbances are common in physical handicap and chronic disease (e.g. Kaufman and Hersler, 1971). Indeed this result might almost be considered as a substantive finding that diabetics have a disturbed body image, if one knew that this variable was validly measured by the Rorschach. Although in psychoanalytic theory the body image and ego development are intimately related (Erikson, 1956) the other discriminating indices were not related to ego weakness, but rather to neurotic reaction, which is interpreted by Vegelius as being the children's way of coping with the disease.

While this study is impressive as a demonstration of the discriminatory power of the Rorschach and the WHIDD method, I cannot altogether agree with the interpretation of the results given by Vegilius (1976). The point at issue is the nature of the control group. In my view, a further control should have been used of a chronically-ill non-diabetic group, so that it would have been possible to separate out the diabetic from the ill effects. It is possible that the poor body image reflects being ill, or having an inefficient pancreas or the effects of having to have injections or any combination of these. Nevertheless if one ignores the interpretative problem, the outstanding placement accuracy is a tribute to the Rorschach test and to the WHIDD method. Actually Vegelius (1976) also used weighted G indices in a comparative study where he obtained much the same results.

Sufficient examples have now been given of the power of G analysis in its various forms to make it clear that it possesses great potential for the psychological study of clinical groups. One of the difficulties with G analysis, as has been observed in all these illustrations, lies in the identification of the factors: a related problem concerns the fact that different studies, perhaps inevitably, usually fail to yield identical factors. These two difficulties need to be overcome before any truly substantive findings can be made with this technique. Before leaving G analysis, I want to briefly discuss the solution to these problems.

The identification of factors is particularly important because an obvious objection to G analysis as a technique is the one that has been consistently used against criterion-keyed tests, such as the MMPI. This is, of course, that any results are purely empirical and have no necessary psychological meaning. The solution to this difficulty demands that one relates any factors discriminating these groups to known dimensions of personality and ability. Thus, one can obtain Q factor scores for each person and put these in an R analysis with variables such as have been discussed throughout this book, i.e. those from factored tests. This external method of verifying G analysis factors is both objective and psychologically meaningful because it locates them within a framework of meaningful variables. This was the method used by Hampson and Kline (1977).

Perhaps more serious is the second difficulty when sometimes the same factors fail to emerge. This can only be resolved by proper sampling of subjects. This is a particular hazard with the G index which for statistical reasons works most effectively with about 30 subjects. It demands, therefore, that G analysis studies are replicated on many different samples. This enables us to see whether the factors are idiosyncratic to the particular sample or not. Since the standard errors of factor loadings ensure that even identical factors about which there is no disagreement, e.g. verbal ability or anxiety, do not have identical loadings from study to study, there has to be some method of factor matching. This can be done statistically or by examining the correlations of the G factor with other factors. Both methods are desirable to ensure that emerging factors from different samples are in fact the same.

If they are not the same, there is the additional problem of whether they should be, as Hampson and Kline (1977) found in their studies of criminals, where the samples were in all probability genuinely different in respect of personality. These problems of replication can only be solved empirically and until a good deal of replication has been done, and until factor differences can be observed in the light of other evidence about the samples, one cannot do much more than be aware of the problem and ensure in G studies that one has adequate means of identifying factors.

THE MMPI

This test has been fully described in Chapter 3 and is notable for the fact that huge numbers of scales can be constructed by criterion-keying from its item pool. By the early 1960s, Dahlstrom and Welsh (1960) could list more than 200, and many more have been developed since. Indeed the MMPI could be regarded as one of psychometrics' major successes, a personality inventory that has been widely used in clinical psychology. However, as I have consistently argued throughout this book, such criterion-keyed scales cannot be psychologically meaningful (other than by chance). Items are utilized in a scale because they discriminate a particular group. Since criterion groups may differ from each other and from normals on a variety of variables, criterion-keyed scales may be psychologically heterogeneous. The fact that schizophrenics differ from controls on a set of MMPI items, the Sc scale, does not mean that this scale should be labelled or conceived of as a schizophrenic scale.

From this it is clear that the psychological meaning of the MMPI scales, both the nine standard clinical scales and any others developed by criterion-keying, is not guaranteed. Any psychological meaning MMPI scales possess is literally there by chance: the chance that only homogeneous items with no response sets or other sources of bias have been used, or the chance that the group discriminated differs from others on only one variable.

This logical, ineluctable limitation to the meaning of any MMPI scales means that any results achieved with the MMPI cannot constitute a contribution to psychological knowledge unless one so narrows that term, that knowledge is defined in terms of differences on empirical scales. This I refuse to do, as it can only harm the development of psychology as a coherent corpus of knowledge.

This incapacity to make a substantive contribution to psychology is particularly unfortunate in the case of the MMPI for there is now a considerable body of research results, many of which have been subjected to careful examination. Over the years the profiles of various groups have been gathered together so that a clinician who obtains a patients' score can simply match it up with the profiles in these collections, profiles which have been coded in a variety of ingenious ways. Perhaps the most enthusiastic of the workers in the field of obsessional empiricism, are Marks and Seeman, whose latest work (Marks *et al.*, 1977) extends this actuarial use of the MMPI down to adolescents.

Even if this argument is accepted, that MMPI profiles as found in the work of Marks *et al.* (1977) cannot provide psychological knowledge of any substance, it can still be objected that they are highly useful for the clinician in that they have diagnostic power. In brief, diagnostic power is a contribution to knowledge. However, this argument will not do. The diagnostic power is illusory knowledge that turns the researcher away from what he should seek. If instead of relying on the MMPI these clinicians aimed to work with the meaningful factors discussed throughout the earlier chapter of this book, then the discriminations that emerged could be interpreted. These factors being the fundamental dimensions of their sphere, whether it is personality or motivation, would provide insight into the nature of the groups and the psychiatric syndrome. If they do not, then one can begin to construct a theory that will account for the differences, as indeed despite all the problems, both Cattell and Eysenck have done. In trying to understand the nature of mammals, is it better to count the hairs of the body and classify their colours than to examine the underlying neural and skeletal structure?

The MMPI discriminations and codebooks, however elaborate and technically sophisticated, are a dangerous chimera. How this can be so when Cattell's abnormal personality sphere and its factors were to a large extent determined by the MMPI. This argument is supported by this argument. For the discriminatory power of the MMPI turns on the fortunate fact that the original items were so skilfully chosen by Hathaway and McKinley that they embraced many of the abnormal temperament factors. This is the reason the test discriminates so well. However, many of the profiles and especially scales, are not factor pure but mixtures of factors which are of unknown relative weight. A carefully conducted multivariate analysis using pure factor scales would reveal far more and, if as is possible, the scales consisted of MMPI items only, the discrimination would be as good as or better than that utilizing the orthodox MMPI procedures.

Another psychometric approach which is radically different from that of the factor analysts, but capable of tying in with it is Foulds' work. The best summary of his position can be found in "The Hierarchial Nature of Personal Illness" (Foulds, 1976) and amplification of the empirical work on which it is based can be found in a variety of papers, notably Foulds and Bedford (1975), Bedford and Foulds (1977) and Bedford *et al.* (1976).

Foulds' book is closely argued and I shall examine the central issues in his thesis, one of which is dependent in part at least, on psychometric evidence which is why it is important in this section.

There is a philosophic basis to Foulds' work—Macmurray (1961) argues that what constitutes personal existence is the personal relation of persons. From this virtual axiom Foulds argues that personal illness must induce a change in one's relationships with other persons and a loss of one's ability to formulate one's actions consonant with other people. This in turn involves changes of attitudes and affects which are the signs and symptoms of what is generally referred to as mental illness. This concept of mental illness as personal illness has been extensively developed by Foulds and his colleagues and put on to an empirical, psychometric basis.

A number of key terms have to be defined before one can fully understand Foulds' position:

> A *Sign* is a qualitative change in bodily or mental functioning (e.g. a delusion) which is not reported as stressful, although the observer can recognize its maladaptive quality.
> A *Symptom* is a qualitative change from a previous condition which distresses the sufferer and is rare in the general population.
> A *State* is a quantitative affective change from a previous condition lasting weeks rather than days and is rare, though more common than symptoms, in the general population.
> An *Attitude* reflects consistency of response to given situations and is usually generally distributed through the normal population.

Foulds and Bedford (1976) argued in the case of depression that the question neurotic or psychotic depression was inappropriate because the relation between these two disorders was inclusive and not exclusive. Evidence was adduced demonstrating that all those with psychotic depressive symptoms neurotic depressive symptoms, although the converse was not true. In depressive illness therefore, there was an hierarchical structure of symptoms.

This is one example of the hierarchical structuring which Foulds (1976) argues, runs through the whole gamut of personal illness, including all the traditional Kraepelinian categories of mental disease.

Foulds (1976) argues that there are four classes of personal illness, each having its own sub-classes, ordered by increasing degrees of adverse change in the person:

Class 1. Dysthymic states: anxiety states, depression states and states of elation. The states refer in these cases to changes in affect and an individual thus affected would be described as emotionally disturbed.

Class 2. Neurotic symptoms: conversion symptoms, dissociative symptoms, phobic symptoms, compulsive symptoms and ruminative symptoms. With neurotic symptoms, a patient is in a state of dissonance— he sees part of his behaviour and experience as akin to his normal self.

Class 3. Integrated delusions: delusions of persecution, delusions of grandeur, delusions of contrition. Here the patient's self-concept has become distorted in some way.

Class 4. Delusions of disintegration: the groups are as in Class 3 except that they suffer from delusions of disintegration as well. Thus a schizophrenic (of the paranoid variety) might suffer from delusions of disintegration and paranoid delusions. At this stage (4) the person has disintegrated to a high degree and he no longer feels himself as agent of his own actions, feelings or thoughts.

Since this is an hierarchical structure, the hypothesis is that a subject with symptoms at any class level will have symptoms at all the lower class levels: conversely a person with no symptoms at a given class level will not have symptoms at any higher class level. Obviously some people at a given level will have no symptoms beyond this level.

These are Foulds' claims concerning the hierarchical structure of mental disorders. As he admits this is not an original theme, although it is one that is generally neglected in writings in abnormal psychology. Bleuler (1950) for example, argued that manic depressive symptoms were present in schizophrenia and Chapman (1966) claimed that among the symptoms of young schizophrenics every kind of neurotic symptom could be found, especially in the early stages of the disease. One aspect of the hierarchical structuring of personal illness is that, at a stroke, it demonstrates why studies of the reliability and validity of psychiatric diagnoses are usually low. Such investigations imply exclusive relationships in contrast with the inclusive relations posited by the hierarchical approach.

Such clinical claims, however interesting, would be of no relevance to this chapter, had not Foulds and his colleagues, over the years, constructed a number of psychometric tests in an attempt to develop and investigate their theoretical position. These tests, indeed, in the view of their authors have confirmed their theories to a striking degree. If their claims are not exaggerated, we have a genuine contribution to psychological knowledge. The empirical bases of their claims and their psychometric tests are scrutinized in the following section.

THE DSSI

In order to put these hierarchical hypotheses to the test, Foulds has developed the Delusions-Symptoms-States-Inventory (Foulds and Bedford, 1975) from a previous measure, the Symptom-Sign Inventory (Foulds and Hope, 1968). The DSSI consists of 12 sets of seven items selected for relevance to the most frequent clinical syndromes, although, of course, the traditional psychiatric classification is not the basis for the item sets. These consist of: delusions of disintegration, persecution, grandeur and contrition; conversion symptoms, dissociative symptoms, phobic symptoms, compulsive symptoms, ruminative symptoms; states of anxiety, depression and elation. All the groups and classes are measured in Foulds' hierarchical classification of personal illness by only seven items. There are two forms: one concerned with recent, the other with previous events.

Before examining the evidence for the validity and reliability of the DSSI, there is one highly interesting feature of this test. Foulds' (1976) description of the hierarchy, indeed any hierarchy *per se* demands precise measurement on a Guttman scale which consists of items so ordered, that if one knows the highest item endorsed by a subject, one knows that he will have endorsed all the items below it. It is therefore, disappointing that the DSSI is not a Guttman scale, another example of the claim by Levy (1973) that the psychometric assumptions of many tests are not in accord with their theoretical rationale. However this is perhaps too strict. A simple inventory of the DSSI variety can demonstrate whether this hierarchical structuring of personal illness occurs or not.

A study is reported by Foulds (1976) which required judges, psychiatrists and psychologists, to allocate the items in the DSSI to syndrome groups. This was a test of the face validity of the items in terms of content. The results indicated considerable agreement that items were relevant to the intended psychiatric syndromes. Only one item created disagreement. A further investigation related responses to the inventory to psychiatric ratings of the patients. Again, there was agreement for all groups except those with phobic, compulsive and ruminative symptoms. The conclusion that can be drawn from these results are that the DSSI items are relevant to the categories they purport to measure, and that responses to them reflect in most instances patients' behaviour, as observed by those working with them. This last finding is the more important and means that the DSSI can be used for research with confidence that the responses are not just test specific. The first result is equivocal in my view since the face validity of personality items is not always a good guide to what is actually measured. However, in view of the later finding, this is not such a critical question. The DSSI can test the hierarchy hypothesis.

In a test of this hypothesis, 480 psychiatric patients (in-patients, out-patients and day-patients in England, Scotland and Canada) were compared with 240 non-psychiatric controls. To fall into a class, at least two of the relevant DSSI items had to be endorsed. In fact for all groups of patients divided by type of treatment and sex, there was a 93·3 % concordance rate with the hierarchy structure. The controls showed a similar pattern although not unnaturally, the majority were simply not personally ill. Indeed the results from this study indicate that in almost all classes membership of a class implies membership of all lower classes, and the converse does not hold. Foulds' (1976) hierarchical hypothesis is supported. Retesting of the in-patients showed that patients had moved down the hierarchy in the main and much more important, that the hierarchical structure remains. This has highly interesting implications for treatment. Thus at Class 3, ECT may be the most effective treatment, while as the patient moves to Class 2, according to the hierarchic model, another treatment may be more effective, e.g. behaviour therapy for phobias.

In conclusion, it seems that these results with the DSSI constitute a major contribution to clinical psychology from psychometrics—namely that psychiatric symptoms are hierarchically structured, a finding with important implications for treatment and for theory, although both these topics are beyond the scope of this chapter.

It must be noted that these results although not based upon factored dimensions, do not suffer from the same difficulties as those concerning the MMPI. The questions on which the MMPI has been brought to bear are essentially those which demand a factor-analytic answer: how do patients in class A differ from patients in class B? However the DSSI has merely provided evidence that patients' symptoms have a hierarchical structure. For this question a factored test is unnecessary. It is also to be noted that if one wishes to expand one's knowledge of the structure of symptoms to investigate its psychological concomitants, then one needs recourse to factored tests and concepts, as shall be seen later. Indeed if there are symptom factors and this would appear likely from the work of Cattell with the MMPI based items in the abnormal personality sphere, then an essential question concerning this symptom structure is how it relates to the established symptom factors. Nevertheless, as it stands, Foulds' results (1976) are an important psychometric contribution, albeit descriptive, to psychological knowledge.

At this point one should mention the SCL-90 which is a factored rating-scale of symptoms (Derogatis *et al.*, 1973). Nine dimensions of symptoms are found: somatization, obsessive, interpersonal sensitivity, depression, anxiety, hostility, phobic anxiety, paranoid ideation and psychoticism. There seems little doubt that these are stable (Derogatis and Cleary, 1977). However, their status relative to the major personality dimensions, especially Cattell's abnormal personality factors, needs to be worked out before their significance and psychological meaning can be assessed.

Another study with the DSSI of the groups used in the hierarchical classification deserves a brief note. It concerned the problem of psychiatric diagnosis which has long been shown to be highly unreliable (e.g. Beck, 1962). However, the notion of the hierarchy suggests that many patients are bound to have symptoms that overlap two or more classes. If using the hierarchy, psychiatrists classify patients by their highest symptom, much of the unreliability disappears. This, however, is of minor interest in this thesis.

The most interesting aspect of Foulds' work is the relation of the classes of personal illness to what he refers to as the "more enduring personality attributes". For this investigation 325 of the original patient sample were further administered the Personality Deviance Scales (measuring extrapunitiveness, intrapunitiveness and dominance) developed from the Hostility-Direction of Hostility Questionnaire (Caine *et al.,* 1967). Unfortunately the validity of these scales, their factorial structure, and their place in factor space remain undetermined, although Foulds has attempted to remedy this defect by administering this personality deviance scale and the 16 PF test to a small sample of young normal subjects. These correlations suggest relationships between these scales and exvia and anxiety. In view of the fact that, as has been demonstrated, the Cattell factors embrace much of the temperamental variance, one should much prefer to see studies directly linking these factors to the DSSI rather than the PDS scales which are idiosyncratic to Foulds, making generalization difficult. So, one is forced to conclude that an investigation is needed which will in a large sample of abnormal patients, link up the DSSI groups to the major dimensions of personality. In fairness to Foulds it must be pointed out that if he was not original and determinedly divergent, the hierarchy of symptoms would not have been so clearly demonstrated. Consequently his use of the PDDS which is symptomatic of these same research traits has to be tolerated. The missing work must be completed by others.

In summary, I would argue that the demonstration of the hierarchic nature of psychiatric symptoms is a valuable contribution to clinical psychology both descriptively and moreover, theoretically, because this structure has to be accounted for. In addition, the links with temperamental dimensions are likely to prove illuminating. The practical implications for diagnosis and treatment are also considerable although these remain to be worked out. Foulds' work constitutes an original contribution to the field and one rooted in psychometrics and in this case—the DSSI.

OTHER PSYCHOMETRIC MEASURES

For reasons that have been fully explicated throughout this book, non-factorial psychometric tests which exist in great profusion, or indeed factored tests which remain unlocated in their relevant factor space are usually unable to contribute much to psychological knowledge. Even the MMPI as we have seen, despite its objective diagnostic capacity (which however is really factored, see Chapter 6), is not advocated here because blindly empirical diagnosis, albeit useful in practice, prevents more important theoretical based diagnosis from being developed. Thus, there is no need to comment on other psychometric tests, however useful some of them may be to practitioners.

One exception has to be made. The Goldberg Mental Health Questionnaire (1972) is used increasingly in the epidemiological survey of mental health on the general population. It can be regarded as a classificatory device for ascertaining how many people in any category show symptoms of mental illness. The results reported in the book describing the development of the scale (Goldberg, 1972) indicate that it can screen out those needing treatment. It is arguable that this is a useful contribution to psychology and to psychological practice, rather than knowledge. The only knowledge to which a scale of this sort can add is statistical. The proportions in various social classes and other groups show various symptoms. Conversely, data of this type could be useful in elucidating environmental, aetiological factors in various different types of psychiatric abnormality. Nevertheless, one would still argue that this psychometric test is of practical rather than theoretical interest and that the results do not constitute a contribution to psychological knowledge.

The main conclusions from this chapter are set out below in the order they have been discussed.

SUMMARY

(1) Questionnaire measures of temperament give useful and meaningful differences between diagnostic groups, $C-$, $E-$, $F-$, $G-$, H, $O+$ and $Q4+$. These are the factors that distinguish neurotics. Psychotics can be discriminated by the abnormal P factors or Eysenck's P which is tentatively related to maleness.

(2) Objective factors important in clinical diagnosis are UI 19, UI 23 and UI 25 (psychoticism), i.e. abnormals are dependent, regressed and psychotic.

(3) Motivational factors have yet to contribute to the psychology of clinical diagnosis.

(4) The psychometric contribution to the study of therapeutic efficiency could be considerable. Research designs were elaborated that would overcome most of the problems in this field.

(5) The specification equations, P analyses and the dynamic calculus described methods and approaches with great potential for clinical theory.

(6) G analysis and related methods were described. The power of G analysis demonstrated how to provide meaningful clinical diagnoses. The power of the Rorschach test in a number of diverse fields was also described. Again, the potential rather than the actual results of such methods were demonstrated.

(7) The dangers of the MMPI classification systems were pointed out.

(8) Foulds' work demonstrated the hierarchic structure of abnormal symptoms, which is considered to be a major psychometric contribution to clinical psychology. The need to relate Foulds' sub-classes to factored personality dimensions was pointed out.

10

Psychometrics and Cross-cultural Psychology

INTRODUCTION

Warren (1977), arguing that cross-cultural psychology is in reality no more than a decade old, defines its purpose as extending psychology "beyond its Western and possibly ethnocentric base". In order to understand the impact and importance of psychometrics in this relatively new branch of psychology, one has to examine the implications of this definition a little further.

First, it may seem strange that cross-cultural psychology is claimed to be so young. Here however there is an important point concerning Warren's general definition of its aim. Previously, as Warren (1977) states, the study of other cultures, especially "primitive" cultures did not aim to extend our knowledge of psychology: on the contrary, psychology was used to inform our research of the culture. Thus, many apparent cross-cultural studies would not be so classified because their aims were different. Was not the objection to the possible defects of the reaction-timers to be used on the Cambridge expedition to the Torres Straights answered sufficiently by their being good enough for savages?

Cross-cultural psychology aims, therefore, to widen the data of scientific psychology. This I would argue, along with Warren (1977) is its real importance and significance in the field of psychology. Western psychology has based so many of its claims on results obtained from students, children and the hooded rat, together with samples of neurotics and psychotics (all groups who cannot escape the experimenter), that if one follows the normal rules of sampling and generalization of results, then it is a specious subject. That is why it is so curious an objection from academic psychology (e.g. Eysenck, 1953) to psychoanalytic theory, that its sampling procedures are bad. Indeed a Freudian could well argue that this objection is itself a defence-projection, i.e. resistance.

By this criterion, to extend the boundaries of psychology, early studies which had not this overt aim, can still be categorized as cross-cultural. For even if they simply applied Western psychology to a new culture, the resulting data and results can be re-used. Knowledge of a different culture can be used to check on various psychological hypotheses. Kline (1977) indeed surveyed a number of such investigations and related the results to psychoanalytic hypotheses, concluding that cross-cultural psychology was a powerful means of putting Freudian theories to the scientific test.

In this chapter, although I agree with Warren's rigorous definition of cross-cultural psychology, the term is used more widely—to include all studies of other cultures because ultimately all such knowledge *can* be used to modify or extend, if necessary, our general psychological Western-based knowledge.

We are now ready to examine the contribution that psychometrics has made and can make to cross-cultural psychology, i.e. to the knowledge of other cultures. Since this is a huge field of knowledge embracing, *inter alia*, anthropology, sociology, social psychology, ethnology, human geography and linguistics, one is forced to examine cross-cultural psychology analytically. To do this it would appear useful to categorize cross-cultural research into types or schools. For if each of these has different aims and different research methodologies, the psychometric contribution to each will obviously vary.

In the paper previously referred to, I examined (Kline, 1977) cross-cultural psychology, with regard to its relevance for putting psychoanalytic theory to the scientific test. In that article I was able to identify four main types of cross-cultural psychology types varying in aims and methods and hence valuable for the purposes of assessing the psychometric contribution to the field. These types were as set out below:

(1) *British social anthropology.* The workers in this school of whom the best known are probably Evans Pritchard (e.g. 1940), Radcliffe-Browne (e.g. 1952) and more recently, Gluckman (1962), all characteristically make highly detailed studies of societies utilizing as few psychological or psychoanalytic explanatory principles as possible. Strictly their work is not psychology at all, but their observations can be valuable for cross-cultural psychologists.

(2) *Hologeistic studies.* This group of cross-cultural investigations utilizes ethnographic and anthropological reports of societies but in a special way. Large numbers of such studies of different societies are collected together and data are abstracted from them and subjected to statistical analysis such that, if the societies reflect all those known to ethnography, statements can be made which truly generalize to all mankind (assuming for the moment that the data are accurate). Whiting and Child's "Child Training and Personality" (1953) is probably the best known hologcistic study: anthropological reports from 75 primitive societies were searched for data relevant to child-training procedures and adult personality characteristics. The resulting ratings were then correlated.

(3) *Culture and personality school.* This group aimed to answer to question, as Spiro (1972) argues, of what culture produced certain personality variables. This contrasts considerably with the first group of social anthropologists who were primarily concerned with the historical and

environmental variables that produced a given culture. This definition of the aims of the personality and culture school (which was an attempt to provide some kind of structure to the enormous body of anthropological data collected over the years) demonstrates clearly that their aims were psychological. Their interest was in the dynamics of behaviour which accounts for the fact that in the main they expressed what was then (the 1930s) the most popular dynamic account of personality—the psychoanalytic.

Incidentally, it should be noted that this group of researchers overlap with another—the psychoanalytic anthropologists (e.g. Roheim, 1947)—who essentially psychoanalyse primitive subjects (rather than Viennese neurotics).

(4) *Cross-cultural psychologists.* This is the most recent category of research workers. They utilize the methods and procedures of experimental psychology, including psychometric tests aimed to test the generalizations of Western psychology, and understand the conditions and experiences that affect development. Much of the work has concentrated on Piagetian developmental concepts, e.g. Cole *et al.* (1971) and Dasen (1977). The reasons for this highlight the strength of the cross-cultural approach. If one can find differences in Piagetian developmental sequences in different cultural groups, a study of the child-rearing procedures and the educational environments in the widest and proper sense of the term, can enable us to relate them to the differences and one has, therefore, obtained a powerful insight in the development of abilities. The advantage of cross-cultural studies in this field should be evident, namely that the variance among cultures is far greater than variance within any one culture for virtually all variables. Thus cross-cultural studies are extremely powerful in the investigation of the affects of the environment; they form part of an ideal research design.

All this assumes, of course, that in practice, as distinct from logic, cross-cultural psychologists are able to construct reliable and valid measures in a wide variety of cultures. In fact this has turned out to be extremely difficult and in a subsequent section of this chapter the difficulties and problems of cross-cultural testing are discussed.

From this brief discussion of four categories of cross-cultural investigation which are not intended to be entirely mutually exclusive or perfectly differentiated but which do, however, categorize most research into four rather separate groups, it is obvious that psychometrics has a major part to play in, and is in fact an intrinsic component of, our last group. In the first group it is clearly not highly relevant while in the other two groups psychometrics has not so far played much part although as I shall argue, it could so do. In the sections that follow the methodological problems involved in carrying out the aims of these four kinds of cross-cultural psychology are outlined so that one can see what value psychometrics is or can be: but first a discussion of those categories where it is evident that psychometrics will play but little part.

As I have indicated, the avowed purposes of social anthropology to account for a culture in terms of historical and environmental variables is actually non-psychological and, as such, psychometrics must be irrelevant to it. However, two points need to be made. While it is true that social anthropology *per se* is not relevant for psychometry, it must be remembered that anthropological data have been used (by the hologeistic workers) to answer psychological questions. If these data were more psychometric in kind, they could be more useful to psychology. This point is probably unfair: one cannot expect researchers to obtain data because others would like them to. The second issue is perhaps more important. As Spiro (1968) has pointed out, social anthropology, despite its claims, is often implicitly psychological. For example, Radcliffe-Browne (1952) who despises psychoanalytic theorizing about the oedipus complex as found in "Totem and Taboo" (Freud, 1913) considered *post partum* fatherhood rituals as symbolic expressions of paternal concern. This however is a psychological hypothesis—that there exists some necessity to symbolize certain human relationships. Furthermore, it is a psychological hypothesis that has no theoretical basis. If in fact social anthropology is implicitly psychological, then it is reasonable to require that it collects pertinent psychological data. If it did so, then possibly psychometrics could have some part to play in it. As it stands however, psychometrics is not relevant and cannot contribute to social anthropological cross-cultural studies.

The hologeistic method makes use of anthropological and ethnographic reports. By nature of dealing with large numbers of societies at a time, it differs from orthodox anthropology. It makes use of, in its standard application, ready-made data so that obviously any data-collecting technique is not relevant to it, thus making psychometry inapplicable. However, if psychometric data were collected in anthropology, then the hologeistic method would become more precise since the accuracy of the original data is clearly one of the major difficulties with the hologeistic method (this has been fully discussed by Campbell and Narroll, 1972).

However, it is possible to use the hologeistic method and collect one's own data although obviously this is a lengthy process. By so doing the research worker from the viewpoint of this discussion, falls into one of the other categories and the contribution to his work from psychometrics will depend upon the particular questions he is seeking to answer. Thus, both social anthropology and the hologeistic method have made relatively little use of psychometrics, although the latter method could be greatly improved by psychometric data.

The culture and personality school whose cross-cultural studies aimed to elucidate the effects of culture on personality are clearly concerned with psychological problems and there is little doubt that, if good cross-cultural personality measures could be constructed, the work of these anthropologists would be more attractive to psychologists.

Most of the researchers who fall into this category are anthropologists of a psychoanalytic persuasion. However, as I (Kline, 1977) have pointed out, the data on which they base their arguments are characteristic of anthropology and lacks quantification. In some cases the provenance of the data is suspect. Parin and Morgenthaler (1969) for example, who studied a variety of African tribes, speaking in all more than 100 languages, rather than learn these, which is a daunting task, obtained their information from local residents in English or French and from interrogation with the help of local interpreters. If these statements can be considered the raw data one can have little confidence in them. How extensive or accurate is the knowledge of their informants? How trustworthy are the responses of subjects to the interpreter? How accurate was the interpretation? How representative a sample were the subjects who were interviewed? All these questions infirm the data of this study.

There can be little doubt that, if the culture and personality school are concerned with personality, they should best measure personality variables psychometrically, if in fact it is possible to do so in the kinds of culture which they study. If they were to do this, the sample from whom the scores were obtained would have to be stated and its adequacy would become obvious. This question of sampling is particularly salient in cross-cultural psychology. Obviously large and representative samples are needed if one wishes to make statements about national differences. Muensterberger (1969) tried to argue that the dependence of the Southern Chinese was linked to their orality. His data were obtained from interviews in English with 15 men and six women living in the Chinese quarters of San Francisco and New York. Is it possible that such a sample of approx. 350 million Southern Chinese (in China alone) is adequate? The collection of psychometric data brings home to the investigator the inadequacy of sampling, at least in respect of numbers.

Thus, I would argue that the culture and personality researchers would be well advised to utilize tests if this is possible in cross-cultural studies. However, if they do so, they would become difficult to distinguish from the last group— the cross-cultural psychologists who try to use standard psychological techniques in non-Western cultures to test and expand psychological Western-based hypotheses.

Given then that the fourth group of cross-cultural psychologists utilize where possible, the standard psychological techniques and methods of the West, and given all the arguments presented throughout this book on the advantages of factored tests over others for meaningful psychological knowledge, it follows that for this group psychometry must have a large part to play, *unless* factorial, psychometric tests fail to work in non-Western cultures. From this it follows that the value of psychometry in cross-cultural psychology must depend upon the extent to which tests and other assessment procedures can be used in cultures different from those where they were developed to provide comparable scores. A discussion of the problems in cross-cultural psychological testing is therefore necessary before one can understand the value of psychometrics in this field.

PROBLEMS IN CROSS-CULTURAL PSYCHOLOGICAL TESTING

The basic problem in cross-cultural testing is simply that a test valid in one culture is not necessarily so in another. Although some of the reasons for this are common to all kinds of test, to some extent tests of different types are plagued by different problems. The discussion will begin with the difficulties that beset virtually all tests and the more specific problems will be examined separately.

Before the cross-cultural problems in testing can be thoroughly appreciated one must note what Triadis *et al.* (1971) have argued: that data collection in anthropological psychology has never taken the emic-etic dilemma seriously enough to obtain the advantages of both approaches. The emic approach, as Spindler (1975) neatly puts it, following claims of Malinowski and Boas, argues that cultures have to be understood within their own terms. Behaviour is studied as it is seen by the member of the culture. A good example can be taken from the field of intelligence testing. Intelligence is a variable that is important and understood by most Westerners. An intelligence test has a definite meaning to Western subjects. Wober (1973) in Uganda, however, has shown that the notion of intelligence held by Ugandans is quite different. To compare the results of Ugandans and Westerners, therefore, on this emic view would not be meaningful. Social anthropology is certainly an emic discipline.

The etic approach, on the other hand, seeks for universal laws of human behaviour. It uses concepts that are culture-free, conceptually equivalent or universal. Psychoanalytic anthropology and theory, the culture and personality school and the cross-cultural psychologist extending psychological theory, exemplify the etic approach. The totally emic worker cannot do cross-cultural research. The etic worker on the other hand, may end up with worthless data of only apparent cross-cultural comparability. An ideal solution to the dilemma, according to Spindler, is to develop emic methods to measure etic constructs. This is fine but one then has to be sure that the emic measures are equivalent.

This distinction which mirrors culturally the better known distinction among measures of individual differences—the idiographic and nomothetic—and the need in any properly conducted cross-cultural study to have elements of both approaches, clarifies some of the problems in cross-cultural testing which will be discussed below.

Cognitive Abilities

Indeed, the conflict between the emic and etic approaches is of the greatest importance when one comes to examine the use of tests of cognitive abilities in cross-cultural psychology. Thus Berry and Dasen (1972) in their concluding remarks to their large collection of readings on culture and cognition demonstrate that orthodox cross-cultural psychology of which they are acknowledged leaders, has begun to form dogma on this issue, dogma with which it seems to psychometrists, it is easily possible to disagree. They argue that the passing of the stage where one culture was compared with another on I.Q. tests is a real achievement, for Western technology has recognized its ethnocentrism, and such simplistic acts of comparison will never be made again. Instead cross-cultural psychology "... laid bare once again the basic problems which were so clearly articulated early in the century: do, indeed, cognitive processes differ, and do levels of competence differ from culture to culture?". Having then agreed that cross-cultural studies of these cognitive processes have not yet produced clear answers to these questions, they claim that "... a major achievement of these studies has been the liberation of cross-cultural cognitive psychology from a distressing concern with intelligence and its *impossible* (my italics) attempts to make it "culturally neutral" through culturally independent ("culture free", "culture fair" or culture-reduced) measures".

Having written off the use of intelligence tests in cross-cultural psychology, and of course by a logical extension of their argument, these strictures would apply to all other tests of the cognitive factors whose identification was regarded in this book as a contribution to psychological knowledge, they prescribe for good cross-cultured research. First, the demonstration of differences between cultural groups on test scores is not useful. Instead the prediction of such differences in terms of cultural variables and a study of the mechanisms involved is a more important aim. One-shot studies are proscribed because they preclude the emic approach and the results cannot be interpreted in the light of the culture. What are required are long-term, carefully-planned and adequately-sampled research projects. A conclusion surely with which none would argue.

Some comments, however, must be made about the assumptions implicit in these views, for if accepted, they mean that psychometry can offer little to cross-cultural psychology.

The first point that must be taken up concerns the "impossibility" of measuring the I.Q. cross-culturally. This statement appears to mistake the nature of the gf factor measured by such tests. As shown in Chapter 4 on ability, this factor is conceived as a basic reasoning ability. Why therefore should it be distressing or impossible to measure this in different cultures? Of course, I do not deny that this ability is emphasized in the West and neglected in many other cultures so that the ability tapped has little relevance for members of such cultures. However this is a psychological fact. To discover a group scoring low on such measures is not branding them as inferior. It is simply demonstrating that the group is poor at this particular reasoning ability. Of course I fully agree with Berry and Dasen that the interesting aspect of such a finding is in examining the cultural and institutional features (if any, for it *could* be genetic) that would account for it.

However, the fact of low g scores for a cultural group is of psychological significance because, as has been demonstrated in the chapter, gf is correlated with a large number of diverse achievements. A group scoring low on g is therefore unlikely to be successful in Western technological enterprises unless appropriate steps are taken in the culture to stimulate its development.

Therefore, it is not true to argue that there is no reason to test g cross-culturally; neither should one regard it an achievement to no longer be interested in testing g cross-culturally. This is especially the case when one considers Berry and Dasen's (1974) claim that they are concerned with cognitive processes, because as has been demonstrated, gf and gc are the main factors in cognitive processes in the West. Unless one tests cross-culturally one cannot examine the factor structure of abilities in other cultures and thus one is unable to make statements about the relative importance of g in other cultures.

In general, therefore, while one agrees with Berry and Daren, that the aim of cross-cultural studies of cognitive processes is to explicate the environmental variables affecting them one can see no reason why this precludes the study of intelligence using intelligence tests.

It is possible, perhaps, that their main argument turned on the difficulty of testing g in other cultures: that this was so difficult (so emic a measure would be needed) that it could never be done properly. This, however, is the counsel of despair; there is no psychometric reason why tests cannot be constructed which can be shown to measure basic reasoning ability in any culture. In this respect in what way does one culture differ from another? If it can be done in one culture (as it can be) it is up to Berry and Dasen to explain why it cannot be done in another. Certainly there are grave practical difficulties of measurement, as there are in other sciences, but these can be overcome as one can see in the discussion of the practical problems concerned in cross-cultural test construction. Certainly, there are problems of matching factors, but again methods have been developed which allow this to be done.

In conclusion, therefore, it still seems true that given the aims of Berry and Dasen for cross-cultural psychology, no case can be made for ignoring the measurement of intelligence.

This emic-etic distinction is in fact intrinsic to the whole question of what is meant by functional equivalence. Indeed, Berry and Dasen (1974) have argued that for making meaningful cross-cultural comparisons of behaviour three criteria have to be met—functional equivalence, conceptual equivalence and metric equivalence. With regard to tests, therefore, it is clear that the emic-etic distinction concerns the functional equivalence of the behaviour being measured. Obsessional cleanliness in one culture may be properly measured by items referring to cleaning under stair rods: a radically different item would be needed even in urban Scotland where there is in some areas, a preponderance of bungalows.

Conceptual equivalence as a problem in cross-cultural studies is seen most obviously in translation. Back translation is helpful where the original is compared with an independently translated-back version. However, as Brislin (1970) has argued this does not guarantee conceptual equivalence since the similarities could arise from other reasons. As a further safeguard for conceptual equivalence Werner and Campbell (1970) have provided rules for constructing items which are likely to be unambiguous.

The last of these criteria is metric equivalence which is important if cross-cultural comparisons have to be made. The simple differences between mean scores can be misleading because in different cultures valid items can have different endorsement rates as Kline and Mohan (1974) showed in a comparison of Ai3Q (see Chapter 5) in India, Great Britain and Ghana. Kline *et al.* (in press) have confirmed this finding with OPQ (see Chapter 5) in India and Great Britain. The method which demonstrates metric equivalence in any two cultures ensures that the item statistics, correlations and factor loadings of any tests are in both cultures the same (within statistical limits of standard errors). This of course also ensures conceptual equivalence for variables with different meaning which would be unlikely to have similar factor patterns. This was the solution that I used both in Ghana (Kline, 1967b) and in Uganda with the EPI and JEPI (Honess and Kline, 1974b). Berry (Berry and Dasen, 1973) also advocates a method which he calls subsystem validation. In this hypotheses are examined both cross-culturally and intraculturally. Although the methods are different, the same rationale underlies both; namely that if variables are the same, then their relationships with other variables will be the same.

Indeed this approach of demonstrating the identity across cultures of factor loadings, effectively does away with all other objections to tests researchers might have. For if the variable in each culture has been shown to be the same, then questions about the adequacy and meaning of the items become irrelevant, as do all other possible sources of error. However, although this is true, this does not mean that one can ignore them. Obviously if these difficulties have not been overcome, then the factors will not be identifiable across cultures. One must now turn after a discussion of general problems in cross-cultural testing to an examination of those more finely-grained difficulties.

Specific Difficulties in the Cross-cultural Testing of Cognitive Abilities

It has been shown that Berry and Dasen (1973) assume that I.Q. tests are emic, Western measures, and that it is mere ethnocentrism to expect to find similar factors in groups reared in environments totally different from those of the West. As one hopes is now evident, this is not the assumption here. My assumption is that the major cognitive factors, gf and c, V, N and K will be present cross-culturally. This assumption is based upon the fact that factors are fundamental dimensions accounting for observed regularities in behaviour, dimensions which would appear to be important in a huge range of culturally common activities. N, one should expect, however, only in societies where numerical thinking occurs. Similarly within culture genetic studies, especially of intelligence (see Chapter 4) lead us to the view that there is in Western cultures, a substantive genetic component, a component expected to appear larger in societies with less emphasis on environmental pressures for achievement. Hence the assumption is that these factors will appear cross-culturally when the specific psychometric difficulties have been removed.

Biesheuvel (1949), one of the most experienced test constructors in the field of abilities among non-Western groups and one who holds similar views to mine concerning the necessity to measure the basic factorial variables, has an admirably pertinent paper on just these points. The confounding factors in tests of ability are: (1) familiarity with the language, (2) habits and knowledge from a specific type of scholastic education and (3) habits and knowledge acquired by living within a given socio-economic context.

Biesheuvel (1949) argues that language familiarity is the easiest to control because, as we have seen from the chapter on ability tests, almost all verbal item types have a non-verbal equivalent. Raven's Matrices (Raven, 1965) would appear to be an ideal g measure for cross-cultural studies. However, the rejection of verbal items does not necessarily overcome the problem. First, Raven's Matrices is not quite non-verbal, although its verbal loadings are low; it is helpful in solving the problem to describe the stimuli in English to oneself. Whether this would affect cross-cultural results is not, however, clear. More important is the fact that the whole idea of sorting patterns into orders by whatever arbitrary rule is so alien to many non-Western subjects that the task is not comprehensible. The point of doing it cannot be grasped. Warburton (1951), in a classic study of the Gurkhas was able to demonstrate this point clearly though here the test concerned was the formboard. The Gurkhas who thought of Warburton as the woodman because of the test materials simply forced any piece through any shape.

Another non-verbal test that might appear useful is the Porteus Mazes (Porteus, 1952) requiring subjects to trace their way through printed mazes with a pencil. As Vernon has succinctly recounted, however, this test has the same difficulty for non-Western subjects as Raven's Matrices: it is an alien task. An old African who was tested was asked to trace the maze, imagining he was to lead his cattle into the kraal. He replied that he would prefer not to, since anyone who built a kraal like that was mad.

In brief, non-verbal tasks in non-Western cultures avoid the language problem but encounter another perhaps more serious problem, when these tasks seem pointless to subjects.

There is, too, a further and even more serious problem with non-verbal, pictorial, intelligence test items in non-Western groups. As Hudson (e.g. 1967) has shown, pictures and patterns may not be seen in the same way by Westerners. Western perspective is not universal and thus repetitive designs such as Raven's Matrices may be totally inappropriate for such groups who may not perceive any design in any of the stimulus drawings. I have referred again to the Raven's Matrices as the example not because it is a bad test, but because as the discussion in Chapter 4 demonstrated, this is one of the best tests of gf (the fluid ability factor) there is, and one which would appear ideally suited to cross-cultural studies. Indeed Cattell has utilized similar items in his Culture-Fair test (Cattell and Cattell, 1960).

In his study of Gurkhas, Warburton (1951) attempting to find some pictorial items which would provide variance, showed his subjects life size pictures of a kukri, the knife which all Gurkhas carry with them. Almost none were able to recognize it. The conclusion from this kind of evidence is simple. If one uses non-verbal pictorial items in testing the g factors of non-Western subjects it is imperative to demonstrate that these items are in fact measuring such a factor before inserting them into a test. To do this one would have to confirm that they discriminate subjects categorized on other criteria as intelligent from those who were not thus described. This evidence makes Cattell's (1959) claims for the culture-free test, that the items are constructed from materials either so overlearned that all subjects know them or so novel that none will have had previous experience of them, irrelevant for cross-cultural testing, although within Western groups these tests are probably among the best for measuring basic reasoning ability.

These general points about the problems of non-verbal testing are made categorically specific in Biesheuvel's (1949) paper based upon his extensive experience of testing in South Africa. He writes: "The use of pencil and paper for any purpose whatever is not permissible unless the groups to be compared have had an equal amount of schooling". Many non-Western groups are so unused to using pencils that tests involving them are bound to be worthless as measures of intelligence. Similarly, the use of non-verbal pictorial material is ruled out on account of the reasons such as have been discussed. As Biesheuvel explains, the picture is but a conventional cultural symbol and the African and many other groups are not raised with this convention. Thus, any attempt to translate non-verbal items into cultural equivalents is doomed to failure. This difficulty with pictures and patterns also means that Koh's blocks (as used in the WISC and WAIS, see Chapter 3) cannot be used because it requires objects which have to be assembled according to plans. Thus Biesheuvel (1949) argues against the use of pencil and paper tests and pictorial material. He also found non-representational drawing, such as Raven's Matrices, or the Porteus Maze test, useless with his African samples. Not only was the object of the matrices, as I have argued, foreign to their experience, but also Biesheuvel argues, that such designs are in the African experience, parts of other objects and are not examined on their own. Similar difficulties mean that tests aimed at assessing skills in spatial relationships are also not powerful, in cross-cultural research. Often in tests, African subjects would choose a solution with the correct object upside down or sideways on—as if the African was using different criteria to complete the task, from those the tester had in mind. Finally, manipulative items such as the form-board are not suited to cross-cultural work because lack of experience in playing with toys as children means that, as we saw with the Gurkhas in Warburton's study, there seems to be no feeling for the task. Not only are shapes forced through inappropriate spaces but also the correct piece is often picked up but facing the wrong way and subjects seem only rarely to think of turning it round; rather, the incorrect orientation is seen as intrinsic to the object which is then abandoned.

With this somewhat devastating critique, Biesheuvel (1949) has effectively eliminated from cross-cultural research virtually all the item types which comprise the best validated Western measures of the major cognitive factors which I argue should appear cross-culturally. In terms of the emic-etic distinction, one needs a highly emic set of tests to be able to make cross-cultural comparison of cognitive abilities in the light of this evidence.

Certain issues which are fundamental to the psychometric study of abilities cross-culturally are raised by Biesheuvel's paper (1949) and these must now be scrutinized. If one accepts Biesheuvel's evidence that Africans (and there is little doubt that these claims would be supported in other cultures than Africa) score lower than Europeans on almost all these item types and hence on the tests of ability which they comprise, two interpretations are possible. One is that Africans are in fact less intelligent than Europeans, i.e. that the tests are valid in that culture. As Biesheuvel argues, it could be the case that non-Europeans have a basic inability to think conceptually, to manipulate symbols and to handle abstract relations. However, this is unlikely because within their own cultural milieu, Africans appear to be well able to do all these things, as evidenced by their skill in language acquisition—an activity which demands all these abilities to a high order. Of course even if one were to accept that they were inferior to Europeans at these skills, this would by no means demonstrate a genetic or racial inferiority. Their environment could be such that such skills were not developed. Studies of music ability for example (Slater, 1968), show that for its full flowering musical experience as early as possible, is essential.

The interpretation favoured by Biesheuvel and adopted implicitly in the creed of the modern cross-cultural psychologist, as discussed above, is of course that Africans are not worse at these skills but that these items fail to tap them in these cultures. If this is so, careful studies of cultures must be carried out in the problem-solving and intelligence relevant behaviours of non-Europeans (such as Hunt (1976), has advocated for the study of intelligence generally, see Chapter 4). Thus, a rationale for writing emic cognitive items can be developed such that items can be confidently written as equivalent for each culture, which it is wished to compare.

One further point does remain however. When used in the West these tests correlate with educational success and its associated technological skills. Even if these items do not tap the abilities of non-Europeans, the correlations may still hold in these cultures. This is why, perhaps because the requisite skills are not culturally imbued, many African and Indian states find it difficult to produce skilled technological and technical manpower, as Foster (1965) shows.

At present, without a sound rationale for cross-cultural cognitive ability test construction the best that would appear practicable is to use our knowledge and experience of the culture as a guideline to writing items, and to retain those that show themselves to be valid in factor analysis and criteria-based studies. Such tests enable the cross-cultural psychologist to elucidate the environmental factors influencing the major ability factors which is one of the stated aims of cross-cultural psychologists. The disadvantage of this approach lies in the fact that such different tests make comparison between cultural groups more difficult to interpret. Ideally one should like to develop a test such as the Culture-Fair (Cattell and Cattell, 1960), which has items purportedly suited to a wide variety of cultures. Until more is known about how cultures affect thinking and reasoning skills, this cannot be done effectively.

Enough has now been written on the major problems of cross-cultural ability testing. Despite all these, a number of researchers have attempted to test the abilities of non-Western groups and to make comparisons. Two of these studies seem to have produced substantive results which represent a contribution to psychological knowledge or at least indicate clearly how such a contribution could be made. These are the researches carried out by Irvine (e.g. 1969a, b, 1960) and Vernon's researches reported in his book, "Intelligence and the Cultural Environment" (Vernon, 1969).

Irvine's work carried out as part of the North Rhodesian Mental Ability Survey (MacArthur *et al.*, 1964) involved testing more than 5000 African children. Irvine and his colleagues have produced a considerable number of papers from these data but the two cited especially the report of Irvine (1969b), are the most pertinent for these purposes. In this paper he compares the results from factor analyses of measures of ability completed by subjects in Rhodesia, Kenya and Zambia with other African researches.

Samples and Tests

The Zambian and Rhodesian samples were drawn from stratified random samples of schools. The Kenyan sample represented the typical boarding school environment in that country. The sample included some specially constructed and standardized tests for African groups together with those that were usable in the West. There were 23 psychological tests which fell into six groups. These groups will be set out below together with one or two example tests.

> Reasoning in English: all these were special tests except the Birkbeck College 1; Reasoning with low verbal content: Raven's Matrices; English Language Skills: including comprehension spelling and vocabulary; Numerical and Mathematical skills: Birkbeck College 3 and 4; Spatial and Perceptual tests: Birkbeck College 5 and 6, and finally, Information and Knowledge: Birkbeck 2.

With a battery of tests such as these, the resulting factor patterns should be simple to compare with their British or U.S. equivalents.

Statistical Analyses

Irvine (1969) describes the sample sizes as all (except one) large running from 1615 to 72. The correlations between the scales were subjected to principal component analyses followed by Varimax rotations to orthogonal simple structure.

Results and Discussion

In the Zambian and Rhodesian samples there was remarkable agreement in the results. In each case four factors were extracted which were highly similar from their loadings in each culture and which accounted for around 65% of the variance. These were labelled g, reasoning; n:ed, numeracy, as taught in the school; v:ed, literacy, as taught in the school and "male educational aptitude" factor, one which accounts for the fact that in Africa males are generally more successful in the school system.

There are several points about these results which deserve comment. In view of all the problems concerning items, the agreement between the two factor analyses in Zambia and Rhodesia is remarkable. Perhaps even more surprising is the fact that three of the four factors are the three largest found in Western studies of the structure of abilities—surprising that is to cross-cultural psychologists who regard intelligence as a variable, which is dangerous if not impossible to test. Of course, these African results powerfully support the claims made throughout this book for the power of factor analysis to uncover fundamental variables which one should not expect to vary considerably from culture to culture.

One further point needs clarification. The sceptic can still argue that these results only demonstrate that four factors account for the variance. How does one know that Irvine has given them accurate labels? However, examination of the factor loadings for each factor demonstrates that there can be no disagreement about identification. The v:ed factor loads, as it would in the West, on comprehension, vocabulary and spelling among the psychological tests. Further confirmation is gained from its loadings on English, History and Geography attainment. The n:ed factor is similarly clear, loading on the computation test and Maths and Science attainment. The g factor loads on all the psychological ability tests except spelling, and is highest on Raven's Matrices. There can be no doubt that in these Rhodesian and Zambian samples, the three main ability factors have been reproduced. There would also appear to be little doubt that Raven's Matrices does measure g in these cultures. This, of course, is further support for Cattell's claims (see Chapter 4) concerning the value of the Culture Fair test where the items are matrices together with other non-verbal types for cross-cultural work. It seems that this first part of Irvine's paper is a substantive contribution to knowledge in that it establishes unequivocally that the structure of abilities in these African children closely resembles that found among British and U.S. samples. This is a useful bedrock in the cross-cultural investigation of cognitive skills.

The similarity of the results between the two countries and the size of the samples make one confident about the replicability of these results. Irvine presents three further sets of results which largely confirm these findings. A small sample (N = 72) of mine workers revealed similar factors, although the proportions of variance each accounted for, was changed in comparison with the previous studies. However, this could well be due to the small size of the sample. Among a Zambian secondary school sample the same factors again emerge, together with a spatial mechanical factor, although once again the relative size of the factors has changed. Finally, similar results are found in the sample drawn from Kenyan boarding schools. From all these studies the results and conclusions seem clear. The structure of abilities in the African samples is largely similar to that found in the West and despite measurement problems factor analysis does seem able to uncover ability factors.

Irvine (1969) is duly cautious about interpreting these results which have been claimed to demonstrate a cross-cultural identity of ability factors in Africa and the West. First, he examines them in the light of orthogonal, varimax rotations of some of the best known earlier studies which had utilized unrotated centroids. The varimax rotation of Macdonald's (1944–1945) study of 1700 East African recruits revealed a large g factor loading of Raven's Matrices and block design, and a mechanical spatial factor. This g factor is partly a function, Irvine argues, of the considerable heterogeneity of the sample. A third factor, loading on pegboard and physical agility was interpreted as a physical factor with a strong manual dexterity component. Biesheuvel's work (1952, 1954) with performance tests for recruits to mining, also produced a general factor. Irvine argues that this general factor is a result of the alien tasks that had to be performed by unselected populations; hence its appearance in the two studies. It should be noted that this statement is very much what one should expect from the nature of g (especially gf), as defined by most of the leading factorists with its stress on problem solving and its separation from culturally learned solutions. Again this work of Macdonald and Biesheuvel supports the existence of g in their non-Western groups.

Against this interpretation, on the other hand, Irvine is able to cite the work of McFie and Brimble. McFie (1961) trained African students on a variety of perceptual and memory skills. After training and experience in the tasks, the importance of the general factor declined. Irvine argues that such a result demonstrates the sample and test dependence of the factors and that it may be unwise to make too much of an African g factor. However, this is not my interpretation of these findings. On a strange task, g is an important factor in performance. However, once the special skills have been learned one can do it almost without recourse to g. For example, for young children numerical skill is more loaded on g when each item has to be worked than among older ones where the particular skills have been learned. A real life example can be taken from psychological statistics where the rate of learning and the speed of grasping the concepts is undoubtedly related to g. Over the years, many a hack psychologist has managed to learn enough to get by. It is this phenomenon which these results confirm; the difference between Newton and Liebnitz who invented calculus and the polytechnic student who labouriously learns to use it.

The second warning study is by Brimble (1963) who gave a battery of pictorial items to a homogeneous sample of Africans. A varimax analysis did not reveal a general factor as would have been expected but three factors, loading on distinct item types. However, the adequacy of the varimax rotation which is orthogonal, takes variance from a general factor and by no means necessarily reaches simple structure, must be called into doubt. A more adequate oblique solution may well have revealed an underlying second-order general factor. It is highly likely that Brimbles' results are little more than bloated specifics, specific to the item types, a phenomenon seen in Guilford's factorial model (see Chapter 4).

In his interpretation of results, Irvine (1969) makes the highly interesting point that these cross-cultural studies of Africans do indicate a general reasoning factor as accounting for the variance in cognitive and educational tests, but he regards this factor simply as a function of the education system: the tests are in English, and the skills they tap are those of the school which teaches in English. The tests in these surveys have "not begun to tap the modes of thought that are the products of African Languages and African Relationships". Indeed, the fact that the school is the sole source of this type of knowledge and skill probably accounts for the third education aptitude factor in the results. To do well a student has to espouse modern, Western, school values and this is more easy for the male to do than the female in African society.

Thus, Irvine's position is that, while the results show, as argued, that g, v:ed and n:ed may be recognized cross-culturally (at least in Africa), it is not necessarily valid to conceive of them as universals. Given Western tasks and tests, it would appear that similar factors account for African and Western performance. This does not mean to say however that in traditional African culture, such abilities play an important part. Just as Jahoda found that the day names of children which have personal qualities were in fact associated with those qualities (Jahoda, 1954) in Ghana, the reinforcement of behaviour in accordance with a belief system, so in the case of intelligence, cultural factors may or may not reinforce its development. In the West, Irvine (1969) argues that the notion of intelligence implies values: highly intelligent implies worth and goodness, usefulness and esteem. In other cultures this may not be so and hence its development may be neglected if not hindered and other variables may become the object of cultural development.

From this discussion, therefore, it appears that despite the findings that in African cultures, g and other major group factors may be found, it is false to argue that they are thus universals of thought. What are needed are emic measures of African culture (assuming that Irvine is correct in thus divorcing school and life). Such is the argument proposed by Irvine (1969).

This position is not antithetical to that proposed by myself. From these results one still argues that g, v:ed and n:ed have been shown to account for psychological and educational test variance in these African cultures, as in the West. If Africans do indulge, as Irvine claims, in cognitive activities that do not involve reasoning ability and abstract thinking, then obviously one should not expect to find the g factor accounting for their variance. Clearly other factors will be needed. Nevertheless, in tasks demanding g, v:ed and n:ed these factors emerge. In this sense they can be regarded as universal. They are still important in these cultures if their members wish to develop in the technological, Western tradition. Studies such as these show clearly that Africans are well able, in terms of factors, to master such tasks. The other intellectual factors, if they do exist, remain to be elucidated and this is likely only to be done by psychologists who are themselves members of the particular cultures.

Irvine (1969b) has elaborated many of the above arguments. In a more detailed survey of African factor analyses, he is able to show clearly not only that the common Western factors emerge, as I have already fully discussed, but also that, in addition, variance in African societies is not simply attributable to environmental influences. Vernon (1969) for example, found that among Hebrideans field independence was correlated with female dominance but with male dominance in Jamaica, to extend work beyond Africa.

Of particular interest to this thesis on the place of psychometrics in the cross-cultural study of ability, is his approach to what was previously referred to as other modes of thinking among African groups. To do this he analysed the wrong responses given by a small sample of Ghona on tests drawn from the Kit of Reference Tests for cognitive factors (French *et al.*, 1963). Unfortunately, the small size of the sample and the large number of variables make the results of factor analysis somewhat dubious and the three second-order factors emerging from the promax analysis do not make obvious sense. This is a method which clearly deserves further research.

Irvine (1969b) also summarizes briefly, modes of African thought as described by anthropologists quoting Evan-Pritchard, (1936) Gluckman (1944) and Colson (1962). It appears that there is some agreement among anthropologists that south of the Sahara, African thought systems have an identity of theme concerning man and his place in the world. Everything that exists contains force. Man and the spirits of his ancestors can activate forces directly and consciously or inadvertently and by accident. Animals, plants, inanimate objects contain forces but these have to be released by man and spirits. Man's eminence lies in control over words which themselves have force, which are the prime movers of actions and transcend space and time, fixing them to one modality. Words themselves can vary their meaning for different speakers. Such is the Weltenschaung of the African, south of the Sahara, according to Irvine (1969b) which is a view with implications of causality different indeed from that of the West. Gluckman (1944) has telling examples which fit this description and demonstrates its opposition to Western thinking. Thus, the teacher who in full understanding of the causes of typhoid was troubled as to why the germs had attacked his son, illustrates the conflict well. What forces had been unleashed to bring the attack about?

Irvine (1969) then examines the nature of 113 Shona beliefs and omens about behaviour, in terms of knowledge required and the consequences of actions. Here it turns out that the most common kind of knowledge is that of natural objects and animals, objects with social functions, knowledge of one's habits or symptoms, and last, knowledge of utensils or utilities. The effects of non-observance rebound on self, kin and community. There is little conscious control of the environment. In such a society intelligent acts are conforming, with reference to relations with the forces of the living and dead.

From this anthropological description of African societies and the empirical study of Shona beliefs, Irvine argues that African children "develop a primary thought mode that perceives events and uses knowledge in a complex field of personal relationships whose organization is essentially affective". As adults they continue to use this and to interpret events accordingly. It is wrong, according to this position, to compare this with animistic thought in the Piagetian sense which stems from ignorance: this Shona belief system simply uses a non-Western framework which happens to be animistic.

This then is the support for Irvine's (1969a) hypothesis that Africans demonstrate the major Western ability factors given Western tests and problems but that there is another set of abilities (and these are the more important for they are in daily use) which lie undefined and untapped by factors. Of course, it should be clear from the descriptions of the two sets of abilities that they are basically antithetical. Just as for Westerners it is difficult to empathize with primary mode thinking, so for Africans it is the case with formal logical abstract reasoning.

The implications of this for psychometric research into cross-cultural abilities are profound. As has been seen throughout this book, if multivariate techniques are to map out areas of psychology successfully it is essential that one samples the whole universe of variables. In the cross-cultural study of abilities, this means that one must include measures of the most important Western factors, as described in Chapter 4, and measures of the special factors which may be present in the culture. This would not only describe such primary modes of thinking but it would also define what their relationship was to the standard Western factors which is even more important.

In summary, I would argue that Irvine's work demonstrates the weakness of the standard cross-cultural approach to the study of abilities, as proposed by Berry and Dasen (1973). First, it is clear that it is possible to measure intelligence and other ability factors in non-Western groups and that these factors can be shown to account for variance in tests of ability and attainment. On the other hand, it would appear likely that it is truly the case that other emic factors account for variance in ability tasks, factors that have not been found in the West.

The role and contribution of psychometrics in the cross-cultural study of ability now becomes clear. Tests of these special factors must be developed not only for Africa but across a wide variety of cultures. Studies of these, together with Western factors will elucidate the relationship between them and enable us to see the educational problems involved in technological development. Finally, a study of the cultural milieu and the utilization of anthropological data along with the psychometric factors must inevitably give us insight into factors affecting cognitive development. It is essential, therefore, that cross-cultural psychologists do not abandon psychometry, believing it to be nothing but intelligence testing. The cross-cultural study of ability is a field in which psychometrics is ready to make a major contribution.

We must next examine the work of Vernon (1969) reported in "Intelligence and Cultural Environment", concentrating on those findings which highlight the problems involved in the cross-cultural study of abilities. Although this research used samples smaller than desirable for factor analysis, it must be pointed out there were in addition, clinical assessments of home conditions which would have been exceedingly difficult with larger samples.

Tests

Verbal and educational tests. Arithmetic, English, spelling, word-learning and information-learning.
Induction tests. Abstraction and creative response matrices.
Concept development tests. Sorting tests (by concept).
Piaget battery. Thirteen tasks tapping the development of most of those concepts which apparently are age-related, e.g. logical inclusion, length conservation.
Creativity tests. e.g. Rorschach inkblots (used as test of imagination), Torrance's incomplete drawings.
Perceptual and spatial tests. Porteus Mazes, picture recognition, Gottschald Embedded Figures test, design reproductions, Koh's Blocks, Draw-a-man test, Vernon Formboard and finally as a reward, the Mischel Delayed Gratification test—chocolate now or double after the session is complete.

Some comments are necessary about this test battery. First, it would appear to cover all the abilities commonly found in Western groups. This enables one to compare the factor pattern within each group of subjects and to see to what extent the tests are valid within each culture. On the other hand, there is no attempt here to measure primary modes of thinking.

These tests were given to samples of 11-year-old children from various cultures, and subjected to factor analysis after all scores had been standardized against a British sample. In the English group, g emerged plus the usual group factors, all related to cultural stimulation in the home. This, then, is the comparative basis against which to judge the other results. Interestingly, among the Hebrideans this factor analysis was not reproduced, for here the g and V:ed factors were not separated. This is interpreted in the light of the correlations with home background as evidence for the widespread affect of a stimulating home affecting all abilities rather than some.

The groups tested were comprised of Jamaicans, Ugandans, Eskimos, Canadian Indians and the British samples. The Jamaicans were notable for being low on non-verbal inductive reasoning tests although they were not equally poor at classroom English. They differed from the Ugandans by their better performance at the Piagetian tasks which is probably due to their greater sophistication, fewer magical beliefs (Irvine, 1969) and greater contact with American and British culture. As with the Hebrideans there was a higher than usual correlation between verbal and other factors thus indicating that school is necessary for all kinds of mental development in this society where there was relatively little home stimulation.

The Ugandan group were low in oral English, three-dimensional picture interpretation and conservation. The structure of abilities was curious in this group, in that verbal ability (in English) was distinct from other abilities, as it was not in all the other samples. This may be due to the sample in that they were acculturated, being urban and selected, for only about one-third of this age-group attend school. The implication from this factor analysis is that the Ugandans do not integrate their English language learning into their thinking but use it as an isolated translation skill. This lack of integration of learning in school is said to be typical of tropical education (Foster, 1965).

Among the Indians and Eskimos attending Canadian schools, the findings were less clear cut. Generally, the Eskimos were within the normal range and superior to the Indians who were apathetic in the testing situation. Boarding Eskimos did better on induction tests and concept development than those in the settlements, a finding attributed by Vernon (1969) to the fact that boarding promotes independence. Indians were particularly poor at the divergent thinking tests, and it appears that there is little encouragement for originality (at least along these lines). The general factor g among the Eskimos was correlated with the amount of schooling and not the characteristics of the home. This last finding is particularly interesting. It supports the claims of the cross-cultural psychologists that the Western notion of general intelligence is not appropriate for other cultures and is little but a stunt which can be learned (as a seal can catch herrings thrown by its keeper) (Anastasi and Foley, 1949). Thus this g factor reflects school and what has been learned there. In the West of course, schools reflect society and hence g is relevant. This is not the case where schools, as in the ex-Colonies, have been imposed on societies by rulers of very different traditions. It also means that, if one wishes to foster g among Eskimos, as a help to technological development, it is essential that all receive as much schooling as possible.

This research by Vernon must be regarded as a pilot study. It demonstrates that by careful selection of a wide variety of tests and by clinical assessments of home background it is possible to elucidate, in cross-cultural studies, some of the factors affecting abilities in ways which would not be possible if one restricted testing to Great Britain or U.S.A. However, in this research the samples are too small to be confident of their representativeness or of the reliability of the results, and this is particularly true of the factor analyses which need large samples. Another weakness lies in the home assessments which were done by a Westerner. Considerably more refined data gathered after years of anthropological observation is really needed if one is going to understand what goes on in a home from an alien culture.

Nevertheless, these results indicate that in non-Western cultures it is meaningful to discuss and compare the major Western ability factors, although clearly studies such as this ignore the primary mode thinking factors discussed by Irvine. However, since these factors are implicated in technological success, the study of the factors influencing their development is not only of theoretical interest but also of considerable practical value.

In summary, therefore, this Vernon (1969) research is clear evidence that a large-scale cross-cultural study of abilities with both emic and etic scales, together with social anthropological data, would yield critical information concerning the structure of abilities and would yield indubitably new ability factors specific to various cultures. The indications of cultural differences noted in the summary of Vernon's findings are sufficient to indicate that a large-scale study would almost certainly locate environmental factors affecting the development of abilities.

Comparisons between Cultures

One further point deserves note. In his attempt to compare one cultural group with another Vernon used British norms as a baseline. The difficulty with utilizing normative groups is that scores on a test are composed of two sources of variance which are generally confounded: item difficulty and the ability of the subjects. This confusion is particularly acute in the case of cross-cultural comparisons where items can be difficult, not through lack of ability in the subjects but because they are culture-bound, and low scores may not reflect the real ability of the group. While this distinction between culture-free and culture-bound items is probably more important in respect of personality test items (this is discussed in the section on cross-cultural personality testing), it is clearly one factor in the performance of non-Western groups on Western tests. Rasch (1960) has developed a model of performance on items which allows of separate estimates for item and subject difficulty. This Rasch scaling enables subject comparisons to be made independent of item difficulty and is thus ideally suited to cross-cultural comparisons. Rasch scaling is used in the New British Intelligence Scale (see Chapter 4) and it would be most interesting to use it in cross-cultural studies.

Before leaving the field of cross-cultural abilities one could summarize the contribution of psychometrics thus. It does enable one to discover the structure of abilities in different cultures and to gain insight into the environmental factors influencing the development of abilities. It has shown that the main ability factors found in the West do appear in non-Western societies but that these are considerably influenced by schooling. It is likely, in the light of this evidence, that there are other ability factors in these cultures which remain as yet undefined.

Race and Intelligence

Before leaving the topic of the cross-cultural testing of abilities one must briefly discuss the problem of race and intelligence, a subject which in recent years has created bitter controversy and no little unreason. Cattell (1971) has claimed to discern two schools in this argument, both equally irrational: racists who assume that one or more races are superior to others (usually those of which they are members) and ignoracists who assume that there are no racial differences. Since whether races differ in intelligence or not is an empirical question, these assumptions are not conducive to scientific appraisal of the question.

As shown so far, in the discussion of the cross-cultural study of abilities, the comparison of mean scores of racial or cultural groups on ability tests is a procedure frought with difficulties. Thus, to discuss the question of whether races differ in intelligence is probably not useful. It is indubitably true that different racial groups have significantly different scores on certain intelligence tests. The origin of these differences is however problematic and hence the interpretation of the results has to be exceedingly cautious. The problems in the question of race and intelligence are identical with many of those discussed in the previous sections on cross-cultural testing, and the arguments are not repeated here. I shall concentrate on the aspect of the question that is most controversial: the difference in intelligence test scores between North American Negroes and Whites. Are Negroes as their detractors would have us believe, innately inferior to Whites in intelligence?

To answer this question a number of points have to be established. Readers who require more information are referred to Loehlin *et al.* (1975) whose views, however, are not in all cases identical to mine. First, the question becomes a nonsense if Negroes are not racially distinct from Whites. It is to this that we first turn.

Racial Differences between Negroes and Whites

There seems to be reasonable agreement that homo sapiens can be subdivided into various races or taxa, although there are various different ways of categorizing groups such that the resulting categories are not necessarily identical. Nevertheless, a negroid group (not always given that title) is recognized by almost all workers in the field, e.g. Garn (1971) who uses the geographical description African, and Baker (1974) who prefers the term negrid. Thus, it is reasonable to assume that there are genetic differences between negroes and whites. From this point of view the question does have meaning.

Scores of Negroes on Intelligence Tests

There seems to be little doubt that Negroes score lower than Whites and indeed most other groups on I.Q. tests. (Eysenck, 1971, Jensen, 1972.) Jensen (1972) has tried to classify abilities into groups (1 and 2, 2 being typical I.Q. tests) such that it is especially on group 2 tests that Negroes are particularly low scoring. However, this division does not seem powerful and does not fit the factorial findings reported in Chapter 3 of this book. However, there is a real problem: Negroes do score lower on I.Q. tests and Negroes are genetically different from Whites. What can be said about the origin of these differences?

Within-group and Between-group Variance

The first point to clarify is that even if one accepts that I.Q. variance within each group is attributable, in part, to genetic influences and that there are genetic differences between the groups, there is no logical means of attributing I.Q. differences between groups to genetic influences. This point, as Loehlin *et al.* (1975) stress is agreed amongst all workers in the field.

Can Cultural Deprivation Account for the Findings?

This is not a likely possibility since, as has been pointed out frequently, e.g. Eysenck (1973) other deprived groups do not score so low. A group for example, who score close to Western norms are the Canadian Eskimos, whose environment cannot be thought of as particularly stimulating. Furthermore, as Jensen (1972) indicates, Negroes do better on measures of gc, i.e. those most likely to be affected by the environment, than they do on gf measures such as matrices. Furthermore, and this applies to the studies of nature-nurture discussed in Chapter 4, although the concept of cultural deprivation is frequently used as an explanatory concept, it has no prior definition.

The Confounding of Race and Culture

By definition, if one belongs to race A one tends to belong to the culture associated with that race. Thus, if Negroes have a characteristic culture it could be the case that it is this cultural factor which produces the differences. This is not necessarily deprivation as suggested in hypothesis (b) above, but it could be a part of Negro culture in the U.S.A. not to try at tests or to be suspicious, and hence nervous, of investigations, and so on. Again, they could be rendered less competitive in general and hence test performance would be lowered. Even if one cannot identify the cultural factors affecting performance, the logical possibility remains that it is the culture not the race that produces the lower scores. Even those attempts cited by Baker (1974) and Loehlin *et al.* (1975) where I.Q. scores are correlated with the percentage of White blood, do not truly separate race and culture, for as the appearance tends to negritude so will treatment and cultural interaction resemble more closely that of Negroes. Thus, the modest correlation of light skin colour and I.Q. does not convincingly demonstrate the hereditarian case. Similarly, studies of illegitimate children in Germany fathered by Blacks and Whites can demonstrate nothing unless the I.Q. of the parent is known.

Loehlin *et al.* could find no clear evidence concerning the I.Q. of black children adopted by white Americans while the Tizard (1974) study of orphan black and white children in institutions, which showed that black children progressed as well as whites up to five years old, is vitiated by the fact that the black parents may not be representative of their racial group and I.Q. testing at five years old is not likely to be so reliable and valid as later scores.

Are the Questions Fair for U.S. Negroes?

This point has been fully discussed early in this chapter, but relative to all groups. Certainly test construction depends on the population on whom the items were tried. If they were real intellectual differences between the two populations, white and black, items tried on each group would appear different with each group on item analysis. This difference could be attributed to items or to populations or to an interaction of both. Conventional item analysis could reject the items giving different item statistics and in this way, Negroes and Whites could be shown to be equal in ability. Similarly, no doubt items demonstrating Black superiority could be developed. Thus, tests developed for Whites could well be unfair to Black populations. However, their validity in these groups appears to stand up in terms of correlations and external criteria, making this an unlikely (though possible) source of bias. Certainly, it makes the comparison of mean scores between Black and White groups of dubious value. A possible solution to this difficulty lies in the scaling procedures of Rasch (1960) where test variance can be analysed into subject and item variance, thus eliminating the different applicability of items for different populations. No examples of this technique, unfortunately, appear in the comparative literature.

All these problems in the interpretation of mean differences in scores and the impossibility in real life of having all the genetic mixes needed (from representative parents), for a good biometric genetic analysis means that for us the question of the genetic or environmental origin of the differences in scores between U.S. Negroes and Whites cannot be satisfactorily answered at present. I agree with the carefully considered unbiased conclusions of Loehlin *et al.* (1975), that the observed differences between Negroes and other groups can be attributed to both genetic differences and environmental differences between groups and problems of testing (which Rasch analysis, I argue, might remove). However, as Loehlin *et al.* show, there are greater within-race differences than between-race differences such that the attribution of a particular intelligence test score based upon social membership would be wildly inaccurate.

Problems in the Cross-cultural Study of Personality and Motivation

In the sphere of personality and motivation, cross-cultural studies have perhaps an even more important part to play than was the case with ability. This is because many theories of personality, as one can see from any popular survey, posit either implicitly or explicitly, that the child's early environment has a profound effect on his later personality (e.g. Hall and Lindzey, 1957) although Orlansky (1949) was unable to adduce any clear evidence confirming this hypothesis. As pointed out elsewhere (Kline, 1972) cross-cultural studies are particularly useful because they provide extreme examples of any child-rearing procedure, compared with the range within any one society, and in addition such cross-cultural extremes are not also abnormal as the extremes within any one society necessarily are. One confounding factor is thus removed by utilizing cross-cultural samples. Unfortunately, however, cross-cultural personality and motivation testing is beset with problems beside which those associated with cognitive tests pale into insignificance.

Before considering the problems in any detail, I shall briefly survey the general difficulties. In the case of projective tests which are usually visual, one has the problem of perception of pictures, which has been discussed in relation to tests such as Raven's Matrices. Hudson's work in Africa (Hudson, 1967) makes it clear that some pictures may not be understood (simply in terms of perspective etc.). Furthermore, TAT type projective tests utilize culturally bound symbols in their drawings with social connotations for Western subjects which would be entirely missed by non-Westerners: the significance of a violin is a good case in point.

Psychometric tests of personality utilizing personality test items are notoriously difficult to use cross-culturally. Even assuming translation is possible and accurate, items such as "Do you enjoy drop the handkerchief" or "Do you sometimes feel tired", must be of dubious and certainly different psychological significance in, for example, India compared with the U.S.A. The first example is simply culture biased to the U.S.A., the second may reflect infection and its resistance in populations subject to bilharzia, malaria and dysentery, as common and unnoteworthy ills. Finally, the attitudes toward revealing personal information and the problems of orally administering tests to illiterate groups are all factors that could influence psychometric personality questionnaires, used cross-culturally.

Objective tests on the other hand, with low face validity as discussed in Chapter 3, have to be demonstrated to be valid in any culture in which they are used. Since many of these tests demand laboratory facilities this rules them out for many kinds of cross-cultural work.

We shall now turn to an examination of the difficulties besetting each kind of test and to the solution of the problems.

Psychometric Tests: Personality questionnaires

The contribution to cross-cultural psychology from personality question-naires must come, if one is true to the multivariate techniques, from the study of the main personality and motivation factors in the West described in Chapters 5 and 6. As was the case in the study of abilities, cross-cultural comparisons should enable one to discover the environmental factors contributing to personality development. In addition one must be prepared to discover other personality factors peculiar to each culture. However, if one considers how the 16 PF test was originally constructed, that its basis lies in a dictionary search for all words describing behaviour, it may be that behaviour does not in fact differ much from culture to culture and that therefore, the Cattell factors do embrace the main personality variance even of non-Western cultures. This is not a matter worthy of speculation since it is empirical. Nevertheless, two conclusions can be drawn from this argument. First one should try to measure established Western factors in non-Western cultures, and that means utilizing in some form or other, the Cattell and Eysenck tests, for in the requisite chapter it has been shown that most of the other personality questionnaires largely measure the same factors. The smaller factors missed by the Cattell test such as in the DPI for example, would be worth measuring in a cross-cultural setting only after the basic personality structure had been established (unless of course some specific hypothesis was under investigation). Secondly, it is clearly essential to attempt to investigate specific cultural factors. Since these two tasks demand different tests and present very different problems, they are discussed separately. The first considerations are the problems of investigating the Western personality structure in the cross-cultural setting.

Culture-bound and Culture-free Items

Since one would be using the Cattell tests, the Eysenck tests and the MMPI item in as much as they cover the abnormal factors, we shall restrict ourselves to a brief study of these items. This distinction (Cattell, 1957) has already been exemplified from the MMPI "Drop the Handkerchief" which is culture-bound to the U.S.A. and causes problems even in Great Britain. If this is a culture-bound item, a culture-free item might be "Have you experienced headaches?", an affliction common to all men. However, this item shows the superficiality of the distinction, or more charitably, the relativity. For, as Whiting and Child (1953) have shown, different cultures have different views concerning the origin and nature of disease so that having a headache is an experience common presumably to all men but one of varying psychological significance and connotation. Thus the culture-bound culture-free distinction is at best only relative.

If one examines the items of the 16 PF test one can see that many are certainly culture-bound to the U.S.A. Items refer to suburban housing, wild animals, classical music, being an engineer, having a job with a large salary that is uncertain, mirrors and holidays, and all these are on the first page. The EPQ is similarly culture-bound: for example, items refer to being in debt, locking up your house, seeing animals suffer, trusting in insurance schemes, dodging taxes and driving carefully. Finally, the MMPI is no better for cross-cultural use. Suffice to say that items concerned with sleeping powders, table manners, Jesus Christ and "Alice in Wonderland" do not go down easily in Utar Pradhesh or the Central African Republic.

It is problems such as these that make the difficulties with translating tests seem relatively trivial. There is simply no point in translating, however accurately, items that have no psychological meaning or referrents. Certainly, given items that are as culture-free as possible, one has to ensure that translations are accurate and idiomatic. In this respect as pointed out earlier in this chapter, back translation usually ensures a reasonable linguistic equivalence. However, since the major Western tests clearly contain items that are culture-bound, how can one overcome this problem and investigate the structure of personality in non-Western cultures?

One solution, and this is the one adopted by most researchers in this field (the results are considered in a later section of this chapter) is to test literate and highly-educated subjects using either a straightforward English version of the test or a translation item by item into the local language. Such a method was adopted, for example, by Tsujioka and Cattell (1965) in Japan with the 16 PF test. Certainly, as was the case with ability tests, literate, Western-educated subjects can understand the items and know enough about Western culture to render the culture-bound items sufficiently meaningful for them to answer. Whether resulting factor analyses reveal the personality structure of a group whose personality has been in some sense changed by their education or whether the group can be said to be representative of the whole national group in terms of personality is not clear.

However, if the strategy of using the test as it is, or translated item by item, is adopted with literate samples, it is essential to show in some way that the variable it measures is still in the new culture what it was in the West. This can be done by demonstrating that the test correlations are similar to those in the West, or that in factor analyses the test loads on the same factors as in the West. Again it is strong support for the validity of the test in the new culture if it can be shown that the same groups have similar scores in the two cultures. All this demonstrates conceptual equivalence. A last resort in small-scale studies is to item analyse the test or to factor the test items. If the item loadings or item statistics are similar to those in the West, it is highly unlikely that the test is invalid in the new culture, although this is not ruled out. If the item analysis is satisfactory, one would have to argue that the test measured, in the new culture, a new variable related to the items just as the former variable: an unlikely hypothesis without some further evidence to support it. If these precautions are taken, showing that the personality questionnaire is still efficient in the new culture, then the measurement of educated, literate, samples does appear to be possible. In a later section of this chapter some results obtained with this type of investigation are examined.

In view of the problems with culture-bound items and the fact that culture-free items are only in most cases relatively culture-free, the ideal strategy for comparing factor structures of personality across cultures is to construct a new test that is equivalent to the Western Test. This, of course, involves demonstrating that the resulting factors have the same correlates in the full sense of the word as their originals. Equivalent items need to be written. For example, where in the EPI there is a stress on parties, it could be the case that in North India one could change the emphasis to discussions over tea, meetings which to some extent fulfil similar social functions although without the sexual overtones. Such items would have to be tried out. Clearly for the construction of such equivalent tests one needs the help of anthropologists and native social psychologists.

Kline and Mohan (1974) carried out a study in North India with Ai3Q (Kline, 1971), a test of obsessional personality traits (see Chapter 5) among a highly educated and literate sample. Here it was found that many of the items failed although they had been successful in Ghana and Great Britain. What is interesting is that although with hindsight *post hoc* explanations of failure could be found, not all failing items were anticipated. Curiously enough a later study (Kline *et al.*, in press) with OPQ, a measure of oral pessimistic personality traits was successful with a female sample of Punjabi students.

These two studies are cited not for their contribution to knowledge but as examples of the difficulty of using personality questionnaires even with educated samples in the cross-cultural setting.

There is a further problem in questionnaire studies in non-Western cultures which must be briefly discussed. This concerns test-taking attitudes.

These have already been mentioned in connection with tests of abilities where it was pointed out that the need for speed and the very purposes of the test were quite foreign to some cultures, so that subjects often made no effort. In the case of personality tests, it is attitudes to self-disclosure and to pleasing people in authority that are relevant. In non-Western societies inexperienced in the conventions of psychological testing such attitudes can easily lead to severe distortion through the medium of response sets, particularly social desirability and acquiescence (Cronbach, 1970). These response sets can endow personality questionnaires with a spuriously high reliability and item analyses can appear sound due to their effects. Even factor analyses of items can yield what is effectively a spurious general factor. Thus again in cross-cultural studies this is a further reason to demonstrate the validity of any test factor against some external criterion.

Even if all these difficulties have been overcome and the investigations with personality questionnaires such as the 16 PF and EPI or EPQ can be shown to yield reliable and valid factors, there remains the problem of sampling. These tests can only be given to literate, educated samples mainly because the items are not meaningful to subjects with only local knowledge. The question here concerns the representativeness of educated samples. Even in the U.S.A. and Great Britain, students' samples are atypical of their age-group. Even more so is this the case in most non-Western societies.

One solution which might appear feasible is to administer tests orally, thus doing away with the necessity for literacy. This, however, in view of the knowledge and sophistication needed to understand the items in most questionnaires, is not likely to be successful. In addition it reduces one of the main advantages of the questionnaire: the exclusion of variance due to differences between testers. Furthermore, there is the problem of test rapport. It is highly likely in such oral test administrations that subjects will ask questions. To answer them is to introduce error variance; to refuse to answer them may induce fear or suspicion in the subjects. All these objections to oral testing can be derived from what is known about the difficulties of projective testing cross-culturally (problems discussed below). Ideally empirical studies are needed. If these were to show that the objections were groundless, then these sampling difficulties can be ignored.

Such are the problems besetting the cross-cultural study of personality using personality questionnaire in the comparison of personality structure in the West and with other cultures—problems of items, factorial equivalence, test-taking attitudes and sampling. Despite their severity, researchers have attempted to use these tests and the findings which have to be interpreted in the light of these difficulties will be considered in a later section of this chapter.

Problems using Psychometric Tests in the Study of Personality Factors Specific to a Culture

Most of the problems with psychometric testing discussed in the previous section arose from the need, in order to compare structures across cultures, to use tests that were in Price-Williams' (1969) phrase "transcultural". However, the study of factors that might be specific to cultures does not raise the same difficulties. Indeed, for this one simply has to follow the rules for sound test construction, fully discussed in Chapter 1. One can develop items that closely fit the experience of the subjects and use the idiomatic vernacular. With items such as these, it would be possible to give the tests orally and thus sample widely. Clearly however the construction of such culture-specific tests can be done only by psychologists with a wide and deep understanding of the particular culture and its languages. This aspect of cross-cultural psychology strongly depends therefore on the education of local psychologists.

The factors resulting from such investigations, as described above, are clearly difficult to interpret in terms of item content. All such studies need full validation of factors against external criteria so that they can be identified. Since investigations of this kind could throw up specific cultural factors and/or Western factors, all test variables must be located in the Western personality sphere. Psychometric work of this kind, for which the techniques now exist, could fully reveal the nature of cultural characteristics, and the cultural factors affecting their development. It is to be noted that the full value from such specific cultural personality factors can only be obtained when they are factored together with the Western personality factors and thus located in personality space, and when they are related to environmental variables.

From this discussion the potential contribution to cross-cultural psychology from research with personality questionnaires can be seen to be large.

Objective Tests in the Cross-cultural Setting

As shown in the discussion of objective tests, this term has been used to embrace what are more often known as projective tests, provided that these are objectively scored. However, because the traditional projective tests have been extensively used in cross-cultural work, we shall examine the use of these tests separately from objective tests as defined by Cattell—objectively scored and their purpose obscure.

Objective Tests (excluding Projective Techniques)

There is little that can be said about the cross-cultural use of these measures. They have not been used in this setting up to the present date although it could well be argued that of all the types of personality tests, some objective tests would be most likely to be valid across a variety of cultures. Nevertheless, since they are not face valid, the validity of all objective test variables has to be demonstrated, a task of peculiar difficulty in a culture where there are no clear marker variables for personality. However, objective tests might be the most effective transcultural measures and are worthy of cross-cultural experiment within a larger research programme with other variables, thus enabling one to identify objective test factors.

Projective Tests

The weaknesses of projective tests as well as their merits have been fully discussed (see Chapters 1 and 3). All these points apply if one uses projective tests in cross-cultural work but they will not be discussed here. Suffice to say that there are grave deficiencies when projective tests are used in the standard way in respect of both validity and reliability—defects which are likely to be exacerbated rather than minimized in the cross-cultural setting. Despite this, however, the attraction of being able to present the same test materials to subjects regardless of culture, has made projective tests popular in cross-cultural psychology. Indeed, such tests have formed the data base of the search for the modal personality, described as the Eldorado of the culture and personality school (e.g. Du Bois, 1944).

The discussion of projective tests for cross-cultural use must, therefore, be concerned with special factors which might render the difficulties in their utilization, in standard scientific research, relatively unimportant. In fact Spain (1972) and Lindzey (1961) have written at length on this question and I shall concentrate on those points of relevance to this thesis.

Unfortunately the special cross-cultural factors are likely to make projective tests even less valuable than in the West. This is not to say that brilliant individual investigators (e.g. Henry (1947) with the TAT) cannot use these tests intuitively with great advantage: this may be so but such cases cannot be used to advocate their use generally. The exacerbating cross-cultural problems can be briefly listed. Most of the TAT pictures and similar derivative tests are highly culture-bound, probably even to a greater degree than psychometric test items. Card 1, for example, portrays a violin, card 13 a staircase, and card 2 shows a ploughing horse. Furthermore the settings are typically American with the unmistakable ambiance of the 1930s. Postures of grief or excitement are Western. Lee (1953) in an attempt to overcome these difficulties has produced an African version of the TAT, but even this is suitable only for certain tribes of that sub-continent and could not be used elsewhere.

Perhaps even more powerful evidence against using the TAT and similar techniques lies in those studies of perception indicating that some African groups have difficulties with picture recognition and depth perception. Kilbride and Robbins (1969) in their study of the Uganda Baganda found a correlation between the ability to percieve depth in pictures and acculturation. Hudson (1960, 1967) working with the Bantu showed that this ability was similarly related to cultural isolation and also to intelligence and perceptual style. Wober (1966) has convincingly demonstrated that field dependence as measured by the rod and frame test plays an important part in this perceptual skill. Furthermore his suggestion that some cultures are not visually oriented but are keyed to other perceptual modes has profound implications for cross-cultural testing which have not been fully worked out. However Wober's notion of sensotypes certainly means that it is idle to hope to be able to compare responses to compare projective test stimuli across cultures and to use the same interpretative bases. Indeed, if the purely perceptual experiments of Hudson (1967) and Deregowski (1968) are correct, it is clear that projective test stimuli are not in any meaningful sense the same stimuli to cultures with different perceptual skills. In conclusion, in addition to the normal problems of reliability and validity, cross-cultural studies with projective tests (of which the vast majority are visual) are subjected to further sources of error arising from perceptual deficits and cultural influences of a more general kind upon perception.

Of course it is possible to construct projective tests that do not employ visual stimuli thus avoiding the specific perceptual problems, discussed above. Sentence-completion is a well-known example of such a test and Phillips (1965) has constructed one designed for a variety of cultures. However it demands literacy if it is to be used as a group test and obviously requires translation. With a large number of different samples, therefore, comparison is not clear cut. Since there is no evidence for the validity of this measure, it would appear that it could at best only be regarded as experimental. Analysis of results would have to be theoretical and objective, utilizing the G analysis which is fully discussed in Chapter 9. Such a test does not appear likely to reveal the substantive knowledge for which psychometrists are looking.

These objections virtually preclude the use of projective tests cross-culturally at least, as normally scored and interpreted, i.e. subjectively. Yet, as the bibliographies in Lindzey (1961) and Spain (1972) reveal, these tests have been widely used. Since not all these users by the laws of probability, can be regarded as brilliant, intuitive investigators, most of this work must be regarded as valueless as scientific evidence and the findings could not, by virtue of the arguments above, be regarded as substantive psychological knowledge. At best the results of projective tests cross-culturally may be useful in formulating hypotheses which can be tested more rigorously.

At this juncture it must be pointed out again that projective tests can yield insightful and valuable information in the cross-cultural setting if used by brilliant investigators, but the value of scientific tests lies in their objectivity—the ability to produce the same results regardless of the tester. Further, this information which is full of insight is not the same as, although it may be more interesting and stimulating, substantive results. An outstanding example of a first-rate cross-cultural study using projective techniques exemplifies this point—Carstairs' (1957) work among the Rajputs in India. Although the sample was self-selected, although the data were Rorschach protocols and perhaps even worse, interviews and biographies, Rajput personality appears to have been revealed. However, Carstairs has a rare combination of anthropological, psychiatric and psychological skills. He also possessed the unfair advantage of knowing the local language. From this it is clear that the results of this investigation cannot be cited to support the general utility of projective tests.

Despite their extensive use, it must therefore be concluded that projective tests are not able to provide the substantive cross-cultural knowledge for which psychometrists are looking. The only hope appears to be to use the methods advocated in the discussion of the Rorschach—G analysis, as described by Holley (1973). It is possible that the empirical investigation of the Rorschach cross-culturally might yield, with G analyses, interesting Q factors. Some of these might be no more than the cultural perceptual factors found by Hudson and Deregowski, but others might well be powerful personality factors. This field deserves to be explored but any other cross-cultural application of projective techniques would not appear to be valuable.

Before examining the substantive findings achieved with any of the personality tests so far discussed in this chapter, one further assessment technique must be briefly scrutinized. In the chapter outlining the basis of the Cattell personality questionnaires, the important place of ratings in that work was noted. Indeed behaviour ratings were the original criteria for assessing the validity of factors and items. Now such behaviour ratings could be most useful in attempting to construct measures of those factors specific to particular cultures. By such careful rating procedures, one ought to be able to capture the behaviour of subjects even when it is strange or alien to one. However I would advocate behaviour rating only as a basis for item writing and test construction.

From this discussion of the problems involving cross-cultural testing of personality and motivation it is clear that the only methods that would produce substantive findings are likely to be personality questionnaires and possibly projective tests if objectively scored and left uninterpreted.

Cross-cultural Results with the 16 PF Test

Table 10.1 sets out the results from a number of cross-cultural researches with the Cattell 16 PF test. This table is taken from the handbook to the test. (Cattell *et al.*, 1970).

Although these results are in some cases based upon large samples, they cannot be regarded as definitive profiles of the various national groups and they throw little light on the currently unfashionable problem of whether whatever personality differences there are, stem from genetic or environmental influences. In fact as such this is an incorrect statement of the question since there is undoubtedly an interaction of culture and genes: it is the extent of this interaction which is unknown.

In the light of all the problems concerning the cross-cultural use of personality tests one can briefly make the necessary warning comments. First in respect of sampling, some of these studies cannot possibly be representative of the designated population. This is not meant as a criticism but as a reflection of hideous sampling difficulties in cross-cultural studies. For example De

TABLE 10.1
CROSS-CULTURAL PERSONALITY PROFILES (STEN MEAN AND STANDARD DEVIATION)[a]

	Sex	Norm pop.[b]	N	A	C	E	F	G	H	Source trait I	L	M	N	O	Q_1	Q_2	Q_3	Q_4
Australian	f	C	579	5.2 1.9	6.2 1.9	5.1 1.9	6.0 2.0	5.6 2.0	4.8 1.9	5.6 1.9	5.4 2.0	4.9 2.0	6.2 2.0	5.9 2.1	5.7 2.0	6.2 2.0	6.0 2.0	5.0 1.9
Australian	m	C	694	5.1 2.0	5.6 2.0	5.2 2.0	5.6 2.1	5.1 2.0	4.5 1.9	5.7 2.0	6.1 2.0	5.3 2.0	6.1 2.0	5.9 2.0	5.6 1.9	6.6 1.9	5.4 2.1	5.5 2.0
Brazilian	f	GP and C	828	4.8 1.9	5.2 2.2	6.0 2.3	4.6 2.3	4.8 2.2	5.5 2.3	6.0 2.3	7.6 2.1	7.1 2.0	5.3 2.2	6.1 2.4	7.4 2.4	6.6 2.1	5.6 2.4	5.6 2.0
Brazilian	m	GP and C	1406	5.6 2.1	4.7 2.5	4.8 2.4	3.7 2.4	5.6 2.1	5.3 2.0	6.4 2.2	7.6 2.0	7.2 2.1	5.0 2.2	6.5 2.5	6.1 2.2	6.1 1.9	5.5 2.3	6.0 2.3
British	m + f	C	204	5.0 1.8	4.5 1.7	4.9 2.7	4.9 2.2	6.4 1.8	6.3 2.4	5.7 2.0	4.9 1.9	4.9 2.0	5.8 1.9	4.1 2.4	5.8 1.8	5.3 2.0	4.8 2.1	4.5 2.0
Canadian	f	C	167	5.6 1.8	5.6 1.8	6.3 2.0	5.6 1.8	4.3 2.0	5.6 1.8	6.2 1.8	4.9 1.8	6.6 2.0	4.5 1.9	5.0 2.0	6.7 1.7	6.4 1.8	5.0 2.0	5.5 1.8
Canadian	m	C	201	5.1 2.1	4.7 2.2	5.7 2.0	5.6 2.0	5.2 2.2	5.1 1.8	5.0 2.2	6.2 1.9	6.0 1.9	6.2 1.9	5.7 1.9	6.1 1.9	6.6 2.0	5.4 2.0	5.7 2.1
Chinese	f	C	285	4.2 1.8	3.9 1.9	5.1 1.9	3.6 1.9	4.4 2.0	4.4 1.9	4.6 1.8	7.8 1.9	5.9 2.0	4.7 1.9	5.4 1.9	6.4 1.9	6.4 1.8	6.1 2.0	5.0 2.0
Chinese	m	C	425	5.4 1.9	3.9 2.0	3.9 2.0	3.8 1.9	5.1 1.9	4.8 1.9	6.1 1.9	7.0 2.0	6.5 1.9	4.6 2.0	5.5 1.9	6.0 1.9	6.2 2.0	6.7 2.0	4.8 2.1
German	m	GP	1000	5.7 1.7	6.1 1.9	4.9 1.8	5.5 1.8	5.5 1.6	5.4 1.7	3.6 1.8	5.7 1.9	4.9 1.7	6.6 2.1	5.7 1.8	6.5 1.9	5.3 1.8	7.1 1.7	4.4 1.8

		Norm[b]	N	A	C	E	F	G	H	I	L	M	N	O	Q1	Q2	Q3	Q4
(Indian)	f	C	100	3.0	3.0	3.6	2.0	4.3	4.2	0.6	3.1	3.6	3.0	4.8	3.4	3.0	3.2	3.9
				1.9	1.5	1.8	1.7	1.6	1.6	2.6	1.9	1.6	2.5	2.1	2.3	1.7	2.4	1.9
Indian	m	C	100	4.6	2.6	3.4	3.5	5.0	4.8	2.4	5.5	5.0	4.2	4.6	5.3	4.7	4.6	3.9
				1.6	2.1	2.3	1.5	1.9	1.8	2.2	1.8	1.8	1.9	2.1	2.3	1.7	2.7	1.8
Italian	m + f	GP	200	5.3	6.3	6.7	5.1	6.1	5.8	4.8	7.0	7.0	7.7	6.0	7.4	6.2	6.3	4.1
				2.1	1.3	1.5	1.6	1.8	1.7	1.5	2.2	1.9	1.5	1.9	2.1	1.8	1.5	1.7
Japanese	m	C	300	4.2	3.3	5.3	3.2	4.5	3.8	6.0	5.9	7.2	5.7	6.7	7.3	6.8	4.6	6.6
				2.0	1.8	1.9	1.9	1.8	1.7	2.0	2.1	2.1	1.9	2.1	2.2	1.8	2.0	2.0
Mexican	m	GP	138	5.6	6.6	4.4	4.7	5.8	5.7	4.7	5.9	7.2	5.4	6.1	5.6	6.3	6.9	4.3
				1.7	2.2	2.0	2.0	1.7	1.9	1.6	2.0	2.5	2.5	2.1	2.1	1.9	2.0	1.6
New Zealand	f	HS	521	5.1	5.4	5.6	5.5	4.6	5.1	5.2	6.0	5.9	5.4	5.7	6.4	5.9	5.6	5.5
				1.8	1.9	2.1	2.0	2.1	1.9	2.0	2.0	2.1	2.0	1.9	2.0	2.0	2.1	1.9
New Zealand	m	HS	611	5.2	5.4	5.5	5.3	4.6	4.9	5.0	5.9	5.8	5.8	5.5	6.4	6.0	5.8	5.3
				1.9	2.0	2.1	2.1	2.0	1.9	2.0	1.9	2.0	2.1	1.9	1.9	2.0	2.0	2.0
Philippine	f	C	2468	5.0	4.8	6.0	3.5	6.1	4.7	6.0	6.8	6.1	5.7	6.5	5.6	5.4	6.8	5.4
				1.3	1.8	1.4	1.4	1.5	1.5	1.7	1.6	1.5	1.7	1.4	1.8	1.7	1.8	1.3

[a] In all cases, mean scores on Factor B have not been reported here. Translators have frequently reported difficulties in doing the B Scale. Consequently, it has not seemed desirable to include the results here.

[b] Symbols in this column indicate the norm tables which were used in converting the raw scores to stens. GP represents general population norms, C represents college student norms and HS represents high school student norms. In each case, raw score profiles were converted to stens on the basis of the most appropriate norm table.

The data for these profiles have been taken from the following sources: Australian—Anderson (1960); Brazilian—de Andrade et al. (1969); British—Cattell and Warburton (1961); Canadian (male)—Butt and Signori (1965a); Chinese—Liu and Meredith (1966); Indian—Kapoor (1964); Italian—Cusin and Novaga (1962); Japanese—Tsujioka and Cattell (1965); Philippine—Vidal (1966). Data for the Canadian (female) profile were supplied by Dr. John Crane (University of British Columbia, Vancouver, Canada). Data for the German profile were supplied by Mr. Gundo Schröder (Deutsche Lufthansa, Cologne, Germany). Data for the Mexican profile were supplied by Mrs. M. E. Resano Hassey (National University, Mexico City, Mexico). Data for the New Zealand profiles were supplied by Dr. Graham Vaughan (University of Auckland, New Zealand). Reprinted with permission of IPAT, Champaign, Illinois.

Andrade *et al.* (1969) studied Brazilian college students. How much do these resemble others of their age-group, particularly in factors such as are likely to affect obtaining college entrance—the chapter on educational psychology indicates that G and C + are important in educational success. Again the work with the Chinese by Liu and Meredith (1966) cannot represent Chinese personality since it was carried out in Hong Kong and Taiwan; and Morris (1956) has demonstrated that there are relationships between personality as measured by the Cattell test and social and political values. As a final example, Kapoor (1964) working with a Hindi version of the 16 PF utilized samples of only 100 of each sex. Not only is Hindi not the sole language and more Indians are ignorant of it than know it, but also a sample of 100 cannot represent adequately the 650 millions on that continent.

For these reasons detailed comparison of the results in Table 10.1 is not likely to yield meaningful or useful contributions to a knowledge of personality. The results are included because they are suggestive of interesting hypotheses which can then be put to the test in more rigorously chosen samples and with measures of the critical environmental variables. The danger of simply comparing mean scores is clearly illustrated by an examination of the Indian samples. Inspection indicates that these have extremely low scores compared with other groups on almost all variables. This could be in fact the case that Indians are thus different on the major personality factors. On the other hand it is more likely that this is an artifact of the Hindi translation, or the particular sample used or the scaling procedures. Here indeed Rasch scaling, as previously advocated, would seem to be necessary. Indian women have an extremely low score on I. Their mean of 0·6 indicates that some large proportion must have scored nothing on this scale. This is possible evidence that this particular scale was not valid in this sample. Certainly in normal item analysis items that fail to discriminate are rejected. If one accepts the finding, one has to consider whether it is psychologically meaningful that Indian women are exceptionally tough-minded.

From these studies reported in Table 10.1 one other interesting feature must be noted. As Cattell *et al.* (1970) point out in the Handbook to the test, in almost all cases, factor analysis revealed that the Western factor structure was applicable in these samples. They argue that these results, although far from definitive, demonstrate that the 16 PF is amenable to translation and thus suitable for further cross-cultural study.

In fact Cattell (1973) is able to report on studies in Italy, New Zealand, Sweden, Czechoslovakia, Chile, Quebec, Peru, Venezuela, Belgium, Switzerland, Mexico, Hungary, Jugoslavia, Finland, Poland, Hawaii, South Africa, Spain and Ghana. However, for reasons of sampling and itemetric difficulties, no substantive findings relative to national personality differences can be made. Nevertheless one clear fact still emerges—namely that the factor structure of the test items remains essentially similar across cultures. What is needed are well sampled studies of different groups within each culture such that comparisons can be made—e.g. between students, between teachers and so on, after the scales have been shown to be valid in each culture, preferably at the item or item parcel levels. Stankov's work with the F scale and the 16 PF test in Jugoslavia (Stankov, 1977) shows how important this is, if proper interpretations are to be made. He found that the F scale in Jugoslavia had essentially, judged against the 16 PF factors, changed its meaning.

One further point merits mention. So far I have argued that if the factor structure of the test remains as it was designed in any cross-cultural investigation, then this is evidence for the validity of the test. This argument does have a logical flaw. Thus while it is true that if the factor structure is different, the scales cannot be valid nor the factors the same; the converse is not always the case. Thus the factor structure could remain the same for the factors account for item variance: the same factor means that the items have been answered in the same way as in the West. However their external correlates may be quite different. Ideally this and the factor structure itself demands investigation. Kline (1967b) working in Ghana with a small sample of Ghanaian students found the factor structure of the test as in Great Britain and also the correlation of extraversion and anxiety with academic success. These two findings together made it seem likely that the 16 PF can meaningfully measure Ghanaian student personality. Similar external correlations have been found elsewhere. As Cattell (1973) claims, the 16 PF does seem to work cross-culturally.

The EPI

As is to be expected, since the primary factors in the 16 PF are cross-culturally valid, the main second-order factors, exvia and anxiety also appear. Since there is, as we have seen, a virtual identity, other than in name, between the Cattell second-orders and the EPI E and N factors, it is no surprise to find that the EPI and JEPI can be used cross-culturally, although in fact there are few such investigations.

The MPI, the forerunner of the EPI has shown itself to be valid in that two factors were extracted in the Lebanon (Rafi, 1965) in Chile (Bolardos, 1964) and in India (Jalota, 1964) who had also used the 16 PF (Jalota, 1957).

The EPI appears to have been used even less in non-Western populations. Orpen (1972) who studied the Bantu found only the work of Kline (1967) in Ghana and Mehyrar (1970) in Iran. However there have been a number of studies using this test in India and Hussein and Mehyrar (1973) actually used P items in Iran. In these Indian studies the EPI was used to allocate subjects to experimental groups (so that the main object was the EPI factors as such). Typical examples are Mohan and Rajinder (1973) where drive and reminiscence was investigated, Mohan and Kumar (1973) concerned with inhibition and Gupta (1976) who studied the effects of drugs. All these studies exemplify the fact that the EPI is valid in Indian samples, since not only did the factors meaningfully discriminate subjects but the experimental predictions about high and low scorers were also confirmed. This is in effect construct validity for the EPI in India.

In the other African populations, the test items appeared to load on the factors as required. Thus inadequate as the samples may be of national populations the conclusion from these studies must be that the EPI is a successful test cross-culturally and that, as with the 16 PF test, non-Western personality can be described along dimensions of E and N and possibly, in Iran, P.

Some interesting points concerning the cross-cultural use of the EPI have emerged from these studies. First the relatively rare use of the EPI cross-culturally stems from its items which are culture-bound, particularly in African societies where they appear, intuitively, particularly inappropriate. However in the study in Ghana, Kline (1967) showed that the EPI was valid (a) by factoring it with the 16 PF, with results as expected from the Western studies and (b) by correlating the scores with academic success. Yet item analyses of the N and E scales revealed that three N and eight E items were unsatisfactory. This means that the validity of scales is not destroyed by a few weak items. However this also indicates that comparison of mean scores on scales in which certain items were not functioning is rendered worthless. In other words the Ghanaian finding demonstrated that the EPI was valid within the culture but not for comparisons between cultures. Indeed this is a conclusion which is probably true for all the 16 PF and EPI results cross-culturally. The factor analyses demonstrate within culture validity but by no means guarantee between culture comparability. For that Rasch scaling is needed. Even so the results show that a similar factor structure exists outside the West. Some recently published work in Japan by Iwawaki, Eysenck and Eysenck (1977) and in Nigeria by Eysenck *et al.* (1977) fully confirms these claims.

As I have argued in the chapter on personality testing, results with children are less trustworthy than with adults mainly because one cannot be as certain whether they understand the items and because they may distort their responses. For these reasons the JEPI has been even less used than its senior version in cross-cultural studies. However, Honess and Kline (1974) administered the EPI to 103 males (18 years old) and 66 female students (17 years old) and the JEPI to 77 boys and 90 girls of mean age 15 years in Uganda, of whom all but a few were Bagandas. Although item analyses revealed the tests to be carrying few poor items, the reliabilities were for both scales in the region of 0·5 to 0·6, rather lower than those reported in the test manuals. For this reason these tests should only be used with groups rather than individuals in Uganda. Nevertheless, as previously discussed, correlations between E, N and academic performance (Honess and Kline, 1974) were in accord with the Western results, thus supporting the validity of these scales. This study must be regarded as some evidence that E and N are useful dimensions of personality among adolescents in East Africa. This result in view of apparent differences between Bagandan and European life-styles is surprising.

Conclusions

The studies and results which have been examined, are typical examples rather than the complete total, all suggest that despite the problems of cross-cultural testing with questionnaires, in non-Western societies, the same personality factors can be found to account for test variance as in the West. However, even if this is correct, it has been shown that cross-cultural comparison of mean scores is unlikely to be valuable, the tests being valid within rather than between cultures. For such a cross-cultural comparison Rasch scaling techniques are necessary. The questions of whether the Western personality structure is situation-bound in many of these cultures (to the questionnaires) and if so what other culturally-specific personality factors can be shown to occur, has not been answered. Generally cross-cultural research with the major personality questionnaires has been unsystematic. What are needed are investigations using the major tests, other "local" questionnaires together with measures of the environment to estimate environmental affects on factor structure and scores. This demands a rare combination of anthropological and psychometric skills.

Results with other Tests

In the list of personality and motivation factors, a number of small factors of great theoretical interest, such as oral and anal factors, surface traits rather than source traits were set out. Although such surface traits were not important in terms of variance accounted for and although their validity was not so highly attested as that of the larger factors, they are of special relevance to cross-cultural psychology. In the Freudian theory of psychosexual development (Freud, 1905, 1908) it is hypothesized that oral and anal characteristics arise from fixation at the oral and anal stages of development and the fixation is itself dependent (in a great part) on weaning and toilet training procedures. As I have extensively argued previously (Kline, 1972, 1977), cross-cultural personality studies are powerful in putting such hypotheses to the test because cultures which are extreme on these child-training variables can be compared in terms of personality traits.

The psychometric tests available for such studies are few in number and generally such as not to encourage their use in the non-Western societies in which the hypotheses are most easily tested. The DPI (Grygier, 1961, see Chapter 2) although simple in item form is culture-bound extensively: hot milk, mixing paints, ballet dancing, flag poles and being a florist, are a random assortment of DPI items. Among the Baganda of the EPI Study (Honess and Kline, 1974) these would be problems.

I carried out a study of anal characteristics (Kline, 1969) among Ghanaian students using Ai3Q (Kline, 1971) as the test. Item analysis of the test showed that it worked well with Ghanaians and a factor analysis with the EPI and 16 PF tests demonstrated good construct validity. However, as a cross-cultural test of Freudian theory it was a failure since we were unable to discover any accurate accounts of Ghanaian pot-training despite the fact that a chapter in Barrington Kaye's study of child-rearing in Ghana is concerned with just this subject (Kaye, 1962). The Ghanaian scores were in fact significantly higher than their British controls. However, whether this mean difference reflected genuine population differences should have been tested with a Rasch analysis which was not carried out.

Kline and Mohan (1974) also attempted to use Ai3Q in India. India was chosen because according to analytically oriented anthropologists Hindu culture is anal (Berkely-Hill, 1921). Certainly the apparent denial of faeces, allows defecation to occur anywhere in a manner startling to those in the West. In this study, however, there was no point in even comparing Indian and British scores, since the item analysis revealed that the test was not working in the Indian sample. In some cases the reasons were obvious. For example one item was concerned with smoking, and smoking is a forbidden practice among the Sikhs, a large part of this sample. Similarly one item was concerned with revolution and during testing in Amritsar, this city became embroiled in the Pakistan–Indian fighting. Some items, however, failed in India, for no obvious reason, given that they had worked in Ghana. These data demand a Rasch analysis which is at present under way.

Finally Kline *et al.* (in press) carried out a study with OPQ, a measure of oral pessimistic traits, with a further sample of female Indian students. Item analysis revealed that this test was working. However, contrary to Freudian theory there were no significant differences between vegetarians and non-vegetarians or Hindus and Sikhs. The hypotheses, for those who try to argue that Freudian theory is untestable, were that the vegetarianism practiced by many Indians stems from oral fixation. Indians constitute a good sample to test this because in that culture vegetarianism is not associated with crankiness, bare sandals, Hampstead and yoga as it is in this country. Similarly it can be hypothesized that the vegetarian Hindu is orally fixated (as a part of the religious attitudes and practices). Although none of the hypotheses was supported, one cannot be certain that the test was valid in India despite the item analysis, and clearly further more systematic and careful research is needed.

I have argued that the contribution of psychometrics to psychology comes from the establishment of factor-analytically derived dimensions. I have included projective tests in these studies because, subjected to a suitable statistical analysis valuable information could be yielded. However despite the large number of projective test studies, none of them met the stringent requirements of multivariate analysis and the results will not be discussed here.

CONCLUSIONS

The problems peculiar to the cross-cultural testing of personality have been fully discussed. Despite these difficulties it does appear that the standard factored personality questionnaires can be used cross-culturally and a factor structure similar to that in the West occurs. However these tests may leave aspects of personality untapped and special tests for each culture should be designed to measure these. Even more important is the assessment of environmental variables so that the effect of these on factorial structure and the factors themselves can be gauged. Comparison of mean scores across cultures is difficult because of the confusion concerning sources of variance. For this Rasch analysis is possibly the answer. From this it can be argued that as yet the cross-cultural use of psychometrics in the study of personality has not contributed much to our knowledge. While this is true, there is equally no doubt that the contribution could be huge. Either scholars are trained in anthropology and psychology (including psychometrics) so that the necessary environmental assessments can be made and the special cultural items written, or else teams will have to be formed with native psychologists to supply the anthropological information. Given this background, psychometrics can make a powerful contribution to cross-cultural psychology.

SUMMARY

(1) A definition of cross-cultural psychology was attempted: four schools were discerned and the problems of each were outlined so that the contribution of psychometrics to the field could be understood.
(2) The problems of cross-cultural testing were defined: the emic and etic approaches were discussed.
(3) The cross-cultural testing of cognitive abilities was discussed in the light of these problems and the question of the intelligence of Negroes was scrutinized. The psychometric contribution could be considerable.
(4) The discussion then turned to the problems of cross-cultural personality measurement: difficulties with questionnaires, projective tests and objective tests were studied. The value of Rasch analysis and G analysis was stressed.
(5) The results achieved with personality tests in the cross-cultural setting were set out and discussed.
(6) It was concluded that, contrary to the arguments of cross-cultural psychology, psychometrics could make an important contribution to cross-cultural psychology.

11

Conclusions

In this book I have shown what the substantive findings from psychometrics have been, and in some case might be, in the fields of abilities, temperament, mood and dynamics. These findings have been examined as they have been applied to theories of learning (which are essentially theories of behaviour) and to educational, clinical and occupational psychology.

This chapter attempts to show whether any coherent account of human behaviour is implicit in these results and to assess other broad theories or approaches to understanding human behaviour in the light of these results. The value of such an endeavour for psychology lies in the fact that these psychometric results even where generally known, are not integrated into psychology, and factor-analytically derived variables have the virtue, from the viewpoint of science, of being quantified, and can be defined operationally by their factor loadings as fundamental dimensions in their field.

ABILITIES

From the study in Chapter 4 of the chief ability factors, the main question is, what coherent account of cognition can be extracted. The first point that has to be made is that in any discussion of factors, one must be careful not to reify them: these factors are not things in the head, although at the higher order especially, they may represent the influence or action of structures and even physiological factors, as in the case of factors of symptoms representing the tubercle of tuberculosis (Eysenck, 1967c).

In Chapter 4 it has been seen how the experimental approach to cognition has yielded findings (where they impinge upon abilities) which are in striking agreement with those of factor analysis. This was demonstrated in the examination of Hunt's (1976) and Carroll's (1976) work, the first of whom certainly argued that cognitive experimental psychology was a better way of grasping the nature of abilities than the factor-analytic method. Here one could see that the abilities demonstrated by experimental psychology corresponded in the main with known ability factors. These however, being necessarily derived from large samples are known to be reliable and replicable, and thus of wide applicability. It was argued, therefore, that the cognitive psychology based upon experiment was an ideal complement to the factor-analytic method because the results provide a precise operational description of the factors. However, examination of the tests loading most saliently on the factors can also do this. Nevertheless, it is the case that the cognitive psychological experiments describe the processes involved in the abilities represented by the factors.

Many of these comments apply even more strongly if one attempts to compare the factorial picture of abilities with the work on cognitive processes by Piaget and the Geneva school. Piaget is concerned with intelligence in much of his work (intelligence as conceived popularly rather than factor-analytically defined) as Furth (1969) has pointed out. Piaget's experiment can be seen as attempts to define and describe the mental processes underlying intelligent behaviour in the cognitive field. Thus to take the simple example of conservation of quantity, as examined in the experiment where liquid in a narrow tall jar is poured into a broad shallow vessel, the age trend of successful solution to this problem is taken as indicative of the attainment of conservation. This itself is a description of a process made possible by certain structures. Thus, in a modification of the typical conservation experiment reported by Piaget (1970), designed to aid the learning of conservation, it was found that such learning depended on initial cognitive level. At the pre-operational level the logical operations necessary for conservation could not be learned—i.e. transitivity and reversability. This experiment from Piaget (1970) is cited to demonstrate that Piaget's methods and concepts are aimed at precise description of mental processes. They are thus, as was the case with the approach of Hunt (e.g. 1976), complementary to the factor-analytic picture of abilities.

However, what is interesting is that tests of Piagetian problems almost invariably load high on g, usually, where possible to say, gf for example (Vernon, 1965, Tuddenham 1970). This must mean that it is the individual's basic reasoning ability which enables him to acquire quickly and successfully, the operations, structures and concepts described by Piaget. In these terms, Piaget's cognitive psychology is a description of how fluid ability is applied to certain problems. Thus conservation might emerge as a factor among young subjects (for whom this was a source of variance), given problems requiring this in their solution, but it would be a narrow specific factor. In other words, conservation problems would be expected to load on gf and s conserv. Thus, I would argue that essentially Piaget is engaged in the clinically detailed description of rather narrow primary factors which are specific to certain classes of problems and closely related to the major ability dimension of gf (in this example).

One should note that Piaget's work is complementary to the psychometric because (a) it is highly detailed, describing processes and (b) relatively narrow. Conservation is an ability peculiar only to a small number of problems. In as much as it depends on reversability for example, it will correlate with other skills thus dependent. In contrast, the psychometric picture of abilities emphasizes the most important factors that are pervasive of a large number of problems and account for much variance. It has deliberately eschewed the picking up of small primary factors because the list will be long and their importance slight.

What is now required are studies linking Piagetian performance to the main factors of ability as discussed in Chapter 4: in this way both approaches will be richly illumined.

The only systematic attempt to weld the factorial findings in the sphere of abilities into a coherent whole, is that of Cattell (1971) employing the ADAC model, the investment theory of abilities and triadic theory. These theories have been fully discussed in Chapter 4. Nevertheless, the theoretical parts of Cattell's work are highly speculative. They represent an imaginative attempt, well in advance of the research evidence, to provide a developmental theory of abilities.

TEMPERAMENT

We must now see what kind of psychological theory is implicit in the temperamental factors that have emerged from psychometrics and how they may be explicitly woven into a theory. Their pertinence to other non-factorial theories of personality must also be noted. All this will be done briefly because at the present stage of research and knowledge, this discussion is inevitably subjective and speculative. The value however, of such an exercise, resides in the fact that the variables are precisely defined in a theory built around factor-analytic findings. If one talks for example, of super-ego, one refers to factor G with its replicable factor loadings and tests of reasonable reliability.

I shall first examine the bearing of these findings on theories of personality. Since such theories are so numerous it is only necessary to discuss those that are generally spoken of with some approbation in what are considered to be the best surveys of personality theory, books such as Hall and Lindsey (1957), Sarason (1972) and Cartwright (1974).

The Number of Factors

The first point to note is that the number of factors which have clearly been isolated by factor analysis is an embarrassment to all theories of personality that may be labelled as psychoanalytic. In as much as precise predictions and clear statements of hypothesis can be derived from such theories (and they can, as Kline (1972) and Fisher and Greenberg (1977) have shown at some length), far fewer factors would have been expected. Further, the argument that perhaps one should consider higher-order factors is reasonable. However, generally the fit of these factors to the theories is not good.

Freudian theory has so many facets (topological, dynamic and psychosexual, for example) that one must be precise in any discussion: blanket rejection is unconvincing. I shall deal briefly with various aspects of psychoanalytic theories separately. For a more detailed treatment readers are referred to Cattell and Kline (1977).

Psychosexual Theory

Psychosexual theory in its developed form (see Fenichel, 1945) supports three temperamental factors—oral, anal and phallic characters. It is possible that the oral and anal factors could each split into two (depending on over-indulged or frustrating training procedures). The major personality factors, described in Chapter 5, can in no way be held to confirm this theory. The primary factors do not resemble closely any of these syndromes, nor indeed do the secondaries. From the factor-analytic research, therefore, it can be concluded that the psychosexual personality syndromes are not of great importance in the description of personality.

On the other hand, my own research has shown that small factors equivalent to oral optimistic and pessimistic character (Kline and Storey, 1977) and anal character (Kline, 1968b) do exist. It is likely, especially in the case of the oral factors, that in terms of Cattell's system they are surface rather than source traits. It is important to notice that these factors have, *per se*, no implication of orality and anality, they merely indicate that certain constellations of personality traits cohere together. Finally it must be stated that so far no studies have ever found evidence in support of the phallic character.

This rejection of psychosexual dimensions by factor analysis as major categories of temperament, inevitably means that similar descriptions to be found in Fromm (1949), Reich (1945) and Horney (1939) are disconfirmed.

Jung's Approach to Temperament

Jung (1923) hypothesized that individuals could be divided into two groups by a basic orientation—outwards, extraversion, or inwards, introversion. This typology could be divided again in terms of four modes of operation—thinking, intuiting, feeling and sensing. Jung, therefore, essentially proposed an eight type theory. This book clearly shows that extraversion together with anxiety is the most important and well-established personality factor. In Chapter 5 even where rotations fall grossly short of the ideal, extraversion emerged. It is, therefore, ironic that Jung of all analysts, the most mystical and least deliberately scientific, should be confirmed more strongly than the rest. However, factorial extraversion is by no means identical to that of Jung, which is why, to avoid confusion, Cattell has called his factor exvia. An important difference is that extraversion as a factor is a dimension. For Jung it was part of a typology. In the factorial work no hint of the orientations has emerged.

Nevertheless factor analysis confirms the basic accuracy of Jung's observations but sharpens his verbal descriptions by defining it in terms of variables loading on the factor.

Eros and Thanatos

Towards the end of his life, Freud went beyond the pleasure principle. A two factor theory of personality, conceived of as the forces of life (eros) opposed to death (thanatos) was proposed. None of the factors discussed in this chapter, even at the highest order confirms these hypotheses. Indeed it would be difficult to say what loadings would define these factors (or a bipolar factor, if it was conceptualized thus).

Topological Theory, Ego, Superego and Id

Here there seems to be better support in the factorial results. Thus Cattell has isolated C and G, ego and superego. As already discussed in Chapter 9 in the application of these findings to clinical psychology, C was low among neurotic groups and it tended to rise among lobotomized patients. Among normals the low scorer on factor C is easily annoyed, feels dissatisfied and generally behaves as befits a person of low ego strength.

Factor G, again, resembles the psychoanalytic concept of superego, a resemblance to which it owes its title. The higher G individual is described as: persevering, dominated by a sense of duty, determined and responsible, a man concerned with moral rules. As Cattell and Kline (1977) have argued this would appear to catch the notion of superego quite well were it not for the fact that when measured by questionnaire, criminals seeking parole score high (even as Myra Hindley impresses Lord Longford), while adolescents in revolt score low, although their behaviour remains typically conscientious. Thus it could be argued that G reflects not superego but middle class mores. However, negative correlations with delinquency and homosexuality and positive correlations with achievement favour the superego interpretation. As already discussed in Chapter 9 on clinical psychology, the typical neurotic scores on G do not support either psychoanalytic theory where it should be high or Mowrer's (1950) learning theory where it should be low. In conclusion then the primary factor patterns of C and G and their associated correlations are some support for topological theory.

The fourth-order questionnaire pilot study by Warburton (1968), was interesting because two factors were revealed: morality (G) *vs* thrust. This, of course, looks not unlike the ego-superego conflict, reality *vs* morality. However, problems of accurate rotation with so few points available at the fourth-order make this research unworthy of more detailed discussion. Even more cautiously one might mention here the third-order factor analysis of T factors carried out by Pawlik and Cattell (1964). Here it was found that three factors emerged tentatively labelled as ego, superego and id. At least there were similarities to the Freudian model. However since the validity of T tests is not clearly recognized, interpretation of third-order factors must be necessarily tentative.

As regards the temperamental aspects of psychoanalytic theory one may with justice conclude that the factor-analytic findings have not given them unequivocal support. As might be expected from such acute observers some of their claims have been confirmed but in general, because they generalized from inadequate samples and because the clinical method is weak compared to multivariate analysis, their conclusions cannot bear close scrutiny.

Other Theoretical Positions

Not all personality theories are psychoanalytically derived, although a surprising number utilize many of the basic concepts and assumptions. However, the temperamental factor-analytic findings are relevant to the claims of two theorists, Allport (1937) and Mischel (e.g. 1973).

Allport has never denied the fact of common dimensions of personality. What he has argued, however, is that what are more important are those aspects of personality stemming from experiences that are unique to each individual. Thus the demonstration of psychometrics of a set of common personality factors neither confirms nor rejects Allport's claims. In his case the critical test is the application of this work. If one can develop specification equations which can predict a wide range of human behaviour utilizing the factors discussed in this book, then Allport is refuted. If it turns out to be impossible then Allport's claims are confirmed. The relevant sections of this book to Allport's work are those, therefore, which examine the application of these findings to clinical, educational and occupational psychology. Here we saw that already, although research in this area is not well advanced, occupational and clinical indices from these factors can be developed. It is likely, therefore, that Allport placed too much stress on the uniqueness of the individual. Two points need to be stressed in relation to this theoretical argument. First, the difference between the psychometric and Allport's position is one only of emphasis. The psychometrist takes account of individual experiences but sees these as having effects via the trait pattern of the individual. Thus experience X has a similar effect on persons with similar traits. Furthermore, the experiences each have are not entirely arbitrary since one exposes oneself to experiences in part depending on one's traits. The high H subject likes powerful motorbikes and is thus more likely to be involved in accidents than the low H individual, for example. Furthermore, the psychometrist assumes that experiences are themselves categorizable. To lose a parent while young, to be maltreated at school or in the family, these are not unique experiences. Each individual experiences a unique instance of a common experience. Finally, in the interplay of a large number of traits and experiences there is ample opportunity for individual differences. Given a large number of traits with a large variance, the number of identical subjects is inevitably going to be small. Thus I would claim that theoretically and practically (as one can see from the application of the factors to education and clinical psychology), Allport's case is over-stated.

Logic of Traits

Mischel (e.g. 1973) has argued that the whole trait position in psychology is based on scientifically naive assumptions. To take adventurousness as an example, if we see a person behaving adventurously, we call him adventurous and explain the behaviour by calling him high on a trait adventurousness for which our only evidence is the behaviour it was invoked to explain. This is logically a sound objection. However this logic is trivial if one demonstrates empirically that such traits are useful behavioural descriptions. In my view it is precisely this that the factor analysis of personality has done.

Inconsistency of Behaviour

Mischel, however, has not restricted his attack merely to logic. He has argued that in the field of personality there is no consistency across situations to support the hypothesis of underlying personality traits. Response patterns may be unrelated even in similar situations. Only in the ability sphere does Mischel allow consistency. The obvious rejoinder that the factors discussed in this book would appear to destroy his point is countered by the claim that the factors themselves are situational—determined by the test-taking situation.

However, commonsense observation tells us that people are consistent. Dockers are not noted as aesthetes or ballet dancers nor are chess-masters renowned as town criers or wrestlers. Such intuitive observation is regarded by Mischel (1968) and by Vernon (1964) as reflecting not reality but the halo effect and the stereotypes of observers. Thus contrary evidence is ignored. However more careful observation in fact supports the notion of consistency. Studies of drivers involved in serious driving offences by Willet (1964), showed that a high proportion of offenders had been previously convicted of other serious crimes. The lunatic driver is the criminal who is not careful of life.

Furthermore if the factors described in this book were test specific how can it be that they correlate with non-test external criteria as discussed in the chapters on the application of these findings. All the large mass of psychologically meaningful differences on factors between occupational and clinical groups would be inexplicable. In my view the situational argument is destroyed by the empirical evidence. Personality factors are not test specific.

Meaning of Ratings

A further argument adduced by Mischel (which is also refuted by the empirical findings) is that the ratings of behaviour reflect not the reality of the behaviour but simply the categories used by the raters to assess behaviour (if ultimately any distinction can be made on this point). His argument has an empirical buttress in that the factorial structure of ratings made on subjects, seen only for a brief period (i.e. imaginary ratings), was the same as ratings seriously carried out. Thus ratings reflect raters rather than subjects.

This objection, however, is not as severe as it seems. If for example we were to have subjects rate for colour and movement, woodland scenes, seascapes and other panoramas, the factor structure of ratings both actual and made from imagination would not be different. It may be that people's perception of what behaviour is like is in general accurate. How closely it fits actual subjects may differ depending whether or not they are actually rated.

Cattell's rating procedures (Cattell, 1957) were however, so based on behavioural observation that it is unlikely that rater's stereotypes could much affect them so that even if Mischel's arguments were accepted, the rating basis of Cattell's factors would not be overturned. Recently Howarth (1976) has subjected Cattell's original ratings to a modern factor analysis and extracted not 12 L factors but only five. He has tried to argue from this that the whole of Cattell's system of factors is suspect because originally it was developed to fit the 12 L factors. However, if one accepts that the ratings in Cattell's original data are best explained in terms of five factors and even if the original 16 PF questionnaire is targeted to reproduce the 12 factors, in fact (see Chapter 5 on personality traits), the Q and T factors have gone far beyond L factors. Cattell and Kline (1977) list 23 Q factors and 12 abnormal Q factors as well-replicated when simple structure is obtained. Thus the fact that the original basis was not as sound as originally thought no longer matters. Certainly, I agree with Howarth's conclusion that, in future, rating studies should be carried out on a wide scale and subject to more refined analyses. However, to argue that these findings overthrow the Cattell factor system is not justified.

Nevertheless, all these arguments about the situational determinants of behaviour seem ultimately to be refuted empirically—by the correlations between temperamental factors and external critiera as Hogan *et al.* (1977) have argued. This is not to deny that situations affect behaviour. How situations affect individuals is determined by their traits. The tough-minded individual (1) is less affected than the tender-minded and so on. Indeed these situational determinants of behaviour are taken into account in the psychometric system by indices which represent the stimulus value of any situation for particular ergs. Where the psychometrist differs from Mischel is that the former takes account of both situation and person. In its crudest form situationalism denies the importance of the person. More recently, however, Mischel (1973 and 1977) does seem to recognize the interaction and essentially again the difference is one of emphasis.

Personality and Physique

Many textbooks on personality describe the work of Sheldon (Sheldon and Stevens, 1942) and Kretschmer (1925) attempting to link personality and physique, an association commonly found in literary accounts of personality typified by Falstaff and Cassio in Shakespeare. In evaluating these theories against the factor-analytic findings two issues are essential: the accuracy of their personality descriptions and the link between these and physique.

Based upon clinical observation of mental patients, Kretschmer postulated two temperamental dimensions with normals at one pole, neurotics in the middle and psychotics at the other extreme. One of these dimensions was the cycloid or circular personality varying from moodiness in the normal to manic depression among the psychotic. His second dimension was labelled schizoid and was characterized by aloofness and coldness at one pole which in the psychotic became the typical schizophrenic withdrawal and loss of reality contact.

These two dimensions are an eloquent tribute to Kretschmer's powers as a clinical observer for they resemble the two main second-order temperamental factors recognized by all theorists—exvia and anxiety. Relevant to this relationship of Kretschmer's and Cattell's descriptions, Howarth (1976) quotes a nice incident: on being told by Cattell of the similarity of results, Kretschmer replied "Ach, Herr Cattell, *now* I believe in factor analysis". However, one aspect of this personality description is not correct. Kretschmer claimed that the psychotic personality was an extreme form of the neurotic personality. In fact, as the studies of the abnormal factors show together with the study of factor P by Eysenck and Eysenck (1976) this is not the case. Normal personality factors discriminate between normals and neurotics but not between normals and psychotics. For this abnormal factors are needed.

As regards the relation of personality and physique, the clinical impressions of Kretschmer have not really been supported. The largest correlation with personality factors and physique is small (around 0·25) being between body breadth and factor F.

The work of Sheldon differs from that of Kretschmer in that he attempted to measure physique objectively, and in such a way that normals could be easily accommodated into the system, whereas Kretchmer's descriptions fitted only extreme examples. Sheldon in fact categorized subjects into three groups depending on which aspect of their physique was the most important— ectomorphy (predominance of the nervous system), mesomorphy (predominance of the musculature) and endomorphy (where the gut is king). These three aspects were rated on a seven-point scale based upon a series of measurements.

Sheldon derived his personality dimensions from ratings and thus the findings should bear a close relation to Cattell's L and Q factors. However Sheldon extracted three clusters from the ratings with no statistical test as to the number of dimensions that would best account for the correlations and this number was presumably chosen because of the three basic physiques described in his system. The fact that the number of dimensions was thus *a priori* selected means that it is likely that they are factorially confused.

In fact cerebronia, the ectomorphic temperament, resembles the primary factor A, withdrawn, aloof, somewhat schizoid, at its negative pole.

Viscerotonia resembles the high A description, cheerful, sociable and good natured as typified by Falstaff. Indeed this temperamental syndrome resembles both extraversion and anxiety, for mood swings are part of viscerotonia. This concept is without doubt factorially complex. Finally somatotonia typified by energy, push and drive comes nearest to the positive pole of E, dominance.

From this brief description and comparison with factorial findings it is clear that Sheldon's dimensions of temperament are important aspects of personality because factor A is the largest primary factor and extraversion and anxiety are the two largest second-order temperamental factors. On the other hand these dimensions are factorially complex as is to be expected with so crude a form of analysis, and in addition a large number of important temperamental factors have been omitted.

Curiously the relation between these Sheldonian groups and temperament has never been fully followed up. The high correlations reported by Sheldon are probably incorrect and contain computing error, as Eysenck has pointed out (Eysenck, 1970b) but nevertheless it would seem a useful exercise to investigate them with greater precision. The Rees-Eysenck index of body, builds a more simple physical measure than the categorization used by Sheldon, has demonstrated only slight relationships between physique and temperament.

In conclusion I can state that the work of Sheldon and Kretschmer on physique and temperament has not been confirmed by factor-analytic research. They have exaggerated the relation between physique and temperament. Furthermore, their descriptions of temperament, though clearly dealing with the major temperamental factors, were factorially confused, and represent a gross over-simplification of a complex field.

Distinction between Normal and Abnormal Factors

In the study of Kretschmer's work, it was mentioned that the factor-analytic study of temperament had unmistakably revealed the discontinuity of abnormal and normal personality. The abnormal factors, of which Eysenck's psychoticism factor is one of the most important, indicate that psychotic personality is qualitatively different from the normal and neurotic personality which are on a continuum.

Since this topic has been fully discussed in Chapter 9 on clinical psychology, one only need comment on the relevance of these findings to theories of personality in as much as these relate to abnormal psychology. Psychoanalytic conceptions of mental disorder are difficult to tie down but in general, they are supported by these results. Thus neurosis is regarded as the outcome of inefficient defence mechanisms. Since defences are part of our everyday strategies in maintaining the dynamic balance of id, superego and id, neuroses can be seen as an accentuation of normal behaviour. Psychosis however, results from the breakdown of the defences and the emergence of id material into consciousness, hence the qualitative distinction between psychosis and normality. Thus this distinction between normal and abnormal factors may be said to give modest confirmation of the general psychoanalytic position on mental disorders.

So far little has been said about the relevance of results with objective test factors to personality theories. This is partly because as yet, the identification of these factors where they do not correspond to the Q and L factors is hazardous, because the validity of T tests is hard to demonstrate. In Chapter 9, many of these factors have been shown to be good discriminators of neurotics, psychotics and normals, and since these tests fit neatly into no personality theory, it must be concluded that they run counter to theories of personality.

To conclude this section on the implication of theories of personality of the temperamental factors isolated by factor analysis, a few simple points can be made:

(1) No clinically based theories were able to pick out the important personality dimensions.

(2) Most of the theories approximate a crude description of the two largest factors, exvia and anxiety.

(3) Some aspects of psychoanalytic theorizing received modest support but in the main they were not confirmed.

(4) Similar negative results obtain with the work on physique and personality.

(5) The claims of Allport and Mischel have been shown to be exaggerated.

(6) Multivariate analysis, as had been earlier suggested, is a more powerful analytic tool than observation of and inference from a few patients.

DYNAMICS

I shall now examine the relevance of the psychometric findings in the field of dynamics to psychological theories. It will be remembered that essentially factor analysis had been aimed at two aspects of motivation: the goals of behaviour and strength of motivation.

Motivation Strength Factors

The factor analysis of motivational strength revealed six factors of which only the first three were named. These were conscious id, ego and superego, all of which have been fully discussed in Chapter 6. The discussion here will be restricted simply to the import of the findings for theories. First, two points stand out. The fact that some of the six factors could not be labelled implies that there is no current way of conceptualizing the results. This alone strongly suggests that current theories of motivational strength are inadequate.

Clearly by a similar argument, the labelling of the first three factors as ego, superego and conscious id, indicates that to Cattell and his colleagues, at least, there is a resemblance in these factors to the psychoanalytic concepts of that name. In Chapter 6, resemblance of these factors to their Freudian counterparts has been fully discussed. It was concluded that there is a degree of similarity, although the conscious id is clearly *not* to be identified with the id which is unconscious. It may be the case that, with further research, the psychoanalytic concepts can be empirically defined, for one of the smaller factors, delta, was possibly identified with the physiological aspects of motivational strength and epsilon, also, seemed to be related to repressed (in the sense of unverbalized), inarticulate conflict. In summary it must be stated that this research gives modes support for the broad psychoanalytic position that our behaviour reflects the outcome of the balance between id, ego and superego, although there are considerable differences on specific points.

As argued in Cattell and Kline (1977) the strength of motivational factors give little support at all for Adlerian or Jungian dynamic theories. There appears to be no way in which these factors could involve concepts such as the collective unconscious, the shadow, social interest or a striving for superiority. These last two Alderian notions may be, in any case, more related to the goals of behaviour than to strength of motivation, a phenomenon which has seemed to interest psychoanalytic theorists more than others. Thus we shall now turn to examine the factored results on this aspect of human dynamics.

Human Drives

As shown in Chapter 6, the factor analysis of drives has revealed about 17 ergs and around 30 sentiments (although this number could be multiplied since human interests, especially across cultures, are very diverse). Not all the ergs and drives were equally important but the largest of them in terms of variance accounted for, can be measured in a standardized test battery; the MAT and the SMAT.

What is the extent to which the psychometric findings support the numerous dynamic theories that have been proposed on the basis of intuition, philosophy and clinical observation, as well as those purportedly stemming from experimental psychology and even biology? First, one must begin with the psychoanalytic theories because it is with the dynamics (rather than the temperament) of human personality that they have been especially concerned.

Freudian theory developed steadily between the 1890s and the 1930s so that there are a number of dynamic hypotheses within it. Without doing too gross an injustice to the complexity and subtlety of Freudian theory, it is probably fair to argue that one would hypothesize one or at the most two basic drives (ergs)—sex and aggression. If one takes the later more metaphysical postulations one should expect again another but different two factor solution—Eros and Thanatos—or even possibly a single bipolar factor.

The number of factors alone clearly indicates that Freud underestimated the diversity of human drives. As his early critics, Jung and Adler, always argued there was too much emphasis on sex. Nevertheless the sex drive is important as is pugnacity. One further point deserves note. Freud claimed that many apparently asexual activities were in fact derived from the sex drive. The dynamic lattice indicates that this can indeed be so. Many activities can serve a number of ergs and sentiments. There is also evidence for the importance of narcism, as Freud claimed.

The later postulation of Eros and Thanatos receives no support from the results. As Fenichel (1945) points out, most psychoanalysts have not utilized the concepts although Melanie Klein is a clear exception: indeed it is central to her theorizing. Fromm (1974) has also worked them into his discussion of Hitler.

In so far as it is possible to develop precise hypotheses from the writing of Jung, there would appear to be no point of contact with the factorial findings and Jung must be considered to remain unsupported by these results. As mentioned previously Adler postulated one all-important motivational factor—the striving for superiority, which in the well-balanced individual was aligned with social interest. The factor-analytic results are not entirely dismissive of this claim since self-assertion is an important erg, and as argued in Chapter 6, the self-sentiment which is clearly related to the Adlerian concept is an organizing principle in motivation. Nevertheless as Freud laid too heavy a stress on the sexual drive, so too Adler over-emphasized the striving for superiority and failed to take into account the other drives that have emerged from factor analysis. Enough has been said to make it clear that the psychoanalysts were wide of the mark in their analysis of motivation. They laid too great a stress on some factors (which may indeed have been paramount in their samples) and ignored others.

The Work of McDougall

McDougall's work is now, in the main, of only historic interest in the mainstream of modern psychology. He has been introduced into this discussion for two reasons. In the first place his findings bear a striking resemblance to those of factor analysis. Secondly, Cattell (e.g. 1957) has attempted to synthesize his factor-analytic findings much as did McDougall. McDougall's views are perhaps most clearly expressed in the "Energies of Men" (1932). Here he argues that native *propensities* are the mainsprings of all human and animal activity. However, few of the *activities* of adult men spring directly from the propensities. Most derive their energy indirectly by means of the *sentiments* within which the propensities are organized. The underlined words emphasize that this claim of McDougall is essentially the principle by which the dynamic lattice and the dynamic calculus were constructed. Cattell has based his work on McDougall.

McDougall's list includes the following propensities: food seeking, disgust, sex fear, curiosity, protection, gregariousness, self-assertion, submission, anger, appeal, constructiveness, acquisition, laughter, comfort, sleep, migration, together with a group concerned with bodily needs. If one compares this list with the hypothesized list of ergs one can see that there is considerable agreement. With regard to sentiments, McDougall had a very large number, although he rightly, it appears, stressed the importance of the self-sentiment as the master sentiment. McDougall's theorizing, therefore, has been generally confirmed by the factor-analytic work, which, however, enables one to measure these variables with some precision. The surprise at the accuracy of McDougall's work is that he was by virtue of his position at Oxford, unable to carry out experiments, the tenure of the Wilde Readership being dependent on not so doing.

Murray (1938) developed what was intended to be a new subject, personology, in which a very large number of needs were postulated. However, unlike McDougall's list, most of these cannot be found in the factor-analytic results. Murray's list of course was derived from data, described in "Explorations in Personality" (Murray, 1938)—essays, biographies, interviews and projective tests—and this makes it likely not that Murray was completely mistaken but that he was describing motivational surface traits rather than source traits. Nevertheless there is virtually no support for Murray's system in the factorial findings. Perhaps as Cattell and Kline (1977) suggested, it would be useful to analyse the type of data used by Murray utilizing multivariate procedures and objective scoring.

Murray postulated, *inter alia*, a need to achieve, N ach, which leads to a discussion of this variable, which has been proposed as a major determinant of high achievement by McClelland and his colleages (e.g. McClelland, 1961). Murray measured need achievement using the TAT but McClelland derived scores from literary and artistic themes in cultures at given historical periods and related these to economic growth. Lynn (1969) and Hundal (1970) have shown that need achievement can be measured by simple questionnaires which will discriminate the entrepreneur from his control executive. In terms of the factorial analysis of motivation it is reasonable to ask why a variable of such apparent potency has not appeared in the lists. The answer to this is relatively simple. Cattell and Child (1975) argue that the achievement motive is a surface trait composed of three factors: self-sentiment, self-assertion and career. Reference to the dynamic lattice will show how activities such as banking or running a business can give outlet for these ergs. To study a factorially complex variable such as the need to achieve without analysis into separate factors, loses much information. What one needs to know is how the various cultural determinants of the need affect the separate factors. Finally, one should note that N ach is highly similar to the variable that Adler considered paramount—the drive for superiority. As with Adler, Murray and later McClelland, have spotted an important aspect of motivation. However human inference alone is not as powerful a technique as multivariate statistics for data analysis and inevitably a confused variable emerged. N ach is better studied through its separate components.

MOODS

Finally a brief mention must be made of the work on moods. Most theories have little to say about moods. However, the discovery of state-change factors was totally unexpected. Clearly some theoretical account is necessary if the findings are clearly replicated. In this sphere, therefore, some entirely new thinking appears necessary.

RELEVANCE OF PSYCHOMETRIC FINDINGS TO THEORIES: CONCLUSIONS

Having discussed the relevance of the psychometric findings in ability, personality and motivation, it is clear that none of the earlier theories relying on clinical observation and intuition, despite the intellectual brilliance of their originators, was accurate. As suggested earlier in Chapter 2 on factor analysis, the fundamental nature of factorial dimensions almost precludes their inference from unaided observation. What is perhaps surprising, is that these investigators even approached unearthing the major variables. Nevertheless, one is forced to the broad conclusion that no pre-factorial theory can stand in the light of the evidence. What therefore is needed is a new theory based upon the factorial findings.

Factor analysis as the name suggests, provides an analytical account of the data upon which it works. This analytic account has been the main body of this book, and in this final chapter the analysis has been fitted to other such accounts. As I have indicated the fit is imperfect. The necessary new theory requires synthesis.

Synthesis and Integration of the Findings

Only Eysenck and Cattell have attempted to synthesize their findings into a coherent theory. These are the two factorists who clearly see the place of factor analysis among scientific methods and who do not, therefore, simply factorize data independently of other results. As the findings in previous chapters relevant to ability, personality and motivation have been examined, so too have the ways in which Cattell and Eysenck have attempted to give the work coherence. In the chapter on learning theory their theoretical accounts were scrutinized in some detail, because clearly learning must be central to any theoretical account of human behaviour.

In the first place it has been demonstrated that Eysenck's factorial findings leave much to be desired and that the basis of his learning theory seems weak (see Chapter 7). This leaves us with the theory developed by Cattell and his colleagues. However, since this book is intended to state the contribution to psychological knowledge from psychometrics, Cattell's theorizing is far too speculative to be regarded under that heading. Nevertheless the essence of the theory can be presented and it will be discussed here as an example of how the factorial findings can be utilized to form a quantified, refutable account of human behaviour. For a further description of Cattell's theory, readers must be referred to Cattell and Kline (1977), where it is reduced to 20 points, embracing 24 propositions.

The Critical Points in Cattell's Theoretical Synthesis

It is possible to make a quantitative statement of trait-action (including ability, temperament and dynamics), to fit an additive specification equation using weighted factor scores *provided that* some account of states is made.

The behavioural specification equation involves stimulus and response, and each act is defined in terms of stimulus, person, response, ambient situation and observer.

Cattell and Child (1975) have a clear example of a specification equation—a young man taking out a sexually desirable but socially uncongenial girl:

$$a_{Ji} = b_{js}E_{si} - B_{jg}E_{gi} - b_{jp}M_{pi}$$

where a = the action, E_s, the sex erg, E_g the gregarious erg and M_p the parental sentiment.

In this example if the behaviour index, b_{js} is large or the sex erg high, the behaviour a_{Ji} will be positive, i.e. he will take the girl out even though b_{Jg} and b_{jp} are negative, again if M_{pi} was very high, he would not take the girl out. This is a simplified equation because the ambient situation has been left out.

A dynamic calculus has been developed for computing the complexity of the specification equations when one takes into account the integrative action (see Chapter 6) of the self-sentiment and superego. The main force of the dynamic calculus lies in the fact that it utilizes vectors to express the emotional quality (direction) and strength of a behaviour (length).

Thus a civilized behaviour in which self-sentiment and superego played a part could be specified:

$$a_{Jik} = b_{je}s_{ne}E_1 + b_{jm}s_{km}M_i + b_{Jss}s_{kss}M_{ssi} + b_{JsE}s_{ksE}M_{sEi}.$$

Here one erg and one sentiment are used for simplicity, apart from the two master sentiments. The S's are the modulators for the dynamic calculus a = response, J = the focal stimulus, i, an individual, k an ambient stimulus and e, m, ss fix the values of b and s for the trait.

The argument here is that if one can specify a behaviour (as in the above equation) then one has fully understood it. In this sense the specification equation is a theory of behaviour. How this theoretical approach was applied in detail to integration learning and structured learning theory has been described in the relevant chapters. Similarly this approach, triadic theory, in the field of abilities has been fully discussed.

Throughout this book I have discussed the theoretical position of Cattell vis-à-vis the main areas of psychometrics because he is one of the few who have attempted to develop a theory based upon the psychometric findings. Nevertheless as has been emphasized in the relevant sections, these theories are speculative. That is why it is only in this final section where there is an attempt to see what kind of coherent account can be made of the findings, that examples of the specification equations which are central to the speculations have been used. These specifications are, in my view, the most powerful summary of the coherence that can be gained from a psychometric work. In the first place, as has been seen in the chapter on educational and occupational psychology, these specification equations can be, as they stand, predictive to an impressive degree. Secondly, and this is the more important reason for concentrating on them, they are sufficiently abstract to enable new findings to be incorporated into them. If new master sentiments were found or new personality traits discovered to be important, or the action of fluid ability in the development of personality patterns explicated, the specification equations could be modified accordingly. Thus these equations are taken as examples of how the psychometric findings can be given coherence. They are not considered to be the final expression of the problem.

In my view the fact that one can point to so many well-established factorially derived traits of temperament, ability and dynamics gives the lie not only to the claims of Mischel (e.g. 1977) but also to Lumsden (1976) who regards the efforts of psychometrists over the years as of little value. From the viewpoint of psychology, as I have argued, it is important to establish the major dimensions of the various fields and this psychometrics has done.

Such then is the contribution of psychometrics to psychological knowledge. It can be summarized in two points:

(1) The main variables in many fields of psychology have been defined and measured.

(2) The numerical relation of these variables to many behaviours has begun to be specified.

In the future the steady development and application of the work should substantially increase our psychological knowledge.

References

Abraham, K. (Ed.) (1921). *In* "Selected Papers of Karl Abraham, 1965" Hogarth Press and Institute of Psychoanalysis, London.

Adler, A. (1927). "Understanding Human Nature" Chilton, New York.

Adler, A. (1930). *In* Murchison, C. (1930).

Adorno, T. W., Frenkel-Brunswick, E., Levinson, D. J. and Sandford, R. N. (1950). "The Authoritarian Personality" Harper, New York.

Allport, G. W. (1937). "Personality: A Psychological Interpretation" Holt, Rinehart and Winston, New York.

Anastasi, A. (1961). "Psychological Testing" Macmillan, New York.

Anastasi, A. (1972). *In* Buros, O. K. (1972).

Anastasi, A. and Foley, J. P. (1949). "Revised Differential Psychology" Macmillan, New York.

Anderson, H. E. (1966). *In* Cattell, R. B. (1966).

Anderson, J. R. and Bower, G. H. (1973). "Human Associative Memory" Halstead Press, New York.

Andersson, A. L., Nilsson, A. Rouuth, E. and Smith, G. J. W. (1972). "Visual Aftereffects and the Individual as an Adaptive System" Gleerups, Lund.

Angst, J. (1969). *Arn-Fors.* **19**, 399–405.

Anstey, E. (1966). "Psychological Tests" Nelson, London.

Appley, M. H. and Trumbull, R. (Eds) (1967). "Psychological Stress: Issues in Research" Appleton-Century Crofts, New York.

Armstrong, J. S. and Soelberg, P. (1968). *Psychol. Bull.* **70**, 361–364.

Ausubel, D. P. (1963). *J. Teacher Ed.* **14**, 217–221.

Baker, J. R. (1974). "Race" Oxford University Press, London.

Baltes, P. B. and Schaie, K. W. (1976). *Psychol.* **31**, 720–725.

Bandura, A. and Walters, R. H. (1963). Social Learning and Personality Development" Holt, Rinehart and Winston, New York.

Banks, C. and Broadhurst, P. L. (Eds) (1965). "Studies in Psychology" University of London Press, London.

Bannister, D. and Mair, J. M. M. (1968). "The evaluation of personal constructs" Academic Press, London and New York.

Bargmann, R. (1953). "The statistical significance of simple structure in factor analysis" Hochschule Fuer Internationale Paedagogische Forschung, Frankfurt-Main.

Barnes, C. A. (1952). *Genet. Psychol. Monogr.* **45**, 109–74.

Barron, F. (1955). *J. Abnorm. Soc. Psychol.* **51**, 478–485.

Barton, K. (1973). The relative validities of the CTS, the EPI and the Comrey Scales as measures of second order personality source traits by questionnaire. *Adv. Pub.* No. **1**. Institute for Research on Morality and Adjustment, Boulder.

Barton, K. (1973b). "The CTS, Core Trait and State Kit" IPAT, Champaign.

Barton, K., Dielman, T. E. and Cattell, R. B. (1971). *Personality* **2**, 325–333.

Bass, B. M. (1955). *J. Abnorm. Soc. Pyschol.* **51**, 616–623.
Bateson, G., Jackson, D., Haley, J. and Weakland, J. (1956). *Behav. Sci.* **1**, 251–264.
Beck, A. T. (1962). *Am. J. Psychiat.* **119**, 210–215.
Beck, S. J. (1952). *In* "Advances in Interpretation. Vol. III. Grune and Stratton, New York.
Bedford, A. and Foulds, G. A. (1977). *Br. J. Med. Psychol.* **50**, 163–172.
Bedford, A., Foulds, G. A. and Sheffield, B. F. (1976). *Br. J. Soc. Clin. Psychol.* **15**, 387–394.
Bellak, L. (1961). *Psychoanal. Quart.* **30**, 519–548.
Bellak, L. and Smith, M. B. (1956). *Psychoanal. Quart.* **25**, 385–414.
Bellak, L., Bellak, S. S. and Haworth, M. R. (1974). "Children's Apperception Test." C.P.S., Larchmont.
Bennet, G. K., Seashore, H. G. and Wesman, A. G. (2nd edn) (1962). "Differential Aptitude Tests." Psychological Corporation, New York.
Bennet, S. M. (1972). The relationship between personality, divergent abilities and academic attainment in ten-to-twelve-year-old children. Unpublished Ph.D. thesis, University of Lancaster.
Bergin, A. E. (1971). *In* "Handbook of Psychotherapy and Behaviour Change." (A. E. Bergin and S. Garfield, Eds) John Wiley and Sons, New York.
Bergin, A. E. and Garfield, S. (Eds) (1971). "Handbook of Psychotherapy and Behaviour Change." John Wiley and Sons, New York.
Berkley-Hill, O. (1921). *Int. J. Psychoanal.* **2**, 306–317.
Bernstein, B. (1967). *In* "Linking Home and School" (Craft, M. and Lytton, H., Eds) Longmans, London.
Berry, J. W. and Dasen, P. R. (1974). "Culture and Cognition: Readings in Cross-Cultural Psychology" Methuen, London.
Biesheuvel, S. (1949). *In* Price-Williams, P. R. (1969).
Biesheuvel, S. (1952). *S.A.J. Sci.* **49**, 25–30.
Biesheuvel, S. (1954). *Occup. Psychol.* **28**, 4–5.
Bilodeau, E. A. (Ed.) (1966). "Acquisition of Skill" Academic Press, London and New York.
Birnbaum, A. (1968). *In* Lord F. M. and Novick, M. R. (1968).
Bleuler, E. (1950). "Dementia Praecox" Allen and Unwin, London.
Blum, G. S. (1949). *Genet. Psychol. Monogr.* **39**, 3–99.
Bolardos, A. C. (1964). *Br. J. Soc. Clin. Psychol.* **3**, 148.
Bowlby, J. (1944). *Int. J. Psychoanal.* **25**, 1–57.
Bowlby, J. (1969). "Attachment and Loss" Vol. 1. Hogarth Press and Institute of Psychoanalysis, London.
Breger, L. and McGaugh, J. L. (1965). *Psychol. Bull.* **63**, 338–358.
Brimble, A. R. (1963). *Rhodesia Livingstone J.* **34**, 23–35.
Brislin, R. (1970). *J. Cross-cult. Psychol.* **1**, 185–216.
Bromley, E. and Lewis, L. A. (1976). *Br. J. Med. Psychol.* **49**, 325–328.
Brown, F. G. (1976). "Principles of Educational and Psychological Testing" Holt, Rinehart and Winston, New York.
Brown, G. W. (1974). *In* Dohrenwend, B. S. and Dohrenwend, B. P. (1974).
Browne, J. A. and Howarth, E. (1977). *Mult. Behav. Res.* **12**, 399–427.
Buck, J. N. (1948). *J. Clin. Psychol.* **4**, 151–159.
Buck, J. N. (1970). "The House Tree Person Technique: Revised Manual" W.P.S., Los Angeles.
Buck, J. N. and Hammer, E. F. (Ed.) (1969). "Advances in the House-Tree-Person Technique: Variations and Applications" West. Psychol. Serv, Los Angeles.

Burdsall, C. (1975). *J. Genet. Psychol.* **125**, 83–90.

Burgess, P. K. (1972). *Br. J. Criminol.* **12**, 74–82.

Buros, O. K. (Ed.) (1953). "The IVth Mental Measurement Yearbook" Gryphon Press, New Jersey.

Buros, O. K. (Ed.) (1959). "The Vth Mental Measurement Yearbook" Gryphon Press, New Jersey.

Buros, O. K. (1971). "Tests in Print" Gryphon Press, New Jersey.

Buros, O. K. (Ed.) (1972). "VIIth Mental Measurement Yearbook" Gryphon Press, New Jersey.

Buros, O. K. (1978). "The Eighth Mental Measurement Yearbook" Gryphon Press, New Jersey.

Burt, C. (1937). "The Backward Child" University of London Press, London.

Burt, C. (1940). "The Factors of the Mind" University of London Press, London.

Burt, C. (1966). *Br. J. Psychol.* **57**, 137–153.

Burt, C. and Howard, M. (1956). *Br. J. Stat. Psychol.* **9**, 95–131.

Butcher, H. J. (1973). *In* Kline, P. (1973).

Butcher, H. J. and Pont, H. B. (Ed.) (1973). "Educational Research in Britian" Vol. 3. University of London Press, London.

Caffelt, D. and Sweney, A. B. (1965). "Motivational dynamics of violent and non-violent criminals measured by behavioural tests" South West Psychology Association, Oklahoma.

Caine, T. M., Foulds, G. A. and Hope, K. (1967). "Manual of the Hostility-Direction of Hostility Questionnaire" University of London Press, London.

Campbell, D. P. (1971). "Handbook for the Strong Vocational Interest Blank" Stanford University Press, Stanford.

Campbell, D. T. and Fiske, D. W. (1959). *Psychol. Bull.* **56**, 81–105.

Campbell, D. T. and Narroll, R. (1972). *In* Hsu, F. L. H. (1972).

Carroll, J. B. (1975). *In* Resnik, R. B. (1976).

Carstairs, G. M. (1957). "The Twice Born: a Study of a Community of High Caste Hindus." Hogarth, London.

Cartwright, D. (1974). "Introduction to Personality." Rand McNally, Chicago.

Cattell, R. B. (1933). *Br. J. Psychol.* **24**, 20–49.

Cattell, R. B. (1943). *Am. J. Psychol.* **56**, 195–216.

Cattell, R. B. (1944). *Psychometrika* **9**, 267–283.

Cattell, R. B. (1946). "Description and Measurement of Personality" Harrap, London.

Cattell, R. B. (1949). *Psychometrika* **14**, 279–298.

Cattell, R. B. (1952). *In* Jackson, D. N. and Messick, S. (1967).

Cattell, R. B. (1957). "Personality and Motivation Structure and Measurement" World Book Co., Yonkers.

Cattell, R. B. (1960). *Psychol. Rev.* **67**, 357–372.

Cattell, R. B. (1963). *J. educ. Psychol.* **54**, 1–22.

Cattell, R. B. (1965). *In* Banks, C. and Broadhurst, P. L. (1965).

Cattell, R. B. (1965b). "The Scientific Analysis of Personality" Penguin, Harmondsworth.

Cattell, R. B. (1966). "Handbook of Multivariate Experimental Psychology" Rand McNally, Chicago.

Cattell, R. B. (1966b). *Multiv. Behav. Res.* **1**, 140–161.

Cattell, R. B. (1967a). *Br. J. educ. Psychol.* **37**, 209–224.

Cattell, R. B. (1967b) *Revue de Psychologie Appliquée* **17**, 135–154.

Cattell, R. B. (Ed.) (1971). "Handbook of Modern Personality Theory" University of Illinois Press, Urbana.

Cattell, R. B. (1971). "Abilities: Their Structure, Growth and Action" Houghton Mifflin, New York.

Cattell, R. B. (1973). "Personality and Mood by Questionnaire" Jersey Bass, New York.

Cattell, R. B. (1973b). A comparison of item and parcel factoring in four studies. *Adv. Pub.* No. **42**. Institute for Research on Morality and Adjustment, Boulder.

Cattell, R. B. (1975). *In* "Current Personality Theories" (Corsini, R. J., Ed.) Peacock Publications, New York.

Cattell, R. B. and Bolton, L. S. (1969). *J. Consult. Clin. Psychol.* **33**, 18–29.

Cattell, R. B. and Butcher, H. J. (1968). "The Prediction of Achievement and Creativity" Bobbs Merrill, New York.

Cattell, R. B. and Cattell, A. K. S. (1955). *Br. J. Stat. Psychol.* **8**, 83–92.

Cattell, R. B. and Cattell, A. K. S. (1959). "Handbook for the Culture Fair Intelligence Test" IPAT, Champaign.

Cattell, R. B. and Cattell, A. K. S. (1960). "The Culture Fair Intelligence Test: Scales 2 and 3" IPAT, Champaign.

Cattell, R. B. and Child, D. (1975). "Motivation and Dynamic Structure" Holt, Rinehart and Winston, London.

Cattell, R. B. and Cross, P. (1952). *J. Personal.* **21**, 250–270.

Cattell, R. B. and Delhees, K. H. (1973). *Multiv. Behav. Res.* **8**, 173–194.

Cattell, R. B. and Foster, M. J. (1963). *Behav. Sci.* **8**, 156–165.

Cattell, R. B. and Gibbons, B. D. (1968). *J. Pers. soc. Psychol.* **9**, 107–120.

Cattell, R. B. and Horn, J. (1963). *Genet. Psychol. Monogr.* **16**, 89–149.

Cattell, R. B. and Kline, P. (1977). "The Scientific Analysis of Personality and Motivation," Academic Press, London and New York.

Cattell, R. B. and Marshall, D. W. (1973). "Supplement to the 16 PF Handbook." IPAT, Champaign.

Cattell, R. B. and Muerle, J. L. (1960). *Educ. Psychol. Meas.* **20**, 569–590.

Cattell, R. B. and Nesselroade, J. R. (1976). *Multiv. Behav. Res.* **11**, 27–46.

Cattell, R. B. and Scheier, I. H. (1961). "The Meaning and Measurement of Neuroticism and Anxiety" Ronald Press, New York.

Cattell, R. B. and Sweney, A. B. (1964). *J. Abnorm. Soc. Psychol.* **68**, 479–490.

Cattell, R. B. and Tatro, D. F. (1966). *Behav. Res. Therap.* **4**, 39–51.

Cattell, R. B. and Vaughan, D. (1973). A large sample cross-check on the factor structure of the 16 PF by item and by parcel factoring. *Adv. Pub. No.* **41**. Institute for Research on Morality and Adjustment, Boulder.

Cattell, R. B. and Warburton, F. W. (1967). "Objective Personality and Motivation Tests" University of Illinois Press, Urbana.

Cattell, R. B., Cattell, A. K. S. and Rhymer, R. M. (1947). *Psychometrika* **12**, 267–288.

Cattell, R. B., Horn, J. and Butcher, H. J. (1962). *Br. J. Psychol.* **53**, 57–69.

Cattell, R. B., Eber, H. W. and Tatsuoka, M. M. (1970). "Handbook for the Sixteen Personality Factor Questionnaire" IPAT, Champaign.

Cattell, R. B., Horn, J. L. and Sweney, A. B. (1970). "Motivation Analysis Test" IPAT, Champaign.

Cattell, R. B., Kawash, G. F. and De Young, G. E. (1972). *J. Exp. Res. Person.* **6**, 76–83.

Cattell, R. B., Schmidt, L. R. and Bjerstedt, A. (1972). *Clin. Psychol. Monogr.* **34**, 1–78.

Cepelak, J. (1973). Cited in Eysenck, H. J. and Eysenck, S. B. G. (1976).

Chapman, J. (1966). *Br. J. Psychiat.* **112**, 225–251.

Cheshire, N. M. (1975). "The Nature of Psychodynamic Interpretation" John Wiley and Sons, Chichester.

Child, D. (1971). "Essentials of Factor Analysis" Holt, Rinehart and Winston, London.

Clyde, D. J. (1963). "Clyde Mood Scale" University of Miami, Miami.

Cochrane, R. (1974). *Bull. Br. Psychol. Soc.* **27**, 19–22.

Cole, M., Gay, J, Glick, J. and Sharp, D. W. (1971)." The Cultural Content of Learning and Thinking". Basic Books, New York.

Colson, E. (1962). "The Plateau Tonga" Manchester University Press, Manchester.

Comrey, A. L. (1961). *Educ. Psychol. Meas.* **21**, 414–431.

Comrey, A. L. (1970). "The Comrey Personality Scales" Educational and Industrial Testing Service, San Diego.

Comrey, A. L. and Duffy, K. E. (1968). *Multiv. Behav. Res.* **3**, 379–392.

Corah, N. L., Feldman, M. J., Cohen, I. S., Green, W., Meadow, A. and Rugwall, E. A. (1958). *J. Consult. Psychol.* **22**, 70–72.

Corman, L. (1967). "Le Gribouillis" Presses Universitaires de France, Paris.

Corman, L. (1969). "Le test P. N. Manuel" Presses Universitaires de France, Paris.

Cortis, G. A. (1968). *Br. J. educ. Psychol.* **38**, 115–120.

Cortot, A. (1935). *Music and Letters* **16**, 124–128.

Cronbach, L. J. (1946). *Educ. Psychol. Meas.* **6**, 475–494.

Cronbach, L. J. (1950). *Educ. Psychol. Meas.* **10**, 3–31.

Cronbach, L. J. (1970). "Essentials of Psychological Testing" Harper and Row, New York.

Cronbach, L. J. and Meehl, P. E. (1955). *Psychol. Bull.* **52**, 281–302.

Cronbach, L. J., Gleser, G. C., Nanda, H. and Rajaratnam, N. (1972). "The Dependability of Behavioural Measurements: Theory of Generalisability for Scores and Profiles." John Wiley and Sons, New York.

Cropley, A. J. (1968). *Br. J. Educ. Psychol.* **38**, 197–201.

Crossman E. R. F. W. (1964). *Br. Med. Bull.* **20**, 32–37.

Crow, J. F. (1970). *In* "Psychological Factors in Poverty" (V. F. Allen, Ed.) Markham, Chicago.

Curran, J. P. (1968). Dimensions of state change in Q data, and chain-P technique on 20 women. Unpublished M.A. thesis. University of Illinois.

Curran, J. P. and Cattell, R. B. (1974). "The Eight State Questionnaire" IPAT, Champaign.

Dahlstrom, W. G. and Welsh, G. S. (1960). "An M.M.P.I. Handbook" Oxford University Press, London.

Darlington, C. P. (1970). *Heridity* **25**, 655–656.

Dasen, P. R. (1977). "Cross-cultural Piagetian Psychology." (Warren, N. Ed.) pp. 155–201. Academic Press, London and New York.

Davis, H. (1974). *Br. J. Psychiat.* **125**, 61–67.

D'Andrade, E. M., De Godoy Alves, O and Ford, J. J. (1969). *Int. J. Psychol.* **4**, 55–58.

Delhees, K. H. and Cattell, R. B. (1971). *Personality* **2**, 149–171.

Delhees, K. H. and Cattell, R. B. (1971b). "The Clinical Analysis Questionnaire" IPAT, Champaign.

Deregowski, J. B. (1968). *Br. J. Psychol.* **59**, 195–204.

Derogatis, L. R. and Cleary, P. A. (1977). *Br. J. Soc. Clin. Psychol.* **16**, 347–356.

Derogatis, L. R., Lipman, R. S. and Covi, L. (1973). *Psychopharm. Bull.* **9**, 13–27.

De Voogd, A. and Cattell, R. B. (1973). Cited in Cattell, R. B. (1973).

De Young, G. E. and Cattell, R. B. (1973). The effect of underfactoring upon the proportion of pseudo second order factors in Rotational Resolutions. *Adv. Pub.* No. **44**. Institute for Research on Morality and Adjustment, Boulder.

Dixon, N. F. (1971). "Subliminal Perception: the Nature of a Controversy." McGraw-Hill, London and New York.

Dixon, N. F. (1976). "The Psychology of Military Incompetence." McGraw-Hill, London and New York.

Dockrell B. (Ed.) (1970). "On Intelligence" Toronto Institute Studies in Education, Toronto.

Dohrenwend, B. S. and Dohrenwend, B. P. (Eds.) (1974). "Stressful Life Events: their nature and effects." John Wiley and Sons, Chichester.

Dollard, J. and Miller, N. E. (1950). "Personality and Psychotherapy" McGraw-Hill, New York.

Dollard, J., Doob, L. W., Miller, N. E., Mowrer, O. H. and Sears, R. R. (1939). "Frustration and Aggression" Yale University Press, New Haven.

Dolliver, R. H. (1969). *Psychol. Bull.* **72**, 95–107.

Dreger, R. M. (Ed.) (1972). "Multivariate Personality Research" Claitor Publishers, Baton Rouge.

Du Bois, C. (1944). "The People of Alor" University of Minnesota Press, Minneapolis.

Eaves, L. J. (1973). *Heredity* **30**, 199–210.

Eberhard, G. (1964). *Psychol. Res. Bull.* (Lund. University) **IV**, 8.

Edwards, A. L. (1957). "The Social Desirability Variable in Personality Research" Dryden Press, New York.

Edwards, A. L. (1959). "The Edwards Personal Preference Schedule" Psychological Corporation, New York.

Edwards, A. L. (1967). "Edwards Personality Inventory" Science Research Associates, Chicago.

Entwistle, N. J. (1972). *Br. J. educ. Psychol.* **42**, 137–151.

Erickson, E. H. (1950). "Childhood and Society" Norton, New York.

Erikson, E. H. (1956). *J. Am. Psychoanal. Ass.* **4**, 56–121.

Evans-Pritchard, E. E. (1936). "Witchcraft, Oracles and Magic among the Azande" Clarendon Press, Oxford.

Evans-Pritchard, E. E. (1940). "The Nuer: a description of the modes of livelihood and political institutions of a Nilotic people" Clarendon Press, Oxford.

Eysenck, H. J. (1952). *J. Consult. Psychol.* **16**, 319–324.

Eysenck, H. J. (1952b). "The Scientific Study of Personality" Routledge and Kegan Paul, London.

Eysenck, H. J. (1953). "Uses and `Abuses of Psychology" Penguin Books, Harmondsworth.

Eysenck, H. J. (1954). "The Psychology of Politics" Routledge and Kegan Paul, London.

Eysenck, H. J. (1957). "The Dynamics of Anxiety and Hysteria" Praeger, New York.

Eysenck, H. J. (1959). "Maudsley Personality Inventory" University of London Press, London.

Eysenck, H. J. (1959). *In* Buros, O. K. (1959).

Eysenck, H. J. (1960). "Handbook of Abnormal Psychology" Pitman, London.

Eysenck, H. J. (1964). "Crime and Personality" Routledge and Kegan Paul, London.

Eysenck, H. J. (1965). "Smoking, Health and Personality" Basic Books, New York.

Eysenck, H. J. (1965b). *Int. J. Psychiat.* **1**, 99–142.

Eysenck, H. J. (1966). *Bull. Br. Psychol. Soc.* **62**, 1–28.

Eysenck, H. J. (1967). *Br. J. Educ. Psychol.* **37**, 81–98.

Eysenck, H. J. (1967b). "The Biological Basis of Personality" C. C. Thomas, Springfield.

Eysenck, H. J. (1967c). *In* Jackson, D. N. and Messick, S. (1967).

Eysenck, H. J. (1970). "Readings in Introversion Extraversion 1" Staples Press, London.

Eysenck, H. J. (1970b). "The Structure of Human Personality" Methuen, London.

Eysenck, H. J. (1971). "Race, Intelligence and Education" Temple Smith, London.

Eysenck, H. J. (1972). *Bull. Br. Psychol. Soc.* **25**, 261–268.

Eysenck, H. J. (1973). "The Measurement of Intelligence" MTP Press, Lancaster.
Eysenck, H. J. (Ed.) (1973). "Handbook of Abnormal Psychology" Pitman Medical, London.
Eysenck, H. J. (1976). *Behav. Res. Therap.* **14**, 251–268.
Eysenck, H. J. (1977). *Psychol. Bull.* **84**, 405–411.
Eysenck, H. J. and Cookson, D. (1969). *Br. J. educ. Psychol.* **39**, 109–122.
Eysenck, H. J. and Eysenck, S. B. G. (1964). "The E.P.I." University of London Press, London.
Eysenck, H. J. and Eysenck, S. B. G. (1965b). "Manual to the E.P.I." University of London Press, London.
Eysenck, H. J. and Eysenck, S. B. G. (1969). "Personality Structure and Measurement" Routledge and Kegan Paul, London.
Eysenck, H. J. and Eysenck, S. B. G. (1975). "The E.P.Q." University of London Press, London.
Eysenck, H. J. and Eysenck, S. B. G. (1976). "Psychoticism as a dimension of Personality" Hodder and Stoughton, London.
Eysenck, H. J. and Rachmann, S. (1965). "The Causes and Cures of Neurosis" Routledge and Kegan Paul, London.
Eysenck, S. B. G. and Eysenck, H. J. (1963). *Br. J. Soc. Clin. Psychol.* **2**, 46–55.
Eysenck, S. B. G. and Eysenck, H. J. (1974). *Br. J. Crim.* **14**, 385–387.
Eysenck, S. B. G. and Eysenck, H. J. (1977). *Br. J. Soc. Clin. Psychol.* **16**, 57–68.
Eysenck, S. B. G., Adelaya, O. and Eysenck, H. J. (1977). *J. soc. Psychol.* **102**, 3–10.
Eysenck, S. B. G., Rust, J. and Eysenck, H. J. (1977). *Br. J. Criminol.* **17**, 169–179.
Fallstrom, K. (1974). *Acta Paedmt. Suppl.* 251.
Fallstrom K. and Vegilius, J. (1976). A discriminatory analysis based on dischotomised Rorschach scores of diabetic children. Unpublished MS. University of Gotëborg.
Fan, Chung-Teh (1952). "Item Analysis Tables" E.T.S., Princeton.
Feldman, F. W. and Lewontin, R. C. (1975). *Science* **190**, 1163–1168.
Fenichel, O. (1945). "The Psychoanalytic Theory of Neurosis" Norton, New York.
Fineman, S. (1977). *Br. J. Psychol.* **68**, 1–22.
Finney, J. C. (1961). *J. Consult. Psychol.* **25**, 327–336.
Fisher, R. A. (1918). *Trans. Roy. Soc.* (Edinburgh) **52**, 399–433.
Fisher, S. and Cleveland, S. E. (1958). "Body Image and Personality" Van Nostrand, Princeton.
Fisher, S. and Greenberg, R. P. (1977). "The Scientific Credibility of Freud's theories and therapy" Harvester Press, Sussex.
Fiske, D. (1971). Cited in Cattell, R. B. (1971).
Fleishman, E. A. (1966). *In* Bilodeau, E. A. (1966).
Flugel, J. C. (1945). "Man, Morals and Society" Duckworth, London.
Foster, P. J. (1965). "Education and Social Change in Ghana" Routledge and Kegan Paul, London.
Foulds, G. A. (1976). "The Hierarchical Nature of Personal Illness" Academic Press, London and New York.
Foulds, G. A. and Bedford, A. (1975). *Psychol. Med.* **5**, 181–192.
Foulds, G. A. and Bedford, A. (1976). *In* Foulds, G. A. (1976).
Foulds, G. A. and Bedford, A. (1977). *Br. J. Med. Psychol.* **50**, 73–78.
Foulds, G. A. and Hope, K. (1968). "Manual of the symptom-sign Inventory" University of London Press, London.
Freedman, A. M. and Kaplan, H. I. (1967), "Comprehensive Textbook of Psychiatry" Williams and Wilkins, Baltimore.

French, J. W., Ekstrom, R. B. and Price, L. A. (1963). "Kit of Reference Tests for Cognitive Factors" E.T.S., Princeton.

Freud, S. (1900). "The Standard Edition of the Complete Psychological Works of Sigmund Freud" Vols 4 and 5. Hogarth Press and Institute of Psychoanalysis, London.

Freud, S. (1905). Vol. 7, pp. 135–243. Hogarth Press and Institute of Psychoanalysis, London.

Freud, S. (1908). Vol. 9, p. 169. Hogarth Press and Institute of Psychoanalysis, London.

Freud, S. (1911). Vol. 12, p. 3. Hogarth Press and Institute for Psychoanalysis, London.

Freud, S. (1913). Vol. 13. Hogarth Press and Institute of Psychoanalysis, London.

Freud, S. (1916). Vols 15 and 16. Hogarth Press and Institute of Psychoanalysis, London.

Freud, S. (1933). Vol. 22. Hogarth Press and Institute of Psychoanalysis, London.

Freud, S. (1940). Vol. 23, p. 141. Hogarth Press and Institute of Psychoanalysis, London.

Frigon, J. Y. (1976). *Br. J. Psychol.* **67**, 467–474.

Fromm, E. (1949). "Man for Himself" Routledge and Kegan Paul, London.

Fromm, E. (1974). "The Anatomy of Human Destructiveness" Jonathan Cape, London.

Fruchter, B. (1954). "An Introduction to Factor Analysis" Van Nostrand, New York.

Fulgosi, A. and Guilford, J. P. (1972). *J. Gen. Psychol.* **87**, 169–180.

Fulker, D. (1975). *Am. J. Psychol.* **88**, 505–537.

Furth, H. G. (1969). "Piaget and Knowledge: theoretical foundations" Prentice-Hall, New Jersey.

Gagné, R. M. (1962). *Psychol. Rev.* **69**, 355–365.

Gagné, R. M. (1965). "Psychological Principles in System Development" Holt, Rinehart and Winston, New York.

Garn, S. M. (1971). "Human Races" Thomas, Springfield.

Gates, A. I. and MacGintie, W. H. (1965). "The Gates-MacGintie Reading Tests" Teachers College Press, Columbia.

Getzells, J. W. and Jackson, P. W. (1962). "Creativity and Intelligence: Exploration with Gifted Students" John Wiley and Sons, Chichester.

Ghiselli, E. E. (1966). "The validity of occupational aptitude tests" Wiley, New York.

Gilmer, B. V. H. (1966). "Industrial Psychology" McGraw-Hill, New York.

Glover, E. (Ed.) (1956). *In* "On the Early Development of Mind" Imago, London.

Gluckman, M. (1944). *Rhod. Sci. J.* **1**, 61.

Gluckman, M. (1962). "Essays on the Ritual of Social Relations" Manchester University Press, Manchester.

Goldberg, D. P. (1972). "The detection of Psychiatric Illness by Questionnaire" Oxford University Press, London.

Gordon, H. (1923). "Mental and Scholastic Tests among Retarded Children" H.M.S.O., London.

Gottheil, E. (1965). *J. Nerv. Ment. Dis.* **141**, 308–317.

Gough, H. G. (1969). "The Californian Psychological Inventory" Consulting Psychologists Press, Palo Alto.

Gray, J. A. (Ed.) (1964). *In* "Pavlov's Typology" pp. 157–287. Pergamon, Oxford.

Gray, J. A. (1967). *Behav. Res. Therap.* **5**, 151–169.

Gray, J. A. (1973). *In* Royce, J. R. (1973).

Grove, G. (1954). *In* "Dictionary of music and musicians" (Blom, F. Ed.) Macmillan, London.

Grygier, T. F. (1961). "The Dynamic Personality Inventory" N.F.E.R., Windsor.

Grygier, T. G., (1970). "The Dynamic Personality Inventory: Experimental Manual" N.F.E.R., Windsor.

Grygier, T. G. and Grygier, P. (1976). "Manual to the Dynamic Personality Inventory" N.F.E.R., Windsor.

Guertin, W. H. (1952). *J. Consult. Psychol.* **14**, 371–375.

Guilford, J. P. (1956). "Psychometric Methods" McGraw-Hill, New York.

Guilford, J. P. (1958). "Fundamental Statistics in Psychology and Education" McGraw-Hill, London.

Guilford, J. P. (1959). "Personality" McGraw-Hill, London.

Guilford, J. P. (1959b). *Am. Psychol.* **14**, 469–479.

Guilford, J. P. (1967). "The Nature of Human Intelligence" McGraw-Hill, New York.

Guilford, J. P. (1975). *Psychol. Bull.* **82**, 803–814.

Guilford, J. P. (1977). *Psychol. Bull.* **84**, 412–416.

Guilford, J. P. and Guilford, R. B. (1934). *J. Abnorm. Soc. Psychol.* **28**, 377–399.

Guilford, J. P. and Guilford, R. B. (1936). *J. Psychol.* **2**, 109–127.

Guilford, J. P. and Hoepfner, R. (1971). "The Analysis of Intelligence" McGraw-Hill, New York.

Guilford, J. P. and Zimmerman, W. S. (1949). "Manual of Instructions and Interpretations" Sheridan, Beverly Hills.

Guilford, J. P. and Zimmerman, W. S. (1956). *Psychol. Monogr.* **70**, 1–26.

Guilford, J. S., Zimmerman, W. S. and Guilford, J. P. (Eds) (1976). "The Guilford Zimmerman Temperament Survey Handbook" Sheridan, San Diego.

Gupta, B. S. (1976). *Br. J. Psychol.* **67**, 47–52.

Guttman, L. (1954). *Psychometrika* **19**, 149–161.

Guttman, L. (1954b). *In* Lazarsfeld, P. F. (1954).

Guttman, L. (1955). *Psychometrika* **20**, 173–192.

Guttman, L. (1957). *Educ. Psychol. Meas.* **17**, 391–407.

Guttman, L. (1966). *In* Cattell, R. B. (1966).

Hakstian, A. R. (1970). *Educ. Psych. Meas.* **30**, 699–701.

Hakstian, A. R. (1971). *Psychometrika* **36**, 175–193.

Hakstian, A. R. and Cattell, R. B. (1974). *Br. J. Educ. Psychol.* **44**, 140–154.

Hall, C. S. and Lindzey, G. (1957). "Theories of Personality" Wiley, New York.

Hamilton, V. (1968). *Research in Higher Education.* Society for Research into Higher Education, London.

Hamilton, V. (1970). *Br. J. Psychol.* **61**, 229–241.

Hammond, K. R. (1970). Cited in "Handbook for Sixteen PF Questionnaire" by R. B. Cattell, H. W. Eber and M. M. Tatsuoka (1970).

Hampson, S. (1975). The Personality Characteristics of Certain Groups of Mentally Abnormal Offenders. Unpublished Ph.D. thesis. University of Exeter, Exeter.

Hampson, S. and Kline, P. (1977). *Br. J. Criminol.* **17**, 310–331.

Hampson, S. and Kline, P. (1977b). "Personality Characteristics of Abnormal Offenders" In Preparation.

Harman, H. H. (1964). "Modern Factor Analysis" University of Chicago Press, Chicago.

Harman, H. H. and French, J. W. (1973). *E.T.S. Tech-Report* PR-73-29.

Harris, C. W. and Kaiser, H. F. (1964). *Psychomet.* **29**, 347–362.

Harris, M. L. and Harris, C. W. (Eds) (1971). *In* "A Structure of Concept Attainment Abilities" University of Wisconsin, Wisconsin.

Hartog, P. and Rhodes, E. C. (1935) "An Examination of Examinations" Macmillan, London.

Hasan, P. and Butcher, H. J. (1966). *Br. J. Psychol.* **57**, 129–135.

Hathaway, S. R. and McKinley, J. C. (1957). "The Minnesota Multiphasic Personality Inventory Manual" Psychological Corporation, New York.

Heilbrun, A. B. (1972). *In* Buros, O. K. (1922).

Heim, A. W. (1975). "Psychological Testing" Oxford University Press, London.

Heim, A. W., Watts, K. P. and Simmonds, V. (1969). "Brook Reaction Test" N.F.E.R., Windsor.

Heim, A. W., Watts, K. P. and Simmonds, V. (1970). "AH4, AH5 and AH6 Tests" N.F.E.R., Windsor.

Heim, A. W., Unwin, S. M. and Watts, K. P. (1977). *Br. J. Soc. Clin. Psychol.* **16**, 253–268.

Henderson and Gillespie, R. D. (1956). "A Test-Book of Psychiatry" Oxford University Press, London.

Hendrickson, A. E. and White, P. O. (1964). *Br. J. Stat. Psychol.* **17**, 65–70.

Henry, W. E. (1947). *Genet. Psychol. Monogr.* **35**, 3–135.

Hentschel, U., Schubo, W. and Zerssen, D. V. (1976). *Arch. Psychiat. Nemenbr.* **221**, 283–301.

Hinde, R. A. and Spencer-Booth, Y. (1970). *J. Child Psychol. Psychiat.* **11**, 159–176.

Hogan, R., Desuto, C. B. and Solano, C. (1977). *Am. Psychol.* **32**, 255–265.

Holland, J. L. (1965). "Vocational Preference Inventory" Consulting Psychologists Press, Palo Alto.

Holley, J. W. (1964). *Scand. J. Psychol.* **5**, 143–148.

Holley, J. W. (1973). *In* Kline, P. (1973).

Holley, J. W. (1975). *Psychol. Res. Bull.* (Lund University) **XV**, 10.

Holley, J. W. and Guilford, J. P. (1964). *Educ. Psychol. Meas.* **24**, 749–753.

Holley, J. W. and Harris, C. W. (1970). *Scand. J. Psychol.* **11**, 255–260.

Holley, J. W. and Kline, P. (1976a). *Scand. J. Psychol.* **17**, 149–152.

Holley, J. W. and Kline, P. (1976b). *Scand. J. Psychol.* **17**, 246–250.

Holley, J. W. and Nilsson, I. K. (1973). *Psychol. Press. Bull.* (Lund University) **13**, 4.

Holmstrom, L. G. (1963). "Musicality and Prognosis" Almquist and Wiksells, Uppsala.

Holtzman, W. H. (1968). *In* Rabin, A. I. (1968).

Holzinger, K. J. (1929). *J. Educ. Psychol.* **20**, 245–248.

Honess, T. and Kline, P. (1974a). *Br. J. Educ. Psychol.* **44**, 74–75.

Honess, T. and Kline, P. (1974b). *Br. J. Soc. Clin. Psychol.* **13**, 96–98.

Horn, J. L. (1967). *Educ. Psychol. Meas.* **27**, 811–820.

Horn, J. L. (1972). *In* Dreger, R. M. (1972).

Horn, J. L. (1976). *Ann. Rev. Psychol.* **27**, 437–485.

Horn, J. L. and Cattell, R. B. (1966). *J. Educ. Psychol.* **57**, 253–270.

Horn, J. L. and Cattell, R. B. (1967). *Acta Psychol.* **26**, 107–129.

Horn, J. L. and Donaldson, G. (1976). *Am. Psychol.* **31**, 701–719.

Horn, J. L. and Knapp, J. R. (1973). *Psychol. Bull.* **80**, 33–43.

Horney, K. (1939). "New Ways in Psychoanalysis" Norton, New York.

Hosseini, A. A. and Mehryar, A. A. (1973). *J. Genet. Psychol.* **122**, 197–205.

Hotelling, H. (1936). *Biometrika* **28**, 321–377.

Howarth, E. (1976). *Br. J. Psychol.* **67**, 213–230.

Howarth, E. (In Press) Technical Background and User Information for State and Trait Inventories" University of Alberta, Alberta.

Howarth, E. and Browne, J. A. (1971a). *Can. J. Behav. Sci.* **3**, 161–173.

Howarth, E. and Browne, J. A. (1971b). *Person. Int. J.* **2**, 117–139.

Howe, M. J. (Ed.) (1977). "Adult Learning" Wiley, Chichester.

Howells, J. G. and Lickorish, J. R. (1962). "The Family Relations Indicator" Oliver and Boyd, Edinburgh.

Hoyt, C. (1941). *Psychometrika* **6**, 153–160.
Hsu, F. L. H. (1972). "Psychological Anthropology" Schenbmann, Cambridge, Massachusetts.
Hudson, L. (1960). *Br. J. Psychol.* **51**, 57–63.
Hudson, L. (1966). "Contrary Imaginations" Methuen, London.
Hudson, L. (1974). *In* Kamin, L. J. (1974).
Hudson, W. (1960). *J. Soc. Psychol.* **52**, 183–208.
Hudson, W. (1967). *Int. J. Psychol.* **2**, 89–107.
Hull, C. L. (1943). "Principles of Behaviour" Appleton-Century Crofts, New York.
Hundal, P. S. (1970). "Rorschach Proceedings" Vol. VII, pp. 173–179. Hans Huber, Berne.
Hunt, E. (1971). *Cognitive Psychol.* **2**, 57–98.
Hunt, E. (1973). *In* "Computer Models of Thought and Language" (Schank, R. and Colby, K., Eds) Freeman, San Francisco.
Hunt, E. (1976). *In* Resnik, R. B. (1976).
Hunt, E., Frost, N. and Lunneborg, C. (1973). *In* "Psychology of Learning and Motivation" (Bower, G. R. Ed.) Vol. 7. Academic Press, New York and London.
Hunt, E., Lunneborg, C. and Lewis, J. (1975). *Cognit. Psychol.* **7**, 194–227.
Hurley, J. R. and Cattell, R. B. (1962). *Behav. Sci.* **7**, 258–262.
Irvine, S. H. (1969a). *J. Biosoc. Sci.* Suppl. 1. 91–102.
Irvine, S. H. (1969b). *Psychol. Bull.* **71**, 20–32.
Irvine, S. H. (1970). *J. Soc. Psychol.* **80**, 23–30.
Iwawaki, S., Eysenck, S. B. G. and Eysenck, H. J. (1977). *J. Soc. Psychol.* **102**, 27–33.
Jackson, D. N. (1967). "Personality Research Form" Research Psychologists Press, New York.
Jackson, D. N. and Messick, S. (1961). *Educ. Psychol. Meas.* **21**, 771–790.
Jackson, D. N. and Messick, S. (Eds.) (1967). "Problems in Human Assessment" McGraw-Hill, New York.
Jahoda, G. (1954). *Br. J. Psychol.* **45**, 192–195.
Jalota, S. (1957). *Science and Culture* **23**, 22–23.
Jalota, S. (1964). *Br. J. Soc. Clin. Psychol.* **3**, 148.
James, W. (1890). "Principles of Psychology" Holt, Rinehart and Winston, New York.
Janson, S. and Vegelius, J. (In Press). *Psychometrika.*
Jencks, C. (1973). "Inequality: A Reassessment of the Effects of Family and Schooling in America" Allen Lane, London.
Jensen, A. R. (1964). "Individual differences in learning: Interference factor" *U.S. Health Education and Welfare Project.* Report no. 1867.
Jensen, A. R. (1970). *Behav. Genet.* **1**, 113–146.
Jensen, A. R. (1972). "Genetics and Education" Methuen, London.
Jensen, A. R. (1974). *J. Educ. Psychol.* **66**, 99–111.
Jensen, A. R. (1974). *Behav. Genet.* **4**, 1–28.
Jinks, J. L. and Eaves, L. J. (1974). *Nature* **248**, 287–289.
Jinks, J. L. and Fulker, D. W. (1970). *Psychol. Bull.* **73**, 311–349.
Joe, V. C. (1971). *Psychol. Reports* **28**, 619–640.
Jolles, I. (1964). "A catalogue for the qualitative interpretation of the HTP" W.P.S., Beverly Hills.
Jones, E. (Ed.) (1923) *In* "Papers on Psychoanalysis" Baillière, Tindall and Cox, London.
Jones, H. G. (1960). *In* "Handbook of Abnormal Psychology" (Eysenck, H. J., Ed.) Basic Books, New York.

Jonsson, H. (1975). *Scand. J. Psychol.* **16**, 125–130.

Jonsson, H. and Franzen, G. (1976). *Psychol. Res. Bull.* **16**, (Lund University) 1.

Juel-Nielsen, N. (1965). *Acta Psychiat. neurolog. Scand.* Suppl. 183.

Jung, C. G. (1918). "Studies in Word Association" Heinemann, London.

Jung, C. G. (1923). "Psychological Types" Harcourt Brace, New York.

Kaiser, H. F. (1958). *Psychometrika* **23**, 187–200.

Kamin, L. J. (1974). "The Science and Politics of I.Q." Penguin Books, Harmondsworth.

Kapoor, S. D. (1964). *Psychol. Stud.* **9**, 124–132.

Katz, M. M., Cole, J. O. and Barton, W. E. (Eds) (1968). "The role and methodology of classification in psychiatry and psychopathology" National Institute Mental Health, Cherry Case.

Katz, M. R. (1972). *In* Buros, O. K. (1972).

Kaufman, R. V. and Herster, B. (1971). *Pediatrics* **38**, 123–128.

Kaye, B. (1962). "Bringing up Children in Ghana: an impressionistic survey" Allen and Unwin, London.

Kiesler, D. J. (1966). *Psychol. Bull.* **65**, 110–136.

Kilbride, P. L. and Robbins, M. C. (1969). *Am. Anthrop.* **71**, 293–301.

Kleinsmith, L. J. and Kaplan, S. (1964). *J. exp. Psychol.* **67**, 124–126.

Kleinsmith, L. J. and Kaplan, S. (1963). *J. exp. Psychol.* **65**, 190–193.

Kline, P. (1966). *Br. J. educ. Psychol.* **36**, 93–94.

Kline, P. (1967). *Br. J. Med. Psychol.* **40**, 193–197.

Kline, P. (1967b). *Br. J. Soc. Clin. Psychol.* **6**, 97–107.

Kline, P. (1968). *Br. J. Med. Psychol.* **41**, 307–311.

Kline, P. (1968b). An investigation of the Freudian concept of the anal character. Unpublished Ph.D. thesis. University of Manchester.

Kline, P. (1969). *Br. J. Soc. Clin. Psychol.* **8**, 201–210.

Kline, P. (1971). "Ai3Q Test" N.F.E.R., Windsor.

Kline, P. (Ed.) (1973). "New Approaches in Psychological Measurement" John Wiley and Sons, Chichester.

Kline, P. (1975). "The Psychology of Vocational Guidance" Batsford, London.

Kline, P. (1975b). "Personality Theories and Dimensions" Open University Press, Milton Keynes.

Kline, P. (1976). "Psychological Testing" Malaby Press, London.

Kline, P. (1976b). *Br. J. Project. Psychol.* **21**, 23–29.

Kline, P. (1977). "The Vampire Test" Unpublished. University of Exeter.

Kline, P. (1977b). *In* Warren, N. (1977).

Kline, P. (1978). *In* Buros, O. K. (1978).

Kline, P. (1978). *Br. J. Med. Psychol.* **51**, 87–90.

Kline, P. and Cooper, C. (1977). *Scand. J. Psychol.* **18**, 148–152.

Kline, P. and Gale, A. M. (1971). *Br. J. Educ. Psychol.* **41**, 90–93.

Kline, P. and Grindley, J. (1974). *J. Mult. Exp. Person. Clin. Psychol.* **1**, 13–32.

Kline, P. and Mohan, J. (1974). *J. soc. Psychol.* **94**, 137–138.

Kline, P. and Storey, R. (1977). *Br. J. Soc. Clin. Psychol.* **16**, 317–328.

Kline, P. and Storey, R. (1978). *Br. J. Psychol.* **69**, 375–383.

Kline, P. and Storey, R. (1978). "OPQ & OOQ" In Press.

Kline, P., Mohan, J. and Storey, R. (In Press). *Psychol. Stud.*

Klopfer, B. (1956). "Developments in the Rorschach Technique" Vol. II. Harcourt Brace, Jovanovich, New York.

Knapp, R. J. (1976). *Psychol. Bull.* **83**, 194–212.

Kraepelin, E. (1907). "Clinical Psychiatry" Collier, Macmillan, New York

Kragh, U. and Smith, G. (1970). "Percept-Genetic Analysis" Gleerups, Lund.

Kretschmer, E. (1925). "Physique and Character" Routledge and Kegan Paul, London.
Kuder, G. F. (1970). "Kuder General Interest Survey" Science Research Associates, Chicago.
Lacey, J. I. (1967). *In* Appley, M. H. and Trumbull, R. (1967).
Laing, R. D. (1960). "The Divided Self" Tavistock, London.
Lazare, A., Klerman, G. L. and Armor, D. J. (1966). *Arch Gen. Psychiat.* **14**, 624–630.
Lazarsfeld, P. F. (1950). Cited in Stoufer, S. (1950).
Lazarsfeld, P. F. (Ed.) (1954). "Mathematical thinking in the social sciences" Illinois Free Press, Glencoe.
Lee, S. G. (1953). "Manual of a Thematic Apperception Test for African Subjects" University of Natal Press, Pietermantzburg.
Levonian, E. (1961). *Educ. Psychol. Meas.* **21**, 937–946.
Levy, P. (1960). *Scand. J. Psychol.* **7**, 239–243.
Levy, P. (1973). *In* Kline, P. (1973).
Lewis, D. G. (1966). *Br. J. Psychol.* **57**, 431–434.
Lindzey, G. (1961). "Projective Techniques and Cross-Cultural Research" Appleton-Century Crofts, New York.
Liu, P. Y. H. and Meredith, G. M. (1966). *J. soc. Psychol.* **70**, 165–166.
Loehlin, J. C., Lindzey, G. and Spuhler, J. N. (1975). "Race Differences in Intelligence" Freeman, San Francisco.
Loftus, E. (1973). "How to catch a Zebra in Semantic Memory" Paper at Minneapolis Conference on Cognition.
Lord, F. M. and Novick, M. R. (1968). "Statistical Theories of Mental Test Scores" Addison-Wesley, New York.
Lorenz, K. (1966). "On Aggression" Methuen, London.
Lorr, M. (1968). Cited in Katz, M. M., Cole, J. D. and Barton, W. E. (1968).
Lorr, M. and Klett, C. J. (1967). "Manual for the Impatient Multidimensional Psychiatric Scale" Consulting Psychological Press, Palo Alto.
Love, T. (1973). Information Processing Characteristics of Good Memorisers Unpublished M.A. Thesis. University of Washington.
Lumsden, J. (1976). *In* "Annual Review of Psychology" Annual Reviews, Palo Alto.
Lynn, R. (1969). *Br. J. Psychol.* **60**, 529–534.
Lytton, H. (1971). "Creativity and Education" Routledge and Kegan Paul, London.
Macarthur, R. S., Irvine, S. H. and Brimble, A. R. (1964). "The Northern Rhodesia Mental Survey, 1963" Institute for Social Research, Lusaka.
McAskie, M. and Clarke, A. M. (1976). *Br. J. Psychol.* **67**, 243–273.
McClelland, D. C. (1961). "Achieving Society" Van Nostrand, Princeton.
McClelland, D. C., Atkinson, J. W., Clark, R. A. and Lowell, E. L. (1953). "The Achievement Motive" Appleton-Century Crofts, New York.
Macdonald, A. (1944–5). "Selection of African Personnel" Ministry of Defence Archives, London.
McDougall, W. (1932). "Energies of Men" Methuen, London.
McFie, J. (1961). *Br. J. Educ. Psychol.* **31**, 232–239.
McGeoch, J. A. (1942). "The Psychology of Human Learning" Longmans Green, New York.
McLeish, J. *Br. J. Psychol.* **3**, 129–140.
Macmurray, J. (1961). "Persons in Relation" Faber and Faber, London.
McPherson, F. M., Presley, A. S., Armstrong, J. and Curtis, R. H. (1974). *Br. J. Psychiat.* **125**, 152–160.
McQuitty, L. L. (1967). *Educ. Psychol. Meas.* **27**, 21–46.
Madan, V. (1967). The relation of neuroticism and extraversion to intelligence and

educational attainment at different age levels. Ph.D. Thesis. University of Punjab, Chandigarh.

Mahrer, A. R. (Ed.) (1970). "New Approaches to Personality Classification" Columbia University Press, New York.

Marks, I. (1969). "Fears and Phobias" Heinemann, London.

Marks, P. A., Seeman, W. and Haller, D. L. (1977). "The actuarial use of the MMPI with adolescents and adults" Williams and Wilkins, New York.

Mather, K. (1949). "Biometrical genetics: The study of continuous variation" Methuen, London.

Mather, K. and Jinks, J. L. (1971). "Biometrical Genetics: a study of continuous variation" Chapman and Hall, London.

May, J. M. and Sweney, A. B. (1965). "Personality and Motivational Changes Observed in the Treatment of Psychotic Patients" S.W. Psychological Association, Oklahoma.

Mayer-Gross, W., Slater, E. and Roth, M. (1967). "Clinical Psychiatry" Cassell, London.

Meehl, P. E. (1955). *Am. Rev. Psychol.* **6**, 357–358.

Meier, C. (1963). "The Meier Art Tests" Bureau of Education Research and Science, Iowa.

Meyer, L. and Kline, P. (1978). *Multiv. Behav. Res.* **12**, 479–486.

Meyer, L., Holley, J. W. and Vegelius, J. (1976). *Psychol. Res. Bull.* **16**(8). (Lund University)

Meyhryar, A. H. (1970). *Br. J. Soc. Clin. Psychol.* **11**, 244–247.

Miles, T. R. (1957). *Br. J. educ. Psychol.* **27**, 153–165.

Miller, R. B. (1965). *In* Gagné, R. M. (1965).

Miller, R. B. (1966). *In* Gilmer, B. V. H. (1966).

Miller, W. S. (1970). "Miller Analogies Test" Psychological Corporation, New York.

Mirels, H. L. (1970). *J. Consult. Clin. Psychol.* **34**, 226–228.

Mischel, W. (1968). "Personality and Assessment" Wiley, New York.

Mischel, W. (1973). *Psychol. Rev.* **80**, 252–283.

Mischel, M. (1977). *Am. Psychol.* **32**, 246–254.

Mohan, J. and Rajinder, S. (1973). *Psychol. Stud.* **18**, 14–17.

Mohan, V. and Kumar, D. (1973). *Psychol. Stud.* **18**, 61–64.

Mohan, V. and Kumar, D. (1976). *Br. J. Psychol.* **67**, 39–398.

Morton, J. (1969). *Psychol. Rev.* **76**, 165–178.

Morris, C. (1956). "Varieties of Human Value" University of Chicago Press, Chicago.

Mowrer, O. H. (1950). "Learning Theory and Personality Dynamics" Ronald, New York.

Muensterberger, W. (Ed.) (1969). "Man and Culture" Rapp and Whiting, London.

Murchison, C. (Ed.) (1930). "Psychologies of 1930" Clarke University Press, Worcester, Massachusetts.

Murray, H. A. (1938). "Explorations in Personality" Oxford University Press, New York.

Murstein, B. I. (1963). "Theory and Research in Projective Techniques" Wiley, New York.

Mussen, P. H. (Ed.) (1970). "Carmichael's Manual of Child Psychology" Vol. I. John Wiley, New York.

Narrol, R. and Cotten, R. (Eds.) (1970). "Handbook of Method in Cultural Anthropology" Natural History Press, Garden City.

Nelson, T. O. (1971). *J. Verb. Learn. Verb. Behav.* **10**, 568–576.

Nesselroade, J. R. and Baltes, P. B. (1972). *Mult. Behav. Res.* **6**, 387–408.

Nesselroade, J. R. and Cable, D. (1974). *Multiv. Behav. Res.* **8**, 273–282.

Newell and Simon (1972). "Human Problem Solving" Prentice Hall, New Jersey.

Newman, H. F., Freeman, F. N. and Holzinger, K. J. (1937). "Twins: a study of heredity and environment" University of Chicago Press, Chicago.

Nichols, R. C. (1965). Cited in Vandenberg, S. G. (1965).

Nowlis, V. and Green, R. F. (1957). "The experimental analysis of mood" Proc. 15 Inter. Congress of Psychol, Brussels.

Nuttall, D. L. (1973). *In* Butcher, H. J. and Pont, H. B. (1973).

Oakley, C. A. and Macrae, A. (1937). "Handbook of Vocational Guidance" University of London Press, London.

Orlansky, H. (1949). *Psychol. Bull.* **46**, 1–48.

Orme, J. E. (1965). *Br. J. Med. Psychol.* **38**, 269–271.

Orpen, C. (1972). *Br. J. Soc. Clin. Psychol.* **11**, 244–247.

Osgood, C. E. (1957). "The Measurement of Meaning" University of Illinois Press, Illinois.

Otis, A. S. (1954). "Quick-scoring ability tests" Harrap, London.

Parin, P. and Morgenthaler, F. (1969). *In* Muesterberger, W. (1969).

Pawlik, K. and Cattell, R. B. (1964). *Br. J. Psychol.* **55**, 1–18.

Pedley, R. R. (1955). "The Comprehensive School" Penguin Books, Harmondsworth.

Phares, E. J. (1976). "Locus of Control in Personality" General Learning Press, Morristown.

Philipps, H. P. (1965). "Thai Peasant Personality" University of California Press, Berkley.

Piaget, J. (1952). "The Origins of Intelligence in Childhood" International Universities Press, New York.

Piaget, J. (1970). *In* Mussen, P. H. (1970).

Pilkington, G. W. and Harrison, G. J. (1967). *Br. J. Educ. Psychol.* **37**, 382–389.

Porteus, S. D. (1952). "The Porteus Maze Test Manual" Harrap, London.

Price-Williams, D. R. (Ed.) (1969). "Cross-Cultural Studies" Penguin, Harmondsworth.

Prociuk, T. J. and Lussier, R. J. (1975). *Psychol. Reports Monog. Suppl.* 1-V37, 1323–1337.

Purdue Research Foundation (1968). "Purdue Pegboard" Science Research Associates, Chicago.

Quereshi, M. Y. (1972). *In* Buros, O. K. (1972).

Rabin, A. I. (Ed.) (1968). "Projective Techniques in Personality Assessment" Springer, New York.

Rachman, S. J. *In* Eysenck, H. J. (1973).

Radcliffe-Browne, A. R. (1952). "Structure and Function in Primitive Society" Free Press, New York.

Rafi, A. A. (1965). *Br. J. S. Clin. Psychol.* **4**, 266–268.

Rasch (1960). "Probabilistic Models for some Intelligence and Attainment Tests" Denmark Institute of Education, Copenhagen.

Raven, J. C. (1965). "The Mill-Hill Vocabulary Scale" H. K. Lewis, London.

Raven, J. C. (1965). "The Crichton Vocabulary Scale" H. K. Lewis, London.

Raven, J. C. (1965). "Progressive Matrices" H. K. Lewis, London.

Reed, E. W. and Reed, S. C. (1965). "Mental Retardation: A Family Study" W. B. Saunders, London.

Reich, W, (1945). "Character Analysis" Orgone Institute, New York.

Reid, R. L. (1960). *Br. J. Psychol.* **51**, 226–236

Resnik, R. B. (Ed.) (1976). "The Nature of Intelligence" Earlbaum, Hillside.

Revesz, G. (1925). "The Psychology of a Musical Prodigy" Harcourt Brace, New York.

Richardson, M. W. and Kuder, F. (1939). *J. Educ. Psychol.* **30**, 681–687.

Richet, G. (1900). "Notes sur un cas remarquable de precosité musicale" Paper at IV Congress Internationale de Psychologie.

Rodger, A. (1952). "The Seven-Point Plan" Paper no 1. N.I.I.P., London.

Roheim, G. (Ed.) (1947). "Psychoanalysis and the Social Sciences" Hogarth Press, London.

Rokeach, M. (1960). "The Open and Closed Mind" Basic Books, New York.

Rorschach, H. (1921). "Psychodiagnostics" Hans Huber, Berne.

Rosenzweig, S. (1951). *Psychol. Rev.* **58**, 213–223.

Rotter, J. B. (1966). *Psychol. Monog.* **80**, (Whole No. 609).

Rothstein, U. (In Press). "A G Analysis of Fear Reactions" Ph.D. thesis. University of Lund.

Royce, J. R. (1963). Cited in Jackson, D. N. and Messick, S. (1967).

Royce, J. R. (Ed.) (1973). "Contribution of Multivariate Analysis to Psychological Theory" Academic Press, London and New York.

Rushton, J. (1966). *Br. J. Educ. Psych.* **36**, 178–184.

Rutter, M. (1972). "Maternal Deprivation Reassessed" Penguin, Harmondsworth.

Sandler, J. (1958). Some notes on delegate analysis. *In* Tacon, S. F. "An investigation of some psychosomatic symptoms in adult neurotic patients" Ph.D. thesis, University of London, London.

Sandler, J. and Hazari, A. (1960). *Br. J. Med. Psychol.* **33**, 113–121.

Sarason, I. G. (1972). "Personality: an objective approach" Wiley, London.

Sarason, S. B., Davidson, K. S., Lighthall, F. F., Waite, R. R. and Ruebush, B. K. (1960). "Anxiety in Elementary School Children" Wiley, New York.

Savage, R. D. (1966). *Br. J. educ. Psychol.* **36**, 91–94.

Saville, P. and Blinkhorne, S. (1976). "Undergraduate Personality by Factored Scales" N.F.E.R., Windsor.

Schonell, F. J. (1944). "Backwardness in the Basic Subjects" Oliver and Boyd, Edinburgh.

Schonell, F. J. (1951). "The Schonell Reading Tests" Oliver and Boyd, Edinburgh.

Schneider, K. (1958). "Psychopathic Personalities" Cassell, London.

Schubo, W., Hentschel, V., Zerssen, D. V. and Mombour, W. (1975). *Archs. Psychiat. Nervenkr.* **220**, 187–200.

Schuerger, J. M. and Cattell, R. B. (1971). "The High-School Objective Analytic Test Battery" I.P.A.T., Champaign.

Schuerger, J. M. and Cattell, R. B. (1975). "The Objective Analytic Test Battery" I.P.A.T., Champaign.

Scott, R. D. and Ashworth, P. L. (1969). *Br. J. Med. Psychol.* **42**, 13–32.

Seashore, C. E. (1919). "The Psychology of Musical Talent" Silver Burdett, New York.

Semeonoff, B. (1973). *In* Kline, P. (1973).

Shapiro, M. B. (1961). "Manual of the Personal Questionnaire" Institute of Psychiatry, London.

Sheldon, W. H. and Stevens, S. S. (1942). "The Varieties of Temperament" Harper and Row, New York.

Shields, J. (1962). "Monozygotic Twins" Oxford University Press, London.

Shuter, R. (1968). "The Psychology of Musical Ability" Methuen, London.

Siegel, B. J. (Ed.) (1971). "Biennial Review of Anthropology" Stanford University Press, Stanford.

Siegel, L. (1972). *In* Buros, O. K. (1972).

Siess, T. F. and Jackson, P. N. (1970). *J. Counsel. Psychol.* **17**, 27–35.

Sjoback, H. (1967). "Defence Mechanism Test" Colytographic Research Foundation, Lund.

Sjobring, H. (1963). "La Personalité. Structure et development" Doin, Paris.

Skinner, B. F. (1953). "Science and Human Behaviour" Macmillan, New York.

Slade, P. D. (1975). An experimental approach to the study of auditory hallucinations. Unpublished Ph.D. Thesis. University of London.

Smith, F. (1971). "Understanding Reading" Holt, Rinehart and Winston, New York.

Smith, G. J. W. and Klein, G. S. (1953). *J. Pers.* **22**, 188–213.

Sneath, P. H. A. and Sokal, A. A. (1973). "Numerical Taxonomy" Freeman, San Francisco.

Snedecor, G. W. (1956). "Statistical Methods" Iowa State College Press, Ames.

Sokal, A. A. and Sneath, P. H. A. (1963). "Principles of Numerical Taxonomy" Freeman, San Francisco.

Spain, D. H. (1972). *In* Hsu, F. L. K. (1972).

Spearman, C. (1927). "The Abilities of Man" Macmillan, London.

Spielberger, C. D. (1966). "Theory and Research on Anxiety in Anxiety and Behaviour" Academic Press, New York and London.

Spielberger, C. D. (Ed.) (1972). "Anxiety: Current Trends in Theory and Research" Academic Press, New York.

Spindler, L. G. (1975). *In* Williams, T. R. (1975).

Spiro, M. E. (1968). *In* "International Encyclopaedia of the Social Sciences" (Sills, S. D., Ed.) Macmillan and the Free Press, New York.

Spiro, M. E. (1972). *In* Hsu, F. L. K. (1972).

Stahmann, R. F. (1971). *J. Counsel. Psychol.* **18**, 190–191.

Stankov, L. (1977). *Br. J. Soc. Clin. Psychol.* **16**, 111–122.

Storr, A. (1976). "The Dynamics of Creation" Penguin Books, Harmondsworth.

Stoufer, S. (1950). "Studies on social psychology in World War II Vol. 4 Measurement and Prediction" Princeton University Press, Princeton.

Stricker, L. J. (1974). *J. Consult. Clin. Psychol.* **42**, 529–537.

Stringer, P. (1970). *Br. J. Med. Psychol.* **43**, 95–103.

Stringer, P., Crown, S., Lucas, C. J. and Supramanium, S. (1977). *Brit. J. Med. Psych.* **50**, 267–274.

Stromberg, E. L. (1951). "Stromberg Dexterity Test" Psychological Corporation, New York.

Strong, E. K. (1943). "Vocational Interests of Men and Women" Stanford: Stanford University Press, Stanford.

Strong, E. K., Campbell, D. P., Berdie, R. E. and Clerk, K. E. (1971). "Strong Vocational Interest Blank" Stanford: Stanford University Press, Stanford.

Sweney, A. B., Cattell, R. B. and Krug, S. E. (1970). "School Motivation Analysis Test" IPAT, Champaign.

Tatsuoka, M. M. and Cattell, R. B. (1970). *Br. J. Educ. Psychol.* **40**, 324–334.

Taylor, C. W. and Barron, F. (Eds) (1963). "Scientific Creativity: its recognition and development" Wiley, Chichester.

Taylor, C. W., Smith, W. R. and Ghiselin, B. (1963). *In* "Scientific Creativity: Its Recognition and Development" (Taylor, C. W. and Barron, F., Eds) Wiley, London.

Teasdale, J. P., Segraves, R. T. and Zacure, J. (1971). *Br. J. Soc. Clin. Psychol.* **10**, 160–171.

Terman, L. M. (1926). "Mental and physical traits of a 1000 gifted children" Stanford University Press, Stanford.

Terman, L. M. and Merrill, M. A. (1964). "Stanford Binet Intelligence Scale Manual" Harrap and Co, London.

Thurstone, L. L. (1931). *Psychol. Rev.* **38**, 406–427.

Thurstone, L. L. (1938). "Primary Mental Abilities" University of Chicago Press, Chicago.

Thurstone, L. L. (1947). "Multiple factor analysis. A development and expansion of the vectors of the mind" University of Chicago Press, Chicago.

Thurstone, L. L. and Thurstone, T. G. (1941). *Psychomet. Monogr.* **2**, University of Chicago Press.

Tinbergen, N. (1951). "The Study of Instinct" Oxford University Press, Oxford.

Tizard, B. (1974). *Nature* **247**, 316.

Torrance, E. P. (1966). "Torrance Tests of Creative Thinking" Personnel Press, Princeton.

Triandis, H., Malpass, R. S. and Davidson, A. R. (1971). *In* Siegel, B. J. (1971).

Truax, C. B. (1963). *J. Consult. Psychol.* **10**, 256–263.

Tryon, R. C. (1939). "Cluster Analysis" Edwards, Ann Arbor.

Tsujioka, B. and Cattell, R. B. (1965). *J. Soc. Psychol.* **65**, 205–219.

Tuddenham, R. D. (1970). *In* Dockrell, B. (1970).

Tyler, L. (1972). *Ann. Rev. Psychol.* **23**, 177–206.

United States Government Printing Office (1970). "General Aptitude Test Battery" Manual. Government Printers, Washington.

Vagy, P. R. and Hammond, S. B. (1976). *Br. J. Soc. Clin. Psychol.* **15**, 121–130.

Van De Geer, J. P. (1971). "Introduction to Multivariate Analysis for the Social Sciences" Freeman, San Francisco.

Vandenberg, S. G. (1965). "Methods and Goals in Human Behaviour Genetics" Academic Press, New York and London.

Vandenberg, S. G. (1966). *Psychol. Bull.* **66**, 327–352.

Van Egeren, L. F. (1963). Experimental determination by P. Technique of Functional unities of depression and other psychological states. Unpublished M.A. thesis. University of Illinois.

Vaughan, D. (1974). On the technical standards of ten representative factor analyses purporting to decide personality theories. Unpublished MS. Department of Psychology, University of Illinois.

Vegelius, J. (1976). "On various G Index generalizations and their applicability within the clinical domain" Acta Universitatis Uppsaliensis 4. Uppsala.

Verma, R. M. and Eysenck, H. J. (1973). *Br. J. Psychiat.* **122**, 573–585.

Vernon, P. E. (1950). "The Measurement of Abilities" University of London Press, London.

Vernon, P. E. (1961). "The Structure of Human Abilities" University of London Press, London.

Vernon, P. E. (1964). "Personality Assessment" Methuen, London.

Vernon, P. E. (1965). *Am. Psychol.* **20**, 723–733.

Vernon, P. E. (1969). "Intelligence and Cultural Environment" Methuen, London.

Vernon, P. E. and Parry, J. B. (1949). "Personnel Selection in the British Forces" University of London Press, London.

Vidal, A. (1972). "BG8 Diagnostic Psychologique a Compte Vendu Programme sur Ordinquteur" Centre de Psychologie Appliquée, Paris.

Waldo, G. P. and Dinitz, S. (1967). *J. Res. Crim. Delinq.* **4**, 185–202.

Wallach, M. A. and Kogan, N. (1965). "Modes of Thinking in Young Children: a study of the creativity-intelligence distinction" Holt Rhinehart and Wilson, New York.

Walsh, J. A. (1972). *In* Buros, O. K. (1972).

Warburton, F. W. (1951). *Br. J. Psychol.* **42**, 123–133.

Warburton, F. W. (1965). *Behav. Res. Therap.* **3**, 129–135.

Warburton, F. W. (1968a). The Structure of Personality Factors Unpublished MS. University of Manchester, Manchester.

Warburton, F. W. (1968b). The relationship between personality factors and scholastic attainment Unpublished MS. University of Manchester, Manchester.

Warren, N. (Edit.) (1977). "Studies in Cross-Cultural Psychology" Academic Press, London and New York.

Wechsler, D. (1958). "The Measurement and Appraisal of Adult Intelligence" Williams and Wilkins, Baltimore.

Werner, O. and Campbell, D. T. (1970). *In* Narrol, L. R. and Cotten, R. (1970).

Whiting, J. W. M. and Child, I. L. (1953). "Child Training and Personality" Yale University Press, New Haven.

Willet, T. C. (1964). "Criminal on the Road" Tavistock Publications, London.

Williams, T. R. (Ed.) (1975). "Psychological Anthropology" Mouton, The Hague.

Wilson, G. D. and Patterson, J. R. (1970). "The Conservatism Scale" N.F.E.R., Windsor.

Wing, H. D. (1936). Tests of musical ability in school children M.A. thesis. University of London.

Wing, H. D. (1953). *In* Buros, O. K. (1953).

Wing, H. D. (1962). *J. Res. Mus. Ed.* **10**, 39–46.

Witkin, H. A. (1962). "Psychological Differentiation: Studies of Development" Wiley, New York.

Wober, M. (1966). *J. Soc. Psychol.* **70**, 181–189.

Wober, M. (1973). *In* Berry and Dasen (1973).

SUBJECT INDEX